England and Germany
in the High Middle Ages

STUDIES OF THE GERMAN
HISTORICAL INSTITUTE LONDON

GENERAL EDITOR: Adolf M. Birke

England and Germany in the High Middle Ages

EDITED BY
ALFRED HAVERKAMP
AND HANNA VOLLRATH

In Honour of Karl J. Leyser

THE GERMAN HISTORICAL INSTITUTE LONDON
OXFORD UNIVERSITY PRESS
1996

Oxford University Press, Walton Street, Oxford OX2 6DP
Oxford New York
Athens Auckland Bangkok Bombay
Calcutta Cape Town Dar es Salaam Delhi
Florence Hong Kong Istanbul Karachi
Kuala Lumpur Madras Madrid Melbourne
Mexico City Nairobi Paris Singapore
Taipei Tokyo Toronto
and associated companies in
Berlin Ibadan

Oxford is a trade mark of Oxford University Press

Published in the United States
by Oxford University Press Inc., New York

British Library Cataloguing in Publication Data
Data available

Library of Congress Cataloging in Publication Data
England and Germany in the High Middle Ages/edited by Alfred
Haverkamp and Hanna Vollrath.
—(Studies of the German Historical Institute London)
Essays derived from the conference 'Germany and England in the
High Middle Ages, a Comparative Approach', which took place in 1987.
Includes index.
1. Great Britain—History—Medieval period, 1066–1485—Congresses.
2. England—Civilization—1066–1485—Congresses.   3. Germany—
History—843–1273—Congresses.   4. Thirteenth century—Congresses.
5. Twelfth century—Congresses.   6. Middle Ages—Congresses.
I. Haverkamp, Alfred, 1937–   .   II. Vollrath, Hanna.   III. Series.
DA175.E54   1996   942.02—dc20   95-25868
ISBN 0-19-920504-3

1 3 5 7 9 10 8 6 4 2

Typeset by Best-set Typesetter Ltd., Hong Kong
Printed in Great Britain
on acid-free paper by
Biddles Ltd.
Guildford and King's Lynn

Foreword

When Alfred Haverkamp (University of Trier), Hanna Vollrath (University of Bochum), and the late Karl Leyser (University of Oxford) asked the German Historical Institute to host a conference on England and Germany in the High Middle Ages, the Institute was pleased to support this undertaking by medieval historians in Britain and Germany. The German Historical Institute London was set up to encourage scholarly dialogue between historians of Britain and Germany, and one of the main ways in which it does this is to promote academic conferences. While the work of the Institute has largely been directed towards the modern and early modern periods, medieval history also features in its programme. From time to time seminars are held on topics of special interest to medievalists, and the Institute's publications have always been open to outstanding contributions from all periods.

The conference *Germany and England in the High Middle Ages: A Comparative Approach* which took place in 1987, and from which the essays collected in this volume derive, was an unusual event. It was a rare opportunity for British and German historians to meet in order to share their research on medieval history. The conference covered the period from the eleventh to the thirteenth centuries, with special emphasis on the twelfth century, a time of great change in almost all areas of life. The volume that has grown out of this conference brings together a number of fine essays on a wide range of topics. The regrettable delay in its appearance goes back to the complicated communications involved when joint-editors prepare an international project of this kind for publication. But it has by no means detracted from the quality of the contributions assembled here.

The conference was generously financed by the Volkswagen Foundation and I should like to take this opportunity to thank the Foundation for its support. I should also like to express my thanks to those who planned and organized the conference, in particular, Alfred Haverkamp, Hanna Vollrath, and the late Karl Leyser, to whose memory this volume is dedicated. Publication would not have been possible without the hard work and help of Dr Eckhart Hellmuth, Dr Hermann Hiery, and Dr Angela Davies, who revised the translations. Thanks are also due to Dr Friedhelm Burgard and Christoph Cluse M.A. (Trier), who also helped with the manuscripts, and to Thorsten Liebelt and Olaf Wiegand (Bochum), who assisted with the Index. I should also like to express my gratitude to Oxford University Press for its expertise in publishing this book.

Adolf M. Birke

Munich, 1995

Contents

Introduction

HANNA VOLLRATH

WITH

J. O. PRESTWICH AND KARL J. LEYSER

Over the last fifty or so years, medievalists have shied away from comparing the kingdoms of medieval Europe. There are, of course, a few exceptions. Among German scholars, the name of Heinrich Mitteis springs to mind. His book, *Der Staat des hohen Mittelalters*, first published in 1940, still stands out. This is essentially a constitutional history of the feudal system, which looks at the internal order of the *regna* as political units ruled by kings. The book has gone through many editions since 1940, but nobody has attempted to emulate its achievement in providing a chronologically structured comparative account of the German Reich, Italy, France, and England.

In Britain, similarly, scholars have had a limited interest in comparative work. There is, of course, the *History of Medieval Europe*, which looks at trends common to the countries of Latin Europe.[1] Examples of fundamental developments are drawn from the various countries and regions of western Europe in order to demonstrate that they were essentially shared. Naturally, this sort of history is less concerned with politics—the actions of people and groups of people—than with longer-term structural changes and more general trends. This type of methodological approach aims to provide a general framework within which western Europe can be understood. A history of medieval Europe written along these lines can be read as a preparation for the comparative analysis of specific periods, but it cannot replace individual

Section V is by J. O. Prestwich, and Section VI by Karl J. Leyser. These sections incorporate commentaries which their authors gave at the conference on which this volume is based. The rest of the introduction is by Hanna Vollrath and was translated by Angela Davies.

[1] *The Oxford Illustrated History of Medieval Europe*, ed. George Holmes (Oxford, 1988); German edn., *Europa im Mittelalter* (Stuttgart and Weimar, 1993).

comparative case-studies. Only individual comparative analyses can answer the question of how problems arising out of general developments were dealt with at specific times in specific countries. Does this mean that we must return to the approach taken by Heinrich Mitteis?

Heinrich Mitteis's method of comparing political orders and constitutional structures will no longer do because scholars today are more interested in different sorts of questions. Medieval historians are no longer primarily concerned with comparing central governmental institutions. Heinrich Mitteis's *Der Staat des hohen Mittelalters* drew upon his earlier book, *Lehnrecht und Staatsgewalt*,[2] and like the earlier study, it interpreted the medieval feudal system as a precursor to a modern constitutional system. It was precisely his comparative approach which led Mitteis to see the feudal system as strongly centripetal, that is, capable of strengthening the central government embodied by a king. His main interest in examining the period from the Frankish kingdom to around 1300, when feudal bonds gave way to 'the growth of corporate organizations, representative bodies, and bureaucratic institutions',[3] was always the size and strength of the king's central government. For him, history was the history of states, of their constitutions and forms of government. In this sense, it was the history of potentially comparable political units. In his view, the great achievement of the Carolingians was that they conceived of feudalism as a state-building agency.[4]

Feudalism, of course, can have a different meaning. Marc Bloch's *La société féodale*[5] was published at about the same time as Heinrich Mitteis's book. The theme of Bloch's work was not legal structures, but the structures of society as a

---

[2] Weimar, 1933.

[3] Heinrich Mitteis, *Der Staat des hohen Mittelalters. Grundlinien einer vergleichenden Verfassungsgeschichte*, 8th edn. (Weimar, 1968), 424. Quotation here taken from the English trans. by H. F. Orton, *The State in the Middle Ages. A Comparative Constitutional History of Feudal Europe* (Amsterdam and Oxford, 1975), 393. On the whole concept, cf. the conference volume, Peter Landau *et al.* (eds.), *Heinrich Mitteis nach hundert Jahren (1889–1989). Symposion anläßlich des hundertsten Geburtstages in München am 2. und 3. November 1989* (Munich, 1991).

[4] Mitteis, *Der Staat*, 64; for a fascinating new approach cf. Susan Reynolds, *Fiefs and Vassals* (Oxford, 1994).

[5] Marc Bloch, *La société féodale* (2 vols., Strasburg, 1939); English trans. published as *Feudal Society* (London, 1961).

whole. This was *histoire totale,* a combination of analysis and understanding.[6] Legal and economic relations as revealed in legal documents, polyptyches, land registers, *leges,* capitularies, and records were seen as elements of a total social reality, which also encompassed the ever-present struggle for sheer survival, the fear of hunger and poverty, the feeling of being at the mercy of supernatural powers and the forces of nature, the darkness of nights without artificial illumination, the smoke, the narrowness, and the cold in uncomfortable houses. All this produced a specific way of living and thinking—that of feudal society. However difficult it may be, international comparisons must also be subjected to the demands of *histoire totale.*

But is this at all possible? Where is the basis of comparison in the medieval *regna,* with their loose structures which had hardly assumed an institutional form and were not linked together into a system? A comparison obviously requires comparable units. But were the *regna* even units? What degree of uniformity was created by allegiance to a king and a royal family, when these were hardly central powers in a position to impose unity? Should we not be comparing regions with comparable natural, climatic, demographic, and social conditions? Of course, the editors of this volume are aware of all these issues. The starting-point of the volume was that specific problems arose at specific times in Latin Europe, and that parallel developments, changes, and transformations took place which can be related to each other. How were these challenges, which were specific to the age, addressed in England and Germany? What means were available in seeking answers to problems, and what were the assumptions on which decisions were based?

I

The twelfth century is an obvious period to select for a comparison of this sort because it has long been regarded as a period of 'renaissance'. The phrase 'renaissance of the

[6] Hartmut Atsma and André Burguière (eds.), *Marc Bloch—aujourd' hui. Histoire comparée et sciences sociales* (Paris, 1990).

twelfth century' was originally used to describe the intellectual developments of the period,[7] but more recently scholars
have applied it to almost all areas of life.[8] Many researchers
have discerned great changes in early medieval structures at
this time. They see this 'Deuxième Age Féodal' as having a
character quite different from that of the 'Premier Age
Féodal'. A significant increase in trade and industry, combined with the growth of towns, changed both the rural
economy and rural social structures. The fact that it was now
possible to move from the country into towns meant that
there was an alternative to an agrarian life-style dominated
by landlords. Other choices also existed. Areas which had
not hitherto been settled were cleared and opened up for
colonization. As urban communities grew, a form of co-
operative organization emerged which soon developed its
own institutions, the council and the consulate. These were
more firmly organized than the loose associations of the
early Middle Ages.

The twelfth century was also an age of increasing mobility.
The popularity of the cathedral schools of the Isle de France
in particular, which turned England into 'a colony of the
French intellectual empire',[9] and the practice of studying law
in Bologna, or medicine in Salerno or Montpellier, are all as
much aspects of mobility as the recruitment of journeymen
to build magnificent churches and cathedrals, spreading
Gothic architecture throughout Europe in the process. The
pilgrims who streamed to the far distant pilgrimage places of
Santiago de Compostela, Rome, Cologne, and, after 1170, to
the grave of the new martyr, Thomas Becket in Canterbury,
possessed a significantly greater degree of mobility as compared with the early Middle Ages. The crusades to the Holy
Land were a completely new type of armed pilgrimage,
which also produced a new type of knightly religious order,

---

[7] Charles Homer Haskins, *The Renaissance of the 12th Century* (London, 1928).

[8] Robert L. Benson and Giles Constable (eds.), *Renaissance and Renewal in the Twelfth Century* (Oxford, 1982).

[9] Thus Richard Southern, 'The Place of England in the Twelfth Century Renais-sance', in id., *Medieval Humanism and Other Studies* (Oxford, 1970), 158–80, quo-tation on 158: 'Culturally the most obvious thing about England in the twelfth century is its dependence on France. It was a colony of the French intellectual empire.'

that of the warrior monks. Their existence is probably the most striking evidence that the idea of the three estates—those who prayed, those who fought, and those who laboured—a notion first articulated around the year 1000 (when it was not a faithful mirror of social reality either),[10] had finally become obsolete.

What set off all these social changes? What was it that made life in the twelfth century more varied, less peaceful, and thus, as people saw it, less secure than earlier? Was climatic change a crucial factor? Did the increased yields from harvests mean that more people survived, with the result that the growing pressure of population encouraged people to break out of their small-scale, narrow ways of life?[11] Or should we seek the crucial factor in the intellectual sphere? Texts were being used in a different way, and the nature and extent of literacy were changing.[12] Recent general accounts, each dealing with one *regnum*, have given different weight to different factors. At least we can all agree that the answer is not clear-cut.

II

In England we see the early emergence of a capital city as the seat of a central administration, the creation of institutionally anchored royal fiscal and judicial systems, and the beginnings of an attempt to monopolize foreign relations. All this gave the English kings a number of instruments of government which did not exist in Germany at the same time. The differences are so glaring that it has often been assumed that England and Germany went in completely different direc-

[10] On these 'three orders of society' cf. esp. the work of Otto Gerhard Oexle, most recently his contribution on 'Stand, Klasse' to the reference work *Geschichtliche Grundbegriffe*, ed. by Otto Brunner *et al.*, vi (Stuttgart, 1990), 183 ff., which contains references to earlier work on the subject.

[11] Georges Duby, *Guerriers et paysans, VIIᵉ-XIIᵉ siècle. Premier essor de l'economie européenne* (Paris, 1973), in particular, points to a 1° rise in average annual temperatures as a factor triggering an improvement in living conditions.

[12] Brian Stock, *The Implications of Literacy. Written Language and Models of Interpretation in the Eleventh and Twelfth Centuries* (Princeton, 1983); id., 'Schriftgebrauch und Rationalität im Mittelalter', in Wolfgang Schluchter (ed.), *Max Webers Sicht des okzidentalen Christentums* (Frankfurt, 1988), 165–86.

tions from the twelfth century. The volume addresses the question of whether significant differences also existed below the level of kingship—for example, in the spread of literacy, in urban and rural economic and social change, in the treatment of non-Christians such as the Jewish minority, and in the crusades. Were differences in what happened at the centre so conclusive that they had a lasting impact on social life at local level?

There are obvious gaps in the range of topics discussed in this volume. In particular, the general area of religion and Church history is missing. We have not been able to offer chapters on the development of the hierarchical Universal Church in the two kingdoms, or on the activities of the new religious orders and the spread of alternative forms of religion, increasingly condemned by the Church as heresies. There are other, no less obvious gaps: historiography and literature; the social, cultural, and political role of the court; aristocratic society and knightly culture; the recruitment of administrative staff; forms of communication and transport routes; the economy and the circulation of money. Even so central a theme as the law is represented only indirectly, subsumed under the topic of maintaining peace. The editors of this volume are fully aware that it cannot provide more than building blocks for a future comparison of the two countries.

III

In England as in Germany, scholars have been greatly interested in the specific forms of literacy in Latin Europe during the Middle Ages. There seems to be general agreement that ways of using texts began to change during the period of the *Investiturstreit*.[13] During the early Middle Ages, texts were most often read as a part of *contemplatio*.[14] Writing holy books for this purpose was considered an ascetic task which was, in itself, pleasing to God. Any consideration of the

---

[13] Stock, *The Implications of Literacy.*
[14] Hagen Keller, 'Vom "Heiligen Buch" zur "Buchführung"', *Frühmittelalter Studien*, 26 (1992), 1–31.

practical uses of such texts was often not decisive. From about the middle of the eleventh century, however, texts began to be read 'with other eyes'.[15] In cases of doubt, texts were consulted as normative points of reference and used, in this practical way, with some regularity. This first happened in the religious sphere. In the twelfth and thirteenth centuries, at different times in different countries, a 'pragmatic form of literacy' emerged.[16] It increasingly involved the use of writing for administrative purposes. What we are witnessing here is the functional integration of texts into social and political life.

Although it is difficult to pinpoint dates for such long-term processes with any accuracy, there is general agreement that in many regions, the secular use of writing began to become more important during the twelfth century. A fundamental point of dispute in distinguishing between different forms of literacy in this way is how to classify the legal documents produced by the Carolingian kings, and in particular, Charlemagne. Similarly, no *communis opinio* has emerged on late Anglo-Saxon law.[17] Specialists on the Carolingian and late Anglo-Saxon periods tend to assume that the texts produced during these periods were of great practical significance. Scholars who study the development of literacy, however, and look at the various ways in which texts were integrated into social life, and at the changing social context in which

[15] A basic text on the changing use of canon law texts is Horst Fuhrmann, 'Das Reformpapsttum und die Rechtswissenschaft', in *Investiturstreit und Reichsverfassung* (Vorträge und Forschungen, 17; Sigmaringen, 1973), 175–201.

[16] The seminal works here are Michael T. Clanchy, *From Memory to Written Record: England 1066–1307* (2nd edn., Oxford, 1993); H. Keller and F.-J. Worstbrock, 'Träger, Felder, Formen pragmatischer Schriftlichkeit im Mittelalter', *Frühmittelalterliche Studien*, 22 (1988), 388–409; Hagen Keller, 'Pragmatische Schriftlichkeit im Mittelalter. Einführung zum Kolloquium', in id. *et al.* (eds.), *Pragmatische Schriftlichkeit im Mittelalter. Erscheinungsformen und Entwicklungsstufen* (Munich, 1992), 1–7.

[17] Simon Keynes, 'Royal government and the written word in late Anglo-Saxon England', in Rosamond McKitterick (ed.), *The Uses of Literacy in Early Medieval Europe* (Cambridge, 1990), 226–57, sees late Anglo-Saxon laws, in particular those of the kings Aethelred (978–1016) and Knut (1016–1035) as instruments of an efficient administration. Patrick Wormald, 'Aethelred the Lawmaker', in *Ethelred the Unready: Papers from the Millenary Conference, BAR* (British Series, 59, 1978), 47–80, is more sceptical; id., 'Lex Scripta and Verbum Regis: Legislation and Germanic Kingship from Euric to Cnut', in Peter H. Sawyer and Ian N. Wood (eds.), *Early Medieval Kingship* (Leeds, 1977), 105–38.

texts were produced over the centuries, are more sceptical about the practical value of administrative texts produced before the twelfth century. Whatever conclusions we draw, there seems to be a general consensus among scholars that in the twelfth century the ordering of social relations began to assume a quality different from what it had been in the early Middle Ages, and that this change was associated with the appearance of administrative documents.

The Roman Church was probably a pioneer in this field. Its popes, schooled in Roman law, drew up legal documents to establish the primacy of their jurisdiction within a hierarchical church which spanned the individual *regna*. But kings, spiritual and secular lords, and urban and rural communities also began to play a more active part than before in shaping their relations with other people. It is obvious that this was associated with a change in the uses of writing, and research on how this happened is in full spate. During the high Middle Ages, 'oral discourse effectively began to function within a universe of communications governed by texts'.[18]

We must assume that the change from a predominantly oral discourse intrinsically interwoven with gestures and ritual to a more textual mode of communication with its definitions and categorizations took place at different times in different places and in different areas of human activity. Many questions remain. But before we consider the implications for social life of the switch to written communication, we must look at the spread of literacy.

To establish the extent of literacy is more difficult than may at first appear, because the designation *literatus*, which to us seems unambiguous, does not, as used in contemporary sources, always mean 'literate'. As Nicholas Orme shows, drawing upon a wide range of English examples, the meaning of this term was not fixed, but covered a variety of ways in which the laity could be exposed to, and influenced by, the written word. In trying to establish what contact lay people had with texts, scholars are largely dependent on random references in narrative sources. This makes any sort of quantification impossible. All we can say is that 'many of the English laity were either literate or involved in literary activi-

[18] Stock, *The Implications of Literacy*, 3.

ties between 1100 and 1300, and it is likely that the number grew significantly during the period' (p. 35).

But roughly how many were there? Do references to literate city-dwellers, country nobility, estate administrators, and even tied peasants allow us to draw any conclusions at all? Merchants and administrators needed to be literate to conduct the practical side of their business from the twelfth century onwards. This points to the economic and social significance of literacy. But at the same time, reading and writing by no means formed a central part of the education of the nobility. These are some of the issues addressed by Alfred Wendehorst's essay in this volume. He does not discuss exactly the same issues as Orme and does not limit himself to lay literacy, but also looks at literacy among the clergy and members of religious orders. Nor does he restrict his investigation to the German area. But as the majority of his sources are German, a comparison is possible. Striking parallels as well as remarkable differences emerge.

One common feature is that the ability to read did not necessarily imply an ability to write, and that the influence of written texts went well beyond those who could read and write themselves. Both authors mention that some people, mostly nobles, preferred to have texts read to them, and to dictate their own. The comparison also demonstrates that for England the contrast between Latin as a written language, and the vernacular as an oral medium is only part of the truth. Quite apart from the many vernacular texts of all types in the Anglo-Saxon period—there is nothing comparable on the Continent—the Norman Conquest produced what was probably a unique situation. A vernacular which was, in effect, reserved for the upper classes established itself in England—namely, French. Orme shows that from the end of the twelfth century, the aristocracy read more and more French texts. Moreover, a reading of the two essays gives the impression that literacy was much more widespread in England than in Germany.[19] What Orme establishes for twelfth-century England appears to tally with what

---

[19] The examples cited, and the whole tenor of the discussion suggest that at the end of the 13th cent. an archbishop who could not write, such as Frederick II of Salzburg (1270–1284), referred to by Wendehorst, would not have been considered representative in England. Conversely, the bondmen who paid fees to send

Wendehorst says of fourteenth-century Germany. Is there any connection between the fact that literacy seems to have been more widespread in England than in Germany, and the establishment of French as the language of the upper classes? Did the connection with France, the country of letters, act as a general stimulus? Did English kings encourage the spread of literacy—especially Henry II, who built up a routine legal and fiscal administration (based on pipe rolls and returnable writs)? Our comparison, which really only allows us to say that there was more of one thing and less of another, leads us to ask how this can be explained.

IV

Since the eighth century at least, kings had been responsible for the maintenance of *pax et iustitia*. But in the early Middle Ages, maintaining the peace was not the same thing as preventing the use of force, feuding, and war. Feuds were a legitimate use of force, and in this sense, a means of re-establishing peace. Anyone whose rights had been infringed considered this a breach of the peace and was obliged to use force in this legitimate way, or lose honour and respect. This began to change in the twelfth century. Kings were now expected to bring feuding under control as part of their responsibility for *pax*. Coming from different backgrounds and with different assumptions, the English and German kings used different methods to achieve this.[20] (See the essays by Hanna Vollrath and David Carpenter.)

their sons to school and the villeins who used legal documents whom Orme mentions for the same period do not fit into the picture drawn by Wendehorst. Cf. also the comments by John Gillingham, who points out that the establishment of schools in towns and villages in 12th-cent. England provided the 'educational environment' for the founding of the universities of Oxford and Cambridge. Similarly, in 15th-century England the bibliophile leanings of a knight like Jakob Püterich von Reichertshausen would no longer have attracted the scorn of his social equals.

[20] Quite apart from the question of practical implementation, 'governing' in the sense of influencing the whole of the body politic, including the attempt to reduce feuding, presupposes that the body politic is conceived of as a whole which can be influenced. This requires a degree of analytical thinking which scholars doubt whether the Carolingian ruling classes of the 9th cent. were capable of (Johannes

The discussion of the extent of Frankish state-building is not yet over, and no *communis opinio* has emerged. But scholars generally accept that in the tenth century any state structures which may have been created during the 'Carolingian renaissance' were no longer there. This applies in particular to the Eastern Frankish Empire, that part of Charlemagne's Empire which had gained some autonomy as a result of the divisions of the ninth century. By the beginning of the tenth century, it had consolidated itself as an independent *regnum* to such an extent that the nobles preferred to elect a non-Carolingian (911) and then a non-Frankish king (919) rather than be tied to the West Frankish Carolingian king. Thus the birth of France and Germany have been dated to the first decades of the tenth century.[21]

The Saxon kings of the Ostreich used its name of Regnum Orientalium Francorum only when the context demanded that it be distinguished from another *regnum*. During the tenth century it became part of an empire which was not associated with the name of a specific people. From Otto I's coronation in 962, its rulers began to prefer the title *Imperator*, which they saw as conferring greater dignity than the title of *Rex*. Together with the former Langobard *regnum*

Fried, 'Der karolingische Herrschaftsverband im 9. Jahrhundert zwischen "Kirche" und "Königshaus"', *Historische Zeitschrift*, 235 (1982), 1–43). Even the most learned of 9th-cent. writers never present the king 'in any way as an organ of the Reich' (Thus Fried, ibid., referring to Hincmar of Rheims). 'Not even in the remotest sense could the king be considered an organ of the Reich' (ibid., referring to the capitularies, esp. the great reform capitulary of 823–5). Nor did the term *res publica*, adopted from the classics, have any specific content. It did not refer to a structure which existed independently of, and at a higher level than, the individuals within it, and which could be described in its own terms' (ibid. 11). There is certainly no agreement among scholars about how the Carolingian kings should be judged, or about the character of the Reich as a political unit. Researchers who concentrate on sources from the time of Charlemagne tend to emphasize the political nature of Carolingian rule. They see the Carolingian kings, and Charlemagne in particular, as rulers who used their limited technical means in a goal-orientated and efficient manner to fulfil their public duties for the good of the whole Reich. (This is argued most strongly by Rosamond McKitterick in her work on royal documents, which she sees as evidence of an administration making efficient use of the written word, *The Carolingians and the Written Word*, Cambridge, 1989.)

[21] Carlrichard Brühl, *Deutschland-Frankreich. Die Geburt zweier Völker* (Cologne and Vienna, 1990); from France's perspective: Karl Ferdinand Werner, *Les Origines (avant l'an mil)* (Histoire de France sous la direction de Jean Favier, pt. 1, Paris, 1984), German trans.: *Die Ursprünge Frankreichs bis zum Jahr 1000* (Stuttgart, 1989).

Italiae and (from 1032) the kingdom of Burgundy, their *regnum*, which essentially stretched from the Rhine to the Elbe, formed the *imperium*. Not until Pope Gregory VII and the German king of the *imperium*, Henry IV, quarrelled towards the end of the eleventh century did the Pope begin to use the designation, common in Italian historiography, of *rex (regnum) Teutonicorum*, or *rex (regnum) Teutonicum*, in order to cut his opponent down to size as an 'ordinary' king of a Reich encompassing only one people.[22] Contemporary controversies concerning the name and title of the rulers of the *regnum* north of the Alps, and of their kingdom within the framework of the *imperium*, mean that unlike other early medieval *regna*, it is now known in terms of a modern structural concept: the East Frankish-German Reich.[23]

It is generally believed that there was a continuity in basic assumptions and mechanisms throughout Ottonian and early Salian times—that is, from the beginning of the tenth to about the middle of the eleventh century. Over the last twenty years, however, scholars have thoroughly revised the picture of the tenth century drawn by Robert Holtzmann. 'The time of the Saxon Kaisers' is no longer seen as a brilliant period when the rulers' power and splendour was unfolding.[24] Instead, the Ottonians are seen as rulers who were able to maintain their kingly position only with great difficulty against the noble warlords, linked by ties of blood or sworn friendship, who were insisting on their autonomous rights. The Ottonian kingdom is now regarded as an 'institu-

[22] Eckhard Müller-Mertens, *Regnum Teutonicum. Aufkommen und Verbreitung der deutschen Reichs- und Königsauffassung im früheren Mittelalter* (Vienna, 1970); Wolfgang Eggert, 'Ostfränkisch-fränkisch-sächsisch-römisch-deutsch. Zur Benennung des rechtsrheinisch-nordalpinen Reiches bis zum Investiturstreit', *Frühmittelalterliche Studien*, 26 (1992), 239–73.

[23] For a discussion of the difficulties of the whole concept of 'German history', and of this terminology in particular, cf. a detailed review article by Johannes Fried, 'Deutsche Geschichte im frühen und hohen Mittelalter. Bemerkungen zu einigen neuen Gesamtdarstellungen', *Historische Zeitschrift*, 245 (1987), 625–59.

[24] A number of assumptions which Holtzmann makes are now being questioned—e.g. that in 973, at the end of Otto I's reign, Europe, after a long period of unrest, was enjoying 'the peace brought to it by the *Imperator pacificus*, the Kaiser as the guardian of peace' (Robert Holtzmann, *Geschichte der sächsischen Kaiserzeit (900–1024)*, reprint of 4th edn., Darmstadt, 1961, 225). Other opinions which are being re-examined are that conditions in the whole of Latin Europe were 'the work of this powerful Kaiser', who 'never allowed the interests of the state to take second place to the views of the Church' (ibid. 227), but developed the Imperial Church as a 'counterweight' to the dukedoms. Holtzmann regards the integration of the duke-

tion without institutions'.[25] Far from being able to impose a comprehensive peace in their Reich, let alone in the whole of Europe, the Ottonians' capacity to act was essentially tied to their physical presence and their ability to spread fear and terror.[26] 'The concrete experience of a nearby ruler far surpassed abstract legitimation from a distance.'[27] In this sense, even the Imperial Church is no longer really regarded as an instrument of rule which focused the various areas of the Reich on the king. Instead, the imperial churches are seen as caught up in their own particular interests and situations. Often, though not always, they are seen as prescribing action to the kings.[28] If we consider the actual conditions under which people lived—in widely scattered settlements, with extremely limited means of communication, in small-scale, agrarian societies dominated by 'mythical fears', in which the lack of any organized food stores made famine a real and constant fear[29]—the Ottonian Reich is more adequately described as an archaic culture than as a state governed by a king.[30]

These basic structures which dominated the Ottonian tenth century seem essentially to have lasted until about the

doms into the state, which the Kaiser had pursued single-mindedly since the 950s, as 'an especially important and effective centrepiece of Ottonian policy' (ibid. 180). Scholars nowadays no longer accept this picture. For an overview, and a summary of more recent approaches, see Johannes Fried, *Die Formierung Europas 840–1046* (Oldenbourg Grundriß der Geschichte, 6; Munich, 1991). Id., *Der Weg in die Geschichte. Die Ursprünge Deutschlands. Bis 1024* (Propyläen Geschichte Deutschlands, 1; Berlin, 1994). Of the literature cited there, see esp. Hagen Keller, 'Zum Charakter der "Staatlichkeit" zwischen Karolingischer Reichsreform und hochmittelalterlichem Herrschaftsausbau', *Frühmittelalterliche Studien*, 23 (1989), 248–64.

[25] Hagen Keller, 'Reichsorganisation, Herrschaftsformen und Gesellschaftsstrukturen im Regnum Teutonicum", *Settimane di studio del Centro italiano di studi sull'alto medioevo*, 38 (1991), 159–201, quotation 163.

[26] Karl Leyser, *Rule and Conflict in an Early Medieval Society. Ottonian Saxony* (London, 1979), 35.

[27] This statement by Peter Moraw, referring to the late Middle Ages, is even more apt for the early Middle Ages, *Von offener Verfassung zu gestalteter Verdichtung. Das Reich im späten Mittelalter* (Propyläen Geschichte Deutschlands, 3; Berlin, 1985), 22.

[28] Timothy Reuter, 'The "Imperial Church System" of the Ottonian and Salian Rulers. A Reconsideration', *Journal of Ecclesiastical History*, 33 (1982), 347–74. This essay provoked a lively discussion. For an overview of this discussion and its present state, see Fried, *Die Formierung Europas 840–1046*, 165 ff.

[29] Marc Bloch, *La société féodale*; Duby; *Guerriers et paysans*.

[30] Hanna Vollrath, *Christliches Abendland und archaische Stammeskultur. Zu einer Standortbestimmung des früheren Mittelalters* (Berta-Benz-Vorlesung, 4; Ladenburg, 1990).

middle of the eleventh century, that is, until Anglo-Saxon
Britain was taken by William the Conqueror and divided up
as booty between his Norman-North French-Flemish army.
The implications of the Norman Conquest for the rule of the
English kings have been discussed for centuries, and cannot
be summed up here. It has been suggested that the pre-
Norman kings possessed a much more efficient government
than their royal contemporaries on the Continent, a system
which covered the whole of their realm and provided en-
forceable sanctions against offenders. But no agreement has
yet been reached on this issue. Is the *Anglo-Saxon Chronicle*,
Ms E, dated 959, the year in which King Edgar ascended the
throne, to be taken literally as referring to more efficient
government when it says that Edgar 'exalted God's praise far
and wide, and loved God's law; and he improved the peace of
the people more than the kings who were before him in the
memory of man'?[31] Should we see the late Anglo-Saxon laws
as norms which people complied with?[32] It has been said
of France that the 'neutral, objective order is very much a
learned value' which did not exist until the mid-thirteenth
century, because only from that time on were conflicts 'being
settled by authoritative courts in accordance with objective
criteria'.[33] Is this not also true of England? However successful or unsuccessful the Anglo-Saxon kings were in maintaining domestic peace by peaceful means of conflict resolution,
there is little doubt that the Norman conquerors were able to
establish relatively strong royal rule just at the time when the
German kingship was fighting for its life in conflicts with the
Pope and the Saxon revolts.[34]

---

[31] Charles Plummer, *Two of the Saxon Chronicles Parallel* (2 vols., Oxford, 1892 and
1899; repr. 1952); the trans. quoted is from Dorothy Whitelock *et al.* (eds.), *The
Anglo-Saxon Chronicle: A Revised Translation* (London, 1961), 74 f.

[32] For the discussion of Anglo-Saxon 'statehood' cf. the literature cited above in
n. 17.

[33] Frederic L. Cheyette, 'Suum Cuique tribuere', *French Historical Studies*, 6
(1970), 287–99, quotations 290 and 289. For forms of conflict regulation in France
in the second half of the 11th cent., cf. also Patrick Geary, 'Vivre en conflit dans une
France sans état. Typologie des mécanisme de règlement des conflits (1050–
1200)', *Annales ESC*, 41 (1986), 1,107–33.

[34] Karl Leyser, 'The Crisis of Medieval Germany', *Proceedings of the British Academy*,
69 (1983), 409–43. Now repr. in id., *Communications and Power in Medieval Europe:
The Gregorian Revolution and Beyond*, ed. by Timothy Reuter (London, 1994).

Similarly uncontroversial is the statement that royal actions, like human actions in general, gained a different quality as part of the twelfth-century renaissance.[35] Ernst Kantorowicz sums up this development for thirteenth-century England thus, referring to Henry de Bracton: 'The ancient idea of liturgical kingship gradually dissolved, and it gave way to a new pattern of kingship centered on the sphere of Law which was not wanting its own mysticism.'[36] Frederick I Barbarossa (1152–1190) in Germany and Henry II (1154–1189) in England are seen as having translated these new movements into strong governmental action. These two rulers, whose almost contemporaneous rules were exceptionally long, both fulfilled the 'modern' demands of the time for more peace, and introduced measures to check feuding and capital crime: Frederick Barbarossa promulgated his *Landfrieden*, and Henry II reformed the law courts. Working from different sources, scholars have given the efforts of these two rulers different labels. Their activities have therefore never really been compared, although they had the same aim of securing the common peace. Against the background of the German situation, where scholars have repeatedly cast doubt on the efficiency of Barbarossa's measures, the Plantagenet's reform of the law courts, where it was mentioned at all, was truly seen as 'The Angevin Leap Forward'.[37]

V

Nevertheless, any attempt to make a comprehensive comparison between the role of kingship in the maintenance of peace in England and in Germany would require volumes rather than a few pages. In the present state of our knowledge it is more important to establish what we are seeking to

---

[35] Karl Leyser, 'Some Reflections on Twelfth-Century Kings and Kingship', in id., *Medieval Germany and its Neighbours 900–1250* (London, 1982), 241–67.

[36] *The King's Two Bodies. A Study in Medieval Political Theology* (Princeton, 1957), 192.

[37] Thus the title of Doris M. Stenton's chapter on Henry II in her book *English Justice between the Norman Conquest and the Great Charter, 1066–1215* (Philadelphia, 1964), 22 ff.

compare than to attempt any premature comparison. English historians have in the past often approached the achievements of the monarchy in the twelfth and thirteenth centuries with marked complacency. The Norman and Plantagenet kings not only accepted that it was their duty to maintain peace and to do justice: they endeavoured to give practical effect to these ideals, with the result that, as Maitland put it, the law of the king's court became the common law. The Anglo-Saxon chronicler had much to say about oppression and perversion of justice in the first three Norman reigns; but nevertheless he conceded in favour of the Conqueror that 'the good security he made in this country is not to be forgotten', while his epitaph on Henry I was that 'he made peace for man and beast'. Under the Plantagenets the lawbook attributed to Glanvill, the treatise of Bracton, and the statutes of Edward I are impressive testimony to the precocious, professional, and enlightened quality of a uniform legal system, ceaselessly expanded and adapted to changing needs. Moreover there is abundant evidence for the network of public courts and law enforcement agencies, and, from the beginning of the thirteenth century, records which show them in operation.

How effective was all this in practice? If we define peace as the absence of rebellion and civil war the record is tolerably creditable. Even in the civil war of the mid-twelfth century Earl Robert of Gloucester was praised by King Stephen's biographer for maintaining at least a shadow of peace in the territory under his control, while Geoffrey de Mandeville was not the champion of anarchy he was formerly held to be.[38] In the civil wars of 1215–17 and 1263–5 what was at issue was not the extent of royal jurisdiction but the definition and control of its operation; and Edward I never faced rebellion at all. But if we define peace more widely as the maintenance of law and order it is difficult to give a confident answer. In the closing years of Edward I's reign there was widespread resort to violence at all levels of society, and it has recently been observed that Edward's policy of imposing stiffer penal-

[38] *Gesta Stephani*, ed. and trans. by K. R. Potter, with an introduction and notes by R. H. C. Davis (Oxford, 1976), 150; and see J. O. Prestwich, 'The Treason of Geoffrey de Mandeville', *English Historical Review*, 103 (1988), 283–317.

ties merely made it yet harder to obtain accusations and convictions.[39] Perhaps this crime wave should be attributed to the effects of Edward's wars on an overstrained administration. But can we be sure that the edicts of 1195 and 1205 on the keeping of the peace were not, like Edward I's statutes and ordinances on criminal law, similarly desperate responses to a widespread threat to order and security? That violence should be endemic in the March of Wales is understandable. But it is a little disconcerting to notice the amount of unrest and disorder in London in the late twelfth and early thirteenth centuries, beginning in the 1170s when the city was terrorized by a large gang, about a hundred strong, consisting of the sons of the leading citizens, whose repeated acts of robbery and murder made it unsafe to venture out at night.[40]And it is even more disconcerting to find that Abbot Samson of Bury St Edmunds, who had served both as a judge delegate and an itinerant justice, impatient of the delay in having a rival market suppressed by due process, sent a well-armed force of almost six hundred men to break up the market and to take captive any buyers and sellers they found there.[41]

It is sometimes suggested that the kings of England during this period were concerned with maintaining peace in England only in as far as it enabled them to exploit its resources for the prosecution of wars of conquest.[42] This is to ignore the extent to which, in varying degrees, they were genuinely actuated by ideals of peace. Henry II's intervention in Ireland in 1171-2 is often described as his conquest of that country. It was not: there was no fighting. We are told that the Irish kings and clergy submitted to Henry because they understood that his whole purpose was to establish and maintain a just peace, and it is unreasonable to think that the Irish were gullible and Henry insincere. Unluckily Henry's

[39] M. Prestwich, *Edward I* (London, 1988), 280–8.

[40] W. Page, *London: Its Origin and Early Development* (London, 1923), 99–126; C. N. L. Brooke, assisted by G. Keir, *London, 800–1216* (London, 1975), 43–51.

[41] *Cronica Jocelini de Brakelonda*, ed. and trans. by H. E. Butler (London, 1949), 132–4 and app. T. Abbot Samson's raid on Lakenheath market took place in 1202 or 1203. Although he was summoned to answer for his action, he does not appear to have been punished.

[42] e.g. by Southern, *Medieval Humanism and Other Studies*, 138–9, 213.

energies were deflected elsewhere, and he never returned to Ireland to complete his work as he had intended.[43] It would anyway be wrong to exaggerate the role of kingship in the maintenance of peace. Indeed it has even been argued that in the thirteenth century royal power contributed to disorder and that the judicial authority of the Crown was a public nuisance.[44] The maintenance of order depended largely on the initiative of local communities: there was much self-government without, and sometimes against, the king's command. A striking example of what could be achieved on a large scale, wholly independently of royal control, is provided by the heterogeneous force drawn from England, Normandy, the Low Countries, and the Rhineland which captured Lisbon in 1147. There was no one leader and only one minor count among the participants; but nevertheless this force was held together by its own ordinances, partly modelled on municipal *leges pacis*, and by the practice of settling policy in debate.[45]

Historians of England in the twelfth and thirteenth centuries have been rightly impressed by the legal and institutional measures of the Crown designed to maintain the king's peace. They have been less concerned to assess the more difficult evidence for the efficacy of those measures against the many different forms of disorder, or to consider the ideals and interests independent of the Crown which contributed to such peace as England enjoyed during these centuries, a peace which was seldom more than a shadow of peace.

VI

War was a primary preoccupation of both the Anglo-Norman aristocracy and of the Hohenstaufen Reich and their numerous military followers. As political societies they sometimes

[43] *Radulfi de Diceto Opera Historica*, ed. W. Stubbs (Rolls Series, 68, 1876), i. 350–1; *Giraldi Cambrensis Opera*, ed. J. S. Brewer, J. F. Dimrock, and G. F. Warner (Rolls Series, 21, 1861–91), v. 285–6.

[44] M. T. Clanchy, 'Law, Government, and Society in Medieval England', *History*, 59 (1974), 78.

[45] *De Expugnatione Lyxbonensi*, ed. C. W. David (New York, 1936).

realized themselves explicitly in their hosts. This is perhaps truer of the Empire than of the Anglo-Norman and Angevin kingdom with its growing plethora of institutions and judicial routines, but even here internal peace could only be armed peace. The royal assembly in Germany was sometimes called *exercitus*. The phrase *domi miliciaeque*, albeit borrowed from Sallust and Cicero, described the two spheres in which any layman of standing was deemed to spend his life. Military obligations and functions could thus serve to define rank within the laity both in England and in the Empire. Yet we must note from fairly early times the discrepancy between actual and sometimes novel modes of warfare, and the existence of obligations that had at one time been designed to meet the military needs of kings and kingdoms. When they ceased to do so, they could not easily be changed. Hence, perhaps, the resort to mercenaries and the professionalism which lay at the core of mercenary warfare. Adalbero of Laon and Gerard of Cambrai in their day defined society as being made up of *oratores*, *bellatores*, and *laboratores*, but not every lay noble or son of a knight was a warrior by choice and inclination, even though he did not wish or was not meant to be a clerk or monk. Yet for a man of this class to be decried as *imbellis* was a severe stigma. In the Reich, with its countless feuds, it was also a luxury few could afford. Demobilization and absorption into the ever-enlarging spheres of local government and judicial functions in shire and hundred came more easily to the descendants of Anglo-Norman foeffees.

Mercenaries were a complex phenomenon (see the essays by Michael Prestwich and Karl-Friedrich Krieger); the receipt of pay by itself cannot be the sole criterion to brand a warrior with this pejorative label. *Milites stipendarii* might be honourable, unenfeoffed household troops and the money fief was always a convenient way to keep a force of *milites* permanently under arms and concentrated, ready for immediate service. This mattered for instance in Outremer.

To understand the uses and employment of mercenaries and their limitations it is necessary to recall one feature of medieval warfare: its character as a form of trial, a manifestation of justice, and vindication of right. Men hired champions to fight their duels; princes could also hire mercenaries to fight their wars, but if they wanted to be seen to have a good cause they had to be there themselves, accompanied by some of their foremost homagers and their vassals' vassals. It would not do to be followed by mercenaries only whose interest and engagement were just their pay and the profits of war.

Like any attempt at comparison, that between the military obligations prevalent in Anglo-Norman England and the Reich, the respective relationship between the use of mercenaries and the military duties of *fideles*, vassals, and freemen as a whole, leads us back to more fundamental divergencies in the history and configuration of their respective societies. The post-Carolingian East Frankish kingdom was the less developed and sophisticated region of Charlemagne's empire. Its military arrangements had to meet the needs of savage frontier warfare, defence, and aggression along the huge eastern borders. That the political centre of gravity in this kingdom had in the ninth century rested for long periods in Bavaria and in 919 moved to Saxony made military sense and expressed the demands of a war situation. To these heavy, standing commitments must be added the Italian expeditions, occasional wars in the East, recurrent armed internal conflicts for and around the kingship, not to mention perennial lesser feuds. The noble warrior alone did not suffice to meet all these calls and this in itself may help to explain the most characteristic feature of German military society, the rise of the *ministerialis* in all his many guises, imperial, episcopal, abbatial, princely, and the knights of lesser lords. Given the ubiquity of *ministeriales* and their serviceableness at least to the end of the twelfth century, there was really less scope or need for hiring mercenaries unless Henry IV's call on Bohemians to fight his civil wars for him can be regarded as an equivalent. What Barbarossa and others did later must have been dictated primarily by considerations of military expedience. Mercenaries were more flexible than the services furnished by lay and ecclesiastical princes. The Brabançons, moreover, were also a weapon of terror and intimidation, and their professional standards defied their critics and judges. At Bouvines 700 of them impassively stood their ground when everyone else on the emperor's side decamped. They seem to have been slaughtered to a man. There was no question of quarter, or offering them terms of surrender.

The military make-up of the Reich was not, and never had been, solely governed by the needs of the emperor and the sworn expeditions he could gather. It came to be shaped more and more by the military requirements of territorial lords of all ranks and by cities. It would also be mistaken to ignore the importance of money in imperial warfare long before the advent of the Hohenstaufen. The *ministeriales* of Bamberg, in their *Dienstrecht* of about 1060, were to receive three pounds per hauberc from their lords when they went on expedition to Italy, and it is clear that this was not unique. Treasure in enormous quantity, sent as a bribe to Henry IV by the Grand Prince of Kiev in the summer of 1075 enabled the king, as Lampert of Hersfeld explained, to reward his warriors lavishly for their recent services in battle against the Saxons, and to mount a second campaign in autumn to force the Saxon princes finally to surrender. The 10,000 marks Henry I sent with his daughter Mathilda when she joined her husband-to-be, Henry V, ensured that the Salian's Roman expedition of 1110 marched out in overwhelming strength. It could coerce and overawe like few others. Henry IV on his march to Italy in 1081 had already relied largely on paid troops.

It is just the contrast with the Reich that reveals how much Anglo-Norman military arrangements were the outcome of conquest and shaped by the invaders' land-hunger, their quest for security, and their rulers' need for swift and reliable service. Without ignoring the plenty of loose-footed knightly manpower available, mercenaries and paid *milites*, all the same the future belonged to a once-and-for-all feudal settlement of the conquerors, the work of two or three decades in the main, willed and imposed from above, formidably monitored, administered, and enduring. If there is a paucity of sources to tell us about the components of Anglo-Norman hosts and the actual performance of service due from knights' fees, there is relatively plentiful evidence for tenurial obligations, their distribution, and the ways and means by which they were surveyed, controlled, and not allowed to fall into oblivion. William I's successors thus disposed over a formidable military asset, the *servitia debita* of their vassals and rear-vassals, the latter tied to them by at least reserved fealty oaths. The kings could employ this asset in different ways, directly by exacting host-service, indirectly by commutation, or by mixtures of the two, as it suited them politically and militarily. The Anglo-Norman Crown commanded more liquid resources than most of its rivals and neighbours, and this ultimately underlay the frequent employment of mercenaries and paid service. Here the Normans only adapted methods already familiar from the later Saxon polity with its housecarls and ships' crews. It is perhaps necessary to distinguish not only between obligatory service and mercenaries, but also between the permanent military companions of a great lord or the king, his *maison militaire*, one might almost call it, and the warriors called upon to attend more or less frequently and regularly.

However many hired knights there were like those envisaged in the treaty with the Count of Flanders, and however early, and however many mercenaries, small standing armies almost, such as fought for Henry I year-in year-out, all the same the *servitia debita* formed the backbone of the system because so many other social and legal obligations besides military service were tied to the tenure of honours, fees, and sergeanties. It was a system that lasted because the vested interests sustaining it were overwhelming. It made social sense even when it became difficult quite soon to raise effective and up-to-date field forces solely by its means.

VII

The eleventh century in Latin Europe witnessed nothing less than a revolution.[46] This was most apparent in the Church.

---

[46] Karl Leyser, 'Am Vorabend der ersten europäischen Revolution. Das 11. Jahrhundert als Umbruchszeit', ed. Timothy Reuter for posthumous publication in *Historische Zeitschrift*, 257 (1993), 1–28. Trans. of this article appears in Karl Leyser, *Communications and Power in Medieval Europe: The Gregorian Revolution and Beyond*, ed. Timothy Reuter (London, 1994).

Limits were not only temporarily stretched by individual excursions into the unknown, they became altogether more permeable for larger ideas and movements. One consequence was the creation of 'many new forms of religious experience and sensibility';[47] another, it must be added, was a new way of marking out as different those whose religion precluded them from taking part in this change in religious feeling. To what extent the exclusion and persecution of religious, non-Christian, and other minorities were linked as characteristic features of the age is the subject of a discussion that has not yet been concluded.[48] In any case, it is a complex phenomenon, and only a fraction of it is discussed in this volume—relations between the kings and the crusades, and between the kings and the Jewish minorities in their respective countries.

The crusades were a religious mass movement (see the contribution by Paul W. Edbury). Not least for this reason, they presented kings with considerable problems. Planning and carrying out a crusade could strengthen the king's authority, or it could demonstrate how little it counted for in his own country. Noble adversaries who remained at home while the king left to go on a crusade, or a crusade tax which was uncollectable—English and German kings were well aware of such dangers, and tried to take precautionary measures. Significantly enough, the German kings, unlike Henry II of England, for example, did not even try to impose a Saladin tithe although, as Rudolf Hiestand shows, they considered the crusades highly important.

In a completely different context, our comparison reveals something striking about the Jewish minorities in both kingdoms. In England, Jews are not mentioned in written sources until after the Norman Conquest. Accounts of Jewish traders in Jewish and non-Jewish sources from the Continent reveal that Jewish merchants pursued their trade as far away as Scandinavia and the Slavic east. Did the Jews deliberately avoid pre-Norman England, and if so, why? The remarkable growth of urban settlements in tenth-century Anglo-Saxon

---

[47] Ibid. 2.

[48] Cf. the discussion stimulated by R. I. Moore's book, *The Formation of a Persecuting Society. Power and Deviance in Western Europe 950–1250* (Oxford, 1987).

England makes it seem far more likely that Jews were involved in the trade which flourished with the cities.

The fragmentary nature of the sources in general makes it
difficult to argue that a specific development deviates from
the norm on the basis of *e silentio*. Paul R. Hyams explicitly
demonstrates this when discussing relations between the
Jewish minority and their Christian environment in England.
Historians in early medieval Europe never intended to
provide a comprehensive description of circumstances and
events. Their selection criteria were not the same as ours.[49]
The principles by which they worked were associative rather
than systematic. The fact that anything in particular is mentioned is, therefore, purely coincidental. It cannot be used as
the basis for assessing whether any specific event was typical
or unique. And certainly the fact that something is not mentioned cannot be taken as evidence that it did not exist. What
medieval historians say or do not say cannot be regarded as
a source for the reality of Jewish life in the Christian Middle
Ages until their work is embedded in a total social context
taking account of intellectual, mental, and general ideological assumptions as well as economic and social conditions.
Only within such a total context can individual events as
well as the legal status of German Jews as *Kammerknechte*
attain significance (see the contribution by Alexander
Patschovsky). The comparison between England and
Germany suggests that the emergence of the Pope's universal episcopate and of a division between Christians and 'enemies of Christianity' during the Pope's campaign to drum
up support for the crusades created a common ideological
basis which made the position of Jews more difficult and
dangerous all over Latin Europe.

VIII

In the constitutional discussions in nineteenth-century
Germany, constitutional categories with their legal distinc-

---

[49] Cf. William S. Brandt, *The Shape of Medieval History* (New Haven, 1966); Nancy
F. Partner, *Serious Entertainment. The Writing of History in 12th Century England*
(London, 1977).

tions were projected back into the Middle Ages. Historians' perceptions of an opposition between the will of the citizens and the rule of a sovereign in their own times led them to equate collective action in the Middle Ages with freedom movements. German towns in the Middle Ages, in particular, were seen as standing for what people aspired to achieve in their own political lives: self-rule by a confident middle class.[50] The beginning of this was dated to an act of liberation in which the domination of the city rulers was cast off. After all, medieval sources provide rousing slogans for what was seen as the essence of the whole movement: 'coniuratio facta est pro libertate.'[51]

German scholars tend to see this idealization of the medieval town, with its emphasis on the creation of the municipality as an organ of self-determination, as a typically German phenomenon which compensated the German middle classes for the political participation which they had long been denied. But a comparative perspective shows that English urban historians, like their German counterparts, have also tended to use modern legal categories in trying to explain the medieval past. Similarly, both German and English urban historians today are interested less in presenting towns and their collective behaviour as an ideal case than in recognizing that collective action 'formed an essential part of all medieval government' (Susan Reynolds, p. 273; see also the contribution by Hermann Jakobs). The old inter-

[50] Interest in medieval towns spread far beyond the circle of professional historians. For liberals, they provided an idealized model of their own times: 'in their view, the towns of the medieval world had given birth to the history of freedom. It seemed to them that the time was ripe for bringing this movement to completion. Its time had come' (Klaus Schreiner, 'Die Stadt des Mittelalters als Faktor bürgerlicher Identitätsbildung. Zur Gegenwärtigkeit des mittelalterlichen Stadtbürgertums im historisch-politischen Bewußtsein des 18., 19. und beginnenden 20. Jahrhunderts', in *Stadt im Wandel. Kunst und Kultur des Bürgertums in Norddeutschland 1150–1650* (Brunswick, 1985), 517–41).

[51] More recent research suggests that this quotation from the *Kölner Königschronik, Recensio II z.J.* 1112, refers to a conspiracy by the princes of the Lower Rhine against Kaiser Henry V in 1114. The citizens of Cologne, together with their archbishop, took a leading role in this conspiracy. Cf. Helmuth Kluger, '1074–1288. Auf dem Weg zur Freiheit. Die Entfaltung des kommunalen Lebens in Köln', in Werner Schäfke (ed.), *Der Name der Freiheit 1288–1988* (Cologne, 1988), 13–24. For a regional historical interpretation cf. also Wolfgang Peters, 'Coniuratio facta est pro libertate. Zu den coniurationes in Mainz, Köln und Lüttich in den Jahren 1105/06', *Rheinische Vierteljahrsblätter*, 51 (1987), 303–12.

pretation of the medieval city was based on the general assumption that *Herrschaft* equals coercion; social mobility was unquestioningly equated with partial or complete freedom from the coercion exercised by a ruler. Against the background of this explanatory model, urban and rural social developments since the twelfth century have been interpreted as a growth of freedom.

Recent historians have been increasingly critical of this concept and the whole terminology associated with it.[52] Research on *coniurationes* and guilds has been vitally important in producing this paradigm shift. For the old school of historians, *coniurationes* were conspiracies directed against the ruler and his rule.[53] More recent research, however, has pointed in a different direction. We have been presented with a new, multi-dimensional picture: *coniuratio, gilde*, and *amicitia* turn out to be synonyms for a specific form of association within a society in which primary ties depended on a blood relationship. It was normally the duty of relatives to offer comprehensive assistance. In these associations, this duty was created by an oath, which formed the basis of an 'artificial relationship'. The community created by eating together at guild dinners, and the religious community established by the commemoration of the dead (*Totenmemoria*) demonstrate that the guilds were associations which encompassed the whole of human existence, and that their members were duty bound to offer many forms of practical help.[54] Arguments on conflict resolution in *dinggenossen-*

[52] Cf. the collection of essays ed. by Johannes Fried, *Die abendländische Freiheit vom 10. zum 14. Jahrhundert* (Vorträge und Forschungen, 39; Sigmaringen, 1991).

[53] It is documented that from the second half of the 11th cent. town-dwellers formed *coniurationes* against their town rulers in Rhenish Flanders. This fact has been built up into a comprehensive explanatory model. Town communities, in the sense of citizens' administrations, were generally seen as growing out of conspiracies against the town rulers. The ringleaders were long-distance traders who, separated from home and kin, developed their merchants' guilds in response to their particular situation. These guilds provided the model of a co-operative association held together by oath. Merchants, who were used to freedom and were not tied to any particular ruler, were seen as the driving force behind the uprisings, and thus as the real creators of urban communities and civic freedoms. Hans Planitz's classic work, *Die deutsche Stadt im Mittelalter. Von der Römerzeit bis zu den Zunftkämpfen* (Vienna, 1954), is based on this tenet.

[54] Cf. the collection of essays ed. by Berent Schwineköper, *Gilden und Zünfte. Kaufmännische und gewerbliche Genossenschaften im frühen und hohen Mittelalter*

schaftlichen courts put forward by legal historians, too, place a large question mark over the idea that early medieval society was, in principle, ruled by coercion.[55] Thus from two completely different starting-points, doubt is cast on the view that twelfth-century processes of social development can be seen as a straightforward movement from coercion by a ruler, to liberation from this coercion and self-determination, or in other terms, from servitude to the liberties of the *ministeriales*, which approximated those of the nobility. Instead, the question of social mobility must be posed in more general terms, and without prescribing a direction.

If we accept John Gillingham's statement that 'the ability of people to rise vertically in society [is] a direct result of moving horizontally' (p. 342), then it is clear that social mobility is directly connected with changes in the manorial system and the growth of towns in the twelfth century. Before asking how economic and social structures changed in the twelfth century, we must be aware of the specific character of early medieval source material. Although as a whole the types of sources available in England and Germany are comparable, the sources which cast light on economic and social structures are very different. The similarity lies in the fact that in neither country do we find written sources preserving data which was routinely collected, and which could be used as the basis for calculating a number of different types of statistics. It is a general feature of the early Middle Ages that in contrast to the modern period, documents were not automatically produced as a by-product of most human activities with the exception of the most intimate, private sphere. In the early medieval period they were produced only in excep-

(Vorträge und Forschungen, 29; Sigmaringen, 1985). In the context of German research, Otto Gerhard Oexle's work was pioneering. His essay, 'Conjuratio und Gilde im frühen Mittelalter. Ein Beitrag zum Problem der sozialgeschichtlichen Kontinuität zwischen Antike und Mittelalter', is in the volume cited above, 113–26.

[55] Jürgen Weitzel, *Dinggenossenschaft und Recht. Untersuchungen zum Rechtsverständnis im fränkisch-deutschen Mittelalter* (2 vols., Cologne and Vienna, 1985); id., 'Gewohnheitsrecht und fränkisch-deutsches Gerichtsverfahren', in Gerhard Dilcher (ed.), *Gewohnheitsrecht und Rechtsgewohnheiten im Mittelalter* (Schriften zur Europäischen Rechts- und Verfassungsgeschichte, 6; Berlin, 1992), 67–86; on the place of Weitzel's research in German legal historiography cf. Karin Nehlsen-von Stryk, 'Zum "Justizbegriff" der rechtshistorischen Germanistik', *Ius Commune*, 17 (1990), 189–222, esp. 213 ff.

tional circumstances, when there was a specific reason for capturing in writing some aspect of a situation or action. At first, this was done almost exclusively by Church institutions and the kings, who had been exposed to a written culture by the clergy at their courts.

As the contributions to this volume which look at forms of writing show, this began to change in the twelfth century. At that time, writing for administrative purposes, as well as by lay people, began to become more widespread. The individual and restricted purposes for which they were drawn up, therefore, means that there are limits to what early medieval documents can tell us. Of course, we can extract information from such documents which their creators did not intentionally convey. But this does not alter the fact that the reason for the drawing up of the document dictated what was communicated. Depending on the purpose for which it was drawn up, a document gives us only glimpses of aspects of the social and economic situation. Thus we must assume, for a start, that the picture which modern historians draw of the medieval economic and social order is also dictated by the nature of the sources.

One type of source which is common to both countries under comparison here is the deed of royal gift. But there are other types of sources for which no equivalent exists in the other country. In Germany, these are notably the late Carolingian *Urbare* (land registers) and the *Traditionsnotizen* (notes recording donations to ecclesiastical institutions). Based on these sources, historians developed the concept of *Villikationsverfassung* as the 'classic, bipartite system of land holding', with *Salland* farmed directly from the manor, and dependent landholdings tied to the lord's manor or to other nearby farms where tribute and service were rendered. Other types of documents, such as manorial laws and records of disputes, show this system in dissolution in the twelfth and thirteenth centuries. The *Salland* might be subdivided and leased out, while tributes and services could be commuted into money rents, thus loosening the structures of the *familia* (Werner Rösener). This picture is not incorrect, but we should take seriously Christopher Dyer's warning. On the basis of his less homogeneous English material, he is suspicious of 'simple unilinear trends', and calls for a 'complex account of social development'. 'Perhaps like all ideal types, the perfect manor is an intellectual construct, that never really existed anywhere, but still serves for us a useful conceptual purpose' (p. 302).

The types of sources available also seem to have had an important impact on the assessment of social change and the social mobility associated with it. In England the Domesday Book is a unique source for the question of social mobility. Before even considering the detailed information it contains, we learn from it that social mobility involves movement in both directions. The army which followed William the Conqueror from the Continent to England, consisting mainly of the younger, and often impoverished, sons of the nobility, rose to become a ruling class. The other side of this coin was that the Anglo-Saxon landlords whose estates they took over suffered social and political decline. As soon as we work with the Domesday Book, we become aware that social mobility involved a change in status relations within a social system. Thus any gain in status on one side always involved a corresponding loss on the other side. Social mobility created new conditions of competition.

In the German-speaking lands the main sources available for studying this topic are records dating from a pre-administrative age and relating to individual cases. Legal documents were generally produced in cases of dispute when it was necessary, for whatever reason, to record the outcome in writing. Thus of all the forms of social mobility, the best-documented are those in which an old obligation is cast in a new legal form after a dispute. As the persons who benefited from this change naturally had an interest in making sure that the decision in their favour was not forgotten, they often took the initiative in having a legal document drawn up, and it frequently reflected their view of things. Studying the records of these cases and manorial law makes social mobility appear essentially a legal phenomenon. This is the source of the close relation which German scholars have seen between social mobility and freedom. After all, in the Middle Ages, the Latin term *libertas* has primarily, but not exclusively, legal connotations, meaning, as it does, an insistence on one's legal status. (For the specific form of *Zensualität*, see the contribution by Michael Matheus.)

The fact that in the sources social mobility appears mainly as an improvement in one's legal status does not, of course, mean that in the twelfth century social mobility was synonymous with an increase in freedom. In both countries under comparison there was also horizontal mobility, both through the colonization of newly opened up land within existing borders, and by movement across the old borders. A closer comparison between the social implications of German settlements east of the Elbe and English 'migrations' to Wales and Scotland would reveal more than individual case-studies can tell us. No one would dispute that the opportunity to move away, whether into towns or to newly settled land, always brought greater freedom with it, in the sense of providing more room for manœuvre. And taking a comparative view prevents us from assuming that developments in any one country were unique.

IX

A number of the phenomena which have prompted the idea of a 'renaissance of the twelfth century' are discussed in this comparative volume. This notion is based on the fact that the state, social structures, and mentalities began to change more rapidly in the twelfth century than before. The question is, how similar or different were the changes in Germany and England? Were the obvious differences at the level of state developments matched in other fields of human activity? The only answer we can give is both banal and modest. The administrative activities of the Angevin court did have an impact, even if it was not always spectacular. They affected a number of spheres, from the spread of literacy among the laity to the internal organization of towns (resulting in greater homogeneity than in Germany), the self-image of the warrior nobility, and social mobility. A comparison shows more clearly than a non-comparative analysis the extent to which the explanatory models developed by historians depend on what information can be extracted from the sources. Further comparative work will both enrich the explanatory models developed for each country and allow us to make more accurate historical judgements.

Part I

MODES OF COMMUNICATION

1

Lay Literacy in England, 1100–1300

Nicholas Orme

The ancient notion of three estates with distinctive functions was well known in medieval England. The clergy prayed, the knights fought, and the peasants laboured. In this tripartite scheme, literacy was seen as the distinctive skill of ecclesiastics; indeed, in the French and English languages, the word 'clergy' meant not only clerks but written learning. Those who practised it were clerks, and 'lay' was a synonym for 'illiterate'.[1] Such ideas had a relationship to real social conditions. They could not have endured without some basis of fact, and it is impossible to disbelieve them completely. Equally, we know that they fail to express the whole truth about a complex state of affairs. Even in medieval times some laymen and women were recognized by ecclesiastical writers as having literary skills, and since the 1930s modern historians have drawn attention to more and more such people: knights, ladies, citizens, and country-dwellers.[2] It is now widely accepted that many of the English laity were either literate or involved in literary activities between 1100 and 1300, and it is likely that the number grew significantly during the period.

---

[1] Louise W. Stone, W. Rothwell, and T. B. W. Reid (eds.), *Anglo-Norman Dictionary* (7 fascs.; London, 1977–92), s.v. *clergie, clerk, lai*; J. A. Simpson and E. S. C. Weiner (eds.), *Oxford English Dictionary* (2nd edn., 20 vols.; Oxford, 1989), s.v. clergy (5), clerk (2a, 4a, 5), lay (3).

[2] Relevant works include V. H. Galbraith, 'The Literacy of the Medieval English Kings', *Proceedings of the British Academy*, 21 (1935), 201–38; J. W. Thompson, *The Literacy of the Laity in the Middle Ages* (University of California Publications in Education, 9; Berkeley and Los Angeles, 1939); H. G. Richardson and G. O. Sayles, *The Governance of Medieval England* (Edinburgh, 1963), 265–84; K. B. McFarlane, *The Nobility of Later Medieval England* (Oxford, 1973); M. B. Parkes, 'The Literacy of the Laity', in D. Daiches and A. Thorlby (eds.), *Literature and Civilisation: The Medieval World* (London, 1973), 555–77; N. Orme, *English Schools in the Middle Ages* (London, 1973); R. V. Turner, 'The *Miles Literatus* in Twelfth- and Thirteenth-Century England: How Rare a Phenomenon?', *American Historical Review*, 83

Defining people's literacy is a difficult matter. Writers of Latin in medieval England inherited the classical word *lit(t)eratus*, meaning 'literate' or 'a literate person', with its counterpart *illiteratus*. A corresponding word in Anglo-Norman French, *lettré*, is found by the end of the twelfth century, and (somewhat later, in the fourteenth century) *lettred and unlettred* appear in English, followed by *literate* and *illiterate* in the fifteenth.[3] In all these languages, however, the words were employed rhetorically and variably as well as precisely and legally. Much depended on the literary context. *Litteratus*, as well as meaning 'literate' in contrast to 'illiterate', could be used to describe a cleric as opposed to a layman, or a choir monk as distinct from a lay brother. At other times it could mean the opposite: a literate layman who was not a cleric, but shared with the clergy their stereotyped ability to read. The word could also imply a standard of learning, and medieval writers sometimes referred disparagingly to people they disliked as *illiterati*. Roger, Bishop of Salisbury (1103–39), Abbot Ording of Bury St Edmunds (1193–1205) and Ralph Nevill, Bishop of Chichester (1224–44) were all accused in this way by hostile witnesses.[4] None is likely to have been absolutely illiterate. Rather, their critics were asserting that they were less learned than they should have been.

Naturally, those who were literate varied in their literary abilities. Dr M. B. Parkes, in an influential article published in 1973, distinguished between the scholar or professional man of letters, the cultivated reader who used books for recreation, and the pragmatic reader who read or wrote in the course of transacting his business.[5] These distinctions are helpful in suggesting the range of literary expertise and

(1978), 928–45; M. T. Clanchy, *From Memory to Written Record: England 1066–1307* (London, 1979; 2nd edn., Oxford, 1993, with recent bibliography); B. Stock, *The Implications of Literacy: Written Language and Models of Interpretation in the Eleventh and Twelfth Centuries* (Princeton, 1983); N. Orme, *From Childhood to Chivalry: The Education of the English Kings and Aristocracy, 1066–1530* (London, 1984); N. Orme, *Education and Society in Medieval and Renaissance England* (London, 1989); and Carol M. Meale (ed.), *Women and Literature in Britain, 1150–1500* (Cambridge, 1993).

[3] Clanchy, *From Memory to Written Record*, 226–30; Stone *et al.* (eds.), *Anglo-Norman Dictionary* s.v.; *Oxford English Dictionary* s.v.
[4] Clanchy, *From Memory to Written Record*, 229–30.
[5] Parkes, 'Literacy of the Laity', 555.

activities, but they fail to do justice to the variety that existed. Everyone's literacy was individual, and setting up simple distinguishing categories can be misleading. Many people must have been both 'cultivated' and 'pragmatic' readers, depending on the occasion, and surviving evidence about the one does not rule out the possibility of the other. There were also linguistic differences. Three languages were written in medieval England—Latin, French, and English—causing further variation, depending on how many one knew and how far. There were those who could read but not write, those who did both, and those who could but did not. Kings, noblemen, and their wives might prefer to be read to and to dictate their writings, because it was easier or accorded better with their status and life-styles. Beyond the 'pragmatic reader' who could understand what he read, there were those who could pronounce a written text but not understand it, and those who used books for devotion by contemplating the letters as icons without being able to pronounce them.[6] So there was not a clear distinction between the literate and the illiterate. And even the illiterate, as Dr Michael Clanchy has shown in his fundamental study of literacy in medieval England, were not necessarily out of touch with literature. They could possess written documents and be present when reading went on.[7]

Some variations in people's literacy were related to their sex, rank, and occupation; certainly, surviving records tell us more about certain social groups than others. The evidence about literacy in medieval England relates to at least four major categories: the male aristocracy, encompassing everyone from the king through the magnates down to ordinary landed or household knights; the female aristocracy across the same range; townsmen; and countrymen. Kings and noblemen are particularly well favoured with records of their literacy, including some of the oldest references. The first great description of the English aristocracy, in Bede's *Ecclesiastical History*, already contains accounts of two seventh-century kings, Sigeberht of the East Angles and Aldfrith of the Northumbrians, who came to the throne having been in

---

[6] Below, n. 68.   [7] Clanchy, *From Memory to Written Record*, chs. 2, 6–10.

close contact with clergy.[8] Aldfrith (685–704), whom Bede informs us was able to read Latin, is the first clear English example of a literate layman. The next great portrayal of the class, the poem *Beowulf* written in the eighth century, does not feature literate noblemen, though its heroes are wise, eloquent, and good-mannered as well as brave and skilled in war. *Beowulf*, however, is a historical story about earlier times which are deliberately depicted as different from that of the audience, and it may already have been out of step with aristocratic education. Indeed, the story was probably written down for a king or lay nobleman to possess and read or hear read. By the early tenth century, the historian Asser was praising Alfred the Great as a literate king who encouraged literacy among his nobility,[9] and by the twelfth century (when large numbers of literary works survive) there is a corresponding increase of writers who recommend literacy as a useful and even a necessary attribute of kings and noblemen. The famous dictum that an illiterate king is a crowned ass (*rex illiteratus, asinus coronatus*) is recorded by William of Malmesbury in about 1125 and by several English writers after him.[10] John of Salisbury wrote in his *Policraticus* (before 1159) that the king should be able to read the laws (though he envisaged illiterate monarchs being given good advice), and he mentioned with approval an opinion that king's children should be educated in liberal studies.[11] Shortly afterwards, the Archbishop of Rouen gave similar counsel to Henry II that his eldest son Henry should have a literary education.[12] With regard to the lesser aristocracy, Peter Alfonsi in his *Disciplina Clericalis* (written in Spain before 1140 but translated into Anglo-Norman by about 1200), wrote that knights should be versed in letters, and not merely

---

[8] Bede, *Ecclesiastical History of the English People*, ed. B. Colgrave and R. A. B. Mynors (Oxford, 1991), 268–9 (bk. 3, chs. 15, 18), 430–1 (bk. 4, ch. 26); B. Colgrave (ed.), *Two Lives of St Cuthbert* (Cambridge, 1940), 237 (Bede's Life, ch. 24).

[9] *Asser's Life of King Alfred*, ed. W. H. Stevenson (Oxford, 1959), 21, 58–60, 67, 73, 75.

[10] Galbraith, 'The Literacy of the Medieval English Kings', 212–13.

[11] John of Salisbury, *Policraticus*, ed. C. C. J. Webb (2 vols., Oxford, 1909), i. 524 (bk. iv, ch. vi).

[12] J. P. Migne (ed.), *Patrologia Latina*, 207 (Paris, 1855), col. 210.

so but in all the seven liberal arts.[13] By the 1180s, the Anglo-Norman poet Hue de Rotelande made the hero of his poem *Ipomedon* a nobleman who could read, and added the significant observation that a man was better thought of if he had mastered *clergie* or literacy.[14]

There were certainly opportunities for young princes and noblemen to learn letters in the twelfth and thirteenth centuries. At this time, most noble education still had a domestic setting. Boys grew up in their parents' households and were sent away as they grew older, for longer or shorter periods, to be educated in the households of other lay noblemen or clerics such as bishops and abbots.[15] Town schools existed in England by the late eleventh century, but their role is less clear in relation to the nobility. They took in noble youths requiring a good literary training for the Church, but we do not know how far they catered for boys intending to become knights.[16] The sons of kings and great lay magnates who were expected to grow up as laymen are usually mentioned being reared in households under the care of a *magister* or *pedagogus*. Sometimes this person was a layman of knightly rank and sometimes a cleric, but in either case he seems primarily to have taught only his pupil since he is always called the *magister* of a specific person, not of a whole school like a schoolmaster (*magister scolarum*).[17] Some modern historians, including H. G. Richardson, G. O. Sayles, and R. W. Turner, have implied that these household *magistri* were literate men capable of teaching letters.[18] This may or may not be true. *Magistri* in romances are often knights praised for their physical prowess and courtesy rather than their scholarship: thus Sabot, the master in the Anglo-Norman romance *Boeve de Haumtone*, is characterized as a rich, strong,

---

[13] E. Hermes (ed.), *The Disciplina Clericalis of Petrus Alfonsi* (London, 1977), 113–15.

[14] E. Kölbing and E. Koschwitz (eds.), *Hue de Rotelande's Ipomedon* (Breslau, 1889), lines 194–212.

[15] On what follows, see Orme, *From Childhood to Chivalry*, chs. 1–2.

[16] Ibid. 67.

[17] Ibid. 18–26. Professor F. Barlow, *William Rufus* (London, 1983), 18–20, identifies the lay and clerical status of these early *magistri* in a different way from me.

[18] Richardson and Sayles, *The Governance of Medieval England*, 272–3; Turner, 'The *Miles Literatus* in Twelfth- and Thirteenth-Century England', 935.

and warlike knight (*chevaler fu riches, fort et combataunt*).[19]
Often, the *magister*'s duties may have been the general ones
of protecting and supervising the boy, or have centred on
non-literary matters such as manners and physical skills.
Some may have taught letters (especially if they were clerics),
or a separate teacher may have been brought in for the
purpose like Matthew, *doctor ducis*, who appears to have done
this task for the young Duke Henry (later Henry II) in the
1140s.[20] But it is probably unwise to assume that the masters
of noble boys were literary teachers when no specific evidence survives to this effect.

Explicit references to noble boys like Henry II learning to
read as a prelude to a lay career are very rare in the twelfth
and thirteenth centuries. This is a problem of evidence, and
does not tell us that such boys were not taught literary skills.
At least a few are likely to have been taught to quite a high
degree, because they were intended to become clergy but
never achieved the aim, due to lack of vocation or a recall to
secular duties because of the deaths of their elder brothers.
Aldfrith's career was of this kind, and there must have been
other examples in later Anglo-Saxon and Norman times.
Such cases become more visible after 1200, when more biographical records survive. Gilbert Marshal, the third son of
the great William Marshal, who was born in about 1200, was
trained to become a cleric and held benefices. Eventually,
however, he inherited the earldom of Pembroke in 1234,
married, and adopted a secular way of life.[21] Thomas de
Clare, a younger son of the Earl of Gloucester, studied at
Oxford in the 1250s but was later knighted and followed a
military career in Ireland.[22] Edmund Mortimer, son of a
Welsh Marcher baron, passed several years at Oxford in the
1270s and held benefices, but abandoned clerical life in

[19] A. Stimming (ed.), *Boeve de Haumtone* (Halle, 1899), 10, lines 223–5.

[20] H. G. Richardson, 'The Letters and Charters of Eleanor of Aquitaine', *English Historical Review*, 74 (1959), 193–7.

[21] G. E. Cockayne, *The Complete Peerage*, ed. V. Gibbs *et al.* (13 vols. in 14; London, 1910–59), x. 371–4; Matthew Paris, *Chronica Maiora*, ed. H. R. Luard (7 vols., Rolls Series, London, 1872–84), iv. 135.

[22] A. B. Emden, *A Biographical Register of the University of Oxford to A.D. 1500* (3 vols., Oxford, 1957–9), i. 425.

1282 on the death of his elder brother and duly inherited the family barony.[23]

In general, however, much more is recorded in this period about the literacy of adults than the education of children, and recent historians have collected many casual references to such expertise from contemporary writers. In the twelfth century, several noblemen are credited with a knowledge of letters: Henry I, his son Robert Earl of Gloucester, the Beaumont brothers Waleran Count of Meulan and Robert Earl of Leicester, and the baronial Brian Fitz-Count.[24] Brian, indeed, is said to have written a manifesto on behalf of the Empress Matilda, and a letter on the same subject survives that is attributed to him. Other allusions throw light on one or two lesser noblemen such as Walter Espec, a Yorkshire landlord, who possessed a Latin text of Geoffrey of Monmouth's British history by 1139, and the unnamed *miles litteratus* from south Wales who liked to compose Latin verses extempore with a companion as a recreation. This man, described by Gerald of Wales and apparently alive in the second half of the twelfth century, had perhaps received a grammar-school education.[25] In the early and mid-twelfth century much of this literacy must have involved the reading and understanding of Latin. Boys were taught to read via the Latin alphabet—a custom which endured until the end of the Middle Ages—and they appear to have got their early reading practice from Latin liturgical books like the psalter. They were thus enabled to understand the Latin liturgy, Latin documents like charters, and Latin literature such as chronicles and saints' lives.

Latin, however, was a difficult language to learn even for French-speakers and much more so for English ones. During the later twelfth century, a large amount of literature in French began to be produced both in France and England, including literary fiction and religious works. This change

[23] Ibid., ii. 1316.

[24] Orme, *From Childhood to Chivalry*, 148–9.

[25] Geoffrey Gaimar, *L'Estoire des Engleis*, ed. A. Bell, Anglo-Norman Text Society, 14–16 (1960), lines 6440–6452; Gerald of Wales, *Opera*, ed. J. S. Brewer *et al.* (8 vols., Rolls Series, London, 1861–91), viii. 310.

may partly have been fuelled by the desire of the laity to read, but to do so more easily than Latin permitted. Boys continued to learn the Latin alphabet and, it seems, to master basic Latin skills: the ability to understand or at least recognize the material in a prayer-book or a Latin charter. But for more extensive reading or writing—religious, recreational, and administrative—they began to prefer French. Hue de Rotelande asserted in *Ipomedon*, in about the 1180s, that the laity hardly understood Latin unless it was translated into French, and Gerald of Wales, addressing his Latin history of the conquest of Ireland to King John (1199–1216) suggested that it should be turned into French for the king's attention (perhaps meaning in an oral translation).[26] By the thirteenth century, noblemen who could read or compose Latin fluently may have been growing rare, save for special cases such as judges or failed ecclesiastics. Matthew Paris mentions Paulin Peivre or Piper (d. 1251), a knight of Henry III who wrote a Latin life of St George, but calls him *miles litteratus sive clericus militaris*, as if he were an unusual kind of hybrid.[27] Sir Stephen de Maulay, a Yorkshire knight, may have been another Latinist since Giles of Rome dedicated to him his academic *Expositio in Aristotelis libros Posteriorum I & II* in 1272–3,[28] and Henry de Bray, born in 1270, of Harlestone (Northants) was certainly a third. He copied out in 1322 a Latin miscellany including English history, geography, and his own cartulary.[29] But other real or alleged knightly writers of the thirteenth century—Luke of Gate (the English knight said to have written the French prose *Tristan*), Walter of Bibbesworth, and Walter of Henley—preferred to write in French rather than Latin, and this preference continued among most of their successors in the early fourteenth century.[30]

Hue de Rotelande tells us in another of his romances, *Protheselaus*, that his patron Gilbert Fitz-Baderon, Lord of

---

[26] Hue de Rotelande, *Ipomedon*, lines 27–9; Gerald of Wales, *Opera*, ed. Brewer, v. 410.   [27] Paris, *Chronica Maiora*, ed. Luard, v. 242.
[28] F. Roth, *The English Austin Friars, 1249–1538: II, Sources* (New York, 1961), 7.
[29] Dorothy Willis (ed.), *The Estate Book of Henry de Bray*, Royal Historical Society, Camden 3rd series, 27 (1916), 3.
[30] Renée L. Curtis (ed.), *Le Roman de Tristan en prose* (3 vols., Cambridge, 1985), i. 8, 39. On the other two authors, see below, n. 36.

Monmouth (1174–91), possessed a collection of books in Latin and French.[31] We do not know their titles and we cannot reconstruct the literary interests and activities of any single nobleman in this period, but we can identify the kinds of literature they read as a class. It is possible they used Latin liturgical books (if only for devout contemplation or as a programme of the service), if we can build on a reference by Chrétien of Troyes in the 1170s to a lady reading from a psalter.[32] Latin prayer-books specially made for the laity, however, are known only from the mid-thirteenth century.[33] By the end of the twelfth century devotional works and lives of saints were available in French. In the thirteenth century Robert of Greatham dedicated a treatise on the seven sacraments, called *Corset*, to an Alain who may have been one of the Montfort family, and Peter D'Abernon addressed his Life of St Richard of Chichester to his kinsman Sir John D'Abernon.[34] French *chansons de geste* and romances were evidently popular, hence Hue's composition of *Protheselaus* for Gilbert, and some families commissioned works to celebrate the deeds of their ancestors. *The History of William the Marshal* and the romances *Gui de Warewic* and *Fouke FitzWarin*, all composed in the thirteenth century, fall into this category.[35] There was also a market for practical works in French. By about 1300 not only had Walter of Bibbesworth written a treatise on learning French and Walter of Henley one on husbandry, but the standard works of the day on kingship and war, the *Secretum Secretorum* ascribed to Aristotle and the *Epitoma Rei Militaris* by Vegetius, had both been translated into Anglo-Norman versions.[36] Composite manu-

---

[31] Hue de Rotelande, *Protheselaus*, ed. F. Kluckow (Göttingen, 1924), lines 1207–11.   [32] Below, n. 60.

[33] Clanchy, *From Memory to Written Record*, 289–90.

[34] M. Dominica Legge, *Anglo-Norman Literature and its Background* (Oxford, 1963), 212–13, 270.   [35] Ibid. 138–75.

[36] Annie Owen (ed.), *Le Traité de Walter de Bibbesworth sur la langue française* (Paris, 1929), corrected by W. Rothwell; 'A Mis-judged Author and a Mis-used Text', *Modern Language Review*, 77 (1982), 282–93; Dorothea Oschinsky (ed.), *Walter of Henley and other Treatises* (Oxford, 1971); Peter D'Abernon, *Le Secre de Secrez*, ed. O. Beckerlegge, Anglo-Norman Text Society, 5 (1944); Lewis Thorpe, 'Mastre Richard, a Thirteenth-century Translator of the "De Re Militari" of Vegetius', *Scriptorium*, 6 (1952), 39–50; M. Dominica Legge, 'The Lord Edward's Vegetius' ibid. 7 (1953), 262–5.

scripts also survive, containing copies of Henley alongside parliamentary statutes, recipes for cookery, lists of measurements, proverbs, moral poems, and other treatises.[37] Finally, any king, magnate, or knight would encounter documents: royal writs, private charters and conveyances of land, letters and wills, the proliferation of which between 1100 and 1300 has been so well charted by Dr Clanchy.[38] Every nobleman must have had muniments relating to his private property and affairs, and many men took up public duties as justiciars, sheriffs, coroners, jurors, and commissioners. Though clerks and clergy were often available to help write and read such documents, recent historians have been unwilling to see the nobility as totally dependent on intermediaries to deal with such material.

There can be no doubt, therefore, that the nobility included some—perhaps many—who could read, and that all of them had to do with literary material at first or second hand. At the same time, literacy should not be overemphasized as an element of male noble culture. Certainly, contemporaries did not unduly stress it. By the second half of the twelfth century writers of romances often describe how heroes such as Horn, Ipomedon, and Tristan were reared and trained. But the process involves a variety of skills and standards—moral, artistic, and physical—and literacy is not singled out for attention. We do not possess the educational sections of the earliest Tristan romances, Thomas's Anglo-Norman version (c. 1155–70) and Beroul's continental one (probably 1190s), but neither shows the adult Tristan as a literate man.[39] The earliest text to handle Tristan's upbringing, Eilhart von Oberge's German version of the late twelfth century, says nothing about the learning of letters, and mentions only courtesy, music, and physical exploits.[40] In contrast, Beroul and Eilhart focus on noble disengagement from literature. When Tristan is in the forest and needs to communicate with King Mark, he gets the hermit Ogrin to write the king a letter. This is duly read to Mark by a chaplain who

[37] For descriptions, see Oschinsky, *Walter of Henley*, 11–50.
[38] Clanchy, *From Memory to Written Record*, ch. 2.
[39] e.g. Beroul, *Tristran*, ed. A. Ewert (vol. i, Oxford, 1939), lines 2278–680.
[40] Eilhart von Oberge, *Tristrant*, ed. Danielle Buschinger (Göppingen, 1976), lines 130–84.

composes a reply which Ogrin reads to Tristan.[41] Neither king nor knight is directly involved. Later writers were more likely to portray their heroes as personally literate. Hue's Ipomedon in the 1180s is 'well lettered' and better esteemed for that reason; Gottfried von Strassburg's Tristan (*c.* 1210) explicitly learns letters in his youth; and in the French prose *Tristan* (*c.* 1215–35) Tristan reads a letter by himself and Lancelot writes one.[42] After this it is common to find passing mentions of noble literacy in romances, but the ability rarely attracts the attention which is given to other accomplishments. Even in the thirteenth century, the young William Marshal is chiefly praised for his singing, good manners, and athletic feats, and Guy of Warwick for his courtesy, generosity, and skill as a hunter.[43]

There are also numerous references to kings and noblemen making contact with literature through other people, rather than personally. The Anglo-Norman poet Denis Pyramus writing in the late twelfth century tells us that the *Lais* (short stories) of Marie of France were popular with earls, barons, and knights who had them recited frequently and took great delight in them.[44] Chrétien de Troyes's *Yvain* (1170s) portrays a girl reading a romance to her noble father and mother,[45] and Gerald of Wales, as we have seen, imagined that his Irish history would reach King John via an intermediary. Writers of romances sometimes adopt the manner of addressing a noble audience by mouth, as in *Boeve de Haumtone*: 'Lords barons, now listen to me . . . If you will hear, I will tell you.'[46] Writing could also be done at second hand, through general instruction or precise dictation, to produce apparently personal letters and even a whole book. Here, the example of Geoffrey de la Tour Landry, the noble author of *The Book of the Knight of the Tower*, is relevant al-

[41] Ibid., lines 4764–901; Beroul, *Tristrant*, ed. Ewert, i. lines 2278–680.

[42] Hue de Rotelande, *Ipomedon*, lines 85–96; Gottfried von Strassburg, *Tristan*, ed. K. Marold and W. Schröder (Berlin, 1969), lines 2062–94; *Le Roman de Tristan en prose*, ed. Curtis, i. 145–6; ii. 16–20.

[43] P. Meyer (ed.), *Histoire de Guillaume le Maréchal* (3 vols., Société de l'Histoire de France, Paris, 1891), i. lines 400–1162; A. Ewert (ed.), *Gui de Warewic* (2 vols., Paris, 1932–3), i. 63–8.

[44] Denis Pyramus, *La Vie Seint Edmund le Rei*, ed. H. Kjellman (Gothenburg, 1935), lines 35–48.

[45] Chrétien de Troyes, *Yvain*, ed. W. Foerster (Halle, 1887), lines 5363–72.

[46] *Boeve de Haumtone*, ed. Stimming, lines 1–5.

though somewhat later in date. The author, who lived in Anjou (France), was walking in his garden one day in 1371 when he decided to write a book to instruct his daughters. He tells us that

I went out of the garden and found on my way two priests and two clerks that I had, and told them that I wanted to make a book and an examplar for my daughters to learn to read French (*roumancier*). So I made them bring me the books that I had, such as the Bible, the deeds of the kings, the chronicles of France, Greece, England and many foreign lands, and I had each book read, and where I found a good example to extract I had it taken out to make this book.[47]

In such a way a man might 'write' a book from sources read to him, perhaps in an extempore translation which he rearranged in his mind and dictated to scribes, without personally undertaking any reading or writing. *The Book of the Knight of the Tower* confirms the importance of literary relationships, as well as personal literacy, in medieval societies. We shall never know if all the male nobility were literate, but it may not matter. They lived with literate people, and many aspects of their lives (religion, public service, private administration, and recreation) were influenced by literary texts that could be brought to them at second hand. The same principle applied to society beneath the nobility.

Literacy among noble women is also well attested, and is now well endorsed by cultural historians. There had been literate and even learned women in classical times, and their existence was remembered in medieval literature which drew on classical sources. The difference between the two eras was that in classical times Latin was a vernacular language, whereas by the later period it was an ecclesiastical and scholarly tongue. For a medieval writer or reader, a Latinate woman suggested an unusual degree of learning and a person who was also of an exceptional kind. The eleventh-century 'vulgate' Life of St Katharine of Alexandria (allegedly martyred in the fourth century), adapted into Anglo-

---

[47] M. A. de Montaiglou (ed.), *Le Livre du Chevalier de la Tour Landry* (Paris, 1854), 4.

Norman by the nun Clemence of Barking towards 1200, uses learning to make the saint seem superhuman; she studies the liberal arts to such effect that skilful scholars could not worst her in debate.[48] In the late twelfth-century continental romance, *Partonopeu de Blois,* Melior, daughter of the Emperor of Constantinople, is portrayed as a prodigy who learnt all the liberal arts from masters before she was fifteen.[49] Morgan and Viviane in the early thirteenth-century French prose *Estoire de Merlin* are depicted learning astronomy, necromancy, and other magic crafts, while Felice, the heroine of *Gui de Warewic,* studies astronomy, arithmetic, and geometry under Premonstratensian canons from Toulouse.[50] Such stories developed and publicized a concept of the well-educated noblewoman but one which is, arguably, meant to create a romantic heroine as much as to sketch a model for readers and listeners to follow. When educationists in France began to discuss the bringing up of noblewomen in the thirteenth century, they did not recommend such high levels of expertise. Vincent of Beauvais advised in the mid-century that girls should be able to read, but did not specify an ambitious range of studies.[51] His successor Giles of Rome, who was more influential in England than Vincent, mentioned even reading only in relation to high-born women unable to work with their needles.[52] Academic education for lay women, by the thirteenth century, was largely confined to the world of romance.

There is nevertheless a good deal of evidence about women's literacy in letters, didactic literature, and even romances where the subject comes up casually and seems more realistic. It points to the skill among women in both the old Anglo-Saxon and the new Norman royal families during the late eleventh and early twelfth centuries. Margaret Queen of

---

[48] E. Eininchel (ed.), *Life of St Katherine,* Early English Text Society, original series. 80 (1884), 8: Clemence of Barking, *Life of St Catherine,* ed. W. MacBain, Anglo-Norman Text Society, 18 (1964), 5.

[49] J. Gildea (ed.), *Partonopeu de Blois* (2 vols., Villanova, Pa., 1967–8), i. 186–8.

[50] H. O. Sommer (ed.), *The Vulgate Version of the Arthurian Romances* (8 vols., Washington, 1909–16): *L'Estoire de Merlin,* ii. 211–12, 253, 338; Ewert, *Gui de Warewic,* i. 147–56.

[51] Orme, *From Childhood to Chivalry,* 157.

[52] Ibid.

Scotland (d. 1093), sister of Edgar the Aetheling, studied sacred writings and discussed hard questions with the learned men of her court.[53] Her contemporary Matilda (d. 1083), the wife of the Conqueror, is said by Orderic to have had a knowledge of letters.[54] Matilda's daughter Adela (d. 1137), the mother of King Stephen, read Latin prose and poetry, and one of her correspondents suggested that she might study St Augustine.[55] Margaret's daughter Matilda (d. 1118), the first wife of Henry I, commissioned a life of her mother in Latin which the author said was intended for her to look at, not merely to hear.[56] Henry's second wife, Adeliza of Louvain, likewise commissioned a life of her husband by the historian David, apparently in French.[57] As the twelfth century proceeds, evidence of literary interests survives from lower down the aristocracy. Constance, the wife of the Lincolnshire magnate Ralph Fitz-Gilbert, and an heiress in her own right, is reported by Geoffrey Gaimar to have given a silver mark for a copy of David's Life of Henry I and to have kept it and read it in her chamber. She was responsible for borrowing Geoffrey of Monmouth's history in Latin and giving it to Gaimar, who employed it to write his Anglo-Norman works on British history.[58] By the middle of the century, Sanson of Nanteuil was translating the Proverbs of Solomon into Anglo-Norman for Alice de Condet, probably the wife of Richard Fitz-Gilbert of Clare, and by its end Guischart de Beaulieu's Anglo-Norman *Sermon* in verse pays compliments to a certain Lady Denise, possibly one of the Hacon family from Hampshire.[59]

At the beginning of the twelfth century the works used by noblewomen were in Latin, like those of noblemen, but gradually French also came to be read. David's Life of Henry I appears to have been in that language, and Sanson's prov-

[53] Thompson, *Literacy of the Laity*, 170–1, 188.

[54] Marjorie Chibnall (ed.), *The Ecclesiastical History of Orderic Vitalis* (6 vols., Oxford, 1969–80), ii. 224–5.

[55] Migne, *Patrologia Latina*, 166 (Paris, 1894), col. 1202; 171 (Paris, 1893), col. 146.

[56] Thompson, *Literacy of the Laity*, 171, 188; Legge, *Anglo-Norman Literature*, 9.

[57] Gaimar, *L'Estoire des Engleis*, ed. Bell, lines 6477–86; Legge, *Anglo-Norman Literature*, 22–4, 28.

[58] Ibid.

[59] Ibid. 36–40, 135–6.

erbs certainly were. As the century wore on, women are likely to have resembled men in reading less in Latin and more in French. If they learnt letters, they would have done so in the form of the Latin alphabet, and some may have read Latin liturgical texts to the extent of pronouncing the words. Chrétien of Troyes's *Yvain* portrays the noble lady reading the psalter.[60] Girls, however, seem to have had less formal schooling than boys, and a true understanding of Latin appears to have grown rare among them by 1200. Marie of France who lived in England in the mid-twelfth century knew Latin but wrote chiefly in French, and at the end of the century Clemence of Barking was able to write her Anglo-Norman Life of St Katharine from Latin sources. But after them there is not much evidence for the understanding of Latin by lay noblewomen in England until the early sixteenth century.[61] Even nuns, though saying the Latin liturgy daily, appear by 1300 to have been more familiar with French or, later on, English.[62] Noble wives and widows involved in the management of their own or their family's affairs must have come into contact with Latin documents and may even have acquired some familiarity with their form and content. But when they read at length or drew up personal letters or wills—usually through a scribe—they too preferred to use French. It is impossible to say whether more noblewomen were literate than men, or spent more of their time reading. The more secluded lives of women may have encouraged literary activities, but men had better formal training to read and a greater need to do so because of their involvement in public life.

In breadth of interests, on the other hand, noblewomen in England came close to their male counterparts. Chrétien's allusion to liturgical text reading is complemented by various references to women's involvement with devotional literature in Anglo-Norman. Robert of Greatham's thirteenth-century *Miroir* (sermons on the Sunday gospels) was written for a Lady Aline who may have belonged to the Montfort

---

[60] Chrétien, *Yvain*, ed. Foerster, lines 1414–15.
[61] For a possible exception, see below n. 64.
[62] Eileen Power, *Medieval English Nunneries c. 1275 to 1535* (Cambridge, 1922), 246–9.

family.[63] John of Howden translated his own Latin medi-tation on Christ and the Virgin into Anglo-Norman for Eleanor of Provence, the queen of Henry III, and Matthew Paris wrote her a Life of St Edward in Anglo-Norman verse. His Life of St Edmund, in the same medium, was written for Isabel, Countess of Arundel (d. 1282), and Isabel even en-couraged Ralph Bocking to write his Latin Life of St Richard of Chichester in 1268–72.[64] Noble ladies liked to read fiction, and one or two may even have written it. Marie of France certainly devised the *Lais*,[65] but the romance *Blandin de Cornoailles* once attributed to Queen Eleanor of Provence, is now ascribed elsewhere.[66] The late twelfth-century poem *Waldef*, a *chanson de geste* in Anglo-Norman, was addressed to a female *duce amie*, and Robert of Greatham said that he wrote his *Miroir* to cure his patroness of her love for *Tristan* and for *chansons de geste* such as *Basin*, *Miainet*, and *Sansonet*. At least one practical work was written for a woman: Walter of Bibbesworth's *Tretiz de Langage* (*c.* 1250), which sought to help Denise de Montchensey teach her children better French.[67] As with men, these examples are random ones and do not tell us what was normal. No doubt there was a range of abilities, from those who read and understood to those who listened to readings like the mother in Chrétien's *Yvain* or who contemplated prayer-books they could not read, as St Elizabeth of Hungary (d. 1251) is said to have done in her childhood.[68] By about 1300 an English vocabulary writer could make the general statement that mothers taught their children to read ('woman readeth child on book'),[69] and later still the motif of the Virgin Mary learning to read from

[63] On the works in this para., see Legge, *Anglo-Norman Literature*, 145, 213, 233, 269–70, and Jocelyn Wogan-Browne, ' "Clerc u lai, muïne u dame": Women and Anglo-Norman Hagiography', in Meale (ed.), *Women and Literature in Britain*, 61–85.

[64] Legge, *Anglo-Norman Literature*, 232–5, 268–9; D. Jones, 'The Medieval Lives of St Richard of Chichester', *Analecta Bollandiana*, 105 (1985), 107.

[65] Marie de France, *Lais*, ed. A. Ewert (Oxford, 1944).

[66] C. H. M. Van der Horst (ed.), *Blandin de Cornouaille* (The Hague and Paris, 1974), 62.

[67] Owen, *Le Traité de Walter de Bibbesworth, passim.*

[68] Jacobus de Voragine, *The Golden Legend*, trans. W. G. Ryan (2 vols., Princeton, 1993), ii. 303.

[69] W. W. Skeat, 'Nominale sive Verbale', *Transactions of the Philological Society* (1903–7), p. *7.

her mother (a fact not recorded in the early apocryphal gospels) became a popular subject in religious art.[70]

From at least the early twelfth century, the wealthier men of the towns had opportunities and reasons for becoming literate. It was there that schools and schoolmasters, independent of religious houses, were chiefly to be found. Such schools appear in English records during the late eleventh century in places such as Canterbury, Dunwich, Lincoln, and Old Sarum, where there were cathedrals or important centres of trade. They can be traced in at least thirty-five English towns during the twelfth century and in at least sixty-nine during the thirteenth.[71] Many (though not all) town schools had ecclesiastical affilations, being often governed by local monasteries or clerical dignities, and many of their pupils must have been studying with careers as clergy in mind. We do not know how many other boys came in as a preparation for lay employment any more than we do in the case of noblemen's sons, but schoolmasters (working for fees) were unlikely to refuse customers and it was cheaper for a town-dweller to send his or her son to school than for most other people. Urban parents had only to pay the master's fees, which were comparatively small, and afford the loss of the child's earnings; the greatest expense of schooling, then as now, was the cost of food and lodging away from home. True, the custom said to have been followed in the English schools up to the mid-fourteenth century, by which French was used as the language for teaching Latin, may have presented an obstacle, but the custom may not have been universal and some of the élite families of the larger towns knew French.[72] Townsmen certainly sent their sons to schools to be trained as clerics— Thomas Becket's schooling in London in the 1130s is a well-known example[73]—and would-be clerics, as we have seen, could pass from school to lay careers if their

[70] Clanchy, *From Memory to Written Record*, 13.

[71] Orme, *English Schools in the Middle Ages*, 293–321; *Education and Society*, p. xiv.

[72] The assertion that Latin was taught in French is made by the 14th-cent. writers Ranulf Higden, Robert Holcot, and John Trevisa, but has been challenged by Tony Hunt, *Teaching and Learning Latin in Thirteenth-Century England* (3 vols., Cambridge, 1991), i. 433–4; cf. the review by N. Orme in *Historiographica Linguistica*, 21 (1994), 199–201.

[73] F. Barlow, *Thomas Becket* (London, 1986), 17–18.

ambitions changed or family arrangements were altered by unforeseen deaths.

Moreover, by the twelfth century the more important male town-dwellers had practical reasons for learning to read. The leaders of urban communities were acquiring charters of privileges from their royal or seigneurial overlords, and receiving letters from those authorities requesting things to be done. Communal activities like the keeping of a judicial court and the imposition of taxes and tolls were beginning to generate documents. The earliest surviving series of town records, the guild rolls of Leicester, begins in 1196, to be followed by (for example) the taxation rolls of Wallingford in 1227, the rolls of the London court of husting in 1252, and the mayor's court rolls of Exeter in 1263.[74] Extant records are often preceded by evidence that towns had clerical staff involved in making and handling documents. Lincoln had two town clerks by 1202[75] and similar functionaries are recorded in London shortly afterwards. A two-volume collection of the laws and customs of the capital was drawn up by a clerk in the city guildhall between 1206 and 1216.[76] Oxford had a clerk by 1227–8 and Exeter one by 1237.[77] Not all literary activity in towns can have been confined to clerks, however, since the citizens who served as chief officers had to be involved with documents and may well have kept private personal records of their property, trade and affairs. It is more difficult to gather the names of individual literate townsmen than it is with the aristocracy, but the references to Vitalis the clerk, sheriff of London in 1161–2, and Eudo the clerk, reeve of Canterbury in about 1205, suggest that

[74] G. H. Martin, 'The Origin of Borough Records', *Journal of the Society of Archivists*, 2 (1960–4), 152; G. H. Martin. 'The Registration of Deeds of Title in the Medieval Borough', in D. L. Bullough and R. L. Storey (eds.), *The Study of Medieval Records: Essays in Honour of Kathleen Major* (Oxford, 1971), 155–8; *Historical MSS Commission, Report on the Records of the City of Exeter* (London, 1916), 406.

[75] J. W. F. Hill, *Medieval Lincoln* (Cambridge, 1948), 196.

[76] Mary Bateson, 'A London Municipal Collection of the Reign of John', *English Historical Review*, 17 (1902), 480–511, 707–30; F. Liebermann, 'A Contemporary Manuscript of the "Leges Anglorum Londoniis Collectae"', ibid. 28 (1913), 732–45.

[77] H. E. Salter (ed.), *Cartulary of the Hospital of St John Baptist, Oxford*, vol. i, Oxford Historical Society, 66 (1914), 364; J. W. Schopp (ed.), *The Anglo-Norman Custumal of Exeter* (Oxford, 1925), 8–9.

both were regarded as clerical and therefore very likely literate.[78] In Bath, a casual mention of Reiner the goldsmith as
scrivener of the guild-merchant in about 1220 points to
another leading citizen able to read and write.[79]

Nor was urban male literacy restricted to documents; it
extended to literature like that in vogue among the nobility.
We do not have as much evidence of works commissioned
by townsmen or dedicated to them as we have for their
superiors, but it is likely that some of the metrical romances
composed in Anglo-Norman and English between 1150 and
1300 were read by the urban élites, particularly English romances. The story of *Havelok* is a case in point. The late
twelfth-century Anglo-Norman version takes its hero (a lost
king's son) to Grimsby and its fishermen, and the late thirteenth-century English redaction adds a scene at Lincoln
where Havelok goes to find work.[80] This second version tells
how fishermen go from Grimsby to Lincoln, how fish and
meat are sold on the High Bridge of the latter city, how
porters wait there to be hired, and how the servants of the
great men who live on the hill come down to buy their food.
Havelok, though partly aristocratic, seems also to speak to
an urban audience familiar with such matters. So too the Life
of Guy of Warwick appealed to Baldwin de Windesore,
a leading citizen of Exeter, who caused a copy of the text to
be written in 1301, probably a vernacular version of this
chanson de geste.[81] Some citizens of London cultivated history
and poetry. A chronicle of city affairs beginning in 1188
was written in Latin between 1258 and 1272, probably
by Arnold Fitz-Thedmar, alderman of Bridge Ward, or
by someone associated with him. It mentions him and his
affairs and is the earliest of a genre of city chronicles produced in London and other towns during the following

[78] C. N. L. Brooke, *London 800–1216: The Shaping of a City* (London, 1975), 220;
W. Urry, *Canterbury under the Angevin Kings* (London, 1967), 438.

[79] C. W. Schickle (ed.), *Ancient Deeds Belonging to the Corporation of Bath* (Bath,
1921), 7.

[80] A. Bell (ed.), *Le Lai d'Haveloc* (Manchester and London, 1925), lines 125–246;
W. W. Skeat and K. Sisam, *The Lay of Havelok the Dane* (2nd edn., Oxford, 1939),
lines 861–908.

[81] R. L. Poole and Mary Bateson (eds.), *Index Britanniae Scriptorum* (2nd edn.,
Cambridge, 1990), 104.

centuries.[82] At about the same time some Londoners founded a guild called the Puy, whose distinctive feature was an annual feast at which each member had to compose a new song or pay a fine. The prize song was displayed in written form at the guild's premises throughout the following year, and the guild maintained a clerk to carry out its secretarial work and a box for its muniments, so necessary seemed such things even in a voluntary guild by the end of the thirteenth century.[83]

Finally, literacy reached some of the male inhabitants of the countryside. True, most of the early records of schools relate to towns, but some of these schools were in small settlements that were virtually rural in character, or sufficiently near to the countryside to be attended without boarding. There was also a tradition of priests instructing pupils,[84] and lay people may well have taught each other to read or even learnt by themselves; not everybody need have got the skill in school or in childhood. Villeins appear as the parents and supporters of scholars. As early as the late twelfth century, Walter Map maintained that rustics were eager to educate their children in the [liberal] arts,[85] and court rolls of the late thirteenth century reveal the payment of fines by bondmen to send their sons to school.[86] Here the intention was probably to train them as clergy, but the usual chance existed of a lay career by accident. The chief practitioners of literacy in the countryside were seigneurial officers: stewards and bailiffs. Manorial courts were keeping rolls recording their business by the 1240s, and within another twenty years there were treatises on court practice which incidentally recommended the keeping of written court records.[87] One such

[82] T. Stapleton (ed.), *De Antiquis Legibus Liber: chronica maiorum et vicecomitum Londoniarum*, Camden Society, 34 (1846), 1–177, 238–42; Antonia Gransden, *Historical Writing in England, c.*500 to *c.*1307 (London, 1974), 509–17.

[83] H. T. Riley (ed.), *Munimenta Gildhallae Londoniensis*, vol. 2, pt. 1 (Rolls Series, London, 1860), 216–28.

[84] D. Whitelock, M. Brett, and C. N. L. Brooke (ed.), *Councils and Synods*, pt. 1: *871–1204* (2 vols., Oxford, 1981), i. 331.

[85] Walter Map, *De Nugis Curialium*, ed. M. R. James, C. N. L. Brooke, and R. A. B. Mynors (Oxford, 1983), 12–13.

[86] Orme, *English Schools in the Middle Ages*, 50–2.

[87] Clanchy, *From Memory to Written Record*, 46–51; F. W. Maitland and W. P. Baildon, *The Court Baron*, Selden Society, 4 (1890), 68, 71–2.

treatise suggests that manorial officials should list in writing their tools and stock each autumn, so as to know what to buy for the coming year, and by the 1270s they were also advised to record the names of all laymen over the age of twelve for the twice-yearly view of frankpledge.[88] In 1285 the Statute of Exeter required bailiffs to provide the king's commissioners with rolls containing the names of villages and hamlets.[89] We do not know how many villeins could read, but they certainly used documents. The Peterborough Abbey cartulary known as *Carte Nativorum* contains copies of many charters issued by one villein to another, conveying tiny pieces of property (an acre, a half-acre or a house), and some villeins even had seals by the thirteenth century, despite their technical inability to possess or convey any land of their own.[90]

Most people nowadays have direct access to literature. Far more of us read than are read too, and personal literacy is an essential skill without which status falls and everyday life is impaired. This was less true in the twelfth and thirteenth centuries, even after the great transition from memory to written record described by Dr Clanchy. Only the clergy were required by law to be literate, and literacy for them was but one of several desirable qualities. The enquiries directed at candidates for ordination concerned their legitimate status, physique, moral behaviour, and economic resources, as well as their ability to read and sing.[91] For many clergy, their major literary task—the saying of the liturgy—was done from memory as much by reading texts. Novice monks, up to at least 1300, spent much of their time learning by heart the weekly cycle of services.[92] Much of the literature relating to kings and noblemen, as has been said, ignored the topic of literacy, and Mark and Tristan were shown depending on others to read without apparently losing status in doing so. It

[88] Oschinsky, *Walter of Henley*, 436; Maitland and Baildon, *The Court Baron*, 68–9.

[89] A. Luders and others (eds.), *The Statutes of the Realm* (10 vols., Record Commission, London, 1810–24), i. 210.

[90] C. N. L. Brooke and M. M. Postan (eds.), *Carte Nativorum: A Peterborough Cartulary of the Fourteenth Century*, Northamptonshire Record Society, 20 (1960).

[91] H. S. Bennett, 'Medieval Ordination Lists in the English Episcopal Registers', in J. Conway Davies (ed.), *Studies Presented to Sir Hilary Jenkinson* (London, 1957), 20; Orme, *English Schools in the Middle Ages*, 15.

[92] D. Knowles, *The Religious Orders in England* (3 vols., Cambridge, 1948–59), i. 285–6.

was the same with merchants and townsmen. The contemporary Life of St Godric of Finchale (d. 1170) by Reginald
of Durham tells of a man of lowly origins who became a
shipman and a merchant, grew skilful in navigation, learnt
French, and went on pilgrimages. His religious knowledge
was based on the Lord's Prayer and the Creed which he knew
by heart, and not until the age of forty did he own a psalter
and begin to learn to read; yet Godric was eventually ac-
claimed as a saint.[93] Among the peasantry, Langland was to
assert in the 1360s that abstinence and conscience—non-
literary disciplines—produced a Plowman better acquainted
with God's word than a literate priest.[94] Right to the end of
the Middle Ages, ecclesiastical writers and legislators recommended the laity to know and repeat by heart the Paternos-
ter, Ave Maria and Creed as their basic devotional aids.

Personal literacy mattered less in this period, because
there was less to read and more opportunity to get someone
else to read it. Literacy was more of a communal skill, less of
an individual one. It is therefore impractical, even if it were
possible, to estimate how many people were literate. Simple
figures would do justice neither to differences of ability nor
to relationships between the literate and illiterate. Most bi-
ographies of lay people have to be constructed and studied
without knowing whether they were literate or not. What Dr
Clanchy and others have now shown beyond doubt is that
English society was collectively literate by 1300. Many genres
of literature, documents, and inscriptions existed, and proliferated in numerous examples. Everyone had some contact
with a literate person, in the shape of a servant, a master, or
an agent such as a priest or bailiff; with a literary forum like
a church or a court where texts were being written or read;
or with literate material. Literacy and literature already
affected everyone's lives.

[93] J. Stevenson (ed.), *Libellus de Vita et Miraculis S. Godrici*, Surtees Society, 20
(1847), esp. 23–38.
[94] William Langland, *The Vision of William Concerning Piers the Plowman*, ed. W. W.
Skeat (2 vols., Oxford, 1954), 244–5 (A. viii. lines 119–20; B. vii lines 131–2).

2

Who Could Read and Write in the Middle Ages?

ALFRED WENDEHORST

When looking at medieval sources on the founding of schools, it is tempting to project back the experiences of our own schooldays. In our mind's eye, we see children tentatively spelling out and reading their first words, perhaps writing letters and numbers on a slate (producing an unforgettable noise), and reciting their multiplication tables. Why are we so sure that while elementary instruction has evolved over more than a thousand years, schools as the setting for organized teaching have maintained some sort of continuity in the face of all these changes?

A more detailed look at medieval sources shakes our certainty that teaching in the Middle Ages was a precursor of present-day schooling. Like Detlef Illmer, we begin to wonder whether the term 'school' 'hides essential discontinuities rather than pointing them up'.[1] Reading and writing are not the only things that can be taught in schools.[2] For example, schools may encourage pupils to take up a particular way of life. They may impart an ideal without providing a general and in the modern sense elementary substructure.[3] Indeed,

---

This is an English version of 'Wer konnte im Mittelalter lesen und schreiben?', originally published in Johannes Fried (ed.), *Schulen und Studium im sozialen Wandel des hohen und späten Mittelalters* (Vorträge und Forschungen, xxx, ed. by Konstanzer Arbeitskreis für mittelalterliche Geschichte; Jan Thorbecke Verlag: Sigmaringen, 1986), 9–33; trans. by Angela Davies.

[1] Detlef Illmer, *Formen der Erziehung und Wissensvermittlung im frühen Mittelalter* (Münchener Beiträge zur Mediävistischen Renaissance Forschung, 7; 1971), 8.

[2] e.g., there are driving-schools, cooking- and sewing-schools, vocational schools in general, music schools, riding-schools, military schools etc.

[3] On learning without books and the *vox viva* as a medium see Helga Hajdu, *Lesen und Schreiben im Mittelalter* (Pécs, 1931), 8–11, 37 f., 60 f. M. T. Clanchy, *From Memory to Written Record* (London, 1979), 214–26.

it is only a relatively recent view that there is no equivalent for this.

In 1521, already into the modern period, Johann Eberlin of Günzburg wrote: 'Alle kind, mägdlin und knäblin, soll man im dritten jar irs alters zu schul tun, bis sie acht jarh alt werden. . . . In den schulen soll man kind leren das christlich gsatz aus dem ewangeli und aus Paulo.' (All children, girls and boys, should be sent to school in their third year, until they are eight. . . . In school, the children should learn Christian teachings from the Gospels and St Paul.)[4] He also lists a number of other things which children should learn at school, including reading. But there is no mention of writing or arithmetic, skills which a civilized person a thousand years before would have possessed.

The highly ordered legal system of the late Roman Empire and its well-developed bureaucracy largely depended on written communication, and this in turn presupposed organized, if private, teaching.[5] As late as the sixth century there were still professional scribes who copied books and documents, and there was a flourishing trade in books.[6] Stonemasons, who sculpted inscriptions, seem occasionally also to have worked as scribes, writing books.[7] Medieval inscriptions, by contrast, sometimes give the impression that the stonemasons did not know what they were chiselling. By the end of classical antiquity, knowledge of cursive, the type of writing in normal use, was so widespread that personally written greetings authenticated private documents. And from the fourth century, personal signatures by the issuer, the wit-

[4] Johann Eberlin von Günzburg, *Ausgewählte Schriften*, 1, ed. by Ludwig Endres, *Flugschriften der Reformationszeit*, 11 (1896), 127.

[5] Cf. Franz Joseph Dölger, *Antike und Christentum*, iii (1932), 62–72: 'Der erste Schreibunterricht in Trier nach einer Jugend-Erinnerung des Bischofs Ambrosius von Mailand'.

[6] Cf. the entries under 'librarius' and 'scriba' in *Paulys Realencyclopädie der classischen Altertumswissenschaften*, 2 series and 15 supplementary vols. (Stuttgart and Munich, 1893–1978), xxv (1926), cols. 137–9, and II (1921), cols. 848–57 respectively. Georg Rhode, 'Über das Lesen im Altertum', in id., *Studien und Interpretationen zur antiken Literatur, Religion und Geschichte* (1963), 290–303. Norbert Brockmeyer, 'Die soziale Stellung der "Buchhändler" in der Antike', *Archiv für Geschichte des Buchwesens*, 13 (1973), cols. 237–48. Lorenz Grasberger, *Erziehung und Unterricht im klassischen Altertum*, ii (1875), is still worth reading because of the wealth of material it contains.

[7] Ludwig Traube, *Vorlesungen und Abhandlungen*, iii (1920), 219.

nesses, and the scribe were all required to authenticate a document.[8] The copperplate facsimiles of papyrus documents from antiquity which Gaetano Marini started to produce in 1805[9] show clearly that the personal signatures which had been required by law since the time of Emperor Justinian I (527–67) were, in fact, usually executed. Only rarely were they replaced by the sign used by those who could not write. The Benedictine monastic rule assumed that novices could read (*c.*38, 48), while for those who could not write themselves, it provided for the document of profession to be drawn up by others and signed with a cross by the professor (*c.*58).[10]

In Italy, where documents continued to be used for a long time after the late Roman period, and schooling merely became more limited, but the ability to write did not become the preserve of one social order as it did north of the Alps, personal signatures remained a method of authenticating business documents until well into the Middle Ages. Documents from the Tuscan monastery of San Salvadore in Montamiata, edited by William Kurze, provide numerous examples dating from 736 to 951.[11] Matilda, countess of

---

[8] Entry under 'subscriptio' in *Paulys Realencyclopädie der classischen Altertumswissenschaften*, II, vii (1931), cols. 490–501. James Westfall Thompson, *The Literacy of the Laity in the Middle Ages* (1939), 1–26. Peter Classen, 'Kaiserreskript und Königsurkunde. Diplomatische Studien zum Problem der Kontinuität zwischen Altertum und Mittelalter", *BYZANTINA KEIMENA KAI MEΛETAI*, 16 (1977), 61 ff.

[9] Gaetano Marini, *I papiri diplomatici* (Rome, 1805). Jan-Olof Tjäder, *Die nichtliterarischen Papyri Italiens aus der Zeit* 445–700, i and iii (Acta Instituti Romani Regni Sueciae, series 4, XIX: 1 and 3; Lund, 1954, 1955). Individual papyri: Wilhelm Arndt and Michael Tangl, *Schrifttafeln zur Erlernung der lateinischen Paläographie*, ii (4th edn., 1906), plate 32 (from the year 166) = Franz Steffens, *Lateinische Paläographie* (2nd edn., 1929), plate 9; *The Palaeographical Society*, 1st series, iii (London, 1873–83), plate 28 (from the year 572).

[10] Herbert Grundmann, 'Litteratus—illiteratus', *Archiv für Kulturgeschichte*, 40 (1958), 23. Harold Steinacker, ' "Tradition cartae" und "traditio per cartam", ein Traditionsproblem', *Archiv für Diplomatik, Schriftgeschichte, Siegel- und Wappenkunde*, 5/6 (1959/60), 1–72. Philipp Hofmeister, 'Die Unterschrift der Analphabeten', *Österreichisches Archiv für Kirchenrecht*, 11 (1960), 96–112 (in a wider context, including the law). Bernhard Bischoff, 'Chirographum', in *Mittelalterliche Studien. Ausgwählte Aufsätze zur Schriftkunde und Literaturgeschichte*, i (1966), 118 f. Illmer, *Formen der Erziehung*, 34 f.

[11] *Codex diplomaticus Amiatinus*, ed. by Wilhelm Kurze, iv, pts. 1–2: *Facsimiles* (1978, 1982). A review by Rhaban Haacke in *Zeitschrift für Kunstgeschichte*, 91 (1980), 417–9, discusses the problems. On the 6th cent., see also Hans Ferdinand Massmann, *Die gothischen Urkunden von Neapel und Arezzo* (1838). For the 8th cent.,

Tuscany, seems to have signed with her own hand a document without a seal, dating from 1106.[12] A document drawn up by a Venetian merchant in Ragusa in 1168 bears the signatures of the merchant, the Archbishop of Ragusa, and five witnesses.[13] In Italy, documents authenticated only by signatures, not by a seal, were accepted everywhere by the notaries who began to establish themselves from the tenth century.[14]

There are many ways of describing the collapse of the Roman Empire. One would be to say that a spoken culture swamped a culture of writing. If we now ask who could read and write in the Middle Ages, our main interest is not in the technique of writing and how it was taught. (We know something about this subject thanks to the detailed researches of Heinrich Fichtenau and Bernhard Bischoff.)[15] Our main concern is to examine the way in which writing was accepted by a society which initially had no writing. We will illustrate this process, which was complicated and anything but uniform and continuous, by reference to (1) rulers, (2) the clergy, (3) knights, and, after a brief glance at (4) the Jews, among whom developments took a different course, (5) the merchants.

also Armando Petrucci, 'Libro, scrittura e scuola', in *La scuola nell'occidente latino dell'alto medioevo. Sett. cent. it.*, xix, pt. I (1972), 313–37, with plates 1–VI. For the later period, Thompson, *The Literacy of the Laity*, 53–81.

[12] Caterina Santoro, 'Le sottoscrizioni dei signori de Canossa', in *Studi di Paleografia, Diplomatica, Stoira e Araldica in Onore di Cesare Manaresi* (Milan, 1953), 259–89, with figures 29–33; fig. 31 = Steffens, *Lateinische Paläographie*, plate 78.

[13] Viktor Nowak, *Latinska Paleografija* (Belgrade, 1952), sl. 78. Many further examples—and counter-examples—from Italy in *Archivio paleografico italiano* from 1882 on. Signatures by witnesses (esp. from the 12th cent.) in the hand of the writer of the document also in *Ecclesiae S. Mariae in Via Lata Tabularium*, ed. by Ludovicus M. Hartmann (3 vols.; 1895–1913).

[14] Armando Petrucci, *Notarii. Documenti per la storia del notariato italiano* (Milan, 1958). A. Amelotti and G. Costamagna, *Alle origini del notariato italiano* (Rome, 1975).

[15] Bernhard Bischoff, 'Elementarunterricht und Probationes pennae in der ersten Hälfte des Mittelalters', in Leslie Webber Jones (ed.), *Classical and Medieval Studies in Honor of Edward Kennard Rand* (New York, 1938), 9–20. Heinrich Fichtenau, *Mensch und Schrift im Mittelalter* (1946), 57–62, 166f., n. 297 and ill. no. 7. Gert A. Zischka, 'Der Vorgang des Schreibens und Lesens im Mittelalter', *Liberarium*, 4 (1961), 138–42. Still worth reading are Ludwig Rockinger, 'Zum baierischen Schriftwesen im Mittelalter', *Abhandlungen der Bayerischen Akademie der Wissenschaften*, 21/1 (1873), 51–4, and Wilhelm Wattenbach, *Das Schriftwesen im Mittelalter* (3rd edn., 1896), 264–70, 274, 283–5.

I

When the rulers of the Germanic tribes who settled on the territory of the Roman Empire after the migration of the nations accepted Roman rule, the process of signing the *Obrigkeitsurkunde* (charter of authority), must have caused them some embarrassment, for with the exception of several Visigothic kings,[16] they were apparently unable to write.[17] We know this with certainty of the Ostrogothic ruler Odovacar,[18] and of Theoderic the Great. The Anonymous Valesianus reports of Theoderic that he had a gold foil stencil made of the word *legi*, which he then traced on to the document as his signature.[19]

In contrast to these rulers, the Merovingian kings, continuing the more recent Roman tradition of private documents, signed diplomas (except *placita*) in person. In the areas under Merovingian rule, the king's signature continued to be what authenticated diplomas.[20] Literary sources, too, provide ample evidence that the Merovingian kings could write. Chilperic I (561–84), the most highly educated of them all and a poet,[21] even devised signs for four sounds which the Latin alphabet lacked (apparently for transcribing non-Latin

[16] Karl Zeumer, 'Zum westgotischen Urkundenwesen', *Neues Archiv der Gesellschaft für ältere deutsche Geschichtskunde*, 24 (1899), 13–38. Classen, 'Kaiserreskript und Königsurkunde', 114 ff.

[17] On the Langobard and Vandal kings, cf. Grundmann, 'Litteratus—illiteratus', pp. 31 f. See also the less general work of Richard Heuberger, 'Vandalische Reichskanzlei und Königsurkunden', *Mitteilungen des Instituts für Österreichische Geschichtsforschung*, supplementary vol. xi (1929), 76–113.

[18] Leo Santifaller, 'Die Urkunde des Königs Odovakar vom Jahre 489', *Mitteilungen des Instituts für Österreichische Geschichtsforschung*, 60 (1952), 1–30, esp. 14; most recent edn.: Tjäder, *Die nichtliterarischen Papyri Italiens*, nos. 10–11.

[19] Anonymi Valesiani pars posterior. MGH AA 9, 326: 'Igitur rex Theodericus inlitteratus erat et sic obruto sensu, ut in decem annos regni sui quattuor litteras subscriptionis edicti sui discere nullatenus posuisset. De qua re laminam auream iussit interrasilem fieri quattuor litteras "legi" habentem; unde si subscribere voluisset, posita lamina super chartam per eam pennam ducebat, ut subscriptio eius tantum videretur.' Grundmann, 'Litteratus—illiteratus', is probably correct to take literally the passage which Wilhelm Ensslin, 'Rex Theodericus inlitteratus?', *Historisches Jahrbuch*, 60 (1940), 391–6, regards as derived from Byzantine sources, which say something similar about Emperor Justin I.

[20] Philip Lauer and Charles Samaran, *Les Diplômes originaux des Mérovingiens— fac-similés phototypiques avec notices et transscriptions* (Paris, 1908).

[21] Gregorii ep. Turonen, hist. lib. V, c. 44 MGH SRM 1, 252 f., 320.

names). He wanted to introduce these signs into general use, and even to have existing texts rewritten incorporating them. Gregory of Tours comments: 'Addit autem litteras litteris nostris, id est ω sicut Graeci habent, ae, the, uui, . . . Et misit epistulas in universis civitatibus regni sui, et sic pueri docerentur ac libri antiquitus scripti, planati pomice, rescriberentur.'[22] A contemporary witness says explicitly that King Dagobert I (623–39) and his son Clovis II (639–57) could both write. When Dagobert wanted to sign a charter for the monastery of St Denis, his hand was so shaky with age that he could not hold the calamus, and he asked his son to sign on his behalf.[23]

Although there are examples of the laity being able to read and write as late as the middle of the ninth century,[24] with the change in dynasty there was a complete change in the ability of rulers to write. The Carolingian major-domos lived without writing at all. Karlmann signed documents with an X.[25] From the time of Pepin, the ruler's personal contribution to signing diplomas was limited to completing the monogram with what came to be known as the 'executive stroke' (*Vollziehungsstrich*).[26] But this non-individualized sign, which could easily be imitated, was no longer a real authentication. According to Roman law, the authenticity of a (private)

[22] Ibid., c. 44, 254; cf. Grundmann, 'Litteratus—illiteratus', 33 f.

[23] Gesta Dagoberi regis Franc. c. 42. MGH SRM 2, 420: 'Nos vero praesens praeceptum iam minime valemus subscribere, quia, invalescente aegritudine, calamus in manu nostra trepidat. Et propterea rogamus dulcissimum filium nostra Hludowicum regem, ut per signaculum sui nominis istam cartam adfirmet.'

[24] In 843 the West Frankish noblewoman Dhuoda wrote to her son: 'plurima volumina librorum tibi acquiri non pigeas, ubi de Deo creatore tuo per sacratissimos doctorum magistros aliquid sentire et discere debeas . . . , haec verba a me tibi directa lege, intellige et opere comple . . . Lege vitas vel dicta sanctorum', *L'Éducation carolingienne: le manuel de Dhuoda*, ed. by Edouard Bondurand (Paris, 1887), 70 f., 92.

[25] Eigilis Vita S. Sturmi, c. 12. MGH SS2. 370: 'Porro rex iussit chartam suae traditionis scribi, quam ipse manu propria firmavit.' On this cf. Arthur Giry, *Manuel de diplomatique* (1894), 717.

[26] Cf. Pepin's document from the year 760 (MGH DD Karol. DP 13) in Franz Steffens, *Lateinische Paläographie*, plate 40. This practice seems to have been adopted from the Merovingian chancellery, where, however, it had been used only by rulers who were minors; cf. Wilhelm Erben, *Die Kaiser- und Königsurkunden des Mittelalters. Handbuch der mittelalterlichen und neueren Geschichte*, ed. Georg Below and Friedrich Meinecke, iv, pt. 1 (1906), 146 f.

document was established by a comparison of the handwriting.[27] After personal signatures ceased to exist, therefore, other means had to be sought of guarding against forgeries. Seals began to be used for authenticating documents. As Oswald Redlich has put it, north of the Alps 'the mighty power of the seal' in the early and high Middle Ages was 'in essence the product of an age that could not write'.[28]

Pepin's son Charlemagne, who commissioned magnificent codices and collected them in a unique library, is said to have mastered both Latin and Greek. But he could not write. His biographer Einhard reports that at an advanced age he struggled with writing exercises during sleepless nights, but without much success: 'Temptabat et scribere tabulasque et codicellos ad hoc in lecto sub cervicalibus circumferre solebat, ut, cum vacuum tempus esset, manum in litteris effigiendis adsuesceret, sed parum successit labor praeposterus ac sero inchoatus.'[29] Louis the Pious, like his father, is believed to have known Latin and Greek.[30] But according to Thegan's evidence,[31] as well as Waldemar Schlögl's researches,[32] unlike his father, he also signed diplomas. Similarly, Louis the German's signature on a document of Charles the Bald is considered to be in his own hand.[33] From then until the turn of the millennium, however, we

[27] Zeumer, 'Zum westgotischen Urkundenwesen', 30–8.

[28] Oswald Redlich, *Die Privaturkunden des Mittelalters. Handbuch der mittelalterlichen und neueren Geschichte*, ed. Georg Below and Friedrich Meinecke, iv, pt. 3 (1911), 123.

[29] MGH SRG (in us. schol.) [25], 30. A different interpretation is put forward by Waldemar Schlögl, *Die Unterfertigung deutscher Könige von der Karolingerzeit bis zum Interregnum durch Kreuz und Unterschrift* (Münchener Historische Studien, Abteilung Geschichtliche Hilfswissenschaften, 16; 1978), 55; cf. also Thompson, *The Literacy of the Laity*, 29.

[30] Thegani vita Hludowici imp. c. 19. MGH SS 2, 594: 'Lingua graeca et latina valde eruditus, sed grecam melius intelligere poterat quam liqui; latinum vero sicut naturalem aequaliter loqui poterat.'

[31] Ibid. c. 10, 593: 'Eodem anno [814] iussit . . . renovare omnia praecepta, quae sub temporibus patrum suorum gesta erant ecclesiis Dei, et ipse manu propria ea cum subscriptione roboravit.'

[32] Schlögl, *Die Unterfertigung deutscher Könige*, 61–9, investigating the diplomas RI ²I 350 (13 June 799) and 643 (817), plausibly suggests that we can assume an autograph signature.

[33] MGH DD Karol. dt. LdD. 32 (14 Oct. 843); Schlögl, *Die Unterfertigung deutscher Könige*, 70–2. The fact that Hrabanus Maurus and other authors dedicated works to

have no evidence that is even relatively reliable that any emperor was able to write.

As the public and organized transfer of knowledge gradually died out with the educational establishments of antiquity, writing increasingly became the business of the clergy. The presence of children in monastic houses has led some scholars to conclude, incorrectly, that they ran schools in the modern sense. While we know that capitularies demanded the opportunity for children to stay in monastic houses for the purpose of instruction, we have no evidence that it ever happened in reality.[34] Consequently, the semantic range covered by the word 'school' must have been different from what it was earlier and later. *Schola* actually meant 'living together'; *scholis tradere* did not mean 'to send to school', but 'to be destined for holy orders', and later also 'to be prepared for a certain type of life'.[35]

The enormous numbers of books dating from the Carolingian period were produced in monastic scriptoria and in those of the cathedral schools.[36] Similarly, the work of

him says little about his ability to read. In fact, one dedication explicitly mentions reading aloud ('coram vobis relegi'). Elisabeth Karg-Gasterstädt's argument in Verf.-Lex., 5 (1955), col. 700, that a copy of Muspilli was made personally by the king is obviously on the wrong track.

[34] Thompson, *The Literacy of the Laity*, 38, and 'Formen der Erziehung und Wissensvermittlung', esp. 21–8, 42–8, 79–86, 100–6.

[35] Cf. Josef Fleckenstein, *Die Bildungsreform Karls des Großen als Verwirklichung der norma rectitudinis* (1958), 28 f. The published proceedings of the conference *La scuola nell'occidente latino dell'alto medioevo* (Sett. cent. it., 19/II; 1972) also convey the impression oulined above.

[36] Cf. Edward Kennard Rand, *A Survey of the Manuscripts of Tours* (2 vols.; Cambridge, Mass., 1929); Karl Preisendanz, 'Aus Bücherei und Schreibstube der Reichenau', *Die Kultur der Abtei Reichenau*, 2 (1925), 657–83; W. M. Lindsay, 'The (Early) Lorsch Scriptorium', *Palaeographia Latina*, 3 (1924), 5–48; id. and Paul Lehmann, 'The (Early) Mayence Scriptorium', *Die Kultur der Abtei Reichenau*, 4 (1925), 15–29; Karl Löffler, 'Die Sankt Galler Schreibschule in der 2. Hälfte des 8. Jahrhunderts', *Die Kultur der Abtei Reichenau*, 6 (1929), 5–66; Leslie Webber Jones, *The Script of Cologne from Hildebald to Hermann* (Cambridge, Mass., 1932); Frederic M. Carey, 'The Scriptorium of Reims during the Archbishopric of Hincman (845–882 AD)', in *Classical and Medieval Studies in Honor of Edward Kennard Rand* (New York, 1938), 41–60; L. W. Jones, 'The Scriptorium of Corbie', *Speculum*, 22 (1974), 191–204, 375–94; Berhard Bischoff and Josef Hofmann, 'Libri sancti Kyliani. Die Würzburger Schreibschule und die Dombibliothek im VIII. und IX. Jahrhundert', *Quellen und Forschungen zur Geschichte des Bistums und Hochstifts Würzburg*, 6 (1952); Bernhard Bischoff, *Die südostdeutschen Schreibschulen der Karolingerzeit*, i (2nd edn., 1960), ii (1980).

the royal chancellery was now done only by clergy; the chancellery became a department of the court chapel.[37] Writing itself changed at exactly this time. Fritz Rörig's description of the change is only slightly exaggerated: 'The Carolingian renaissance had no space for cursive writing. The demand for speed, characteristic of every period when writing was widely practised, decreased as its use for worldy purposes—commerce, administration, and education—shrank, and it was used by fewer secular practitioners. The peace and seclusion of the religious life, and its need for quality, meant that it could make do with the type of writing used for books. In other words, the hasty character, and especially the ligatures, of cursive writing were deliberately eliminated. In general, all of these processes had a conscious and artificial quality.'[38] To a certain extent, the writing used for documents came to resemble the writing used in books. As always, these changes took place at different times in different places. 'In documents, the classical domain of cursive writing', Rörig continues, 'cursive disappeared'.[39] From the Carolingian period on, it was the clergy who wrote, but in a new way. Letters were placed individually on the parchment. Before we carry on this thread of the argument, however, we will return to the kings and emperors and their ability to write.

From Louis the German to Charles IV, there are few literary sources which throw any light on the ability of rulers to write. But together with Waldemar Schlögl's findings, based on his sophisticated analysis of diplomas, they allow us to draw a few conclusions about the Hohenstaufen period as a whole.

From the time of Pepin, with few exceptions (to be discussed soon) diplomas drawn up in chancelleries were not, in general, expected to be signed by the issuer. His participation was limited to completing the monogram.[40] But as this

[37] On this see most recently Josef Fleckenstein, 'Die Hofkapelle der deutschen Könige 1', *Schriften der Monumenta Germaniae historica*, 16/I (1959), 8f., with n. 31, 74–9, 229, 231.

[38] Fritz Rörig, 'Mittelalter und Schriftlichkeit', *Welt als Geschichte*, 13 (1953), 29–41, quotation on 31.

[39] Ibid. 32.

[40] From the time of Lothar III (1125–1137), this stroke was no longer executed by the issuer in his own hand; MGH DD Loth. III. introduction, xxvii.

stroke had become a fixed feature of the diplomas, its presence does not necessarily mean that the ruler issuing the document could not write.

Signatures by kings and emperors are found on relatively few documents, such as the *placita*, which acquired a fixed form from the time of Otto III,[41] on synod protocols, *pacta*, and papal documents. But the material available for comparison is often so limited that no firm conclusions can be drawn. According to Schlögl, twenty-four signatures by rulers on diplomas dating from Louis the Pious to Conradin can be regarded as autograph.[42]

It is necessary to point out here that these signatures did not consist simply of names. They were declarations of assent, which included the writer's name. If he had simply signed a name, we would hesitate to see them as sufficient evidence of the ability to write. What can we now say about the ability to write on the basis of all the sources, including literary ones?

We know with certainty that Otto the Great could read,[43] and this was probably also true of Otto II.[44] The first signature by a ruler since Louis the German which has survived in the original is by Otto III, on papal document JL 3888, dated 9 May 998. It reveals an unsteady hand, obviously not practised in shaping and spacing letters.[45] Signatures on another papal document, of which only a copy has survived,[46] and on two *placita*,[47] of which again, only copies have survived, are highly likely to have been in the ruler's own hand.[48] Henry II, who had been educated for holy orders,[49] is known to have been able to read[50] and write. He is believed to have signed

---

[41] Harry Bresslau, *Handbuch der Urkundenlehre*, ii (3rd edn., 1958), 180f.

[42] Schlögl, *Die Unterfertigung deutscher Könige*, 51.

[43] Rest gestae Saxon., MGH SS 3, 292.

[44] Casus s. Galli, MGH SS 2, 146; on both, see Thompson, *The Literacy of the Laity*, 83, and Siegfried Spring, 'Die literarische Bildung Heinrichs I., Ottos I. und Ottos II.' (PhD thesis, University of Munich, 1943, typescript).

[45] Schlögl, *Die Unterfertigung deutscher Könige*, 83–5.

[46] JL 3863.

[47] MGH DD O. III. nos. 339, 396.

[48] Schlögl, *Die Unterfertigung deutscher Könige*, 77–89.

[49] Siegfried Hirsch, *Jahrbücher des Deutschen Reiches unter Heinrich II.*, 1 (1862), 90f. with nn. 3 and 4.

[50] Thompson, *The Literacy of the Laity*, 84, 103.

two documents, neither of which, however, has survived in the original.[51] Five documents which are not signed in the conventional way have survived (two in the original) from the time of Henry III, who describes the person continuing the *Chronicon Novalese* as 'bene pericia litterarum imbutus', in contrast to his father, Conrad II ('per omnia litterarum inscius atque idiota').[52] It is highly likely that Henry III signed one of these documents, *plactium* DH. III. no. 318, in his own hand.[53] The fact that we have so much evidence in the case of Henry IV has not yet been satisfactorily explained. It is striking in the context of the whole of the Middle Ages. On his own testimony,[54] and on that of the monk Ebo from Kloster Michelsberg near Bamberg,[55] Henry IV could read. And according to Schlögl, there is no doubt that five of the emperor's original signatures have been preserved. Of all rulers' signatures until far beyond the interregnum, Henry IV's hand looks the most fluent and practised.[56]

It is extremely likely that Henry V signed two *placita* in his own hand in 1116. The writing is clumsy.[57] He tried to sign another *placitum*, but instead of 'Heinricus' he managed to put only two groups of letters, 'Hec' and 'cus', on the parchment.[58] Even the crosses reveal Henry V's hand as unsteady.[59]

No signatures have been preserved by Lothar von Supplinburg, or the Hohenstaufen emperors Conrad III and

---

[51] MGH DD O. III. no. 227, MGH DD H. II. no. 225; see Schlögl, *Die Unterfertigung deutscher Könige*, 90–8.

[52] MGH SS 7, 128 = Fonti 32 (1901), 304 f. Wipo, Gesta Chuonradi, c. 6, MGH SRG (in us. schol.) [61]³, 28: 'Quamquam litteras ingoraret. . . .'

[53] MGH DD H. III. no. 318, Schlögl, *Die Unterfertigung deutscher Könige*, 99–115.

[54] In his letter to Bishop Gebhard of Speyer in 1106, in which he asks him for a *Kanonikat* in Speyer: Helmoldi Chon. Slav., MGH SRG (in us. schol.) [32], 64: 'Da mihi prebendam apud Spiram . . . Novi enim litteras et possum adhuc subservire choro.'

[55] Ebonis Viat Ottonis ep. Bambergen, I, 6: 'Erat enim imperator litteris usque adeo imbutus, ut cartas, a quibuslibet sibi directas, per semetipsum legere et intelligere prevaleret.' Jaffé, BRG 5, 595; cf. Thompson, *The Literacy of the* Laity, 89 and Grundmann, 'Litteratus—illiteratus', 45.

[56] Schlögl, *Die Unterfertigung deutscher Könige*, 116–32 with ill. 6–9, 11, 12.

[57] Stumpf-Brentano, no. 3129 (11 Mar. 1116), and no. 3139 (13 May 1116); Schlögl, *Die Unterfertigung deutscher Könige*, 157–61, 168–72, with ill. 20a, 20b.

[58] Stumpf-Brentano, no. 3132 (18 Mar. 1116); Schlögl, *Die Unterfertigung deutscher Könige*, 161–4 with ill. 21a, 21b.

[59] Schlögl, *Die Unterfertigung deutscher Könige*, 143–81, ill. 14–27.

Frederick Barbarossa, whose second wife Beatrix was considered to be a 'litterata'.[60] At best, Barbarossa learnt to read a little at an advanced age.[61] But Charlemagne is not the only illustration that not being able to write was not equated with being uneducated. John of Salisbury has King Conrad III repeat the proverb 'quia rex illiteratus est quasi asinus coronatus'.[62] This does not mean that a king who cannot write is a crowned ass, but that an uneducated king is a crowned ass. In the Latin tradition, one could be educated without having acquired one's knowledge through the medium of writing.

The sources are equally scanty for the late Hohenstaufen emperors. We probably have one signature in the hand of Henry IV.[63] Philip of Swabia, destined to take holy orders, was elected Bishop of Würzburg in 1190, and later became king.[64] He was certainly able to read because of his training for the Church.[65] Similarly, Frederick II, whom Riccobald of Ferrara called 'satis literatus',[66] could undoubtedly read, but we have no signature by him,[67] whereas Conradin's signature on his diploma for Pisa in June 1268 is generally considered to be in his own hand.[68] After the interregnum, none of the rulers from Rudolf of Habsburg[69] to Louis the Bavarian, who said 'sicut miles scripturarum et litterarum subtilitatum ignari (sumus)',[70] and Frederick the Beautiful,[71] seems to

[60] Acerbi Morenae Historia, MGH SRG NS 7, 168.

[61] Herbert Grundmann, 'Die Frauen und die Literatur im Mittelalter', *Archiv für Kulturgeschichte*, 26 (1936), 142 with n. 37.

[62] Iohannes Saresberiensis, *Policraticus (IV, 6)*, ed. C. C. J. Webb, i (Oxford, 1909), 254; cf. Grundmann, 'Litteratus—illiteratus', 50–2, and Laetita Boehm, 'Das mittelalterliche Erziehungs- und Bildungswesen', in *Propyläen Geschichte der Literatur*, ii (1982), 144.

[63] Stumpf-Brentano, no. 5003 (10 June 1196); Schlögl, *Die Unterfertigung deutscher Könige*, 202–4.

[64] Alfred Wendehorst, *Das Bistum Würzburg*, i (Germania Sacra, NF, 1; 1962), 179.

[65] Thompson, *The Literacy of the Laity*, 95.

[66] Muratori, *Historia Imperatorum*, ix, col. 132.

[67] Schlögl, *Die Unterfertigung deutscher Könige*, 202–4.

[68] RI V 4854; Schlögl, *Die Unterfertigung deutscher Könige*, 205–7.

[69] Oswald Redlich, *Rudolf von Habsburg* (1903), 732.

[70] *Vatikanische Akten zur deutschen Geschichte in der Zeit Kaiser Ludwigs des Bayern*, ed. by Sigmund von Riezler (1891), 639, no. 1841.

[71] Max Vanca, 'Angebliche eigenhändige Unterschriften deutscher Könige um die Wende des 13. und 14. Jahrhunderts', *Mitteilungen des Instituts für Österreichische*

have been able to write, except for the sons of Rudolf of Habsburg, Albrecht I and Hartmann. They ratified their father's treaty with Pope Nicholas III on 14 February 1279 with signatures which are obviously in their own hands.[72] Scholars have come to similar conclusions for rulers outside the Holy Roman Empire, with cultural differences between east and west, and north and south.[73]

Not until the second half of the fourteenth century do we see rulers becoming literate at a rapid rate. Before that time, there had been no continuous development in this direction. Charles IV, who read the canonical hours like a clergyman, was a polyglot and had been educated in Paris. He probably wrote down the first fourteen chapters of his autobiography,[74] that is, the part which is written subjectively, in his own hand.[75] In any case, as a king he signed some of his documents personally.[76] As chancery additions became more differentiated and numerous in the fifteenth and sixteenth centuries, rulers' signatures appeared on the documents again. But there was no continuous development in the Reich chancellery from the time of Charles IV on, because there was not enough common ground among those who had been elected.

In his *Concordantia Catholica* of 1433, Nicholas of Cues

Geschichtsforschung, 17 (1896), 666–8. Hans Wibel, 'Zur Frage eigenhändiger Namensunterschriften in deutschen Königsurkunden', *Mitteilungen des Instituts für Österreichische Geschichtsforschung*, 39 (1923), 236–8. Grundmann, 'Litteratus—illiteratus', 11. Schlögl, *Die Unterfertigung deutscher Könige*, 197.

[72] Heinrich von Sybel and Theodor von Sickel (eds.), *Kaiserurkunden in Abbildungen*, instalment 8 (1891), plate 10 (print: MGH Const. 3, 204–6, no. 221). I am grateful to Prof. Heinz Dopsch (Salzburg) and Dr Winfried Stelzer (Vienna) for this reference.

[73] V. H. Galbraith, 'The Literacy of the Medieval English Kings', *Proceedings of the British Academy*, 21 (1935), 201–38 (on the whole, too positive). France: Thompson, *The Literacy of the Laity*, 125–33, with an important reference to Vincent of Beauvais († c. 1264), *De eruditione filiorum nobilium*, ed. Arpad Steiner (The Medieval Academy of America, Publ. 32; Cambrige, Mass., 1938). (The children of the nobility should be able not only to read, but also to write.) Kretschmayr, *Venedig*, i. 198. (We have evidence that until into the twelfth century some of the Venetian Doges were completely illiterate; others most likely were.)

[74] Zivot cisare Karla IV. Vita Karoli IV. imperatoris. *Fontes rerum Bohemicarum*, ed. J. Emler (7 vols., Prague, 1873–1907), iii (1882), 323–417.

[75] Cf. Anton Blaschka, 'Kaiser Karls IV. Jugendleben und St. Wenzels-Legende', *Geschichtsschreiber der deutschen Vorzeit*, 83 (1956), 3rd edn., 13.

[76] Erben, *Die Kaiser- und Königsurkunden des Mittelalters*, 258.

proposed that the king of the Romans should be elected by secret and written ballot. But provision had to be made for the electors to bring secretaries with them, as it could not be assumed that all the prince electors could write,[77] even a man such as Prince Elector Ruprecht I of the Palatinate, who had founded the University of Heidelberg in 1386.[78]

The first prince who regularly authenticated important documents in his own hand was Charles IV's son-in-law, Duke Rudolf IV of Austria (1358–65), founder of the university of Vienna.[79] After his death, Austrian princes no longer signed their documents, until Duke Frederick V revived the practice. When he was elected king of the Romans in 1440, this Austrian practice was adopted by the Reich chancellery.[80] Thus from the time of Frederick III, in whose hand we have something which is more like a notebook than a diary,[81] diplomas drawn up by chancelleries again bear the signatures of rulers. We have the books from which his son, Maximilian I, learned to read, and in *Weißkunig*, his autobiography, he reports that he taught himself to write.[82] From now on, there are no rulers who cannot write. Since the Merovingians, we have come full circle. We are confronted with a striking homogeneity which, however, 'has not the least to do with imitation or dependence'.[83] It is simply the homogeneity of a late cultural period.

II

Canon law made few demands concerning the education of the clergy, and they were reduced even further in practice,

[77] Lib. III. c. 37: 'Acceptis itaque scedulis per electores trahat quisque ad partem solus et secrete cum secretario, si literas ignorat . . .'

[78] Grundmann, 'Litteratus—illiteratus', 63 f.

[79] Anton Chroust, *Monumenta Palaeographica II/18* (1915), plates 1a and 1b; cf. Franz Kürschner, 'Die Urkunden Herzog Rudolfs IV. von Österreich', *Archiv für Österreichische Geschichte*, 49 (1872), 1–88, esp. 22–6.

[80] Chroust, *Monumenta Palaeographica II/18*, plate 9b; further, Erben, *Die Kaiser- und Königsurkunden des Mittelalters*, 259 and Bresslau, *Handbuch der Urkundenlehre*, ii, 169.

[81] Alphons Lhotsky, 'AEIOV. Die "Devise" Kaiser Friedrichs III. und sein Notizbuch', *Mitteilungen des Instituts für Österreichische Geschichtsforschung*, 60 (1952), 155–93; repr. in Lhotsky, *Aufsätze und Vorträge* (1971), 164–222.

[82] Heinrich Fichtenau, *Die Lehrbücher Maximilians I. und die Anfänge der Frakturschrift* (1961), 8 f.   [83] Rörig, 'Mittelalter und Schriftlichkeit', 36.

and by the glossists.[84] It did, however, prescribe that no 'ignorans literas',[85] no 'inscius literarum',[86] and no 'illiteratus'[87] could become a priest. This is the place to ask what canon law meant by 'illiteratus'. Did it refer to someone who could neither read nor write?

A particular group of documents can help us to answer this question—those which, in addition to a seal, are meant to bear the signature of the issuer as authentication. Such documents record the sale of Church property, and according to regional Church regulations, every voting member of the religious institution which was selling something was required to sign them.[88] Although documents of this sort are not common north of the Alps, a diligent search produces enough examples to demonstrate without any doubt that not all members of the clergy could write.

Documents of this type show, for example, that in 1291, 1293, and 1297 some members of the convention of the Abbey of St Gallen could not write.[89] However, the proportion of those who could write to those who could not write does not emerge clearly. In the Alsatian abbey of Murbach, it seems that not a single member of the convention could write in 1291.[90] It was the same in the Deutsches Haus in Freiburg i. B. in 1299. No one, not even one of the five priests, could write.[91] On its own admission, the entire convention of St Georgen in the Black Forest, including the abbot, was unable to write in 1313.[92] In 1324, eleven of the forty-seven members of the convention of a Cistercian Abbey

---

[84] Friedrich Wilhelm Oediger, *Über die Bildung der Geistlichkeit im späten Mittelalter* (1953), 46–57, 80–7.

[85] c. 10 d. 34 (Corpus Iurio Canonici).

[86] c. 3 d. 55 (Corpus Iurio Canonici).

[87] c. 4 in VI[to] I 9; cf. also c. 1 d. 38, c. 15 X I 14, and c. 29 X III 5.

[88] Georg v. Below, *Die Entstehung des ausschließlichen Wahlrechts der Domkapitel* (1883), 21. Bernhard Schmeidler, 'Subjektiv gefaßte Unterschriften in deutschen Privaturkunden des 11. bis 13. Jahrhunderts', *Archiv für Urkundenforschung*, 6 (1918), esp. 229f. Peter Johanek, 'Zur rechtlichen Funktion von Traditionsnotiz, Traditionsbuch und früher Siegelurkunde', in *Recht und Schriftlichkeit im Mittelalter* (Vorträge und Forschungen, 23; 1977), 162.

[89] *Urkundenbuch der Abtei St. Gallen*, ed. Hermann Wartmann, iii (1882), 267, no. 1073, 277, no. 1083, 292, no. 1100.

[90] *Der Geschichtsfreund. Mittheilungen des historischen Vereins der fünf Orte Lucern, Uri, Schwyz, Unterwalden und Zug*, 1 (1843), 212.

[91] *Freiburg Urkundenbuch*, ed. Friedrich Hefele, ii (1951), 336, no. 269.

[92] *Fürstenbergisches Urkundenbuch*, v (1885), 271f. no. 299/2.

of Bildhausen in Lower Franconia could not write a declaration of consent in their own hand. This document clearly reveals different levels of ability to write. One of the signatories leaves off in the middle of the declaration, allowing someone with better writing skills to complete it on his behalf. Other hands are so clumsy and the writing so full of errors that it gives the impression that placing their signatures on the document is almost more than the writers can manage.[93] The editor of such a document faces a number of difficult problems, especially when it comes to transcribing names, because some of the writers were incapable of writing what they wanted to write. A further example from a chapter house: on 30 January 1335 the Provost of the cathedral in Zurich sent the Bishop of Constance the papers electing a lay priest. On them he had noted: 'manu magistri Johannis Episcopi de Thurego clerici, notarii nostri, conscriptum, quia singuli de capitulo scribere nescimus.'[94]

Things were no different south of the Alps. In 1320 no less than sixteen out of eighteen monks in the Benedictine Abbey at Saint-Pons near Nice declared that they could not write. Of these sixteen, ten expressly styled themselves priests.[95] In Montecassino a few more people could write. There only six of the thirty members of the convention could not write their names in 1331.[96] It would be easy to multiply the number of examples, which take us up to about the middle of the fourteenth century.[97]

Earlier, it was less common to find explicit declarations of an inability to write. But there is no doubt that a large proportion of the clergy could not write. From the eighth until well into the thirteenth century, there are a considerable number of documents in which the *signa* and signatures

---

[93] Alfred Wendehorst, 'Monarchus scribere nesciens', *Mitteilungen des Instituts für Österreichische Geschichtsforschung*, 71 (1963), 67–75 (including part of a facsimile).

[94] *Urkundenbuch der Stadt und Landschaft Zürich*, xi (1920), 492, no. 4614.

[95] E. Cais de Pierlas, *Chartrier de l'abbaye de Saint-Pons* (Monaco, 1903), 129–31, no. 115.

[96] *Regesto de S. Leonardo di Siponto*, ed. by F. Camobreco (Rome, 1913), 180f., no. 252.

[97] Cf. J. Brunner, 'Die Ordnungen der Schule und Propstei Zürich im Mittelalter', in *Festgaben zu Ehren Max Büdinger's* (1898), 246f., note 6.

of witnesses, including clergymen, were written in the hand of the scribe who drew up the document.[98]

The same was true of bishops both within the Holy Roman Empire and outside it. Thus, for example, the signatures of the bishops on a document of William the Conqueror's, dated 1091, are in the hand of a scribe. Only the accompanying crosses were in the hands of the bishops themselves.[99] The same applies to the declarations of obedience made by the suffragan bishops of Canterbury in the period 1086 to 1133.[100] We get the same picture from the declarations of obedience made by the suffragan bishops of Sens in the thirteenth century (1223–7, 1296–9); only the crosses are autograph.[101] Similarly, the minutes of the Reich synod of Frankfurt (1 November 1007), which confirmed the newly founded bishopric of Bamberg and was attended by almost the entire episcopate of the Reich, do not have a single autograph signature. Again, only the crosses give the impression of being in the signatory's own hand.[102]

It is true, of course, that 'not everyone who signed with a cross did so because they could not write',[103] especially as autograph signatures were often irrelevant for the transaction of the Reich's business. And from the end of the twelfth

[98] Oswald Redlich and Lothar Gross, *Privaturkunden. Urkunden und Siegel in Nachbildungen für den akademischen Gebrauch*, ed. by Georg Seeliger, iii (1914), plate IIa (document from St Gallen, 744). Anton Chroust, *Monumenta Palaeographica II/5* (1910), plate 3 (document by Archbishop Udo from Trier for the Simeon monastery in Trier, *c.* 1075). Further examples in Oskar Freiherr von Mitis, *Studien zum älteren österreichischen Urkundenwesen* (1912), 74 f. and Bresslau, *Handbuch der Urkundenlehre*, ii. 190 f.

[99] *The New Palaeographical Society*, 1st series, ii (London, 1903–12), plate 45a.

[100] Ibid., 2nd series, ii (London, 1913–30), plates 67a–f and 65a–e with commentary.

[101] Ibid., 1st series, ii, plate 37.

[102] MGH DD H. II. no. 143.

[103] Schlögl, *Die Unterfertigung deutscher Könige*, 57. Nobody would think that the Church Fathers and medieval theologians were not able to write because we have no examples of their writing in most cases, and very few in others. As a rule, they dictated to secretaries. Cf. esp. Eligius Dekkers, 'Les autographes des Pères Latins', in *Colligere Fragmenta. Festschrift Alban Dold* (1952), 127–39. In addition, Martin Grabmann, 'Das Albertusautograph in der k. und k. Hofbibliothek zu Wien', *Historisches Jahrbuch*, 35 (1914), 352–6, and Heinrich Ostlender, 'Das Kölner Autograph des Matthäuskommentars Alberts des Großen', *Jahrbuch des Kölnischen Geschichtsvereins*, 17 (1935), 129–42. Further examples: Paul Lehmann, 'Autographe und Originale namhafter lateinischer Schriftsteller des Mittelalters', in Lehmann, *Erforschung des Mittelalters*, i (1941), 359–81 (first pub. in 1920).

century, Popes who are known to have been able to write hardly bothered to contribute personally to the drawing up of their documents.[104]

Of course, there were bishops who could write, not only in Italy,[105] but also in France,[106] in England,[107] and in the Holy Roman Empire.[108] But the fact remains that for centuries, crosses appear on documents followed by signatures in the hand of a scribe. Together with explicit admissions of an inability to write, this suggests that during the early and high Middle Ages, only a small proportion of bishops had mastered the *ars scribendi*. We should regard Archbishop Frederick II of Salzburg (1270–1284), who admitted that he could not to write,[109] as fairly typical until well after 1300.

The ability to write was even less common among canons than among bishops. (Admittedly, except for the incumbents of sacerdotal prebends canons did not have to be priests.) In 1294, three of the eighteen Minden canons could not write; in 1324, the figure was eight out of fourteen.[110] This illustrates a statistical tendency, which was not always expressed in specific cases, for fewer people to be able to write. In Würzburg, five out of six canons could not write their signatures in 1333. Three could not write at all, and the other two could not write 'propter trepidacionem manuum', or 'propter dolorem manuum'.[111] In Meissen, nine out of fourteen canons could not produce a signature in 1350; by

---

[104] Bruno Katterbach and W. M. Peitz, 'Die Unterschriften der Päpste und Kardinäle in den ⟨Bullae maiores⟩ vom 11. bis 14. Jahrhundert', in *Miscellanea Francesco Ehrle* 4. *Studi e Testi*, 40 (1924), 177–274.

[105] For cardinals, see Katterbach and Peitz, ibid.

[106] Alain de Boüard, *Manuel de diplomatique. Album*, 2ᵉᵐᵉ série (Paris, 1952), plate vii (document dating from 1066 with the signatures of French bishops).

[107] *The Palaeographical Society*, 1st series, iii (London, 1873–83), plate 170 (royal document dating from 1072 with the *signa* of William the Conqueror and Queen Matilda, and obviously autograph signatures of archbishops and bishops).

[108] Bernhard Schmeidler, 'Subjektiv gefaßte Unterschriften in deutschen Privaturkunden des 11. bis 13. Jahrhunderts', *Archiv für Urkundenforschung*, 6 (1918), 194–233.

[109] RI IV. 1062. It is also documented that Patriarch Peregrin I of Aquileia (*c.*1130–61) and Bishop Dietmar of Trieste (1135–45), both of German origin, were unable to write, cf. Kretschmayr, *Venedig*, i. 197f.

[110] *Westfälisches Urkundenbuch*, vi, 483, no. 1523.

[111] *Monumenta Boica*, ed. by Bayerische Akademie der Wissenschaften (Munich), xxxix, no. 241, 14f.

1358 the figure had dropped to five out of thirteen.[112] In 1370, not a single member of the Brixen cathedral chapter could apparently write his name, whereas in 1407, this was still true of only two out of eleven.[113] At the Bamberg *Wahlkapitulation* (electoral arrangement) of 1422 the proportion was still six to six,[114] but this was no longer typical of the times.

Is the fact that so many monks, bishops, and canons could not write a symptom of decline, as Albert Hauck has claimed?[115] Many other scholars have echoed him. Surely it was an offence against canon law, which would have required dispensation? When we look at the few medieval and early modern documents of profession which have been preserved from north of the Alps, however, we see that they are all signed with a cross. None bears a personal signature,[116] as the *regula s. Benedicti* (*c.*58) prescribes. This alone makes us wonder.

If canon law made it impossible for an *illiteratus* to become a priest,[117] then the obviously widespread inability to write among the clergy must have generated large numbers either of dispensations, or of defrockings, with an appropriate explanation. But we cannot find a single example. In fact, however, *illiteratus* did not have as wide a meaning as the modern term 'illiterate'. This is confirmed by a number of papal pronouncements of the thirteenth and fourteenth centuries. A decree by Alexander IV to the Archbishop of Cagliari, dated 18 August 1255, states: 'nonnulli prelati Sardine et Corsice literarum patientes defectum, utpote qui *legere* nesciunt.'[118] Similarly, a decree of 22 September 1339 by Pope Benedict IX, which summoned Abbot Peter of Lodi to appear before the apostolic throne to answer a charge,

---

[112] Cod. Dipl. Saxoniae Regiae 2/I, 369–73 no. 452; 2/II, 14–16 no. 506.

[113] Leo Santifaller, *Das Brixner Domkapitel in seiner persönlichen Zusammensetzung im Mittelalter* (Schlernschriften, 7; 1924), 109f.

[114] Wilhelm Engel, 'Georg Graf von Löwenstein, Domherr zu Würzburg und Bamberg († 1464)', *Altfränkische Bilder*, 52 (1953), unpaginated, with 3 ills.

[115] Hauck, 5/1, 243.

[116] Paulus Weissenberger, 'Die Regel des hl. Benedikt in ihrer Bedeutung für das Urkunden- und Archivwesen der Benediktinerklöster', *Archivalische Zeitschrift*, 59 (1963), 14 n. 11.

[117] Paul Hinschius, *System des katholischen Kirchenrechts*, i (1869), 19f., 55.

[118] C. Bourel de la Roncière, *Les Registres d'Alexandre IV*, i (1920), 225 no. 735.

brought by a *visitator*, that 'tantum in litteratura . . . defectum', stated 'ut omnino *legere* scivit'.[119] From this it follows
that under canon law, an *illiteratus* was a priest who could not
read. And in the thirteenth and fourteenth centuries, there
seem to have been more of these in Italy than elsewhere.[120]
The *defectus scientiae* or *literarum* for which bishops were de-
frocked seem largely to have come down to an inability to
read.[121] Ever since Boniface found a priest in Bavaria who was
baptizing 'in nomine patria et filia',[122] a large number of
general and specific statutes had prescribed that clergy, at
least from sub-deacon upwards, had to be able to read.[123] But
as Peter Johanek has pointed out in a different context, the
requirement that clergy also had to be able to write is found
only in one of Charlemagne's capitularies,[124] and it seems to
have been forgotten again immediately.

Quite apart from these legal considerations, there is sufficient evidence going far beyond the Middle Ages that reading and writing were taught and learned separately.[125] The
writing and illumination of books, even if both processes

[119] J.-M. Vidal, *Benoit XII, Lettres communes*, ii (1910), 213 no. 7476.

[120] Thompson, *The Literacy of the Laity in the Middle Ages*, 72, 80 n. 97.

[121] Cf. the decrees of Pope Honorius III (1216–1227), c. 15 X 1, 14 (defrocking
of a bishop who cannot be identified more closely, who 'confessus est coram nobis,
se nunquam de grammatica didicisse nec etiam legisse Donatum et per evidentiam
facti usque adeo de illiterarura et insufficientia sua constat, quod contra Deum esset
et canonicas sanctiones'). The Gest. abb. Trud. cont. tertia, pars II (MGH SS 10,
403) report on the defrocking of Henry of Geldern, Bishop of Liège in 1274: 'Qui
presentie tandem pape Gregorii accersitus, presentibus ibidem [in Rome] precipuis
theologis, Thoma de Aquino ordinis Predicatorum, et Bonaventura ordinis fratrum
Minorum, exclusa comitiva suorum nobilium, episcopus solus asstitit. Appositus
ergo illi liber est ad examinandum, sed illiteratus repertus ab episcopatu destituitur,
et reddito anulo recedere iubetur.' To qualify for admission to holy orders a
candidate had to be able 'bene legere et bene cantare'; cf. Santifaller, 'Die Urkunde
des Königs Odovakar vom Jahre 489', 109 n. 26 and Herbert Paulhart, 'Eine
päpstliche Reservation von 1389', *Mitteilungen der Gesellschaft für Salzburger
Landeskunde*, 99 (1959), 153–7; also Hauck, 5/1, 243 n. 4, and Oediger, *Über die
Bildung der Geistlichkeit im späten Mittelalter*, 54 with n. 3 and 80–97.

[122] *Die Briefe des hl. Bonifatius und Lullus*. MGH Epp. sel. 1, 141 no. 68.

[123] Ludovicus Thomassinus, *Vetus et nova ecclesiae disciplina*, ii (Venice, 1773),
159–66.

[124] MGH Cap. 1, 235 no. 117: 'Quae a presbyteris discenda sint . . .'; no 15:
'scribere artas et epistulas.' Cf. Johanek, 'Zur rechtlichen Funktion von
Traditionsnotiz, Traditionsbuch und früher Siegelurkunde', 141.

[125] Pierre Riché, *Les écoles et l'enseignement dans l'Occident chrétien de la fin de Ve siècle
au milieu du XIe siècle* (Paris, 1979), 298. Thompson, *The Literacy of the Laity in the
Middle Ages*, 119, 196. Franz Anton Specht, *Geschichte des Unterrichtswesens in*

were carried out by the same person, were considered to be a handicraft.[126] At the end of this strand of development we find the writing master. But there was another strand which ran alongside it.

Once *scribere* stopped being an *ars*, and, even in simplified form, began to be considered a general accomplishment, it is rare to come across clergy who cannot write. From the end of the fourteenth century, more and more noble canons started attending university, although they did not necessarily aspire to take a degree. (A degree could be a disadvantage.) Hajnal, Fichtenau, and Engelsing point out that around the middle of the fifteenth century not all students at German universities could write,[127] although academic study in Germany, in contrast to the Romance countries, already consisted largely of taking notes at lectures. But the number of such students decreased rapidly. By the time of the reform councils of Constance and Basle, stating that a bishop could not write was regarded as a criticism.[128]

Times had changed, and so had writing. From the second half of the fourteenth century, the only clergymen who could not write were members of the older generation at cathedral chapters. As the great reforms spread out from the monasteries at Melk, Kastl, and Bursfelde, writing once again began to

Deutschland (1885), 70. Helga Hajdu, *Lesen und Schreiben im Spätmittelalter* (Pécs, 1931). Heinrich Fichtenau, *Die Lehrbücher Maximilians I. und die Anfänge der Frakturschrift* (1961), 7 f. (school ordinance of St Stephan in Vienna, 1446). Hansjürgen Kiepe, '"Ettwas von Buchstaben" Leseunterricht und deutsche Grammatik um 1486', *Beiträge zur Geschichte der deutschen Sprache und Literatur* (Tübingen), 103 (1981), 1–5. August Kluckhohn, 'Beiträge zur Geschichte des Schulwesens in Bayern vom 16. bis zum 19. Jahrhundert', *Abhandlungen der Bayerischen Akademie der Wissenschaften*, 12/3 (1875), 182–8 (school ordinance of Wasserburg, 1562). In the second half of the 18th cent. in Franconia, boys learned to read and write, while girls were taught only to read; cf. e.g. Josef Hasenfuss, 'Aus dem "Gedenkbuch" der Pfarrei', in August Gehrsitz and Johannes Schreiber (eds.), *1150 Jahre Neubrunn* (1965), 147.

[126] Cf. also Jonathan James Graham Alexander, 'Scribes as artists', in *Medieval Scribes, Manuscripts and Libraries. Essays presented to N. R. Ker* (London, 1978), 87–116.

[127] István Hajnal, *L'Enseignement de l'écriture aux universités médiévales* (2nd edn., Budapest, 1959), 60–116. Fichtenau, *Die Lehrbücher Maximilians I.*, 8. Rolf Engelsing, *Analphabetentum und Lektüre* (1973), 12.

[128] Remigius Bäumer, 'Paderborner Theologen und Kanonisten auf den Reformkonzilien des 15. Jahrhunderts', in *Paderbornensis Ecclesia—Festschrift für Lorenz Kardinal Jäger* (1972), 165.

be a function of monasteries. This helped to secure their possessions, not only by the drawing up of land registers and cartularies. It is no coincidence that numerous *modus scribendi* come from reformed monasteries, and date from the time when they adopted the reform.[129]

III

'A quill pen in the hand of a young knight . . . an impossible notion. Read . . . the *Nibelungenlied*, and then try to imagine Siegfried or Hagen at a desk.'[130] There was no Gratian and no diocesan synod to dictate to knights that they had to possess the rudiments of writing. In looking at the knights, we shall consider mainly those who possessed some sort of connection with the written word, or at least seemed to have.

The poet Wirnt von Grafenberg († 1220) had his sources read out to him.[131] This alone does not allow us to infer anything about his ability to read. But on his own admission, Ulrich von Lichtenstein († *c.*1275) could not read. For ten days a letter from his adored one (who could obviously write, as befitted a lady who belonged to courtly society) lay unread because his scribe was away.[132] Wolfram von Eschenbach's († around 1220) confessions about his relationship with the written word—in *Parzival*: 'ichne kan deheinen buochstap'[133] and in *Willehalm*: 'Swaz an den buochen stêt geschriben, des bin ich künstelôs beliben'[134]—have sometimes been interpreted as merely stereotyped self-deprecation, or as general statements saying something like: I lack all scholarly learning. But a Viennese professor of German studies, Blanka Horacek, has come to the conclusion that these statements should be taken literally. In other words, Wolfram von Eschenbach could not read, or at least, he did not get be-

<hr />

[129] Cf. H. S. Steinberg, 'Instructions in Writing by Members of the Congregation of Melk', *Speculum*, 16 (1941), 210–15.

[130] Wolfram von den Steinen, 'Der Neubeginn', in Braunfels, *Karl der Große*, ii (3rd edn., 1967), 9.

[131] Blanka Horacek, 'Ichne kan deheinen buochstap', in *Festschrift Dietrich Kralik* (1954), 131 with n. 12.

[132] Ulrich von Lichtenstein, *Frauendienst*, Str. 166–76, cf. also 115, 1.

[133] *Parzival*, v. 115, 27.

[134] *Willehalm*, v. 2, 19f.

yond the rudiments. Of all attempts to solve this puzzle,[135] this interpretation has remained the most convincing. The poet often misunderstood his sources because he knew them only from hearsay and consequently had to rely on his memory. Moreover, 'in the course of his narrative, he later simply ignored . . . important elements of the plot'. Finally, argues Horacek, syntactical and metrical incongruities, in particular, the frequent use of an anteposed *nominativus pendens* which has no place in the construction of the sentence, suggests that it was composed without being written down. In general, she identifies this as the source of Wolfram's 'dark style'.[136]

Even among knights who composed poetry, one who could read is the exception that proves the rule. Heinrich von Veldeke († around 1190), Hartmann von Aue († 1210/20) and—the presumably non-noble—Gottfried von Strassburg († *c.* 1220) emphasize rather self-consciously, and repeatedly, that they can read.[137] But probably none of them could write. In introducing himself as a learned knight, Hartmann von Aue, for example, does not claim to be able to write, but that he 'so geleret was, daz er an den buochen las, swaz er daran geschriben vant'.[138] Even for the poet Oswald von Wolkenstein, who died as late as 1445, a recent and highly sophisticated study concludes that there is 'no evidence that he could read and write, and no reason to assume it'.[139]

---

[135] Friedrich Ohly has identified verse 2, 19 f. of *Willehalm* as a quotation from Ps. 70, 15 (Wolfram's prayer to the Holy Ghost at the entrance of the Willehalm; *Zeitschrift für Deutsches Altertum*, 91 (1961/2), 1–37), and has therefore cast doubt on the correctness of the confession. Similarly, H. Eggers, 'Non cognovi litteraturan (zu Parzival 115.27)', in *Festschrift für Ulrich Pretzel* (1963), 162–72. But this does not invalidate Horacek's interpretation; cf. H. Grundmann, 'Dichtete Wolfram von Eschenbach am Schreibtisch?', *Archiv für Kulturgeschichte*, 49 (1967), 391–405: 'Even in the Middle Ages authors who were not completely dim-witted used traditional formulae and *topoi* only where they seemed appropriate for what they want to say' (402).

[136] Horacek, 'Ichne kan deheinen buochstap', 137 f.

[137] Ibid. 136. Grundmann, 'Die Frauen und die Literatur im Mittelalter', *Archiv für Kulturgeschichte*, 26 (1936), 140: Hartmann von Aue's 'explicit reassurance that he can read can only have failed to have struck his audience as ridiculous and simple-minded bragging if it was, indeed, the exception.'

[138] *Der arme Heinrich*, v. 1–3; a similar passage in *Iwein*, v. 21 f.

[139] George Fenwick Jones, 'Konnte Oswald von Wolkenstein lesen und schreiben?', in *Gesammelte Vorträge der 600-Jahrfeier Oswalds von Wolkenstein. Seis am Schlern 1977* (Göppinger Arbeiten zur Germanistik, 206; 1978), 39–79, quotation on 67.

To sum up, we can quote Wieland Schmidt: 'Middle High German poetry' and, we can add, the epic as well, was 'listened to and disseminated in the form of sung and spoken words. It grew out of an oral culture.'[140] Neither the Greeks of classical antiquity, nor the medieval world doubted that someone could compose an epic of the size of the *Iliad*, as Wolfram von Eschenbach puts it—completely 'âne de buoche stiure'.[141] And George Fenwick Jones points out that the miniatures in the Manesse manuscript do not depict a minstrel sitting at a desk or standing at a lectern. At most, they are dictating to a scribe, whose subaltern position is indicated by his position in the picture, and his size.[142]

Knowledge of letters held a lowly position, if it figured at all, in the scale of German knights' priorities. This scant regard is summed up in the twelfth century by the author of the *Vita* of Saint Eckenbert of Worms: 'literarum peritia nemini militaturo obesse, seculum relicturo plurimum prodesse.'[143] Jakob Püterich of Reichertshausen († 1469), a Bavarian knight, had a passion for collecting books—not only chivalric romances and books about horses and hunting, but also books of theology and hagiography. At that time, this was still completely untypical behaviour for someone in his position, and it earned for him the scorn, even the contempt, of his equals.[144] A knight surrounded by books was in the wrong sort of world. As Herbert Grundmann has shown, apart from the clergy, women and nuns valued the ability to read and write.[145] In the value scale of knights, jousting, riding, hunting, and dancing ranked as appropriate activities. Reading and writing were despised and regarded as tasks to be delegated, as the examples collected by George

[140] Wieland Schmidt, 'Vom Lesen und Schreiben im späten Mittelalter', in *Festschrift für Ingeborg Schröbler* (1973), 314.

[141] *Parzival*, v. 115, 30. Cf. also M. T. Clanchy, *From Memory to Written Record* (London, 1979).

[142] George Fenwick Jones, 'Konnte Oswald von Wolkenstein lesen und schreiben?', 58.

[143] 'Vita s. Eckenberti', in *Monumenta Wormatiensia*, ed. by Heinrich Boos (1893), 130; cf. Thompson, *The Literacy of the Laity in the Middle Ages*, 93.

[144] *Mittelalterliche Bibliothekskataloge Deutschlands und der Schweiz IV/2* (1979), 705, 713.

[145] Grundmann, 'Die Frauen und die Literatur im Mittelalter', 129–61.

Fenwick Jones demonstrate.[146] Knights continued to have nothing but contempt for the whole business of writing until well after the Middle Ages. In his well-known book *De re diplomatica libri VI* (published in 1681), Jean Mabillon introduces the chapter on signatures (lib. II, c. XXII) thus: 'Fuit olim tempus, nec fortasse multum abest a nostro, cum quidam nobiles et ingenui homines scribendi peritiam contemptui haberent.'

IV

Before turning to the merchants, the last social group to be discussed here, I should like to point out that we shall have to be content with a few brief remarks about the Jews, a religious and social minority within Christian Europe. This is not because I consider the Jews unimportant within the context of my topic, but because developments among the Jewish community took a completely different direction, and are essentially uncontroversial. In the Middle Ages, as at other times, even ordinary Jews as a rule learned to read and write Hebrew.[147] We shall simply mention two significant phenomena. First, in Yiddish, the synagogue is called a 'Schul' (school),[148] because the house of prayer was also a school in which reading and writing (in Hebrew) were taught. Secondly, documents among (non-assimilated) Jews in the Middle Ages were unsealed. As they were authenticated instead by the personal signatures of those issuing the document and of witnesses, they form part of a tradition of private documents going back to late antiquity.[149]

---

[146] Jones, 'Konnte Oswald von Wolkenstein lesen und schreiben?', esp. 41–7.

[147] Moritz Güdemann, *Geschichte des Erziehungswesens und der Cultur der abendländischen Juden*, i (1880), 50–61. Israel Abrahams, *Jewish Life in the Middle Ages*, ii, ed. by Cecil Roth (London, 1932), 364–80. R. Edelmann, 'Jüdisches Geistesleben am Rhein', *Monumenta Judaica. 2000 Jahre Geschichte und Kultur der Juden am Rhein. Handbuch* (1963), 668–712.

[148] Siegmund Andreas Wolf, *Jiddisches Wörterbuch* (1962), 181.

[149] Rudolf M. Kloos, 'Eine hebräische Urkunde zum Finanzwesen des Hochstifts Bamberg im 14. Jahrhundert', *Berichte des Historischen Vereins Bamberg*, 103 (1967), 341–86, esp. 347.

V

By the end of the eleventh century, some of the merchants' guilds in the towns of Flanders were served by a clergyman acting as a *Notarius* who wrote for them anything that needed to be written.[150] This suggests that merchants' lives were so fundamentally different from those of the clergy that merchants felt it inadvisable to send their children and other dependents to schools in monastic houses, preferring to employ clergy, as did the nobility, if anything needed to be read or written.[151] In Rudolf of Ems's epic, *Der guote Gêrhart*, which dates from after 1230, we hear of a long-distance trader (trading as far afield as Russia, Livonia, Prussia, the Levant) who takes a priest with him on his journeys to act as a scribe.[152] But soon, as their business became more extensive and complicated large traders started to work from an office, where they employed scribes, or did their own writing. In the late thirteenth century, account books began to be kept in the area covered by the Hanse.[153] The oldest commercial accounts in Germany to be kept continuously over a number of years, from 1304 to 1307, were kept by a Nuremberg firm, the Holzschuher (which traded mainly in cloth from Flanders) because it needed reliable information, especially on outstanding debts. The editors of these accounts believe that in addition to the four owners of the firm they can identify three assistants acting as scribes.[154] From the mid-fourteenth century on, account books become more common throughout the whole of Upper Germany.[155]

[150] Henri Pirenne, 'L'Instruction des marchands au moyen-âge', *Annales d'histoire économique et sociale*, 1 (1929), 13–28.

[151] Thompson, *The Literacy of the Laity in the Middle Ages*, 92.

[152] *Der guote Gêrhart*, verses 1, 184–99. Cf. also Grundmann, 'Litteratus— illiteratus', 22 f., 60.

[153] Gustav Korlén, 'Kieler Bruchstücke kaufmännischer Buchführung aus dem Ende des 13. Jahrhunderts', *Niederdeutsche Mitteilungen*, 5 (1949), 102–12. Ahasver v. Brandt, 'Ein Stück kaufmännischer Buchführung aus dem letzten Viertel des 13. Jahrhunderts (Aufzeichnungen aus dem Detailgeschäft eines Lübecker Gewandschneiders)', *Zeitschrift des Vereins für Lübecker Geschichte*, 44 (1964), 5–34.

[154] *Das Handlungsbuch der Holzschuher in Nürnberg*, ed. by Anton Chroust and Hans Proesler (Veröffentlichungen der Gesellschaft für Fränkische Geschichte, 10/1; 1934), x f.

[155] Wolfgang v. Stromer, 'Das Schriftwesen der Nürnberger Wirtschaft vom 14. bis zum 16. Jahrhundert', in *Beiträge zur Wirtschaftsgeschichte Nürnbergs*, ii (Beiträge zur Geschichte und Kultur der Stadt Nürnberg, 11/II; Nuremberg, 1967), 751–99.

Nor did the public administrations which the bearers of power had established lag behind private industry in the use of writing during the second half of the fourteenth century.[156] In the Reich chancellery, and even more in the chancelleries maintained by territorial rulers and the towns, the production of documents increased as different departments were set up and began to keep records of various sorts. In commerce as well as the administration it is true to say that around the middle of the fourteenth century, during the reign of Charles IV, written communication began to develop more quickly.

Except among the clergy, the motive for learning to read, write, and calculate was no longer a religious one. Emancipation from an education system dominated by the Church, as can be observed in Flanders from the end of the twelfth century, in Lübeck from about the middle of the thirteenth, and elsewhere soon afterwards,[157] was both a consequence and a cause of this secular, commercial motivation. 'By the first half of the fifteenth century, all Nuremberg merchants above the level of small trader, and their senior staff had to be able to read, write, and calculate.'[158]

Latin schools which were secular, or only formally under the supervision of the Church, were first set up in a number of large towns. In the fourteenth century they were established in many middling-sized towns, mainly by the merchant élite, who shaped the curriculum to their own needs.[159] In 1356 we first see teachers asssociated with an attribute which

[156] Hans Patze, 'Neue Typen des Geschäftsschriftgutes im 14. Jahrhundert', in *Der deutsche Territorialstaat im 14. Jahrhundert*, i (Vorträge und Forschungen, 13; 1970), 9–64. Gerhart Burger, *Die südwestdeutschen Ratsschreiber im Mittelalter* (Beiträge zur Schwäbischen Geschichte, 1–5; 1960). Manfred J. Schmied, *Die Ratsschreiber der Reichsstadt Nürnberg* (Nuremberg, 1979).

[157] Johann Warnecke, 'Mittelalterliche Schulgeräte im Museum zu Lübeck', *Zeitschrift für Geschichte der Erziehung und des Unterrichts*, 2 (1912), 227–50. The town school in Breslau, by contrast, which had been established as early as 1267 by the town council, was strongly influenced by the Church and more old-fashioned in style (*Breslauer Urkundenbuch*, ed. G. Korn, 1870, xxxv, no. 32).

[158] v. Stromer, 'Das Schriftwesen der Nürnberger Wirtschaft', 765. Cf. also Horst Pohl, 'Das Rechnungsbuch des Nürnberger Großkaufmanns Hans Praun von 1471 bis 1478', *Mitteilungen des Geschichtsvereins von Nürnberg*, 55 (1967/8), 77–136.

[159] Edith Ennen, 'Stadt und Schule in ihrem wechselseitigen Verhältntis vornehmlich im Mittelalter', *Rheinische Vierteljahrsblätter*, 22 (1957), 56–72. Friedrich Wilhelm Oediger, 'Die niederrheinischen Schulen vor dem Aufkommen der Gymnasien', *Düsseldorfer Jahrbuch*, 43 (1941), 75–124, esp. 86–9. R. R. Post,

has since become firmly attached to the profession—the rod appears as an iconographic motif on the seal of a school in Höxter, Westphalia.[160] The town schools, which had rapidly increased in number since the beginning of the fifteenth century, and the German schools which teachers ran themselves, placed more emphasis on the acquisition of elementary knowledge, reading, and writing than did the monastic and cathedral schools. And arithmetic was no longer used mainly for computing the correct date for Easter, but also for commercial purposes. Since the fourteenth century, Arabic numbers[161] had increasingly come to replace the unwieldy[162] Roman numerals[163] which had made any sort of computation so complicated. Cursive writing was used. A cross-check by Henri Pirenne has demonstrated that in the late Middle Ages the places where cursive writing was not used were those, such as Ireland, where only the clergy could write.[164]

In highly urbanized Italy there had always been more non-Church schools than in the Reich. As early as the first half of the eleventh century Wipo († after 1046), writer and curate

Scholen en Onderwijs in Nederland gedurende de Middeleeuwen (Utrecht/Antwerp, 1954). Aloys Schmidt, 'Zur Geschichte des niederen und mittleren Schulwesens im Mittelalter im Moselland und am Mittelrhein', *Rheinische Vierteljahrsblätter*, 22 (1957), 73–81. Klaus Leder, *Kirche und Jugend in Nürnberg und seinem Landgebiet 1400–1800* (Neustadt, 1973), esp. 21–6. Franz Xaver Buchner, *Schulgeschichte des Bistums Eichstätt vom Mittelalter bis 1803* (1956) (not very informative on the Middle Ages). The older literature is listed in Friedrich Wilhelm Oediger, *Über die Bildung der Geistlichen im späten Mittelalter* (1953), 68 n. 3.

[160] Klaus Arnold, *Kind und Gesellschaft in Mittelalter und Renaissance* (Sammlung Zebra, B 2; 1980), 80.

[161] *Das Handlungsbuch der Holzschuher* has only Roman numerals.

[162] Calculations with large figures were very often incorrect in the Middle Ages while only Roman numerals were used. The reader is urged to try adding up a few large numbers written in Roman numerals, or to attempt a simple division sum using Roman numerals over 100.

[163] Ignaz Denzinger, 'Einiges über die Entstehung und den Fortgang des Gebrauchs der arabischen Ziffern im Würzburgischen', *Archiv des Historischen Vereins von Unterfranken*, 9/II (1847), 163–84. Balduin Penndorf, *Geschichte der Buchhaltung in Deutschland* (1913), 38f. George Francis Hill, *The Development of Arabic Numberals in Europe exhibited in 64 Tables* (Oxford, 1915). A. P. Juschkewitsch, *Geschichte der Mathematik im Mittelalter* (1965), 346–57. Patze, 'Neue Typen des Geschäftsschriftgutes im 14. Jahrhundert', 64.

[164] Henri Pirenne, 'Le Commerce du papyrus dans la Gaule mérovingienne', *Comptes rendus des séances de l'Académie des inscriptions et belles-lettres, Paris* (1928), 178f.

to the first Salians, claimed that in Italy all children were sent to school, whereas the Germans sent only those of their children to school who were destined for the priesthood.[165] In any case, in the fourteenth century the number of children who went to school in Italy was both absolutely and relatively greater than in Germany.[166]

After the numerous urban schools which taught mainly, but not exclusively, the basics, the first universities were founded. In the fifteenth century, their number increased at a rate unmatched until the 1970s and 1980s. At them, the sons of non-nobles and nobles studied not only theology, but also jurisprudence, and medicine. And as the surviving *reportata* reveal, this gradually came to mean taking notes at lectures.

During the fifteenth century, the great century of university foundations, the need for knowledge became broader. A new phenomenon, the 'educated man' (*Gebildeter*) emerged. Neither a 'scholar' (*Gelehrter*) nor an 'uneducated man' (*Ungelehrter*), the *Gebildeter* 'required a certain amount of knowledge for life in society, but did not want to devote himself entirely to scholarly pursuits'.[167] The demand for

---

[165] Wiponis Tetralogus, MGH SS 11, 251 (v. 190–200). To Henry III:

> Tunc fac edictum per terram Teutonicorum,
> Quilibet ut dives sibi natos instruat omnes
> Litterulis, legemque suam persuadeat illis,
> Ut cum principibus placitandi venerit usus,
> Quisquis suis libris exemplum poferat illis.
> Moribus his dudum vivebat Roma decenter,
> His studiis tantos potuit vincire tyrannos:
> Hoc servant Itali post prima crepundia cuncti,
> Et sudare scholis mandatur tota iuventus:
> Solis Teutonicis vacuum vel turpe videtur,
> Ut doceant aliquem nisi clericus accipiatur.

[166] Amintore Fanfani, 'La Préparation intellectuelle et professionelle à l'activité économique en Italie de XIVᵉ au XVIᵉ siècles', *Le Moyen Âge*, 57 (1951), 327–46. An iconographic motif which we find in 14th-cent. Italy does not appear north of the Alps until later: the child Jesus carrying a bag of books, a slate, and a stylus. See Hans Wentzel, 'Ad infantiam Christi—Zu der Kindheit unseres Herren', in *Das Werk des Künstlers, Studien zur Ikonographie und Formgeschichte. Hubert Schrade zum 60. Geburtstag dargebracht* (1960), 134–60.

[167] Alphons Lhotsky, 'Zur Frühgeschichte der Wiener Hofbibliothek', *Mitteilungen des Instituts für Österreichische Geschichtsforschung*, 59 (1951), 329–63, quotation on 343 (repr. in Lhotsky, *Aufsätze und Vorträge*, i (1970), 149–93, quotation on 166).

books rose, stimulating the business of those who wrote for money, both north and south of the Alps.[168] About 70 per cent of all surviving literary manuscripts date from the fifteenth century.[169] The general availability of cheap paper instead of expensive parchment also encouraged writing.[170] At the beginning of the fifteenth century, the price ratio of parchment to paper seems to have been about 10:1.[171]

Of course, the rapid increase in the amount of writing had an impact on writing itself. The Italian humanists took as their ideal the Carolingian minuscule style, which they incorrectly believed dated from classical antiquity. They deplored its 'degeneration' into *Bastarda* and cursive styles, and accused those who used them of being 'dilettantes'.[172] The need to write more brought with it the need to write quickly, and the old *ars scribendi* became a preserve of the writing master.[173]

Almost at the end of this essay, I shall repeat the question which Robert W. Scribner asked at a conference on the social history of the Reformation held by the German Historical Institute London in 1978: 'How many could read?'[174] It seems to me that the figures suggested by Engelsing,[175] and

---

[168] Wilhelm Wattenbach, *Das Schriftwesen im Mittelalter* (3rd edn., 1896), 470–88. Brothers of Common Life were also engaged in writing for money. See Helga Hajdu, *Lesen und Schreiben im Spätmittelalter* (Pécs, 1931), 20–7.

[169] Rolf Engelsing, *Analphabetentum und Lektüre* (1973), 10.

[170] Leo Santifaller, *Beiträge zur Geschichte der Beschreibstoffe im Mittelalter*, i (Mitteilungen des Instituts für Österreichische Geschichtsforschung, supplementary xvi/I; 1953), esp. 144–52. Patze, 'Neue Typen des Geschäftsschriftgutes im 14. Jahrhundert', 60–4. Learning by heart was probably so common in the Middle Ages because pupils, as a rule, had no books. And the reason for this seems to have been the high price of parchment.

[171] Bernhard Kirchgässner, *Wirtschaft und Bevölkerung der Reichsstadt Esslingen im Spätmittelalter. Nach den Steuerbüchern von 1360–1460* (Esslinger Studien, 6; 1964), 55 f.

[172] Wattenbach, *Das Schriftwesen im Mittelalter*, 484–6.

[173] Werner Doede, *Bibliographie der deutschen Schreibmeisterbücher von Neudörffer bis 1800* (1958). Walter M. Brod, *Fränkische Schreibmeister und Schriftkünstler* (Mainfränkische Hefte, 51; 1968), with an extensive bibliography.

[174] Robert W. Scribner, 'How Many Could Read?', in Wolfgang J. Mommsen, Peter Alter, and Robert W. Scribner (eds), *Stadtbürgertum und Adel in der Reformation. Studien zur Sozialgeschichte der Reformation in England und Deutschland; The Urban Classes, the Nobility and the Reformation. Studies on the Social History of the Reformation in England and Germany* (Veröffentlichungen des Deutschen Historischen Instituts London, 5; Stuttgart, 1979), 44 f.

[175] Engelsing, *Analphabetentum und Lektüre*, 6, 19 f.

further supported by Scribner, are probably pretty accurate. Taking all the variations into account, they propose a fairly conservative estimate: at the beginning of the Reformation, 10 to 30 per cent of the urban population could read.[176] If we go on to ask how many could write, there is reason to believe that the gap which had opened up during the early and high Middle Ages had almost closed by the end of the medieval period. The number of people who could write, that is, those who could write cursive, was probably not far short of the number who could read.

In conclusion, I should like to suggest two main reasons why the knowledge of reading and writing increased gradually throughout the Middle Ages, and took off from about 1350. Contempt for illiteracy initially came from the Church, for Christianity (like Judaism and Islam) is a religion of the book, based on holy scriptures. But the old dispute, kept alive by the Holy Scriptures themselves, about whether the scholar should be ranked above the simple man of faith, prevented the emergence of a general consensus not only about the value of reading and writing, but of scholarship in general.[177] In the early modern period, Martin

[176] In England, the figure was probably somewhat higher. Cf. John William Adamson, 'The Extent of Literacy in England in the Fifteenth and Sixteenth Centuries', *The Library*, 4th series, 10 (1930), 163–93 (repr., with additions, in Adamson, *'The Illiterate Anglo-Saxon' and Other Essays on Education, Medieval and Modern* (Cambridge, 1946), 38–61); similarly, we can assume somewhat higher figures for Italy and France; cf. Hajdu, *Lesen und Schreiben im Spätmittelalter*, 40–3, 51. We shall take one example as a test for our figures. If the chronicler Heinrich Deichsler can be believed, Nuremberg lay towards the top end of the assumed range. Deichsler tells us about the boys and girls, supervised by German scribes and women teachers, who sang for the Kaiser in the castle when Frederick III visited Nuremberg at the end of May 1487. At his request, 'pei vier tausent lerkneblein und maidlein' went 'nach der predig in den graben unter der vesten' on 27 May ('Jahrbücher des 15. Jahrhunderts', *Die Chronik der deutschen Städte vom 14. bis ins 16. Jahrhundert*, ed. by Historische Kommission bei der Bayerischen Akademie der Wissenschaften Göttingen, x (1872), 382 f.). The number of adults in Nuremberg who could read and write certainly equalled the number of pupils, which gives a total figure of 8,000. If we relate this figure to the number of people counted as residents of Nuremberg in 1497 of *c.* 28,000—see Otto Puchner, 'Das Register des Gemeinen Pfennigs (1497) in der Reichsstadt Nürnberg als bevölkerungsgeschichtliche Quelle', *Jahrbuch für fränkische Landesforschung*, 34/5 (1975) (Festschrift für Gerhard Pfeiffer), 930—then about 30% of the population was able to read and write.

[177] Friedrich Wilhelm Oediger, *Über die Bildung der Geistlichen im späten Mittelalter* (1953), 5: 'Do we need . . . special doctrine to penetrate into the scriptures? Is not

Luther's Scola-Scriptura principle undoubtely further encouraged the spread of reading and writing.[178] The second
reason has profane roots. In the late Middle Ages, as business
got more complicated and the administration became more
differentiated traders and territorial administrations could
no longer manage without the written word and written
figures.

The price of this increase in the amount of writing was
such a large change in the nature of writing itself that the
palaeographer of the early and high Middle Ages soon found
himself displaced. His complicated categories and nomen-
clatures became irrelevant in an age which simply wrote
things down, put them on paper, entered them in the books,
made drafts, crossed things out, corrected them, brought
them up to date, and made a note of them.

simple faith enough? Did not Christ praise the father for hiding this from the wise,
but revealing it to the ordinary people? Did he not select uneducated fishermen to
proclaim the happy news?' On the contempt of some Franciscans for book learning,
and a certain hostility to books of some brands of mysticism, see Hajdu, *Lesen und
Schreiben im Spätmittelalter*, 16–20.

[178] On the complex relations and interaction between oral and printed communication and non-verbal communication during the Reformation, cf. Robert
W. Scribner, 'Flugblatt und Analphabetentum. Wie kam der gemeine Mann
zu reformatorischen Ideen?', in Hans Joachim Köhler (ed.), *Flugschriften als
Massenmedium der Reformationszeit* (Spätmittelalter und Frühe Neuzeit, 13; 1981),
65–76.

Part II

WAR AND PEACE

Kingship and the Maintenance of Peace

3
Ideal and Reality in Twelfth-Century Germany

HANNA VOLLRATH

When kingship was Christianized in Carolingian times, clerics began to theorize about the king's secular role and function. The maintenance of *pax* and *iustitia* were considered fundamental royal virtues.[1] Although the implications of promoting peace and justice have changed considerably over the centuries, this has remained a central aspect of public power ever since. In Carolingian times the concept of peace and justice held magico-sacred connotations, as Cathuulf's letter to Charlemagne,[2] and many statements by his contemporaries demonstrate.[3] These connotations eventually disappeared in the process of 'demythicization' which took place during the high Middle Ages, but it was never denied that ultimate responsibility for peace and justice lay with the king.

In Germany, as elsewhere, kingship remained 'the only universally agreed upon source of legitimacy of all government and rule'.[4] The king's paramount legal and judicial position, as laid down by Frederick Barbarossa in his Roncaglia code of 1158,[5] was unchallenged throughout the

[1] H. H. Anton, *Fürstenspiegel und Herrscherethos in der Karolingerzeit* (Bonn, 1968); E. Ewig, 'Zum christlichen Königsgedanken im Frühmittelalter', *Das Königtum: Seine geistigen und rechtlichen Grundlagen* (Vorträge und Forschungen, 3; Darmstadt, 1963), 7–73.

[2] MGH Epp iv, no. 7, 501–5, here 503.

[3] Ewig, 'Zum christlichen Königsgedanken', 54 f.

[4] P. Moraw, 'Die Verwaltung des Königtums und des Reiches und ihre Rahmenbedingungen', in K. A. Jeserich, H. Pohl, and G. C. v. Unruh (eds.), *Deutsche Verwaltungsgeschichte*, i: *Vom Spätmittelalter bis zum Ende des Reiches* (Stuttgart, 1983), 23.

[5] MGH D.F.I. no. 238; cf. V. Colorni, 'Le tre leggi perdute di Roncaglia (1158) ritrovate in un manoscritto parigino (Bibl. Nat. Cod. Lat. 4677)', *Scritti in memoria di Antonino Giuffrè*, i (Milan, 1967), 111–70. German trans.: *Die drei verschollenen Gesetze des Reichstages bei Roncaglia* (Aalen, 1969).

Middle Ages. A royal grant continued to be an essential prerequisite for the exercise of high justice.[6] But in 1220 and 1231–2 Frederick II confirmed the customary right of the princes of the realm (*Reichsfürsten*) to wield the regalia in their territories,[7] and in the *Landfriede* (truce of the land) proclaimed in Mainz in 1235 he explicitly acknowledged their claim that exercising high justice was one of the regalia. In 1278 King Rudolf of Habsburg repeated that the right to exercise high justice was included in the regalia granted to the princes.[8] The grant of the regalia was an integral part of the symbolic act establishing the feudal relationship between the king and the princes as his Crown vassals. As the relationship between lord and vassal was a personal one, it denied the lord the right to act directly in his vassal's benefice unless he had specifically reserved certain rights to himself and had incorporated them into the feudal contract.[9] Normally, however, a lord could act only *through* his vassal. This applied not only to a benefice that consisted of a grant of land, but also to the regalia. Thus in this field a right according to the law (*Rechtskompetenz*) cannot automatically be equated with the right to act (*Handlungskompetenz*). It creates a paradox in our understanding of political competence. As royal responsibility was delegated according to feudal law, it virtually prevented the king from taking direct legal action in the princely territories. Feudal competence excluded the right to act.[10]

[6] K. F. Krieger, *Die Lehnshoheit der deutschen Könige im Spätmittelalter* (Aalen, 1979), 245 ff., 265 ff. This did not change throughout the Middle Ages, despite the fact that high justice itself changed considerably when physical penalties began to replace the old system of compensations in the 12th cent.. A classic account of this change is H. Hirsch, *Die hohe Gerichtsbarkeit* (1922, repr. Darmstadt, 1958); cf. V. Achter, *Die Geburt der Strafe* (Frankfurt, 1951).

[7] Para. 10 of the law for the ecclesiastical princes, *Confoederatio cum principibus ecclesiasticis*, dated 1220, deals with the use of the *regalia*. The equivalent passages in the *Statutum in favorem principum* of 1231–2 for the lay princes are found in 6–8. For the interpretation of the *Fürstengesetze* as formal recognition of long-established legal practices see E. Klingelhöfer, *Die Reichsgesetze von 1220, 1231/2 und 1235* (Weimar, 1955).

[8] MGH Const. iii, no. 205; cf. Krieger, *Lehnshoheit*, 252; E. Kaufmann, 'Bannleihe', *Handwörterbuch zur deutschen Rechtsgeschichte*, i (Berlin, 1971), 314 f.; R. Scheying, *Eide, Amtsgewalt und Bannleihe* (Cologne and Graz, 1960).

[9] Krieger, *Lehnshoheit*, 391 ff.

[10] H. Thieme, 'Friede und Recht im mittelalterlichen Reich' (1945), repr. id., *Ideengeschichte und Rechtsgeschichte: Gesammelte Schriften*, 2 vols (Cologne and Vienna, 1986), i. 213–29.

In the later Middle Ages, therefore, there is a discrepancy between the king's *Rechtskompetenz* and his *Handlungskompetenz*. This should warn us against assuming that when kings presented themselves as legislators in the earlier Middle Ages, this included a competence to act politically. We must realize that acting out traditional roles did not necessarily mean that political decisions were implemented. If we want to know whether the *Landfrieden* proclaimed in the twelfth century were translated into royal political actions, it will not be enough simply to look at the codes. We will also have to ask whether the Salian and Hohenstaufer kings developed adequate administrative methods for transforming acts of law-giving into political actions.

According to the *Landfrieden* issued from 1103 on, the king's aim was to promote peace.[11] However, this concept meant different things to different people, especially in the eleventh and twelfth centuries, as this article will show. Like all global terms, 'peace' needs to be qualified and interpreted. In the eleventh and twelfth centuries it was not enough for a king to exercise his paramount responsibility for 'peace' and 'justice' by admonishing his people to act 'justly' and observe the 'peace' as something they could all agree upon. Any legislation on his part could have the force of a law only if he possessed the means to make people accept *his* definition of peace as against that of others. Historians tend to speak of the measures taken by the German kings in the twelfth century as forming part of a peace movement, in the sense that rulers took legislative measures in response to popular demands, and that these measures were enthusiastically supported by the people. While French narrative sources on the 'peace of God' indeed suggest that large crowds were emotionally involved,[12] contemporary German historians generally devote only a few sentences to the phenomenon. The most important sources are the royal

---

[11] E. Wadle, 'Heinrich IV. und die deutsche Friedensbewegung', in J. Fleckenstein (ed.), *Investiturstreit und Reichsverfassung* (Vorträge und Forschungen, 17; Sigmaringen, 1973), 141–73.

[12] H. Hoffmann, *Gottesfriede und Treuga Dei* (Stuttgart, 1964); H.-W. Goetz, 'Kirchenschutz, Rechtswahrung und Reform: Zu den Zielen und zum Wesen der frühen Gottesfriedensbewegung in Frankreich', *Francia*, 11 (1983), 193–239; O. Engels, 'Vorstufen der Staatwerdung im Hochmittelalter—Zum Kontext der Gottesfriedensbewegung', *Historisches Jahrbuch*, 97–8 (1978), 71–86.

peace codes (*Landfriedensgesetze*). The first of these was issued
in 1103 by King Henry IV.[13] Although there were many differences between the codes, common to all was a ban on
certain acts of violence on penalty of death or mutilation. In
his law Henry IV revived the tradition of the 'truce of God'.[14]
Such truces had been launched on the initiative of episcopal
synods in southern France since the end of the tenth century. Their aim had been to reduce violence by outlawing
certain acts which, when committed in a feud, had hitherto
been regarded as lawful. Ecclesiastical as well as lay princes of
the Reich had accepted these new notions earlier than
Henry IV, issuing truces of God and truces of the land
(*Landfrieden*).[15] Given his traditional responsibility as the
guardian of *pax* and *iustitia*, the king had to meet these
initiatives with legislative acts of his own. Henry's peace code
of 1103 was probably a response to this challenge.

All twelfth-century German kings gave orders for the maintenance of the peace. Only a few of these have survived as
law-codes with detailed paragraphs. In addition to King
Henry's peace, we have those issued by Frederick I
Barbarossa in 1152, 1158 (Peace of Roncaglia), 1179, and
1186 (*Brandstifterbrief*—letter against incendiaries).[16]
The main theme of these legal codes can be summarized
as follows. Henry IV's peace was a typical *pax* in the sense in
which this term was used in the truces of God. Acts of violence against certain groups of people who needed protection were prohibited for four years on pain of physical
punishment. Barbarossa's peace codes had an additional
aim. In every case, the outlawing of violent self-help was
accompanied by an order to seek redress for grievances by
judicial process. This was the case whether acts of violence

---

[13] MGH Const. i, no. 74, 126.   [14] Wadle, 'Friedensbewegung'.

[15] H.-W. Goetz, 'Der Kölner Gottesfriede von 1083. Beobachtungen über
Anfänge, Tradition und Eigenart der deutschen Gottesfriedensbewegung',
Jahrbuch des kölnischen Geschichtsvereins, 55 (1984), 39–76. J. Gernhuber, *Die
Landfriedensbewegung in Deutschland bis zum Mainzer Reichslandfrieden von* 1235
(Bonn, 1952), xii, and E. Wadle, 'Frühe deutsche Landfrieden', in R. Kottje and
H. Mordeck (eds.), *Überlieferung und Geltung normativer Texte des frühen und hohen
Mittelalters* (Sigmaringen, 1986), 71–92; R. Kaiser, 'Selbsthilfe und Gewaltmonopol:
Königliche Friedenswahrung in Deutschland und Frankreich im Mittelalter',
Frühmittelalterliche Studien, 17 (1983), 55–72.

[16] MGH DD F.I. nos. 25, 222, 774 and 988.

were forbidden without exception and temporal limitation as in the laws of 1152 and 1158, or whether only specific acts were banned, as in the laws of 1179 and 1186. While King Henry's law tried merely to limit the consequences of feuding, Barbarossa's apparently attempted to change the legal system by making a judicial process mandatory in cases of conflict. This implied that self-help was to be replaced by action in courts.

In investigating what Frederick Barbarossa did to achieve this end we shall start by examining the notion of law-giving upon which his activities were founded. His laws were given as general rules to be observed in the whole Reich. Actions forbidden by these laws were condemned as illegal. This reflects a new understanding of law and justice,[17] one which also entered the legal vocabulary.[18] In the earlier Middle Ages, the legal order consisted of a summary of innumerable single titles owned by certain individuals and groups of people. Sharing the same type of rights and thus forming a *Rechtskreis* (legal community) was a powerful element in creating the various *Personenverbände* (groups) that made up medieval society. The titles and honours which a person possessed constituted his *Rechtsstand* (legal status). This was determined by birth, origin, and customary use, and could be bettered by the addition of new titles.[19] People were per-

[17] H. Krause, 'Gesetzgebung', *Handwörterbuch zur deutschen Rechtsgeschichte*, i (1971), 1606–20; W. Ebel, *Geschichte der Gesetzgebung in Deutschland*, 2nd edn. (Göttingen, 1958); C. H. Haskins, *The Renaissance of the Twelfth Century* (1927, repr. Cleveland, New York, 1967), 193 ff.; H. Hattenhauer, *Die Bedeutung der Gottes- und Landfrieden für die Gesetzgebung in Deutschland*, Ph.D. thesis (Marburg, 1958/60), 93 ff. argues that the peace movement grew out of a change in beliefs. As the belief in magico-sacred sanctions began to fade, other kinds of sanctions had to take its place. 'Die Wirren des 12. Jahrhunderts haben ihre Ursache in der Entheiligung des alten Rechts, in dem Fehlen von Kräften, die das Gebot der Rechtsordnung hätten erzwingen können', ibid. 95, 170 ff. The observations made by G. Landwehr, 'Königtum und Landfriede', *Der Staat*, 7 (1968), 84–97, here 97 concerning the later Middle Ages also apply to the 12th century; cf. E. Wadle, 'Über Entstehung, Funktion und Geltungsgrund normativer Rechtsaufzeichnungen im Mittelalter', in P. Classen (ed.), *Recht und Schrift im Mittelalter* (Vorträge und Forschungen, 23; Sigmaringen, 1977), 503–18.

[18] K. Kroeschell, 'Recht und Rechtsbegriff im 12. Jahrhundert', *Probleme des 12. Jahrhunderts* (Vorträge und Forschungen, 12; Stuttgart, 1968), 309–35.

[19] H. Krause, 'Königtum und Rechtsordnung in der Zeit der sächsischen und salischen Herrscher', *Zeitschrift der Savigny-Stiftung für Rechtsgeschichte, Germ. Abt.*, 82 (1965), 1–98.

mitted (and expected) to avenge the (real or imagined) infringement of their rights in a feud. 'Justice' and 'injustice', then, were defined by reference to a particular *Rechtsstand.* Of course, general rules did exist in the earlier Middle Ages, in particular, in the Church. Horst Fuhrmann has suggested, however, that before Gratian (1140) canon law 'was accepted in theory but not obeyed in practice'.[20] This means that even within the Church general rules were hardly understood as normative, and that in many cases local customary law took precedence over the universal law of the Church. When Church reformers, especially the Roman reform group around Pope Leo IX, 'realized the flagrant contradiction between norm and reality',[21] the process of re-establishing the normative value of general rules was greatly advanced. Unlike in a customary legal system, this meant that all individual cases were subject to the norms which applied to everyone. This type of legal thinking was first revived within the Church. Its influence on German lay rulers was increased by their contact with late Roman imperial law and its reappearance in northern Italy. The *Landfriedensgesetze* demonstrate this twofold influence. They, too, defined 'right' and 'wrong' not only in terms of an individual's *Rechtsstand* and any injury to it, but also in terms of violating the law as a general rule.

Thus the concept of 'peace' also acquired a new dimension. In traditional, customary law, 'peace' was considered to reign when everybody was able to enjoy their own rights. Feuds were seen as a means of re-establishing peace after a breach of these rights. In this respect feuding parties consid-

---

[20] H. Fuhrmann, 'Das Reformpapsttum und die Rechtswissenschaft', in J. Fleckenstein (ed.), *Investiturstreit und Reichsverfassung* (Vorträge und Forschungen, 17; Sigmaringen, 1973), 175–204, here 178.

[21] The quotation is from R. Schieffer, *Die Entstehung des päpstlichen Investiturverbots für den deutschen König* (Stuttgart, 1981), 36. R. Schieffer shows how difficult it was even for the Church to understand legal clauses as containing general norms that applied to various individual cases. He describes the *Wormser Konkordat* as a text 'der weniger dazu bestimmt [war], eine Rechtslage erst zu schaffen, vielmehr sie zu fixieren, zu beschreiben, zu bekräftigen, ohne doch ihren längerfristigen Wandel hindern zu können' (that was intended to establish legal concepts rather than to create new ones. However, it was unable to prevent them changing in the long term), 'Rechtstexte des Reformpapsttums und ihre zeitgenössische Resonanz', *Überlieferung und Geltung,* 51–69, quotation 68.

ered feuds and the violence which accompanied them to be serving the peace. Presumably not even the blood-thirstiest knight would have objected to 'peace' as such, provided it did not prevent him from committing what he regarded as legal violence in a lawful feud. The *Landfriedensgesetze*, however, declared acts of violence, even in a feud, to be criminal 'breaches of the peace', regardless of whether the feuding party claimed to have been provoked by an enemy's assault upon its rights. The movement for the truce of God had redefined 'peace' in this way, in an attempt to promote a new consciousness of 'right' and 'wrong'.

Early in the movement's life, the bishops had imposed ecclesiastical penalties for breaches of the peace. It soon became apparent, however, that these were not enough to enforce the new notion of peace. The formation of 'peace armies' led by the clergy shows how much opposition there was to this change in values. The German rulers adopted this new notion of peace in their *Landfriedensgesetze*.

In a legal system that includes the observance of general rules, a number of specific measures are essential to guarantee that it actually functions, while a system based on customary law can dispense with such measures. First, an act of legislation producing a new law to be observed by all must be made known to all. Customary law, on the other hand, as the customs practised by a legal community, is known by experience and through the collective legal memory. Laws promulgated as general rules depend on organized dissemination. How did the German kings attempt to ensure that this happened?

Secondly, unlike customary law, in which the collective memory of the legal community as a whole guards against falsification, any given law is in danger of adulteration, deliberate or inadvertent.[22] A legislator aware of this problem must not only provide an authentic text, but also control its implementation and ensure that supplementary legal acts eliminate any ambiguities and contradictions that appear as

---

[22] In this context the question of whether Charlemagne and his successors established authenticated texts of the capitularies and organized their dissemination is of interest. Several papers in the volume *Recht und Schrift im Mittelalter* deal with these questions.

the law is applied. All this requires that the legislator receives information from wherever in his realm the law is valid. Do the sources indicate that the German rulers were aware of this problem, and developed means to solve it?

Thirdly, lawgiving that redefines right and wrong as the *Landfrieden* do can no longer rely on the uninstitutionalized mechanisms of peer pressure. These are effective means of control in a society regulated by unquestioned customs. Heinrich Fichtenau has demonstrated that in the tenth century such peer pressure (*Ordnungszwänge*) was much stronger than institutionalized legal control (*Rechtszwänge*). 'Anyone who did not submit to the rules of the community excluded himself from the social group, or at least felt the opposition of the "good" ones so strongly that his social existence became exceedingly difficult.'[23] This sort of informal pressure presupposes an unequivocal set of social values, and these no longer existed after the *Gottesfrieden* (peace of God) and *Landfrieden* had redefined the notions of peace and justice. Consequently the problem of enforcing the law was far more urgent than before. How did rulers attempt to deal with it?

In assessing whether the *Landfrieden* were effective measures of royal peace-making, we must establish to what extent the necessary supporting measures referred to above were implemented. As our sources contain no direct information about the real effectiveness of royal peace-making, I propose to change focus and look instead for the *possibility* of effectiveness. Were the methods employed adequate to make substantive results likely?

Our first question concerns the dissemination of the laws. In his *Landfrieden* of 1152 Frederick Barbarossa takes it for granted that the law as a document will reach bishops, dukes, counts, markgraves, and judges,[24] whom he addresses in the *intitulatio* in the following terms: 'To the bishops etc., to whom this text will come.' There is no indication in our

---

[23] H. Fichtenau, *Lebensordnungen des 10. Jahrhunderts*, 2 vols. (Munich, 1984), i. 48; cf. T. Luckmann, 'Personal identity as an evolutionary and historical problem', in von Cranach (ed.), *Human Ethology* (Cambridge, 1980), 56–74.

[24] The 'intitulatio' reads: 'episcopis, ducibus, comitibus, marchionibus, rectoribus, ad quos littere iste pervenerint', MGH D. F.I. nos. 25, 41.

sources, however, that Frederick devised effective methods of reproducing and distributing the law as a document. It seems to me that we should therefore understand the *intitulatio* not as referring to an adminstrative act, but as a traditional formula found in many royal diplomas addressed to 'all the faithful, both present and to come'. As the kings who used this formula did not notify the addressees,[25] so Barbarossa, as far as we know, did not use any administrative means to notify those of his magnates who were not present at the royal council that issued the code. The fact that Bertold of Zähringen included the sanctions laid down in the 1152 code in the municipal code when founding Freiburg[26] does not contradict this. No one disputes that some people were aware of the provisions of the code. The question is whether, after the code was issued, adequate means existed to distribute it to *all* those whom it might concern.

Heinrich Appelt has recently suggested that the 1152 code should not be seen as a legislative act at all, but as a communal judgement (*Weistum*), that is, as a formal pronouncement of what was considered legal as far as people remembered. Striking parallels with the provisions of some German truces of God in the eleventh century support this interpretation. If this were the case, it would indeed render the whole discussion superfluous, for it would rule out any substantial royal political role in the *Landfrieden* altogether. The king would not have legislated, but would have confirmed by his authority accepted legal notions—accepted at least as far as their theoretical expression in formal Latin was concerned. What happened in everyday life was probably a different story. Latin theory and vernacular practice did not necessarily coincide.

I believe that there is much to be said in favour of Appelt's opinion. According to this view royal peace-making in the

[25] Cf. the remarks by H. Boockmann on the general prohibition on destroying bridges and hindering traffic contained in a diploma addressed by Otto II to the merchants of Magdeburg: *Einführung in die Geschichte des Mittelalters*, 2nd edn. (Munich, 1981), 76.

[26] H. Keller, 'Die Zähringer und die Entwicklung Freiburgs zur Stadt', *Die Zähringer: Eine Tradition und ihre Erforschung*, 2 vols. (Sigmaringen, 1986), i. 17–29, here 24.

twelfth century was no more than a demonstration of royal virtues. This might not have been totally ineffective, but it certainly does not justify assessing the *Landfrieden* as altogether novel political acts on the part of the German kings. This, however, is what they are usually taken for. And until Appelt's theory has been fully debated, it is this *communis opinio* among scholars which we must address.

If the *Landfrieden* are considered legislative acts in the modern sense, the question of organizing their distribution is vital. There is nothing in the 1152 code, or anything relating to it, however, that suggests that an attempt of this kind was made. In fact, the manuscript tradition suggests the opposite.[27]

As the laws of 1103 and 1158 required every male aged between 18 and 70 in the realm to take an oath of peace, the issue of dissemination becomes even more relevant.[28] Even if we assume that the royal councils were extraordinarily well attended, we can virtually exclude the possibility that every male between these ages was present. But the code of 1158 required all of them to swear an oath of peace. Did royal officers travel the land with an authorization to take the oath from those who had been absent? And what happened if somebody absented himself in order not to have to swear the oath? Neither Henry IV nor Frederick Barbarossa seem to have made any provision for these cases.

This leads to the second question, that of supervising the implementation of the code all over the realm and of gathering the information necessary for effective control. There is no indication whatsoever in our sources that the German rulers who legislated in the twelfth century had any more

---

[27] For the tradition of the different texts see Wadle, 'Frühe deutsche Landfrieden'.

[28] It has been observed that in the earlier Middle Ages a solemn oath was considered indispensable for the making of a new law. By this oath people bound themselves under peril of damnation to observe what everybody had agreed upon. Cf. W. Ebel, *Die Willkür* (Göttingen, 1953) and, with regard to the peace movement, T. Körner, *Iuramentum und frühe Friedensbewegung (10.–12. Jh.)* (Berlin, 1977), who argues against Gernhuber, *Landfriedensbewegung*, 60. In Gernhuber's view the peace codes were acts of 'conscious lawgiving' based on an official royal order. Cf. Landwehr, *Königtum und Landfrieden*, 91 and n. 28, and Wadle, 'Frühe deutsche Landfrieden', 87, who follow Ebel and Körner in seeing the oath as binding people to uphold the *Landfrieden*.

information available to them than their predecessors, who had moved through their kingdoms and, as supreme judges, had listened to the complaints of those who managed to gain access to their person. In order to go beyond this limited dispensation of justice and to achieve lasting effects, kings would have needed regular information about and communication with their subjects. Only administrative routine could make the king a dependable supreme judge, and turn his goodwill as expressed in the codes into effective political action. There is nothing to suggest that any of the German kings in the twelfth century ever attempted this.

The same applies to the third problem, that of enforcing the law. All the codes from 1103 to 1186 express an order either in general terms or in the passive voice. Henry IV commands that all those who break the peace 'are to lose their eyes or hand' (*oculos vel manum amittent*) and that those who defend the culprit are to suffer the same penalty. Henry IV does not specify who is to put out eyes or to cut off hands. Whether traditional legal officers such as dukes or counts were meant or, as is more likely, all those who had taken the oath of peace and thus become members of the peace army, it was certainly not the king who exercised corrective control. Having demonstrated his love of peace by issuing a peace code, the king left it to others to put his commands into effect. The whole peace initiative rested, it seems, on the unspoken assumption that all people of goodwill would want the same thing. The code makes no provision for the possibility of people holding different opinions about what was good, and therefore refusing to co-operate.

The same is true of Barbarossa's codes. Paragraph 1 of the 1152 code stipulates that the penalty for killing someone is capital punishment—*capitalem subeat sententiam.* As judges (*iudices*) are mentioned in the following paragraphs, we can assume that they were responsible for the executions. But how is this supposed to have worked? Presumably if somebody killed a person (in a feud ?) he was to be brought before the judge—but by whom? In most cases the killer preferred to stay out of reach of the law. The code makes a revealing provision for this case. The possessions of anyone who flees from judgement are to go to his heirs (paragraph

2). The heirs are named as his executioners, despite the fact
that they were the natural feud-helpers. The king seems to
have believed that they would co-operate against their own
blood relations because they had a chance to come into their
inheritance prematurely. Similarly, the code appoints feudal
lords as executioners for vassals who were accused of breaking the peace. There is no doubt, however, that the most
powerful bonds in the earlier Middle Ages were those between blood relations on the one hand and between lord
and vassal on the other. These relationships were based on a
far stronger loyalty than that towards king and State. Yet
Barbarossa made the implementation of his *Landfrieden*
depend upon people setting aside these traditionally strong
ties in favour of the king's concept of peace and justice.
Barbarossa's code makes no provision for the case that they
should refuse to do this.

It is clear that I doubt whether the *Landfrieden* were effective legislative measures. Rather, I see them as demonstra-
tions of the traditional royal responsibilities in the areas of
peace and justice, presented in the form—modern at the
time—of an official code. It seems that Barbarossa was of the
same opinion. Barbarossa asked his uncle, Otto of Freising,
to write an account of his rule. In response, Otto in 1157
asked Barbarossa to send him a list of what he had actually
achieved in the Holy Roman Empire since his election in
1152.[29] In this document Barbarossa says a great deal about
his wars against the enemies of the Reich, about destruction
and pillage. All this conformed with the notion that any
infringement of rights called for revenge, and that it was the
emperor's duty to defend the *honor imperii*. In listing his royal
deeds, however, he did not even mention his *Landfrieden*.
Barbarossa, it seems, did not count issuing a peace code
among his practical achievements.

[29] Otto von Freising, *Die Taten Friedrichs*, ed. F.-J. Schmale (Ausgewählte Quellen
zur deutschen Geschichte des Mittelalters, 17; Darmstadt, 1965), 82–9.

4

England in the Twelfth and Thirteenth Centuries

David A. Carpenter

The maintenance of the peace had been a duty of kings in England since the earliest Anglo-Saxon times. 'It is related', wrote Bede, 'that there was so great a peace in Britain wherever the dominion of king Edwin reached that as the proverb still runs, "a new-born child could walk throughout the island from sea to sea and take no harm"'.[1] Edgar at his Coronation in 973 swore that 'the church of God and the whole Christian people may by my will preserve true peace for all time', a similar oath being taken at their Coronations by all subsequent kings of England.[2] Henry I reiterated the point in his Coronation charter: 'I place a firm peace in all my kingdom and order it henceforth to be kept.'[3]

Peace could be looked at from two points of view. When Henry III in 1261 declared that for forty-five years he had laboured to preserve the 'peace and tranquility' of each and everyone, he defined that peace and tranquility as the absence of 'hostility and general war'.[4] In the twelfth and thir-

I am most grateful to Mr J. O. Prestwich and to Dr Paul Brand for commenting on a draft of this paper. They are not responsible for errors of fact and interpretation which remain.

[1] *Bede's Ecclesiastical History*, ed. B. Colgrave and R. A. B. Mynors (Oxford, 1969), 193.

[2] J. W. Legg, *English Coronation Records* (London, 1901), 14–29. Dr Nelson has shown that the *ordo* used at Edgar's coronation was itself derived from earlier English and West Frankish rituals. See J. L. Nelson, 'The Earliest Royal *Ordo*: Some Historical and Liturgical Aspects', *Festschrift for Walter Ullman*, ed. M. Wilks and B. Tierney (Cambridge, 1978), repr. in Nelson, *Politics and Ritual in Early Modern Europe* (London, 1986).

[3] W. Stubbs, *Select Charters, and Other Illustrations of English Constitutional History*, 9th edn., rev. by H. W. C. Davis (Oxford, 1913), 119.

[4] *Foedera, Conventiones, Litterae inter reges et alios*, ed. T. Rymer, new edition revised by A. Clarke and F. Holbrooke, i, pt. 1 (London, 1816), 408.

teenth centuries, as J. O. Prestwich has observed, kings of England were tolerably succesful in maintaining this type of tranquility, the only periods of general civil war being between 1139–54, 1215–17, and 1263–7. There was secondly, however, peace in what might be called the 'police' or 'law and order' sense. It was to that that Edgar turned in the second clause of his Coronation oath when he 'forbad to all ranks thefts and injustices'.[5] It is essentially with peace in this second sense that I will be concerned in this paper. In terms of theory there was little difference here between German and English kingship. 'All through the Middle Ages', as Hanna Vollrath has said, 'it was never denied that the German kings possessed supreme responsibility for peace and justice.' In terms of practice, on the other hand, the contrast was marked. In Germany competence for criminal jurisdiction was part of the 'Regalia' which were formally recognized as belonging to the princely fiefs in 1220 and 1230–1. In England, by contrast, the kings of the twelfth and thirteenth centuries developed an impressive legal and administrative apparatus through which *they* could try and punish serious crime throughout the country and settle a wide variety of civil disputes. They had, therefore, both the theoretical obligation to maintain the peace and the practical ability to do something about it. In what follows I will consider briefly the development of this royal system of justice before questioning its real scope and effectiveness.

The achievement of the twelfth and thirteenth centuries was built on pre-Conquest foundations. By 1066 kings of England claimed more than a vague duty to maintain the peace. They also stressed a narrower and more potent concept of 'the king's peace' which, originally given to particular places and individuals, had come to extend throughout the realm. In the twelfth century this peace was breached, according to *Glanvill*, by homicide, arson, robbery, rape, and forgery. These serious crimes (or felonies) formed the 'pleas of the Crown' which could be tried only in the king's court. In the next century *Bracton* gave a similar list though adding

---

[5] Legg, *English Coronation Records*, 14.

that wounding and wrongful arrest and detention could also involve breaches of the peace and be included amongst the pleas of the Crown.[6] In England, therefore, serious crimes, be the wrongdoer the lowliest peasant, were for the king to try not the princes.

The theory was one thing but the Anglo-Saxons had also created a network of hundred and county courts where the king's pleas could be heard in the presence of royal officials. Again twelfth-century kings built on these foundations.[7] Henry II tightened up the procedures of criminal justice by extending the use of the jury of presentment, a jury composed of twelve men from each hundred whose duty was to bring to light breaches of the peace within the hundred, and name the perpetrators before whoever was to hear the pleas of the Crown. In the 1190s the coroners were introduced to hold inquests on all violent and suspicious deaths and keep a record of pleas of the Crown until their hearing. On the civil side the petty assizes and the grand assize were evolved under Henry II, bringing a huge mass of litigation into the king's courts and contributing to the maintenance of the peace by discouraging the immediate resort to self-help. In the thirteenth century the forms of legal action continued to develop. From 1258 onwards the government made widely available a straightforward procedure whereby men could commence actions (other than those over land) by simple verbal complaint (a *querela*), thus dispensing with the difficulty and expense of obtaining writs. It was possible, moreover, to use this procedure to redress a wide range of minor injuries by alleging that the action complained of, while not serious enough to be a felony, constituted a trespass, that is

[6] Stubbs, *Select Charters*, 86 (Cnut, Secular Dooms, cc. 12, 14), 125 (*Leges Henrici Primi*, X, i); H. R. Loyn, *The Governance of Anglo-Saxon England 500–1087* (London, 1984), 126–7; *The Roll of the Shropshire Eyre of 1256*, ed. A. Harding (Selden Soc., 96, 1980), lii–liii; *The Treatise on the Laws and Customs of England commonly called Glanvill*, ed. G. D. G. Hall (London, 1965), 3, 171–7; *Bracton on the Laws and Customs of England*, ed. G. Woodbine, trans. and rev. S. E. Thorne (Cambridge, Mass., 1968), ii. 327–449. *Lèse-majesté*, forgery, and the concealment of treasure trove were also pleas of the Crown.

[7] For recent surveys of Anglo-Saxon, Norman, and Angevin government, see Loyn, *The Governance of Anglo-Saxon England* and W. L. Warren, *The Governance of Norman and Angevin England 1086–1272* (London, 1987). Another valuable general survey is A. Harding, *The Law Courts of Medieval England* (London, 1973).

had been committed by force and in breach of the king's peace.[8]

New legal actions were combined with new types of judges. Early in the twelfth century both the pleas of the Crown and a variety of civil litigation were heard in the county courts by the sheriffs or by local justiciars. By the 1120s, however, Henry I was hiving off this business to judges sent from the centre who travelled from county court to county court hearing 'all pleas'. This use of justices in eyre or itinerant justices was revived and extended by Henry II and their visitations round the counties of England continued until the end of the thirteenth century. They heard the presentments of the hundred juries, the *queralae* of individuals, the petty and grand assizes, and an array of other civil cases pleaded by writ. In the intervals between their visitations (in the thirteenth century a customary seven years) it became increasingly common to appoint justices of assize, gaol delivery and oyer and terminer and these came to share with the eyre (and the bench and the court *coram rege*) the burden of dispensing criminal and civil justice in England.[9]

The reason for these impressive developments was not simply the king's obligation to maintain law and order. In 1227 one of the justices in eyre in Cumberland, William of York, wrote as follows to the Chancellor: 'my lord, on Satur-

[8] For these developments, see Warren, *The Governance of Norman and Angevin England* and Harding, *The Law Courts of Medieval England.* More specialist works include N. Hurnard, 'The Jury of Presentment and the Assize of Clarendon', *English Historical Review*, 56 (1941), 374–410; *Royal Writs in England from the Conquest to Glanvill*, ed. R. C. van Caenegem (Selden Soc., 77, 1958–9), introduction, on the early history of the common law; D. W. Sutherland, *The Assize of Novel Disseisin* (Oxford, 1973); R. F. Hunnisett, *The Medieval Coroner* (Cambridge, 1961); S. F. C. Milsom, *The Legal Framework of English Feudalism* (Cambridge, 1976); *The Roll of the Shropshire Eyre 1256*, ed. Harding, introd. xxxii–lviii on the origins of trespass. For the development of trespass pleaded by writ in the 13th cent. see S. F. C. Milsom, 'Trespass from Henry III to Edward III', *Law Quarterly Review*, 74 (1958), 195–224, 406–36, 561–90.

[9] For these developments see again Warren, *The Governance of Norman and Angevin England* and Harding, *The Law Courts of Medieval England.* More specialist works include J. A. Green, *The Government of England under Henry I* (Cambridge, 1986); W. T. Reedy, 'The Origins of the General Eyre in the Reign of Henry I', *Speculum*, 41 (1966), 688–724; P. Brand, *The Origins of the English Legal Profession* (Oxford, 1992); D. Crook, *Records of the General Eyre* (London, 1982); D. Crook, 'The Later Eyres', *English Historical Review*, 97 (1982), 241–8; R. B. Pugh, *Imprisonment in Medieval England* (Cambridge, 1968), chs. xii, xiii.

day after the Exhaltation of the Holy Cross I left Carlisle, having finished all the king's business. We were there nine days and obtained 40 marks a day for the king, the total of the eyre being 360 marks or more'.[10] The fact was that justice was profitable. In the 1240s Dr Stacey has shown that it sometimes contributed as much as 20 per cent of the king's annual revenue.[11] On the civil side the writs inaugurating the various procedures had to be paid for while individuals convicted of disseisins and other offences were amerced. It was, however, criminal justice which was most lucrative. On the 1241 Surrey eyre, for example, civil pleas were worth £102 to the Crown, criminal pleas £212.[12] The *murdrum* fine and a whole series of amercements for false accusations, concealment, and so forth could be imposed on the juries of presentment while the chattels of outlaws and convicted felons belonged to the Crown.

The king, therefore, had the strongest possible motive to maintain and develop his control over justice. But there was nothing inevitable about his success in doing so. Indeed, just as the theory about the king's responsibility for the maintenance of the peace was the same in both kingdoms, so the practice in England might also have paralleled that in Germany. The Norman and Angevin kings were frequent absentees just like the Hohenstaufens. Neither kingdom enjoyed unchequered father-to-son succession on the lines of the Capetians. The Investiture dispute had its parallel in the anarchy of Stephen's reign, the German civil war of the 1200s in the English civil war of 1215–17.

In both these periods of war English monarchy faced strong centrifugal tendencies.[13] Under Stephen and Matilda

[10] C. A. F. Meekings, 'Six Letters concerning the Eyres of 1226–8', *English Historical Review*, 65 (1950), 499, repr. in *Studies in 13th Century Justice and Administration* (London, 1981).

[11] R. Stacey, *Politics, Policy and Finance under Henry III 1216–1245* (Oxford, 1987), 206. For estimates of the value of the eyre in the 1230s and 1240s see *The 1235 Surrey Eyre*, vol. i, ed. C. A. F. Meekings (Surrey Record Soc., 31, 1979), 135–6; *The Crown Pleas of the Wiltshire Eyre 1249*, ed. C. A. F. Meekings (Wiltshire Archaeological and Natural History Soc., Records Branch, 16, 1960), 112.

[12] *The 1235 Surrey Eyre*, i. 135. In addition the county's 'common fine' was £ 40.

[13] For Stephen's reign, see R. H. C. Davis, *The Reign of Stephen* (London, 1967); H. A. Cronne, *The Reign of Stephen: Anarchy in England 1135–54* (London, 1970); E. King, 'King Stephen and the Anglo-Norman Aristocracy', *History*, 59 (1974), 180–94.

Geoffrey de Mandeville's ambition was to combine a place at
court with a principality in the home counties over which the
king was to have little control.[14] Apart from the earldom of
Essex he was to hold in hereditary right the Tower of
London and the sheriffdoms of London–Middlesex and Essex–Hertfordshire. Equally he was to hold in hereditary right
the local justiciarships of London and the three counties.[15]
That meant he would hear all pleas, criminal and civil, which
under Henry I had been heard by the justices in eyre. On the
criminal side the empress struggled to retain a vestige of
control, insisting that she could send one of Geoffrey's peers
to see that 'her pleas', presumably the pleas of the Crown,
were justly treated. Stephen, however, made no reservation
on the point.[16] On the civil side Geoffrey ordered a recognition by good men of the neighbourhood into the claim
of the canons of St Martin-le-Grand that they had been
disseised of five acres of land. He thus anticipated the petty
assizes of Henry II. Within Geoffrey's pricipality there was no
need for a king to provide such procedures. Geoffrey would
provide them himself.[17] At the beginning of Henry II's reign,
as Professor Warren has observed, rather than unity being
forged under the Crown 'it was more likely that the realm of
England would, as Germany did after a civil war, disintegrate
into principalities'.[18]

The same prospect reappeared in the 1215–17 civil war
and the early minority of Henry III.[19] When William
Longespee, Earl of Salisbury, entered the faith of the young
king in March 1217 he was promised Sherborne castle and
the counties of Devon and Somerset merely for 'homage and
service'.[20] As sheriff and self-styled Earl of Cornwall, Henry

[14] For Geoffrey as a *curialis*, see J. O. Prestwich, 'The Treason of Geoffrey de
Mandeville', *English Historical Review*, 113 (1988), 283–317.
[15] *Regesta Regum Anglo-Normannorum*, vol. iii, ed. H. A. Cronne and R. H. C. Davis
(Oxford, 1968), nos. 273–6.
[16] However, Mr Prestwich observes that Stephen's silence 'cannot be interpreted
as surrender': Prestwich, 'Geoffrey de Mandeville', 305.
[17] *Royal Writs in England from the Conquest to Glanvill*, 84, 277.
[18] W. L. Warren, *Henry II* (London, 1973), 362.
[19] See D. A. Carpenter, *The Minority of Henry III* (London, 1990).
[20] *Patent Rolls 1216–25*, 38, 86–7. The concession to Salisbury was 'salvo regali
nostro' but what this constituted was not specified. The earls, barons, knights, and
freemen of the counties were to swear homage and fealty to Salisbury saving their

Fitz-Count enjoyed all the financial issues of the county and appointed his own judges to hear petty assizes.[21] Perhaps the model to which these men aspired was that of Cheshire. The king's judges did not enter the county, the earl administering himself both criminal and civil justice and pocketing the proceeds. He had his own justiciar and his own writs to initiate the petty assize procedures.[22]

In admiring the achievements of the Anglo-Saxon, Norman, and Angevin kings in defeating these centrifugal forces and constructing the system of justice outlined above, we need, however, to retain a sense of proportion. The apparatus seems impressive but how effective was it in maintaining law and order? In 1285 the answer appeared to be 'not very', the Statute of Winchester stating bluntly that 'from day to day robberies, homicides and arsons are more often committed than they used to be'.[23] Whether in fact the situation was worse towards the end of the thirteenth century than it had been earlier is impossible to prove or disprove.[24] What seems certain, however, is that throughout the century large numbers of criminals were never brought to justice.[25] On the

fealty to the king and to answer to him henceforth as their lord. Salisbury also claimed to hold the county of Wiltshire in hereditary right.

[21] *Patent Rolls 1216–25*, 202–3.

[22] Bodleian Library MS. Dodsworth 31, fol. 88, a reference I owe to Dr David Crouch. For the authority of the earl in the early 13th cent. see B. E. Harris, 'Ranulph III, Earl of Chester', *Journal of the Chester Archaeological Society*, 58 (1975), 99–114. For the comparable liberty of the Bishop of Durham see G. T. Lapsley, *The County Palatine of Durham* (Cambridge, Mass., 1900).

[23] Stubbs, *Select Charters*, 464.

[24] See below, n. 38.

[25] The work of trying apprehended criminals was increasingly taken in the 13th cent. by justices of gaol delivery, whose rolls do not survive in any number until late in the reign of Edward I. Thus the impression given by eyre rolls that very few criminals were actually caught may be misleading. While an eyre would have to deal with all the unsolved cases since its last visitation perhaps seven years away, it might have only a year of apprehended criminals to try if the justices of gaol delivery had been making regular visitations, as they often did. See Pugh, *Imprisonment in Medieval England*, 277, 258–61. (The county gaol at Salisbury was delivered five times between the eyres of 1241 and 1249: *Crown Pleas of the Wiltshire Eyre 1249*, 56.) Hangings ordered by justices of gaol delivery were not presented on any regular basis at the eyre or, if they were, they were not regularly recorded: *The 1235 Surrey Eyre*, i. 106; *Crown Pleas of the Wiltshire Eyre 1249*, 56. This problem of the evidence, however, is less acute in the early 13th cent. when the eyres made more frequent visitations making commissions of gaol delivery less necessary. Equally, Meekings suggests that cases of homicide *were* reserved for the eyre until at least the 1250s:

Lincolnshire eyre of 1202 over a hundred reported homicides led to only two executions. Approaching fifty of the murders were committed by men who were either unknown or more often had simply fled and remained uncaptured.[26] On the Gloucestershire eyre of 1221, which admittedly covered the period of the 1215–17 war, 330 homicides were presented. These resulted in one man being mutilated and fourteen hanged. For the rest, about 100 orders were given to outlaw men who had not been produced before the judges while 166 of the crimes were attributed to unknown malefactors.[27] In those cases where malefactors were known yet still at large they could, of course, be outlawed. On the 1235 Surrey eyre the judges ordered the hanging of only five people. They ordered ninety (sixty-six accused or larceny and nineteen of homicide) to be outlawed for failing to appear before them.[28] But if outlawry was itself a punishment and one which tight-knit local communities could make effective,[29] it also encouraged rather than prevented further crime. The outlaw, in the words of the Trailbaston song,

Crown Pleas of the Wiltshire Eyre 1249, 5–6, 56. The early eyre rolls, therefore, may give an impression of the numbers of those accused of murder who were actually brought to justice.

[26] These figures are based on A. L. Poole, *Obligations of Society in the XII and XIII Centuries* (Oxford, 1946), 82 (citing I. L. Langbein in the *Columbia Law Review*, 33, (1933), 1337, n. 24) supplemented by my own calculations from the roll, *The Earliest Lincolnshire Assize Rolls*, ed. D. M. Stenton (Lincoln Record Soc., 22; 1926), 93–194. The previous eyre in Lincolnshire had been in 1198. For a commission to deliver Lincoln gaol in 1207 see *Rot. Lit. Claus.*, i. 83 b. No hangings resulted from over eighty cases of robbery in the 1202 roll. In many instances the appellants withdrew their appeals which may indicate they were using the procedure to secure private settlements, such settlements being sometimes formally sanctioned by the justices; *The Earliest Lincolnshire Assize Rolls*, lviii–lix; *The Roll of the Shropshire Eyre 1256*, xxxiii.

[27] F. Pollock and F. W. Maitland, *The History of English Law before the Time of Edward I*, 2nd edn. (Cambridge, 1898), ii. 557. For the roll see *Pleas of the Crown for the County of Gloucester 1221*, ed. F. W. Maitland (London, 1884). On the Shropshire eyre of 1256 180 cases of homicide were presented. There were nineteen executions. In 160 cases townships were amerced for failing to arrest or pursue malefactors. Numerous crimes were committed by *malefactores incogniti*; A. Harding, 'The Origins and Early History of the Keeper of the Peace', *Transactions of the Royal Historical Society*, 5th ser., 10 (1960), 86.

[28] *The 1235 Surrey Eyre*, i. 126.

[29] This is one of the themes of H. R. T. Summerson's 'The Structure of Law Enforcement in Thirteenth-Century England', *American Journal of Legal History*, 23 (1979), 313–27.

'kept within the woods in the beautiful shade', and joined the ranks of the *malefactores incogniti*.[30]

The king, therefore, could try criminals and he could outlaw them, but frequently he could not catch them. The problem lay not with the judges but with the police. The ultimate responsibility for the arrest of criminals in a county rested with the sheriff. But he had many other tasks and from the 1190s the government had attempted to give him assistance. Under an Ordinance promulgated in 1242, for example, 'so that the [king's] peace may be firmly observed', constables were to be appointed in every village and a chief constable in every hundred. The village constables were to raise the hue and cry and pursue and arrest 'disturbers of the peace, robbers and malefactors in parks and fish-ponds'. All this was combined with an elaborate system of 'watch and ward' with at least four men in each village being ordered to be on guard throughout the night and arrest any stranger. Measures such as these, however, tended to be prompted by particular circumstances and be of short duration.[31] The occasion for the 1242 Ordinance was the king's absence in Gascony. The Ordinance itself is evidence that there was no prior system of village constables and it did not set one up on any permanent basis.[32] Much of the 1242 Ordinance was repeated in the Statute of Winchester in 1285.[33] Two years later keepers of the peace were appointed in each county but their task was not to catch criminals themselves but to see

---

[30] *Anglo-Norman Political Songs*, ed. I. S. T. Aspin (Oxford, 1953), 73.

[31] Stubbs, *Select Charters*, 257–8, 276, 362–5; Harding, 'The Keeper of the Peace', 87–8. The provisions of 1242 were a development of earlier measures in 1195 and 1205; Stubbs, *Select Charters*, 257–8; *The Historical Works of Gervase of Canterbury*, ed. W. Stubbs (Rolls Series, 73, 1879–80), ii. 96–7. The 1205 ordinance 'for the common defence of the kingdom and the preservation of the peace' laid down that there shoud be chief constables in each county, a constable in each hundred and city, and a constable for each neighbourhood where there were *minores villae*, meaning presumably a constable for each group of villages. This scheme was prompted by a fear of French invasion which did not materialize and probably little concrete resulted from it; see J. Tait, *The Medieval English Borough* (Manchester, 1936), 253 and n. 4.

[32] There are very few references to village constables in *The Roll and Writ File of the Berkshire Eyre of 1248*, ed. M. T. Clanchy (Selden Soc., 90, 1972–3), *Crown Pleas of the Wiltshire Eyre 1249*, and *The Roll of the Shropshire Eyre of 1256*.

[33] Stubbs, *Select Charters*, 362–5.

that others bore the arms and performed the watches en-
joined by the 1285 Statute. Ultimately the office developed
into the justice of the peace, a branch of the judiciary rather
than the police force.[34] The king himself had no financial
incentive to develop a local constabulary. He made his profit
from the chattels of the criminal whether or not the criminal
was caught. The local communities were positively hostile to
the idea that they would have to pay for a police force. In the
1220s the county of Shropshire fought a vigorous campaign
to limit the number of serjeants in the county charged with
keeping the peace.[35]

It was, however, on the local communities, in the absence
of any effective police force, that the burden of maintaining
law and order rested. In the twelfth and thirteenth centuries,
under a system dating back to Anglo-Saxon times, the inhabitants of each village were placed together in groups
(tithings) of ten or twelve. Each tithing was responsible
for the good behaviour of its members and their pursuit
and arrest if they committed crime. At the raising of
the hue all the villagers were supposed to join in the pursuit
of a malefactor.[36] The value of the tithing system, however,
was limited since it only embraced the unfree population.
Equally outside it were the *vagantes* and *extranei*, who were
responsible for a high proportion of thirteenth-century
crime outside the cases of purely domestic violence.[37] Given
the wooded nature of much of rural England, it must
have been easy for such men to make their escape.
They may also have been increasing in numbers as
the expanding population of the thirteenth century out-

---

[34] Harding, 'The Keeper of the Peace', 85–109; B. H. Putnam, 'The Transformation of the Keepers of the Peace into the Justices of the Peace', *Transactions of the
Royal Historical Society*, 4th ser., 12 (1929), 19–48.

[35] R. Stewart-Brown, *The Serjeants of the Peace in Medieval England and Wales* (Manchester, 1936), 66–7. There was also opposition to schemes in 1253 and 1285 to
make local communities give compensation to those who suffered robberies in their
areas and they proved abortive; *Matthaei Parisiensis . . . Chronica Majora*, ed. H. R.
Luard (Rolls Series, 57, 1872–84), v. 368–9, 410–11; Stubbs, *Select Charters*, 464.

[36] W. A. Morris, *The Frankpledge System* (Cambridge, Mass., 1910).

[37] It is often difficult in the eyre rolls to distinguish between domestic violence, or
violence in the home, and 'professional' crime. Equally what appears to be a
'professional' robbery may be a deed committed as part of some wider dispute over
lands and rights.

stripped the supply of land.[38] Hence perhaps the feeling, expressed in the Statute of Winchester, that crime was increasing.

Even where the local communities knew the identity of the criminals, however, it did not follow that they were keen to see them arrested and convicted. It is true that an elaborate system had evolved to ensure that crime was actually brought to light.[39] The coroners were to hold their inquests in the presence of all males over the age of twelve in the four vills nearest to where the body was found. Sessions of the hundred court were held every three weeks and there the tithingmen (the heads of the tithings) presented all cases of disorder where the hue had been raised since the last meeting of the court. Every six months, at Easter and Michaelmas, in the hundreds under his control, the sheriff would hold his tourn, an especially full session of the hundred court. At the Michaelmas tourn he held the 'view of frankpledge', checking that the population was properly arranged in tithings. At both sessions a jury of twelve free men, having obtained information from tithingmen or representatives of the vills, presented to the sheriff details of cases where the hue had been raised, focusing particularly on serious crimes. They indicted the supposed culprits 'so that they could be arrested and either imprisoned or bailed until the next gaol delivery or eyre'.[40] Further presentments took place at the sessions of the county court. Finally at the eyre, as we have seen, the hundred juries appeared again to present serious crimes which had occurred since the last visitation. Tithings, vills,

[38] The proportion of homicides and thefts committed by strangers and vagrants doubled between the Essex eyres of 1272 and 1285 from 1:7.5 to 1:3.5; see Summerson, 'Law Enforcement in Thirteenth-Century England', 326. Comparatively few of the crimes presented on the 1202 Lincolnshire eyre were said to be committed by those who were unknown; *The Earliest Lincolnshire Assize Rolls*. Another hypothesis is that crime increased in the late 13th and early 14th cents. as a result of Edward I's wars and the political upheavals in the reign of his son. See the discussion in R. W. Kaeuper, 'Law and Order in Fourteenth-century England: The Evidence of Special Commissions of Oyer and Terminer', *Speculum*, 54 (1979), 735–7 and R. B. Pugh, 'Some Reflections of a Medieval Criminologist', *Proceedings of the British Academy*, 59 (1959), 83–104. The absence of the gaol delivery rolls for much of the 13th cent., however, makes it impossible to chart fluctuations in crime over the period.

[39] See Summerson, 'Law Enforcement in Thirteenth-Century England', 318–24.
[40] Ibid. 319.

and hundreds which had failed to arrest criminals would be amerced.

The fact was, however, that hope of favour or fear of reprisal often gave the local communities the strongest possible motive for brazening it out in the face of this hierarchy of courts and protecting as far as possible the perpetrators of crime. For the criminals were not simply *vagantes*. They were also local men, indeed sometimes powerful local men. We may suspect that a fair proportion of the *malefactores incognoti* were very well known indeed. Nor did criminals always prey on their neighbours, the preferred targets often being merchants and others passing through the locality. Matthew Paris alleged that a famous highway robbery at Alton in Hampshire in 1249 was the work of wealthy men of the locality and Dr Clanchy's researches have shown this was indeed the case.[41] Two of the three principals (themselves men of knightly status) and at least twenty of the sixty or so persons indicted as accessories were freemen of the Alton region. Despite his close personal interest in the case, the king found extreme difficulty in preventing the local community closing ranks around the criminals. In numerous instances the juries would not indict, or pronounced acquittals, while many of those accused fled or escaped. The Statute of Winchester in 1285 laid the blame for the increase of crime on local jurors who refused to accuse people of their neighbourhood of felonies especially when the victims were strangers, precisely the circumstances prevailing at Alton.[42]

In the Alton case it was local gentry who were the leading law-breakers. Elsewhere it was the great magnates and their stewards who exercised a sometimes lawless rule. In 1257, for example, the sheriff of Sussex was quite unable to restore to Robert of Cliffe 'in accordance with the law of the land . . . as

[41] *Matthaei Parisiensis . . . Chronica Majora*, v 56–60; M. T. Clanchy, 'Highway Robbery and Trial by Battle in the Hampshire Eyre of 1249', *Medieval Legal Records edited in Memory of C. A. F. Meekings*, ed. R. F. Hunnisett and J. B. Post (London, 1978), 42–6. For other studies of gentry involvement in crime see R. H. Hilton, *A Medieval Society: The West Midlands at the End of the Thirteenth Century* (London, 1966), 248–61; E. L. G. Stones, 'The Folvilles of Ashby Folville, Leicestershire, and their Associates in Crime, 1326–41', *Transactions of the Royal Historical Society*, 5th ser., 7 (1957), 117–36; N. Saul, *Knights and Esquires: The Gloucestershire Gentry in the Fourteenth Century* (Oxford, 1981), ch. v.
[42] Stubbs, *Select Charters*, 464.

his office required' cattle taken by the steward of the Earl of Surrey, John de la Ware. Robert and the sheriff complained to the exchequer which authorized the seizure of the steward's cattle until he made restoration to Robert. The result was that the steward first arrested Robert's groom and when Robert himself came to Lewes to get him freed 'seized him and beat him monstrously and treated him foully all the way to Lewes castle and put him in stocks and kept him there from the Friday till the Wednesday . . . and took from him a horse worth ten marks and forty shillings in money'. Robert put his total losses at 200 marks.[43] The fact was that the apparently splendid advances of Norman and Angevin government had not deprived magnates and gentry of the ability to exercise a large measure of rule in the shires of England.

One element in this rule was the jurisdiction which lords retained in their own courts, like that held by the Earl of Surrey at Lewes. Certain types of serious crime, as we have seen, were the monopoly of the Crown. But this left lords, according to *Glanvill* and *Bracton*, with jurisdiction over brawlings, beatings, and woundings where no breach of the king's peace was alleged.[44] These offences against what *Bracton* called 'the lord's peace' must have embraced a high proportion of local disorders.[45] Jurisdiction over them was enjoyed by large numbers of lords for it was part and parcel of the competence of the ordinary manorial court. It could also be exercised in honourial courts and in hundred courts which were in private hands. Indeed, the jurisdictions of these three types of private court were sometimes intertwined and contemporaries did not distinguish clearly between them.[46] Lords of private hundreds—and half the hundreds of England in the thirteenth century were in private hands—also held the annual view of frankpledge and

[43] *Select Cases of Procedure without Writ under Henry III*, ed. H. G. Richardson and G. O. Sayles (Selden Soc., 60, 1941), 126–7; for John de la Ware, see N. Denholm-Young, *Seignorial Administration in England* (Oxford, 1937), 75–6.

[44] *Glanvill*, 4; *Bracton*, ii. 436.

[45] For cases of this type in private courts and references to the lord's peace, see *Select Pleas in Manorial and other Seignorial Courts*, ed. F. W. Maitland (Selden Soc., 1, 1889), 17–20, 27, 30, 56, 64–6, 92, 96, 113, 118–19, 167, 178.

[46] For a discussion of the types of private courts and their jurisdiction see ibid., introduction; H. Cam, *The Hundred and the Hundred Rolls* (London, 1930), 205–13.

controlled the business of the hundred court. View of frankpledge was a liberty equally enjoyed by many lords of manorial courts whose men were thus exempted from the jurisdiction of the hundred court. In Devonshire in 1238 seventy-eight lords had the right to hold the view of frankpledge.[47]

An even more prestigious liberty was that of 'infangtheof', the lord's right to have a private gallows and hang a thief taken red-handed on his property. This again was a liberty possessed by large numbers of lords of manors. In Devonshire in 1238 there were sixty-five private gallows. Were more men executed in the thirteenth century by private or public hangmen?[48] One may suspect that if a thief was not taken red-handed he was often not taken at all, but the question is unanswerable because few records of private courts survive and the hangings they sanctioned were not regularly presented at the eyres.[49] It is only incidentally that the Devon eyre roll of 1238 reveals seven hangings authorized by two private courts. Other evidence is more anecdotal. In 1270 four tenants of Newenham Abbey performed the following services in return for their tenements. One conducted the prisoner to the gallows, one put the gallows up, one supplied the ladder, and one performed the actual hanging.[50]

Private courts still retained civil jurisdiction over debt and detinue up to the value of 40 shillings as well as having total competence in everything concerning the lands and services of the unfree peasantry. Enjoying the view of frankpledge, infangtheof, and the criminal jurisdiction over brawlings, beatings, and woundings, these courts, as Dr Summerson has observed, 'covered a substantial proportion of the quarrels, lawsuits and business concerns of those who came within their jurisdiction, and allowed the privileged possessor of

---

[47] Cam, *The Hundred and the Hundred Rolls*, 260–85, 210; *Crown Pleas of the Devon Eyre of 1238*, ed. H. R. T. Summerson (Devon and Cornwall Record Soc., n.s. 28, 1985), xix. Private hundreds took a variety of forms. In some, for example, the sheriffs were excluded altogether, in others they had the right to attend when the view of frankpledge was held.

[48] *Crown Pleas of the Devon Eyre 1238*, xix. For private jurisdiction in the West Midlands, see Hilton, *A Medieval Society*, 227–41.

[49] *The 1235 Surrey Eyre*, i. 106.

[50] *Crown Pleas of the Devon Eyre 1238*, xxiii, xx.

that jurisdiction an important degree of social and judicial control over his tenants'.[51] Lords, moreover, were far from merely clinging to this jurisdiction. On the contrary, during the personal rule of Henry III between 1234 and 1258 there is abundant evidence that great magnates were vigorously increasing the numbers of those who owed suit to their courts.[52]

If their own courts constituted one hand with which the magnates and gentry dispensed and manipulated justice in the localities, the other was formed by their increasing control over the apparatus of criminal and civil justice evolved by twelfth- and thirteenth-century kings. The legal developments of these centuries—the possessory assizes, the *querela* procedure and the law of trespass—essentially originated in response to demands from the gentry and those below them in local society. In 1215 Magna Carta called for more royal justice not less—two judges were to visit the counties four times a year to hear the petty assizes. But if the localities encouraged the king to provide certain legal procedures, they wished to control for themselves their actual implementation. In part, of course, by staffing the juries of presentment and assize they had always done so. But in 1215 Magna Carta also stipulated that the two judges sent to hear the petty assizes should sit with four knights of the county elected in the county court. Such demands were part of a wider aspiration in the shires to control the whole running of local government, one of the most persistent demands in the thirteenth century being that the sheriff should be a native of the county and a substantial member of the gentry.[53] In large part, as we shall see, the counties had their way, although the pattern of rule in the shires which emerged differed according to local circumstances. In some areas the gentry, in harmony or competition, could manage affairs themselves. In others a great local magnate could exercise a more or less stable rule through corrupting

---

[51] Ibid. xix–xx.

[52] D. A. Carpenter, 'King, Magnates and Society: The Personal Rule of King Henry III 1234–1258', *Speculum*, 60 (1985), 62–6.

[53] J. C. Holt, *Magna Carta* (Cambridge, 1965), 53–8; for the aspirations of local society after 1215 see J. R. Maddicott, 'Magna Carta and the Local Community 1215–1259', *Past and Present*, 102 (1984), 25–65.

the juries and retaining the gentry who held office as sheriffs, coroners, and judges.[54]

Corruption of the juries, on which the whole working of criminal and civil justice depended, had always been one method by which magnates and gentry could manipulate the judicial system, as we have seen in the Alton case. A petition in the parliament of 1305 from the 'poor men of England' complained that juries were 'so commonly corrupted by the gifts of the rich that no truth could be known by them'. It was not, moreover, simply a question of gifts. The year before judges were commissioned to enquire into who had hired malefactors to assault people in public places for simply telling the truth on assizes, juries, recognitions, and inquests concerning felonies, with the result that jurors feared to give verdicts or make indictments.[55]

Responsibility for empanelling juries in civil cases and for executing the verdicts belonged to the sheriffs. They also presided over the county court which still preserved a wide civil jurisdiction.[56] In the Norman and Angevin period sheriffs had often been drawn from the ranks of *curiales*. The latter brought to the office the prestige and power derived from their close association with the king and enjoyed abundant financial resources since they usually retained the revenue which they collected above their county farms. After 1236, however, the king decided that the financial cost of the curial sheriff outweighed his other advantages and they were replaced by local gentry and minor professional administrators.[57] Such men were already well tried in shrieval office but they lacked the prestige and resources which had enabled the curial sheriffs to stand up to the mightiest in the land. The consequent weakness of the sheriffs in the 1240s and

[54] For the web of control which the lords of Berkeley spread in Gloucestershire see Saul, *The Gloucestershire Gentry in the Fourteenth Century*, esp. 152–8. But Dr Saul, 97–102, also shows that many knights and esquires were unattached to the Berkeleys or any other magnate family.

[55] A. Harding, 'Early Trailbaston Proceedings from the Lincoln Roll of 1305', *Medieval Legal Records edited in Memory of C. A. F. Meekings*, 151, 145.

[56] e.g. *Glanvill*, 150, 153, 167, 170. For the jurisdiction of the county court, see R. Palmer, *The County Courts of Medieval England 1150–1350* (Princeton, 1982), pt. II.

[57] D. A. Carpenter, 'The Decline of the Curial Sheriff in England 1194–1258', *English Historical Review*, 91 (1976), 1–32.

1250s, when they had to deal with great magnates, was one reason why the latter were able to withdraw the suit of their men from the courts of shire and hundred as well as usurp other local government liberties. In the 1260s Henry III justified the temporary reappointment of curial sheriffs on the grounds that they would have the power both to defend his own rights and protect the men of the counties against the oppression of great magnates. By and large, however, the sheriffs of the later thirteenth and fourteenth centuries were drawn from the ranks of the knights and esquires.[58]

During the thirteenth century gentry and magnates also developed a hold over the judiciary. In 1215 Magna Carta, as we have seen, demanded that four knights of the county elected in the county court should sit with the two judges sent four times a year to each county to hear the petty assizes. This stipulation was modified in the Charter of 1217 but down to 1241 its spirit was fulfilled in numerous commissions to four local knights to hear individual assizes. Thereafter, until 1273, when the system was changed again, it became increasingly the practice to issue such commissions to professional judges though these might co-opt local knights as colleagues.[59] In the case of gaol delivery the system of 'four knights' lasted from the earliest commissions in the 1220s down to 1292. For long periods in the thirteenth century, therefore, the gentry had a major role as judges in dispensing the king's criminal and civil justice in the localities. There were obvious pressures for such men to judge cases in their own interests, or in those of their lords, the more so since there is evidence that the parties to disputes could apply for the appointment of particular justices. In 1292, when such commissions were abandoned, the four gaol delivery knights were accused of trying prisoners by

[58] *Foedera*, i, pt. 1, 408–9; Carpenter, 'The personal rule of King Henry III', 66–7. For an analysis of the sheriffs between 1326 and 1337, see W. A. Morris, 'The sheriff', *The English Government at Work*, ed. W. A. Morris and J. R. Strayer (Cambridge, Mass., 1947), ii, 51–3.

[59] Pugh, *Imprisonment in Medieval England*, 257, 265, 278–9; C. A. F. Meekings, *Calendar of the General and Special Assize and General Gaol Delivery Commissions on the Dorses of the Patent Rolls, Richard II (1377–99)* (Nendeln, Liechtenstein, 1977), i–iv. However, one of the 'four knights' might sometimes be a professional judge with local connections. This was also true of the petty assize commissions.

means of juries tainted, suborned, or drawn from areas far from where the prisoners had been arrested. A statute of 1330 laid down that justices of assize and gaol delivery should not be local men, a requirement intended to prevent 'corrupt alliances between justices and local magnates'. Ten years later another statute limited such commissions to justices of the two benches or king's serjeants.[60]

Pressures even more pronounced were brought to bear on the justices of oyer and terminer. From the 1270s these shared with the eyre the burden of hearing complaints of trespass, now more often presented by written 'bill' than by word of mouth. The second Statute of Westminster in 1285 laid down that justices of oyer and terminer must be drawn from the ranks of the king's professional judges—in 1275 only just over half had been. But the Statute was not adhered to, 34 per cent of the commissions in 1300 and 25 per cent in 1316–17 still having no professional judge at all. Indeed, the number of professionals as a proportion of the whole steadily declined—68 per cent in 1275, 42 per cent in 1300, and 32 per cent in 1316–17. Meanwhile a significant proportion of the judges were drawn from the ranks of the gentry, twenty-eight of the seventy-four judges appointed in 1275 and fifty-one of the 140 appointees in 1300 being of this status. The opportunities for corruption were increased because the plaintiffs who sought the oyer and terminer commission were able to name their own judges. Such commissions were often devices in local battles of power, with gentry and magnates accusing rivals of trespass and getting the cases heard by their own judges.[61] In the parliament of 1315 the community of the realm complained that 'when a "great lord or man of power" wished to ruin a man, he simply alleged a trespass by him or maintained someone else to do so and bought commissions of oyer and terminer by justices favourable to himself'.[62]

[60] Pugh, *Imprisonment in Medieval England*, 279–80, 282–3. See *Patent Rolls 1225–32*, 151 and the accusation in 1264 that magnates could obtain whatever judges they asked for, *Documents of the Baronial Movement of Reform and Rebellion 1258–1267*, ed. R. F. Treharne and I. J. Sanders (Oxford, 1973), 272–3.
[61] Kaeuper, 'Law and Order in Fourteenth-Century England', 752–3, 759.
[62] Harding, 'Early Trailbaston Proceedings', 151.

In the thirteenth and fourteenth centuries the king was clearly concerned to maintain the presence of his professional judges on local judicial commissions. The implication was that they were both more expert and less corrupt than the gentry and others who might be employed instead. The presence of professionals was no guarantee of probity, however. In 1225 the Bishop of Winchester spent 20s. on presents for the judge Martin of Patishall when he was hearing pleas in which the bishop was involved at Oxford.[63] Probably judges accepted such presents from all litigants; perhaps they were not unduly influenced by them. But by the 1260s serious allegations, which cannot be dismissed out of hand, were being made against the king's judges. It was said that they were placed and maintained in office by great magnates and were their *tributarii*. As a result lesser men (*minores*) could not secure justice against the great.[64]

In the thirteenth century, therefore, gentry and magnates were able to maintain and develop their rule in the counties of England both through their own courts and through manipulating the system of royal justice and administration. They could corrupt the juries and either hold office themselves as sheriffs and judges or retain and control those who did. In the fourteenth century the pattern was slightly different but the effect much the same. The king, as we have seen, tried to ensure that justices of assize and gaol delivery were now professionals. The justices of the king's bench moved round the country dealing with cases of serious crime.[65] On the other hand the eyre came to an end and the gentry began to dispense criminal justice in the localities as justices of the peace.[66] English kings might worry that they were

---

[63] County Record Office, Winchester, Eccles. II 159279, r. 14 (the Bishop of Winchester's pipe roll).

[64] *Documents of the Baronial Movement of Reform and Rebellion*, 272–3. These charges are discussed in Carpenter 'The Personal Rule of King Henry III', 45–9. For the retaining of judges see J. R. Maddicott, *Law and Lordship: Royal Justices as Retainers in Thirteenth and Fourteenth Century England* (Past and Present Suppl., 4; Oxford, 1978).

[65] For the activities of the king's bench in Gloucestershire see Saul, *Gloucestershire Gentry in the Fourteenth Century*, 171–2.

[66] Putnam, 'Transformation of the Keepers of the Peace', 19–48. See, however, W. M. Ormrod, 'Edward III and the Recovery of Royal Authority in England, 1340–60', *History*, 72 (1987), 12–13. For crime in the 14th cent., see J. Bellamy, *Crime and*

failing to maintain law and order, but up to a point
they could accept magnate and gentry rule in the localities
with comparative equanimity. With revenue coming increasingly from the customs and parliamentary taxation, there
was less need for the eyre to provide judicial revenues and
for curial sheriffs to force great magnates to pay their
debts.[67] Conversely there were good reasons for conciliating
those who voted taxation by giving way to the demand
for 'self-government at the king's command'. How far
individual members of the gentry enjoyed the fruits of
their victory depended on whether they ended up on the
right side of the battles for local control. The losers were
behind the numerous complaints of corruption of the
judicial process made at fourteenth- and fifteenth-century
parliaments, complaints which make it appear that the
worry was now over too little royal government whereas
in the twelfth and early thirteenth centuries it had been
over too much. As for the great magnates they had weath-
ered the storm raised by the new legal actions and the sometimes aggressive kingship of the twelfth and thirteenth
centuries. The threat posed by the petty assizes had been
removed in part by the early decision that those who performed labour services were unfree and could not make use
of them. Disputes over villein lands and services remained
thenceforth the exclusive concern of the courts of lords.
That still left, of course, all free men, many of them peasants
as poor or poorer than their unfree fellows, to make use of

Public Order in the Later Middle Ages (London, 1973). The end of the eyre in the
1290s has been seen as marking a decisive stage in handing justice in the localities
over to the gentry—see Harding, *Law Courts of Medieval England*, 86–92; *The Roll of
the Shropshire Eyre 1256*, xxv—but whether the contrast between the 13th and 14th
cents. was that marked is open to question. For a rather different emphasis on the
importance of the later eyres see Crook, 'The Later Eyres', 247–8. See also, however, Kaeuper, 'Law and Order in Fourteenth-century England', 782–4, and now E.
Powell, *Kingship, Law, and Society. Criminal Justice in the Reign of Henry V* (Oxford,
1989), 10–20. The question awaits analysis of Edwardian eyre rolls and an estimate
of how far the presentments at an eyre were a means by which the judges genuinely
checked and reviewed the administration of justice in a county since their last
visitation, as opposed to simply providing an opportunity to impose amercements.

    [67] There is some evidence that the financial proceeds of the eyre diminished in
the later 13th cent.—Crook, 'The Later Eyres', 247—but the whole question needs
further investigation.

the possessory assizes and later the *querela* procedures.[68] Here the great magnates found a different means of blunting the effect. They accepted the new procedures but corrupted them through their influence over the judges, the sheriffs, and the juries. England had not divided into semi-independent principalities on the German model. But the great magnates had achieved the same results by different means.

---

[68] For the free and unfree peasantry, see J. Hatcher, 'English Serfdom and Villeinage: Towards a Reassessment', *Past and Present*, 90 (1981), 3–39.

The Kings and their Armies

5

Money and Mercenaries in English Medieval Armies

Michael Prestwich

The assumption that during the medieval period there was a steady progression from an economy based on labour services to one dominated by the use of money and the payment of wages does not command much acceptance from present-day historians of the English medieval economy. Yet students of military organization have little doubt that such a development did take place with regard to the recruitment of armies. Where they differ from one another, is over the precise chronology of change.

For H. J. Hewitt, the period of the Hundred Years War was decisive, for then armies came to be recruited by means of a contract system, and 'obligatory service was superseded by voluntary service'.[1] J. E. Morris, writing rather earlier, considered that it was under Edward I that the nature of English armies had been transformed, and that in this process, 'the key was the use of pay'. He argued that in the later thirteenth century, 'the feudal system had to be supplemented by the use of pay'.[2] Professor J. C. Holt argued that the change was taking place still earlier, and that at the start of the thirteenth century King John 'was being compelled increasingly to ensure the performance of the military service of his liege men by the provision of cash rewards.'[3] The shift from feudal to paid service provides a disconcerting moving target. Matters become no clearer when the twelfth century is considered. J. Boussard pointed to the importance of mercenaries in Henry II's armies, seeing a military revolution take place in

---

[1] H. J. Hewitt, 'The Organisation of War', *The Hundred Years War*, ed. K. Fowler (London, 1971), 78.

[2] J. E. Morris, *The Welsh Wars of Edward I* (Oxford, 1901), 68, 108.

[3] *Pipe Roll 17 John and Praestitia Roll 14–18 John*, ed. R. A. Brown, J. C. Holt (Pipe Roll Soc., n.s. 37, 1961), 79.

his reign.[4] Yet J. O. Prestwich argued that paid troops, mercenaries, were quite as important in the late eleventh and early twelfth centuries as they were a century later.[5] Some scepticism is justified about a change which, according to these opinions, was clearly well under way in the early twelfth century, but was still not completed by the fourteenth. Did any such transition take place? Were there perhaps cyclical changes, with feudal service preferred in some periods, and paid troops at others, much as there were fluctuations in the relative importance of labour service and wage labour in the agrarian economy? Alternatively, it may have been the case that different systems of military obligation and recruitment co-existed side by side for a long period. This essay will seek to provide some answers with regard to the cavalry, one element, but arguably the most important, in English armies.

Although J. H. Round, at the end of the nineteenth century, considered that he had proved that the introduction of feudal military tenure took place in England under William the Conqueror, debate still continues.[6] The issues concerning the date of this introduction, and the degree of continuity with earlier, Anglo-Saxon, military institutions, have perhaps tended to overshadow examination of the actual importance of feudal service in its early stages in England. There is no full record of the performance of service prior to the thirteenth century. Only one writ of summons, the celebrated request for service from the Abbot of Evesham, survives from the Conqueror's reign.[7] It is only because William II complained about the quality and suitability of the knights provided by Archbishop Anselm for one of his expeditions to Wales that it is known that a feudal

[4] J. Boussard, 'Les Mercenaires au xiie siècle: Henri II Plantagenet et les origines de l'armée de métier', *Bibliothèque de l'école des chartes*, 106 (1945–6), 189–224.

[5] J. O. Prestwich, 'War and Finance in the Anglo-Norman State', *Transactions of the Royal Historical Society*, 5th ser., 4 (1955), 19–43.

[6] J. H. Round, 'The Introduction of Knight Service into England', *Feudal England* (London, 1895). For two recent contributions to the debate, see J. Gillingham, 'The Introduction of Knight Service into England', *Anglo-Norman Studies*, 5 (1982), 53–64; J. C. Holt, 'The Introduction of Knight Service into England', *Anglo-Norman Studies*, 6 (1983), 89–106.

[7] *Select Charters*, ed. W. Stubbs, 9th edn. (Oxford, 1913), 97.

summons had been issued.[8] Stenton considered that 'it is easy to underestimate the frequency with which the feudal army was summoned by the Norman kings', and he pointed to the fact that even at the end of the twelfth century chroniclers might well fail to record such a summons.[9] Arguments from silence are always difficult, but it is striking that the evidence for mercenary and paid troops from the late eleventh and early twelfth centuries is very much stronger than that for feudal service.[10]

The total feudal service due to the English Crown consisted, at least in theory, of roughly 5,000 knights.[11] Whether such a level was ever attained in practice must be open to doubt. Certainly, references to scutage from the very end of the eleventh century show that it was possible to make a payment in place of service from an early date. By Henry II's reign, a proportion of the full quota, in place of the full total, might be requested. A well-known passage from Robert de Torigni's chronicle records the king's request in 1157 for one third of the total service due. Two years later, according to the same chronicler, Henry II preferred to take scutage from the bulk of his tenants, rather than requiring *agrarios milites* to go on the Toulouse expedition. Round pointed out, however, that record evidence showed that the majority of lay tenants-in-chief did in fact provide service on this occasion.[12] The king certainly did not abandon feudal service. In

[8] F. Barlow, *William Rufus* (London, 1983), provides the most recent account of this incident.

[9] F. M. Stenton, *The First Century of English Feudalism 1066–1166* (Oxford, 1932), 177.

[10] J. O. Prestwich, 'War and Finance in the Anglo-Norman State', 19–43, provides much evidence for the use of paid troops and mercenaries in this period. C. W. Hollister, *The Military Organization of Norman England* (Oxford, 1965), 116–25, discusses the evidence for the use of feudal armies in this period, and concludes that they were 'overshadowed by mercenaries or contingents of native Englishmen'. S. D. B. Brown, 'Military Service and Monetary Reward in the Eleventh and Twelfth Centuries', *History*, 74 (1989), 20–38, analyses both paid service and contemporary attitudes towards mercenaries.

[11] Recent computerized calculations by T. K. Keefe, *Feudal Assessments and the Political Community under Henry II and his Sons* (Berkeley and Los Angeles, 1983), 64, 82–6, have provided confirmation for Round's estimate in his *Feudal England*, 292.

[12] *Chronicles of the Reigns of Stephen, Henry II, and Richard I*, ed. R. Howlett (Rolls Series, 82, 1884–9), iv. 193, 202; Round, *Feudal England*, 221.

1166 he ordered the most far-reaching inquiry into feudal obligation that was ever carried out in England. His motives for doing so may have been in large measure fiscal, but knight service was duly detailed in the return.[13] Feudal service was requested for the expedition to Ireland in 1171, and for that to Galloway in 1186. At the very end of the reign all the knights in England, even if feeble and poor, were summoned, or so it was reported, to serve in France.[14] If so, this makes a striking contrast with the policy of 1157.

The period of the late twelfth and early thirteenth centuries was one of monetary inflation. Military costs were rising sharply. It was increasingly difficult for magnates to supply the very large numbers of men traditionally due when the king summoned the feudal host. The relatively brief period of service, forty days, was no longer in tune with the realities of warfare. What Richard I required was three hundred knights for a year to fight in France, not a huge host which departed within six weeks of mustering.[15] By John's reign, if not earlier, the Crown had to be content with the tenants-in-chief appearing on campaign with a fitting contingent, which was much smaller than the traditional obligation. For the Irish expedition of 1210, for example, Geoffrey Fitz-Peter provided ten knights, not the ninety-eight and a third that he owed technically. In the Poitou campaign of 1214, the Earl of Devon served with twenty knights, not the eighty-nine of his formal obligation.

There was no standard proportion by which the old quotas of service were reduced. A scheme was suggested in the Unknown Charter, which probably dates from the negotiations preceding the issue of Magna Carta, whereby anyone whose obligation exceeded ten knights would have their service reduced appropriately, with baronial advice.[16] In practice the reductions appear to have been a matter for individual bargaining. A demand for service in 1229 yielded

---

[13] Keefe, *Feudal Assessments*, 13–14, argues that the inquiry was related to the king's need to collect an aid on the occasion of his daughter's marriage.

[14] Ibid. 46–7; *The Historical Works of Gervase of Canterbury*, ed. W. Stubbs (Rolls Series, 73, 1879–80), i. 447.

[15] *Chronica Rogeri de Houedene*, ed. W. Stubbs (Rolls Series, 51, 1868–71), iv. 40.

[16] S. K. Mitchell, *Studies in Taxation under John and Henry III* (Oxford, 1914), 97, 110; J. C. Holt, *Magna Carta* (2nd edn., Cambridge, 1992), 427. Part of the

a force of some 500 or perhaps 600 cavalry in all, and by the time of the Welsh campaign of 1245, most of the new re-duced quotas appear to have been established.[17] By Edward I's reign, better records survive detailing the performance of feudal service. For the first Welsh war in 1277, 228 knights and 294 sergeants were provided by the feudal tenants-in-chief for forty days of unpaid service (two sergeants were counted as the equivalent of one knight). From then until 1327 feudal service was summoned with some regularity, though it was not a feature of every campaign. The numbers of those who served varied: more tenants-in-chief might pay fines instead of serving on one occasion than on another. The proportion of knights to sergeants shifted steadily, until there were very few knights performing service. Quite sub-stantial numbers of men were recruited by means of feudal summonses: in 1310 about 440 cavalrymen were performing feudal service, and in 1322 there were roughly 500 such men with Edward II on his futile expedition to Scotland. The total size of the cavalry forces is not easy to estimate, but it seems likely that those doing feudal service might amount to very roughly a quarter of the entire force.[18]

Feudal service was, in theory, not rewarded with pay. Curi-ously, Stubbs chose for his *Select Charters* a return to the inquest of 1166 which did specify service *ad custom vestrum*, but this was highly abnormal.[19] Under King John prests, or advances of cash, were given to those performing feudal service in his armies. In time, these would have had to be repaid, but Holt has argued that the demands of war in this period were such that changes were needed in the military system, and that money payments were required to ensure

evidence for the new reduced quotas is provided by what Holt tems a 'roll of summonses' for the Poitou expedition of 1214, printed in *Pipe Roll 17 John and Praestitia Roll 14–18 John*, 101–3. This resembles later records of feudal musters much more closely than any list of summonses, and may be an early example of a marshal's roll.

[17] The development of the new quotas is fully discussed by I. J. Sanders, *Feudal Military Service in England* (Oxford, 1956), 59–90. The 1229 muster roll is discussed and printed ibid. 115–29.

[18] M. C. Prestwich, *Edward I* (London, 1988), 179; M. C. Prestwich, 'Cavalry Service in Early Fourteenth Century England', *War and Government in the Middle Ages*, ed. J. Gillingham and J. C. Holt (Woodbridge, 1984), 148.

[19] Stubbs, *Select Charters*, 174.

service. He implied that the use of prests may have been an acceptable means of rewarding men who considered that their status would have been adversely affected if they accepted wages in the full sense. A modern analogy might be the payment of lavish 'expenses' to sportsmen anxious to preserve their amateur standing. In the case of the army which mustered at Dover in 1213, the summons did not take the normal feudal form, and therefore some type of pay might have been expected, though Geoffrey de Neville was no doubt surprised to receive a prest of fifteen marks 'on the hairs of his head'. In other cases, however, such as the Irish expedition of 1210, prests were certainly paid to an army which had mustered in response to a normal feudal summons.[20] This practice, however, did not prove to be a stage in a transformation of feudal service from an unpaid to a paid character. It was not followed up under Henry III, or Edward I, under whom feudal service consisted of the traditional forty days without pay. It was only through a clerical error that in 1300 one knight, Hugh of St Philibert, succeeded in being enrolled as performing feudal service at the same time as he was receiving royal pay.[21] Under Edward I, prests were made as advances against wages, whereas under John, they were probably meant in many cases as advances against the scutage that magnates and knights could expect to collect from their tenants.

There were both advantages and problems in making use of feudal service. It was convenient to have a system whereby tenants-in-chief were obliged to provide service, with no question of their having any right of refusal, or of there being any need to obtain their consent. The collection of scutage, or of fines, from those who did not wish to serve in person might be financially lucrative, as was particularly the case under John. The tenants-in-chief also benefited in financial terms, for they could collect scutage from their sub-tenants. This helps to explain why it was that the magnates on occasion displayed a preference for feudal summonses under Edward I.

There were, however, in the view of many magnates, cus-

[20] *Pipe Roll 17 John and Praestitia Roll 14–18 John,* 77–80, 98.
[21] M. C. Prestwich, *War, Politics and Finance under Edward I* (London, 1972), 82.

tomary limitations on where service might be done. The king's right to summon men to fight overseas was a controversial one. The Unknown Charter of John's reign included a clause stating that, outside England, service might be performed only in Normandy or Brittany. At the end of the thirteenth century, Edward I found it impossible to send feudal troops to Gascony. Further, when a feudal muster did take place, the fact that service was for a period of forty days only could well prove inconvenient. The quality of the troops provided by the tenants-in-chief might be low. Although too much emphasis should not be placed on those comic figures from Edward I's musters who insisted on performing curious sergeant services, such as appearing with a side of bacon, and then departing once it was eaten up, or coming with a bow and only one arrow, it was the case that the Crown had little control over feudal recruitment.[22] Further, in an army recruited by means of a feudal summons, the hereditary marshal and constable claimed various rights, both to command, and to the profits of war. It is not clear how important these claims were in the twelfth century, but there is no doubt that for Edward I the claims of the marshal and constable were inconvenient and unhelpful, extending as they did to the right to attend councils of war, to maintain order in the host, to arrange billeting and sentry duty, and to receive various perquisites and profits.[23] The case for or against using feudal summonses was not always the same: circumstances varied in different periods. It was not until the reign of Edward III that the system was finally abandoned, and armies were entirely paid by the Crown.

One way round the difficulties created by feudal service was to introduce some alternative system of obligation. It was possible for rulers to appeal to the general principle that all free men should be prepared to bear arms in defence of their country, a principle similar to the French *arrière-ban*. Henry II's Assize of Arms of 1181 set out the military equipment that men of different ranks were expected to possess. Although the knight was defined as a man who held a knight's fee, rather than in terms of wealth, the non-feudal

---

[22] Ibid. 75–6, 81–2; Holt, *Magna Carta*, 303.
[23] Prestwich, *War, Politics and Finance*, 263 n.

character of this enactment was clear from the requirement
that all free men should swear to bear their arms in the king's
service at his command.[24] Henry's intention may have been
at least as much to do with keeping the peace in the realm as
with making war, but in 1205 and 1213 John was able to
appeal to this principle of a general obligation to fight when
French invasion threatened.[25] It did not prove possible, however, to extend this concept into an effective means of raising
armies which could replace the normal feudal obligation.
This was demonstrated very clearly in 1297, when Edward I's
use of a form of summons which did not make due reference
to fealty and homage in normal feudal manner provoked
widespread opposition, as did his attempt to persuade all
those who held land worth at least £20 a year to fight for him
on the Continent.[26]

The obvious alternative to the use of unpaid feudal service
was to pay troops. To do so might be costly, but many
problems would be avoided. It is important to distinguish
between types of paid service, even though the lines marking
off one kind from another are often blurred. All too often
historians write of 'mercenaries', when they mean no more
than 'paid soldiers'.[27] There was a difference between the
king paying his own subjects, or his own household knights,
and recruiting allies from overseas by means of formal treaties. Then there were also the true mercenaries, men who
would serve any master as long as he gave them their due
reward. Wages might be worked out on a daily basis, or men
might enter into contracts to serve for extended periods for
agreed sums.

The king's own household contained knights who were
accustomed to serving for pay, and recent work has demonstrated the central importance of these men throughout the
period under discussion. In the Norman period, as much
later under Edward I, household knights were retained by

---

[24] Stubbs, *Select Charters*, 183.
[25] M. R. Powicke, *Military Obligation in Medieval England* (Oxford, 1962), 58–60.
[26] Prestwich, *War, Politics and Finance*, 84–6.
[27] See e.g. Hollister, *Military Organisation of Norman England*, 167, where the definition of mercenary is deliberately broadened to include all who fought for pay. See also M. Chibnall, 'Mercenaries and the *Familia Regis* under Henry I', *History*, 62 (1977), 15–23.

means of annual fees, and were paid wages when active in the king's service. The size of this *familia regis* cannot be calculated with precision for the Norman period, though it was clearly substantial. It provided one out of the three divisions of the army at the battle of Brémule in 1119, and one detachment alone of the household was said to have numbered two hundred knights. Wages were paid under Henry I, according to the later evidence of Walter Map, at a rate of 1 s. a day with annual fees of at least £5 a year.[28] There is little to distinguish this system from the so-called bastard feudalism of later medieval England. The absence of surviving household accounts from Henry II's reign makes it impossible to calculate the number of his household knights, but during the 1173–4 rebellion seventeen such men were paid £9 16 s. 8 d. in compensation for their losses. The household accounts of John's reign reveal the payment of fees to household knights, along with *dona*, or gifts. The *Misae* roll of 1209–10 enables at least thirty-six household knights on the Scottish campaign to be identified, while it is probable that John had some forty-five with him in Ireland in the following year. A muster roll for 1215 lists forty-seven household knights.[29] The numbers of these men varied in the course of the thirteenth century according to the needs of the day, and the financial situation. Under Henry III there were rarely less than thirty, and never more than seventy, while under Edward I there were at one time just over a hundred.[30] These men were the permanent core of the paid element in an army. The evidence from Edward I's reign shows that they would all bring their own retinues with them on campaign, and that the paid forces of the household were capable of being expanded very considerably in wartime. The army that the king took to Flanders in 1297, for example, numbered at the outset some 475 cavalry provided by the household itself,

[28] J. O. Prestwich, 'The Military Household of the Norman Kings', *English Historical Review*, 96 (1981) , 8–12.

[29] S. D. Church, 'The Knights of the Household of King John: A Question of Numbers', *Thirteenth Century England V*, ed. P. R. Coss and S. D. Lloyd (Woodbridge, 1992), 152–4; *Rotuli de Liberate ac de Misis et Praestitis*, ed. T. D. Hardy (London, 1844), 125–6.

[30] C. Given-Wilson, *The Royal Household and the King's Affinity* (London, 1986), 21, 204–5.

while additional *forinsec*, or non-household, troops totalled only 195. All were paid through the household department of the wardrobe.[31] At the battle of Falkirk in 1298, the paid forces of the royal household formed one of the four cavalry divisions of the army. The household provided some 800 horse, while the *forinsec* paid element numbered 564.[32] It is not possible to produce figures with equal precision for earlier periods, but the indications are that there was nothing exceptional in this aspect of Edward I's armies, and that the paid element provided by the royal household had been of similar importance since the time of the Conquest.

More attention has been paid by historians to the employment of paid mercenaries from overseas than to the payment of wages to the king's own subjects. J. O. Prestwich pointed to the very considerable evidence for the use of mercenaries in the eleventh and early twelfth centuries. The Conqueror used mercenary knights in the late 1060s, and brought many from France to meet an invasion threat in 1085. The treaty with the Count of Flanders of 1101 assured Henry I of the service of 1,000 knights in return for an annual cash payment. Breton mercenaries played an important part in Henry I's military campaigns.[33] A situation of civil war was obviously attractive to mercenaries, and it is clear that professional soldiers from the Low Countries and elsewhere found England under King Stephen much to their liking. The most notable among them was William of Ypres, illegitimate son of the Count of Flanders. Many were also lured to England by the hope of rich rewards during the rebellion of 1173–4. Boussard pointed to the importance of mercenaries under Henry II, most of them so-called *routiers* recruited from the Low Countries, although Welshmen were also hired.[34]

Richard I and John used mercenaries extensively. Mercadier, Richard I's famous mercenary captain, described his service to the king in these words: 'I fought for him with

[31] N. B. Lewis, 'The English Forces in Flanders, August–November 1297', *Studies in Medieval History presented to F. M. Powicke*, ed. R. W. Hunt, W. A. Pantin, and R. W. Southern (Oxford, 1948), 314.

[32] Prestwich, *War, Politics and Finance*, 52, 68.

[33] J. O. Prestwich, 'War and Finance in the Anglo-Norman State', 19–33.

[34] Boussard, 'Les Mercenaires au xiie siècle', 189–224.

loyalty and strenuously, never opposed to his will, prompt in obedience to his commands; and in consequence of this service I gained his esteem and was placed in command of his army.' Letters on behalf of the mercenary Louvrecaire under John reveal the importance to such men of the profits to be made from booty. Special instructions were given to safeguard his loot as it was carried through Normandy. John also held a Spaniard, Martin Algais, in high regard. His booty was protected, his merchants were quit of customs duties, and he was given the high office of seneschal of Gascony and Périgord. John wrote of him 'We esteem the service of Martin Algais more highly than any other person'.[35]

The precise terms and conditions of service of John's mercenaries no doubt varied. Many knights from the Low Countries were paid retaining fees and offered other rewards. In 1202 promises of money and land were made. A writ to the Provost of Bruges in 1203 summoned all those in receipt of fees to come to the king at Easter.[36] The loss of Normandy did not see John abandon his mercenary troops. Small companies of crossbowmen were stationed in particularly strategic castles, and some of them were highly rewarded.[37] John used mercenaries in his Irish campaigns. In 1210 the records show that he had some sixty-five knights from the Low Countries with him in Ireland.[38] His reliance on mercenaries in the political crises of the last years of the reign was great, hardly surprising given the unreliability of his own subjects. The household *Misae* roll of 1212–13 contains the names of about 115 knights from Flanders and elsewhere in the Low Countries who were in receipt of annual fees; the highest ranked was the Duke of Limburg. Walter le Buk, who had served in Ireland in 1210, brought four knights and thirty-five sergeants from Flanders to join the king's service; he would serve again in 1216. A house-

---

[35] *Rotuli Litterarum Patentium in Turri Londonensi asservati*, ed. T. D. Hardy, 15, 17, 20–1, 24. These men are also discussed by F. M. Powicke, *The Loss of Normandy* (2nd edn., Manchester, 1960), 337–43.

[36] *Rotuli Litterarum Patentium*, 12, 26.

[37] *Pipe Roll 8 John*, p. xix.

[38] *Rotuli de Liberate ac de Misis ac Praestitis*, 177–228. In some cases this record identifies men as Flemings, but in others it does not do so. Nor is it clear that all mentioned were knights, though this seems probable.

hold record from 1212–13 names about 115 Flemish knights in receipt of money fees. Foreign soldiers began to pour into England from Poitou as well as from the Low Countries in 1214. A muster list dating from 1215 names no less than 375 knights, most of whom appear to have come from the Low Countries.[39] Precise definition of a mercenary becomes difficult in John's reign. It could be argued that some of the captains he employed who originated from the Angevin and Norman lands on the Continent were not true mercenaries as they were in a sense his own subjects, but it is hard not to classify men such as Philip Mark, Savary de Mauléon, Falkes de Bréauté, Robert de Gaugi, and Engelard de Cigogné as soldiers of fortune.

The skill of mercenaries provided one strong motive for employing them, though it is not easy from the sources to identify their special contribution. Their use of the crossbow may have been one significant element, but hardened expertise acquired over many campaigns was presumably what gave them their real advantage over less practised soldiers. The *Gesta Stephani*, whose author was no admirer of such men, reported Robert Fitz-Hubert's ingenious capture of Devizes castle by the use of leather scaling-ladders, a 'remarkable feat'. The defeat of Ralph of Fougères and the Earl of Chester, and the subsequent fall of Dol in 1173, were largely explained by Robert de Torigni in terms of Henry II's use of Brabançon mercenaries. Men such as Hugh de Boves, news of whose death in 1215 caused King John to have one of his notorious fits of temper, were celebrated for their military ability, if hated for their pride and iniquity.[40]

It is not easy to calculate the numbers of mercenaries who were recruited by the English Crown. Chroniclers provide impressive figures. Jordan Fantosme suggested that at the time of the rebellion of 1173–4, Henry II had 10,000 Brabançons in his host, but such large numbers cannot be

[39] Church, 'The Knights of the Household of King John', 160; S. D. Church, 'The Earliest English Muster Roll, 18/19 December 1215', *Historical Research*, 67 (1994), 6–17; *Documents Illustrative of English History in the Thirteenth and Fourteenth Centuries*, ed. H. Cole (1844), 238, 242, 266.

[40] *Gesta Stephani*, ed. K. R. Potter, rev. R. H. C. Davis (Oxford, 1976), 105; *Chronicles of the Reigns of Stephen, Henry II and Richard I*, iv. 260; *Chronica Rogeri de Wendover*, ed. H. G. Howlett (Rolls Series, 84, 1886–9), ii. 147–8.

credited. Boussard argued for a maximum number of perhaps 6,000 in Henry II's day, but much of his case rests on a
statement in the pipe roll that William de Mandeville, with
the royal military household (*Familia Regis*), crossed the
Channel in thirty-seven ships. It is unlikely that all this force
consisted of foreign mercenaries, and still more unlikely that
each ship carried between 100 and 150 men, as Boussard
supposed. A much more plausible guess is that each vessel
carried up to forty passengers, and that the maximum
number of mercenaries on this occasion was about 1,000.[41]
Pipe roll entries such as that recording the supply of cloth to
166 sergeants from overseas provide further clues to the
probable number of mercenaries engaged by the king for
the suppression of the great rebellion of 1173–4.[42] The
record of the payment of prests shows that when John went
to Ireland in 1210, he probably had less than fifty knights
and sergeants from the Low Countries with him.[43]

In some circumstances, particularly those of civil war,
mercenaries might prove more loyal than English troops, but
in general they were regarded as unreliable and untrustworthy. Gerald of Wales clearly regarded the semi-mythical
figures of Hengist and Horsa as archetypal mercenaries, with
their treachery towards their master, Vortigern.[44] The author
of the *Gesta Stephani* considered mercenaries as 'utterly
steeped in craft and treachery'. In the case of Devizes, already mentioned, he described the way in which the mercenary Robert Fitz-Hubert, having taken the castle, then

---

[41] *Chronicles of the Reigns of Stephen, Henry II, and Richard I*, iii. 208; Boussard, 'Les
Mercenaires au xiiᵉ siècle', 218–20. The evidence, not cited by Boussard, is provided
by *Pipe Roll 20 Henry II* (Pipe Roll Soc., 21, 1896), 135. The argument about the
number of men a ship could carry is based on Mediterranean evidence, and the
suggestion that northern ships were much smaller is wrongly dismissed. In 1297,
almost 340 ships were needed to transport an army of some 9,000 men, with
equipment and horses, across the Channel (Prestwich, *War, Politics and Finance*,
142). This suggests that even 40 men per ship is an overestimate.

[42] *Pipe Roll 20 Henry II*, 8.

[43] *Rotuli de Liberate ac de Misis et Praestitis*, 210–11, for prests issued at Drogheda.
Working from lists of those in receipt of prests earlier in the campaign, S. Painter,
The Reign of King John (Baltimore, 1949), 265, calculated a lower figure of thirty
three.

[44] *Giraldi Cambrensis Opera*, viii: *De Principibus Instructione Liber*, ed. G. F. Warner
(Rolls Series, 21, 1891), 97. The Saxons, not actually named by Gerald, are described as *stipendiarios milites*.

refused to hand it over to the Earl of Gloucester as he had promised to do. The same chronicler provides another example of an untrustworthy mercenary in Robert Fitz-Hildebrand, who seduced the wife of the man he had been sent to assist. If not properly rewarded, they were likely to prove unsatisfactory: those brought to England by the future Henry II in 1147 were not paid wages, and so 'accomplished nothing of note, but were always sluggish and remiss in all their doings'.[45] Mercenaries were men used to living off the land, and might well prove hard to discipline. An entry in the 1174 Pipe Roll dealing with the provisioning of Dover castle provides one small illustration of what must have been a widespread problem, when it records the loss of wheat and cheese to a value of 41 s., *per rapina Flandrensium*.[46] Although mercenaries generally fought well in order to preserve their reputation, in the last resort they were anxious to save their own skins. At the siege of Rochester, under John, it was the mercenary Savary de Mauléon who argued that the defeated garrison should not be hanged, in case he might suffer the same fate should the fortunes of war be reversed.[47]

The use of mercenaries attracted widespread hostile criticism. The Brabançons and others were condemned for their wicked ways in the Third Lateran Council of 1179. Walter Map accused them of many horrors, including heresy.[48] The main military textbook used in the Middle Ages, the late Roman work of Vegetius, advised against the employment of such men, with the argument that it was far better for a ruler to train his own subjects, 'than to take and reteyn under him grete foison of strange souldeours that he knoweth not'.[49] The grants of lands and offices to mercenary captains made by King John added to the hostility directed against them, and the expulsion of all such men was promised in Magna Carta.

[45] *Gesta Stephani*, 104–6, 150–2, 188, 205.
[46] *Pipe Roll 20 Henry II*, 2.   [47] *Wendover*, ii. 150.
[48] P. Contamine, *War in the Middle Ages*, tr. M. Jones (Oxford, 1984), 243–4; William of Newburgh, in *Chronicles of the Reigns of Stephen, Henry II and Richard I*, i. 209–10; *De Nugis Curialium*, ed. M. R. James (London, 1914), 56–7.
[49] The quotation is from Caxton's translation of Christine de Pisan's reworking of Vegetius, *The Book of Fayttes of Armes and of Chyvalrye*, ed. A. T. P. Byles (Early English Text Soc., O.S. 189, 1932), 26.

Mercenaries were used very little by the English in the rest of the thirteenth century, even in the civil wars of the 1260s. Prince Edward did, it is true, return to England in 1263 from France with a force of foreign knights. They were used on a campaign in Wales. The Marcher lords are said to have taken umbrage as a result, and refused their assistance. Later in the year Edward garrisoned Windsor Castle with these mercenaries, and it is possible that it was because of the need to pay their wages that he resorted to the desperate financial expedient of robbing the Temple in London. It was only when the mercenaries had been dismissed that Edward was able to win the support of an important group of magnates, among whom the Marchers were dominant.[50] After Edward came to the throne, true mercenaries hardly featured in his many campaigns. The valiant troop of Gascons who fought in Wales in 1282–3 were the king's own subjects, and were hardly professional soldiers like the *routiers* of the twelfth century. There were a few foreign knights who entered the king's service, but men such as Pascual of Valencia, known as the *Adalid*, were scarcely equivalent to King John's mercenary captains.[51] In the fourteenth century, with the Hundred Years War, the situation changed again. Some men in Edward III's service, recruited overseas, such as Walter Mauny and Eustace d'Aubricecourt, might well be considered as true mercenaries. At the same time, men such as Robert Knollys, Hugh Calveley, and the notable John Hawkwood provide examples of Englishmen themselves becoming professional mercenary soldiers.[52]

One problem which has not often been considered in discussion of soldiers' pay is that of whether it was sufficient. In the twelfth century, rates appear to have been relatively sensitive to economic change, and may have therefore re-

---

[50] For a fuller discussion, see Prestwich, *Edward I*, 39–41.

[51] Prestwich, *War, Politics and Finance*, 46. In the 1280s there were two Germans who served among Edward's household knights, their names being given as Eustace de Jardin and Rainald Macere: *Records of the Wardrobe and Household 1285–1286*, ed. B. F. and C. R. Byerley (London, 1977), 165.

[52] For a recent discussion, see C. T. Allmand, *The Hundred Years War* (Cambridge, 1988), 73–6. It is interesting to note that when d'Aubricecourt took service with the King of Navarre in 1366, he promised to serve against anyone except Edward III or the Black Prince: J. A. F. de Larrea Rojas, *Guerra y Sociedad en Navarra durante la Edad Media* (Bilbao, 1992), 144.

flected the real cost of serving in the army. They rose from at least 8*d.* a day for a knight under Henry I, to 1*s.* a day under Henry II, and up to 2*s.* a day under King John. Thereafter, however, they changed very little. Some high rates are recorded for the period of the Barons' Wars in the 1260s, but under Edward I a knight was paid 2*s.* a day, a sergeant 1*s.* and a common foot soldier 2*d.* For a short period at the start of the Hundred Years War, Edward III paid double wages, in recognition perhaps of the inadequacy of the normal rates. This soon proved too costly, and he reverted to the levels of his grandfather's day for the knights and sergeants, with mounted archers receiving 6*d.* a day each, and ordinary infantrymen 3*d.*[53] The increasing use of contracts, which were administratively simpler than the process of working out wage costs on a daily or weekly basis, did not have any substantial effect on the pay scale of soldiers. It is striking that a knight in the fourteenth century received half as much in wages for fighting as he could expect to receive as expenses if he was elected to parliament as an MP. One indication of the real cost of fighting is provided by the fact that it cost a bishop £100 in 1322 to hire ten sergeants (the equivalent of five knights) to perform feudal service. This works out at 10*s.* a day for a knight.[54] It must be remembered that a knight would not only have to feed himself and supply his armour and equipment, but would also have to provide for his horses and servants. The Earl of Arundel in 1297 clearly considered that the offer of wages for fighting in Flanders was quite inadequate to meet his costs: he reckoned that he would have to lease out a minimum of £500 worth of land to maintain himself in the king's war.[55] From at least as early as Edward I's reign, knightly pay was clearly inadequate. Later, rates of pay became worth still less in real terms: they

[53] For Edward I's reign, Prestwich, *War, Politics and Finance*, 41; for Edward III, *The Wardrobe Account Book of William Norwell. 12 July 1338 to 27 May 1340*, ed. B. Lyon, M. Lyon, and H. S. Lucas (Brussels, 1983), xcvi–xcvii, 325.

[54] Prestwich, 'Cavalry Service in Early Fourteenth Century England', 149; H. M. Cam, *Liberties and Communities in Medieval England* (London, 1963), 327. Contamine, *War in the Middle Ages*, 94–5, provides evidence of the inadequacy of knightly wages in Gascony in 1253.

[55] *Documents Illustrating the Crisis of 1297–98 in England*, ed. M. C. Prestwich (Camden Soc., 4th ser., 24, 1980), 142.

were largely unchanged even after the Black Death, when other wage rates rose sharply. The fact that under Edward III English armies were almost entirely composed of paid troops, often serving under contract, scarcely begins to explain why men were prepared to fight, much less why they were so successful.

It was not the offer of wages alone which persuaded men to fight. Evidence from Edward I's reign shows that there were many men who did not need this inducement at all. It is also clear that many of those who fought without pay did not do so because of any formal feudal obligation. For the period of Edward I's Scottish wars it is possible to show by means of a comparison of pay records, feudal muster rolls, and heraldic lists of those actually present on campaign, that the majority of the magnates neither accepted royal pay, nor performed feudal service. Instead, they served voluntarily. For the 1300 campaign, the evidence of the pay account shows that the royal household provided about 850 cavalry who received royal wages. Twenty-four of these held the high rank of banneret. A heraldic poem, the *Song of Caerlaverock*, lists in contrast eighty-seven bannerets on the campaign (the author added that there were more, whose names he could not recall), of whom only three are listed on the constable's record of feudal service as serving under a formal obligation for forty days. The only possible conclusion is that the majority, probably about three-quarters, of the bannerets did not accept pay for themselves or their retinues. Only sixty of the bannerets named in the *Song* had actually received summons for the campaign at all. Analysis of the evidence for the Falkirk campaign of 1298, and for the 1304 campaign, provides similar conclusions.[56] Examination of the summonses issued by Edward I for his campaigns shows that when feudal service was called for, the writs asked men to muster in accordance with the fealty and homage they owed. If the feudal quotas were not required, unpaid service was politely requested by appealing purely

[56] The accuracy of the *Song of Caerlaverock* is demonstrated by the fact that it gives the names of twenty-three of the twenty-four bannerets listed in the pay record (*Liber Quotidianus Contrarotulatoris Garderobiae*, London, 1787), as being on the campaign.

to the fealty that was due to the Crown, with no reference to homage.

Similar evidence for what may best be called voluntary service is lacking for earlier periods. B. E. Harris suggested that many important men 'carried out essential administrative and military duties on their own initiative, and presumably at their own expense' in the difficult days of the minority of Henry III, but they were able to set many of their expenses against their receipts from sheriffdoms.[57] William Marshal's accounts for this period show that he did not meet the costs of knights, sergeants, and footsoldiers out of his own pocket. These were paid from the resources of the Crown. There is no indication, however, that he took wages for himself.[58] A much earlier account of the Marshal's, for 1193, shows that he accepted royal pay on behalf of a considerable number of troops under his command, though again, there is no evidence that he was himself paid a daily wage.[59] On the other hand, the fact that the Earl of Salisbury received an annual fee from King John suggests that he probably had no compunction about accepting royal wages.[60] It is unlikely that much voluntary service would have been performed during the period when the feudal quotas were substantial, save that on occasion men may have remained on campaign at their own expense after the end of the formal forty day period of service. The situation must have been transformed, however, by the radical reduction of the quotas for service which took place in the early thirteenth century. It is hard to imagine that great men would have been prepared to campaign with the very small numbers specified by the new quotas if they attended in person. The Earl of Winchester, though obliged to attend with only three and a half knights, produced a contingent of ten for the Welsh campaign of 1245. He usually had half a dozen household knights in regular attendance, although in all, almost thirty knights can be counted as being connected to his *familia*. On

---

[57] *Pipe Roll 4 Henry III*, ed. B. E. Harris (Pipe Roll soc., n.s. 47, 1987), xii–xiii.
[58] *Roll of Divers Accounts for the Early Years of Henry III*, ed. F. A. Cazel, Jr. (Pipe Roll Soc., n.s. 44, 1982), 34.
[59] *Pipe Roll 5 Richard I*, 148.
[60] *Rotuli de Liberate ac de Misis et Praestitis*, 223.

the same campaign, Peter of Savoy acknowledged that he owed the service of five knights, but provided an additional seven *de gratia*. The evidence from Edward I's reign suggests that great magnates might well take retinues at least fifty strong with them on campaign.[61]

Changes in methods of military recruitment, particularly those affecting magnates and knights, were bound to have political implications. Demands for service could impose a considerable burden on individuals and on communities, and it is not surprising that the matter might arouse strong feelings. The summons to serve in Poitou in 1214, with the subsequent request for scutage, did much to spark off the rebellion of the northern barons, which led to the civil war at the end of John's reign. In 1297, Edward I's demands for service overseas were one of the elements which provoked the major constitutional crisis of that year. Yet Magna Carta of 1215, and the *Confirmatio Cartarum* of 1297, contain very little on the subject of military service. This was not, however, a reflection of the importance of the issue. The Unknown Charter dealt very explicitly with the need to reduce the level of service demanded under the old quotas, and the opposition complaints in the Remonstrances of 1297 laid due emphasis on the question of military service.[62] The Crown was always extremely reluctant to make formal concessions on this issue. In practice, in the years after 1215, and again after 1297, the government went some way towards meeting the demands made of it. The quotas of service which applied after Magna Carta were very low, as the magnates wished, and the novel summonses of 1297 were not used again, but formal concessions were avoided in a matter which affected the security of the realm. Edward I reverted to thoroughly traditional methods of military recruitment in the years after 1297.[63]

The formal obligations derived from fealty and homage, and the financial rewards provided by pay, are not sufficient

[61] Prestwich, *War, Politics and Finance*, 62–4; G. G. Simpson, 'The *Familia* of Roger de Quincy, Earl of Winchester and Constable of Scotland', *Essays on the Nobility of Medieval Scotland*, ed. K. J. Stringer (Edinburgh, 1985), 102–23; Sanders, *Feudal Military Service in England*, 134.

[62] Holt, *Magna Carta*, 427; *Documents Illustrating the Crisis of 1297–98*, 116.

[63] Prestwich, *War, Politics and Finance*, 86–90.

to explain why men went to war. There were a great many
other reasons. Different forms of pressure could be put on
men to compel them to fight. In 1213 John made a number
of arrangements whereby he agreed to pardon debts in exchange for military service. These were sufficient to enable
him to mobilize a force of over 150 knights, with twenty
sergeants, for a year. Edward I compelled a group of magnates headed by the Earl of Arundel to go to Gascony in
1295, under the threat of collecting very substantial debts
due to the Crown, some of which dated back even as far as
John's reign.[64] There were also benefits that the Crown could
offer. Those who went on campaign were placed under special royal protection, so that no one could, for example,
bring legal action against them. Those who participated in a
successful campaign might well expect rewards in the form
of grants of land in the conquered territory. Booty might be
won in war, and there was the hope of obtaining ransoms
from the vanquished. In addition, there were the intangible
but none the less vital motives that sprang from the cultural
identity of medieval nobles and knights. The chivalric virtues
of prowess and honour might be displayed in the world of
the tournament, but were best demonstrated by fighting in
a just cause. The noblest cause of all was, of course, the
crusade, and it is interesting to see how, by the thirteenth
century, secular conflicts attracted elements taken from the
crusade. The rebels of 1215 termed themselves 'the army of
God and Holy Church', and in Edward I's Welsh wars, arm-
bands distributed to the infantry bore not the king's arms,
but the religious emblem of the cross of St George.[65] There
must have been powerful social pressures on men to fight.
There might also be baser motives for fighting, as well as
those of honour and chivalry. A rebuke addressed by Edward
I to John Fitz-Marmaduke is highly suggestive: 'You are a
cruel man, and I have several times had to rebuke you for the
delight you take in the death of your enemies.'[66] Such men
needed little persuasion to fight.

[64] Holt, *Magna Carta*, 192–3; Prestwich, *War, Politics and Finance*, 76.
[65] Holt, *Magna Carta*, 226; Prestwich, *Edward I*, 199–200.
[66] *The Chronicle of Walter of Guisborough*, ed. H. Rothwell (Camden Soc., 3rd ser.,
89, 1957), 325.

The methods of cavalry recruitment used in medieval England were certainly not static, but they do not fit easily into a simple pattern of development. Different methods existed side by side at the same time, and there was no steady linear progression from a feudal to a paid system. The greatest element of continuity was provided by the royal household knights, who provided the core of English armies throughout the period under discussion. There was even a substantial element of family continuity within the household, with, for example, the names of Cantilupe, Clifford and Tibetot being found among the household knights of both John and Edward I.[67] Mercenary troops, in the strict sense of the word, were not used to the same extent throughout the period, and there are some grounds for doubting whether they were recruited in the very large numbers sometimes claimed. The heyday of the *routiers*, the professional soldiers mostly recruited in the Low Countries, was in the twelfth and early thirteenth centuries: for a variety of reasons England was not a successful hunting-ground for them under Henry III or his successor Edward I. In a broader sense, pay was undoubtedly important throughout this period, although it was not until the 1330s that English armies were normally wholly paid by the Crown. Feudal service continued to be demanded by English kings for the whole period from the reign of the Conqueror until that of Edward II, but the nature of that service changed very considerably, with a radical reduction of the quotas of knights taking place in the early thirteenth century. The system was, however, far from obsolete even as late as Edward I's reign, and it is interesting to note that Edward tried to introduce a form of feudal service into Scotland, as part of his attempted settlement there.[68] Voluntary unpaid service, which can be well documented for the later part of Edward I's reign, is elusive for

[67] *Rotuli de Liberate ac de Misis et Praestitis*, 125; Prestwich, *War, Politics and Finance*, 43–5, 49.
[68] M. C. Prestwich, 'Colonial Scotland', *Scotland and England, 1286–1815*, ed. R. A. Mason (Edinburgh, 1987), 9. In English-held Normandy in the 15th cent. the exploitation of feudal obligation was 'one of the lynch-pins of military arrangements': A. Curry, 'English Armies in the Fifteenth Century', *Arms, Armies and Fortifications in the Hundred Years War*, ed. A. Curry and M. Hughes (Woodbridge, 1994), 64.

earlier periods, but may well have developed in response to the reduction in the levels of feudal service.

There are many ways in which the various elements of military service can be categorized, but attention should be drawn to one early fourteenth-century attempt. Walter de Milemete, an obscure clerk in royal service, commissioned a fine illuminated manuscript at the end of Edward II's reign to present to the heir to the throne. The book is celebrated as it contains what is probably the earliest representation of a cannon. The text of Milemete's treatise, dull and derivative for the most part, has attracted little attention. Yet the analysis of military service is interesting. Walter defined three types of service, voluntary, paid, and compulsory. Of these, the most commendable was the first, performed as it was through natural inclination. Paid troops, who might either be the subjects of the king, or vassals of some foreign ruler, formed the second category, and the third, and to Walter the least important, was compulsory service, owed as a duty to the monarch. In all cases, he argued, a prudent ruler should reward and thank those who fought for him, making a due distribution of lands to all who assisted in the conquest of a foreign country.[69] Such a tripartite division no doubt owed something to the conventions of the schools, and oversimplified a complex reality, yet it makes more sense than the conventional bipartite division into feudal and paid service.

---

[69] *The Treatise of Walter of Milemete*, ed. M. R. James (Roxburghe Club, 1913), xvii, fol. 27b–30.

6

Obligatory Military Service and the Use of Mercenaries in Imperial Military Campaigns under the Hohenstaufen Emperors

KARL-FRIEDRICH KRIEGER

Before he set out on his Italian campaign in October 1166, Emperor Frederick Barbarossa recruited a force of 1,500 Brabançon mercenaries. These men made up a substantial proportion of the army which Archbishop Christian of Mainz was to lead against Rome, and which, together with the troops of the Archbishop of Cologne, Rainald of Dassel, achieved a resounding victory over the Romans at Tusculum.[1]

That Frederick Barbarossa resorted to the use of mercenaries on this expedition is in itself remarkable. It raises a number of questions. Why should the emperor sign up mercenary soldiers if, as is often pointed out, his subjects were legally obliged to provide military service, either under the terms of universal conscription, or for some other reason?[2] Does the fact that mercenaries were recruited suggest that the obligation to render military service was not enforced in practice? Could the use of mercenaries indicate that the military order of the Holy Roman Empire was crumbling? These questions suggest that obligatory military service and

---

[1] Cf. Vinzenz of Prague, MGH SS xvii, 683 (1167): Otto Morena (continuatio anonymi), *Das Geschichtswerk des Otto Morena und seiner Fortsetzer über die Taten Friedrichs I. in der Lombardei*, ed. F. Güterbock (MGH SS rer. Germ. n.s. 7; Berlin, 1930), 196, now also ed. by F.-J. Schmale (Ausgewählte Quellen zur deutschen Geschichte des Mittelalters, 17 A; Darmstadt, 1986), 218 ff. On this issue see also H. Grundmann, 'Rotten und Brabanzonen. Söldnerheere im 12. Jahrhundert', *Deutsches Archiv für die Erforschung des Mittelalters*, 5 (1942), 442–3, who also provides further evidence.

[2] See below, p. 153 ff.

the place of paid service in the Hohenstaufen military system need to be examined in greater detail.

In this chapter, I shall address three specific problem areas:

1. Who was under obligation to take part in imperial campaigns, and why? Under what conditions were they expected to fulfil this duty?
2. What was the legal basis upon which mercenaries were hired? What advantages and disadvantages did this practice bring the Crown?
3. What does obligatory military service and the hiring of mercenaries reveal about the military system of the Holy Roman Empire?

I shall first look at the problem of obligatory military service on imperial expeditions (defined here as all campaigns instigated by the king, with the exception of crusades, which were subject to special regulations). In the past most historians assumed that this duty had a legal basis, and they were interested mainly in establishing its nature. A number of suggestions were made. This duty could have been based on a general constitutional duty binding all freemen to perform military service;[3] on the possession of land and social standing;[4] on a feudal relationship with the king;[5] or on the princes' consent given when the king held court.[6]

More recently, scholars have attempted a new approach. In a regrettably unpublished dissertation Günter Gat-

---

[3] Cf. R. Scholz, *Beiträge zur Geschichte der Hoheitsrechte des deutschen Königs zur Zeit der ersten Staufer (1138–1197)* (Leipzig, 1896), 34 ff.; H. Conrad, *Geschichte der deutschen Wehrverfassung*, vol. i (Munich, 1939), 84 ff., 111 ff.; id., *Deutsche Rechtsgeschichte*, vol. i, 2nd edn. (Karlsruhe, 1962), 260 ff.

[4] See e.g. L. Weiland, 'Die Reichsheerfahrt von Heinrich V. bis Heinrich VI. nach ihrer staatsrechtlichen Seite', *Forschungen zur deutschen Geschichte*, 7 (1867), 115–74; G. Rosenhagen, *Zur Geschichte der Reichsheerfahrt von Heinrich VI. bis Rudolf von Habsburg* (diss. University of Leipzig; Meißen, 1885), 28 ff.; G. Waitz, *Deutsche Verfassungsgeschichte: Die deutsche Reichsverfassung von der Mitte des neunten bis zur Mitte des zwölften Jahrhunderts*, vol. viii (Kiel, 1878, reissue 1955), 124 ff., esp. 144.

[5] Cf. J. Ficker, *Vom Reichsfürstenstande*, ii, pt. 1, ed. P. Puntschart (Innsbruck 1861–1923; reissue 1961), 236 ff.; M. Baltzer, *Zur Geschichte des deutschen Kriegswesens in der Zeit von den letzten Karolingern bis auf Kaiser Friedrich II.* (diss. University of Strassburg; Leipzig, 1877), 16 ff.

[6] Cf. R. Knussert, *Die deutschen Italienfahrten 951–1220 und die Wehrverfassung* (diss. University of Munich; Öttingen, 1931), 18 ff., esp. 27, 29.

termann, for example, uses documentary evidence and chronicles to classify those who took part in imperial campaigns and those who stayed at home.[7] Gattermann is rightly wary of assuming that participation in a campaign implied the existence of a legal obligation. There were many other reasons for going on campaigns, such as the prospect of payment for services, or the hope of rewards of a different kind, such as booty, or imperial favour. Some, indeed, may have joined a campaign for family reasons, or in order to raise their social standing. Gattermann argues: 'We do not want to know how it was meant to be, but how it actually was.'[8]

In this chapter, however, it has been assumed that both questions—'how it was meant to be', or what legal norms and standards of behaviour existed, and 'how it actually was', or what happened to these norms in reality—are of equal interest to the historian. In many cases we can fully understand constitutional reality only when the difference between theory and practice is made clear.

Like earlier historians, I assume in this chapter that the legal obligation to render military service determined who was liable, and defined the extent of their duties.[9] Unlike the older school of historians, however, I argue that this obligation rested not just on one law, but on several. This means that different groups of people could have had different duties. In this chapter I shall examine how obligatory military service related to a number of different types of law: feudal law, *iure ministerialium*, and other laws.

It is well known that one of the most important principles of feudal law was that in return for his fief, a vassal owed his lord not only loyalty, but also 'help and advice' (*consilium et*

---

[7] G. Gattermann, 'Die deutschen Fürsten auf der Reichsheerfahrt: Studien zur Reichskriegsverfassung der Stauferzeit', 2 vols (unpublished diss., Frankfurt am Main, 1956). Compare also B. Töpfer, 'Kaiser Friedrich I. Barbarossa und der deutsche Reichsepiskopat', in A. Haverkamp (ed.), *Friedrich Barbarossa. Handlungsspielräume und Wirkungsweisen des staufischen Kaisers* (Vorträge und Forschungen, 40; Sigmaringen, 1992), 422 ff., J.-P. Stöckel, 'Reichsbischöfe und Reichsheerfahrt unter Friedrich I. Barbarossa', in E. Engel and B. Töpfer (eds.), *Kaiser Friedrich Barbarossa. Landesausbau—Aspekte seiner Politik—Wirkung* (Forschungen zur mittelalterlichen Geschichte, 36; Weimar, 1994), 63 ff.

[8] Ibid. i. 18.   [9] See nn. 4–6.

auxilium).[10] In this context *auxilium* was understood to include armed service when required, regularly taking the
form of knights' service.[11] This also applied to imperial
vassals in their relations with their feudal lord, the king.
However, a closer look reveals that a distinction must be
made between: (*a*) tenants-in-chief, that is, vassals directly
invested by the king, and (*b*) the tenant-in-chief's own vassals, who were also invested with imperial fiefs, but who held
them from their own immediate overlord rather than directly from the king.

We shall first consider the tenants-in-chief. They were directly answerable to the king, and could be summoned by
him to take part in a military campaign. This group included
all secular nobles of sufficient social standing to be considered members of the 'new princely Estate'—a twelfth-
century constitutional development.[12] It also included holders of smaller fiefs who had been directly invested with them
by the king.[13] Those with ecclesiastical responsibilities—archbishops, bishops, abbots, and abbesses—whose secular authority derived from regalia granted directly by the king,
were also counted as tenants-in-chief. Indeed, they constituted a substantial contingent. In practice, however, the in-
mates of nunneries were generally exempted from armed
service, while sub-vassals were obliged to provide service only
when summoned by their immediate feudal lord.[14]

[10] On the origins and significance of this phrase see H. Mitteis, *Lehnrecht und
Staatsgewalt* (Weimar, 1933; reissue 1958), 59 ff. and K.-F. Krieger, 'consilium und
auxilium', *Lexikon des Mittelalters*, iii (1986), 162.

[11] Cf. Mitteis, *Lehnrecht und Staatsgewalt*, 592 ff.; F. L. Ganshof, *Was ist das
Lehnswesen?*, 4th edn. (Darmstadt, 1975), 90 ff.; K.-H. Spieß, 'Lehnsaufgebot',
'Lehn(s)recht, Lehnswesen', *Handwörterbuch zur deutschen Rechtsgeschichte*, ii (1978),
1698 ff., 1725 ff.; K.-F. Krieger, *Die Lehnshoheit der deutschen Könige im Spätmittelalter
(c. 1200–1437)* (Untersuchungen zur deutschen Staats- und Rechtsgeschichte, n.s.
23; Aalen, 1979), 413 ff.

[12] For a concise summary see G. Theuerkauf, 'Fürst', *Handwörterbuch zur deutschen
Rechtsgeschichte*, i (1971), 1337–51; Krieger, *Lehnshoheit*, 156 ff. as well as the more
recent anthology *Vom Reichsfürstenstande*, ed. W. Heinemeyer (Cologne and Ulm,
1987), previously appeared in *Blätter für deutsche Landesgeschichte*, 122 (1986), and
B. Arnold, *Princes and Territories in Medieval Germany* (Cambridge, 1991), 14 ff.

[13] Instances of this are cited in Krieger, *Lehnshoheit*, 175–6.

[14] Cf. C. Spannagel, *Zur Geschichte des deutschen Heerwesens vom Beginn des zehnten bis
zum Ausgang des zwölften Jahrhunderts* (diss. University of Leipzig; Leipzig, 1885),
58 ff. and Mitteis, *Lehnrecht und Staatsgewalt*, 600–1; W. Kienast, 'Lehnrecht und

Under the terms of feudal law, the military service owed by vassals to their lord was unlimited and unpaid, and had to be performed in person. However, the nature of vassalage as a link of mutual loyalty obliged the lord to operate within a framework of what is nowadays called 'good faith', which placed limits on his claims. This meant that the vassal's theoretically unlimited duty was in practice subject to specific conditions and numerous limitations.[15] For example, the king first had to persuade the vassals he wished to enlist that the expedition was necessary. This involved assembling at court the spiritual and temporal dignitaries who would, if need be, swear to take part in the planned campaign.[16] A further condition for enlisting the vassal's service was that he should be given reasonable notice before being formally summoned by the king or his feudal lord.[17] Moreover, the notion of loyalty permitted the vassal to refuse to participate in particular personal circumstances, such as in cases of 'genuine need', defined by the *Sachsenspiegel* as illness or imprisonment.[18]

From the point of view of the Crown, however, the prob-

Staatsgewalt im Mittelalter: Studien zum Mitteis'schen Werk', *Historische Zeitschrift*, 158 (1938), 31 ff.; Ganshof, *Was ist das Lehnswesen?*, 102.

[15] Cf. Mitteis, *Lehnrecht und Staatsgewalt*, 43 ff., 79 ff., 481–2, 532 ff.; Ganshof, *Was ist das Lehnswesen?*, 35 ff., Krieger, *Lehnshoheit*, 391 ff.

[16] Note, e.g., Emperor Frederick's summons of 1160 to the Patriarch of Aquileia, in which he indicates 'Quod omnes principes Alemanie expedicionem nostram promiserunt et iuraverunt', *Die Admonter Briefsammlung*, ed. G. Hödl and P. Classen (MGH Die Briefe der deutschen Kaiserzeit, 6; Munich, 1983), no. 51, 102, now also MGH DD F.I. no. 317. Also on this point Scholz, *Beiträge zur Geschichte der Hoheitsrechte*, 36 ff.; Conrad, *Deutsche Rechtsgeschichte*, i. 261.

[17] See e.g. the feudal laws of the years 1154 and 1158: 'indicta publice expeditione', MGH DD F.I. no. 91 (1154); no. 242 (1158), and, as examples of written summons, MGH DD F.I. nos. 162, 163 (1157). The 'constitutio de expeditione Romana', a legal document which claimed to be a law introduced by Charlemagne although it was actually produced privately for the abbey of Reichenau in about 1158, records that the length of notice given for the Italian campaign amounted to one year and six weeks. See MGH Const. i. 661 ff. For a summary of the 'constitutio de expeditione Romana' indicating further literature on the issue, see G. Theuerkauf, 'constitutio de expeditione Romana', *Handwörterbuch zur deutschen Rechtsgeschichte*, i (1971), 634 ff. The *Sachsenspiegel* similarly assumed a period of notice of one year, six weeks and three days in the case of the Rome expedition, see *Sachsenspiegel Lehnrecht*, ed. K. A. Eckhardt, 3rd edn. (MGH Fontes iuris germanici antiqui, n.s. 1, 2; Göttingen, 1973), 43. In contrast, a campaign in Germany required a mere six weeks advance notice, ibid., 4 §1.

[18] Ibid., 24 §7.

lems created by conflicting duties as a result of multiple vassalage were more significant.[19] Since many tenants-in-chief were vassals of a number of feudal lords at the same time, a conflict between the king and one of these lords could lead to refusal to serve. The same might happen if a tenant-in-chief enlisted in an imperial campaign was simultaneously called on to serve by another lord who needed support in settling a feud. The institution of liege homage in western Europe, an aspect of feudal law, had eased this situation by obliging the *homo ligius* to serve his liege lord *contra omnes homines*.[20] This practice, however, had made little headway under Hohenstaufen rule, at least within the Empire's German stronghold.[21] A further demand made in the Roncaglian decrees of 1158 was that the king was expressly to be included in all oaths of fealty (that is, whenever homage was sworn).[22] Yet even this stipulation, in so far as it was known within the actual *Regnum Teutonicum,* did not mean that the king's claim for service gained precedence over other obligations.[23] Only in the case of one group of tenants-in-chief—the imperial princes as defined by recent law[24]— did the Hohenstaufen Crown succeed in implementing anything like liege homage. This was because if the imperial princes wanted to avoid certain disadvantages that might result from their legal position, they were constrained by the *Heerschildordnung,* which stipulated that they must not owe homage to members of their own Estate.[25] Thus at least in

---

[19] Cf. Krieger, *Lehnshoheit,* 393 ff.

[20] On the liege system see C. Pöhlmann, *Das ligische Lehnsverhältnis* (Heidelberger Rechtswissenschaftliche Abhandlungen, 31; Heidelberg, 1931); Mitteis, *Lehnrecht und Staatsgewalt,* 315–16, 434 ff. 557 ff.; V. Henn, *Das ligische Lehnswesen im Westen und Nordwesten des mittelalterlichen deutschen Reiches* (diss. University of Bonn; Munich, 1970); V. Henn, 'Das ligische Lehnswesen im Erzstift Trier von der Mitte des 12. Jahrhunderts bis zum Ausgang des Mittelalters', *Kurtrierisches Jahrbuch,* 11 (1971), 37 ff.; B. Diestelkamp, 'Homo ligius', *Handwörterbuch zur deutschen Rechtsgeschiche,* ii (1978), 234 ff.

[21] Cf. the concise summary in Krieger, *Lehnshoheit,* 396.

[22] MGH Const. i, no. 177, Art. 10 = MGH DD F.I. no. 242, 36: 'Illud quoque sanccimus, ut in omni sacramento fidelitatis nominatim imperator excipiatur.'

[23] See Krieger, *Lehnshoheit,* 394, 397 ff.

[24] Cf. n. 12 above.

[25] For a detailed presentation of the *Heerschildordnung* and its significance in constitutional and political terms see Krieger, *Lehnshoheit,* 117 ff., 125 ff. (with references to earlier research).

the case of the non-princely tenants-in-chief, the king could not count on his feudal obligations receiving precedence. To ensure a successful campaign, therefore, the king had to put an end to the numerous feuds in his country, at least for the duration of the campaign.[26]

Initially, obligatory military service in an imperial campaign was still, in principle, regarded as a strict personal duty. In 1161, for instance, Emperor Frederick Barbarossa reminded the Archbishop of Salzburg, who hoped to commute his duty to participate in the Italian campaign into a cash payment, that he was under obligation to serve the emperor 'not with money, but with people and weapons', and that he was thus expected to appear before the emperor with an appropriate retinue.[27] Yet in the Roncaglian decrees of 1158 the same emperor had laid down that vassals could make a payment amounting to half the annual value of their fiefs in lieu of serving in person.[28] Reports of Otto IV's Rome campaign show that numerous tenants-in-chief paid for their discharge from military service,[29] while the *Sachsenspiegel* assumed that a vassal was able to buy his discharge from service. By that time the payment was no more than a tenth of the annual value of the fief.[30]

Tenants-in-chief were expected to respond to the king's call to arms *cum honesta milicia*,[31] that is, with an appropriate number of their own vassals, summoned by them for this purpose. Even if the Crown had clear ideas about the size of the contingents which were to accompany tenants-

[26] Gattermann, 'Die deutschen Fürsten auf der Reichsheerfahrt', i. 88 substantiates this.

[27] 'Cum igitur quantumcumque religiosus ab ipsa veritate que sunt cesaris, cesari reddere iubeatur et tua dignitas non solum qualicumque pecunia, sed et personis et armatura laboribus nostris adesse debeat, per hec imperialia scripta tue fidelitati . . . mandamus', *Die Admonter Briefsammlung*, no. 57, 110 = MGH DD F.I. no. 341. Moreover, in his address to the Patriarch of Aquileia mentioned above, n. 16, the Emperor indicated 'quod nulli principum expedicionem remittemus, quamvis multi querant absolvi, et quicumque remanebit, contra nostram voluntatem remanebit'.

[28] MGH Const. i, no. 77, Art. 5 = MGH DD F.I. no. 242, 36.

[29] See Arnold of Lübeck, *Chronica*, MGH SS xxi, 248.

[30] *Sachsenspiegel Lehnrecht*, 4 §3.

[31] Summons by Frederick I to the Patriarch of Aquileia, *Die Admonter Briefsammlung*, no. 51, 102.

in-chief,[32] it seems that numbers of knights, or minimum contingents, were not specified during the Hohenstaufen period. Instead, it seems to have been left to the sense of duty of the individual tenant-in-chief to decide how many vassals he should enlist, and to what extent to enforce the obligation to render military service within his region.

The discrepancy between the theoretical requirements for service and their realization in practice, arising out of conflicting loyalties, eventually led vassals to demand that their obligation to provide service be defined more precisely. The regulations in the *Sachsenspiegel* provide an example. Vassals with holdings in the region east of the Saale needed to serve only against the Wends, Poles, and Bohemians, and the length of such service was limited to six weeks.[33] As Gattermann has shown, however, during the Hohenstaufen period such regulations should be interpreted more as part of a programme of demands on the part of the vassals than as legal precepts which actually bound the king.[34] Except for cases in which the king made concessions to individual tenants-in-chief, such as the elevation of Austria to the status of a duchy in 1156,[35] tenants-in-chief could neither insist on serving close to home, nor simply return home after six weeks' service if the campaign was not finished.

In general, this also applied to 'transmontane' (or Italian) military campaigns. By their very nature, these demanded special sacrifices from vassals. The *Sachsenspiegel* states that in principle German vassals were not obliged to participate in military campaigns in Italy, with the exception of those with the specific purpose of acquiring the Imperial crown from Rome.[36] Again, however, the practice of the Hohenstaufen

[32] There are some indications that the numbers of troop to be produced specified in Otto II's famous summons of 981 were still familiar during the Hohenstaufen era. Compare K. F. Werner, 'Heeresorganisation und Kriegführung im deutschen Königreich des 10. und 11. Jahrhunderts', *Settimane di studio del centro italiano di studi sull' alto Medioevo*, 15, 2 (1968), 834 ff., reprinted in id., *Structures politiques du monde franc (VI*ᵉ*–XII*ᵉ *siècles)* (London, 1979), 791 ff.

[33] *Sachsenspiegel Lehnrecht*, 4 § 1.

[34] Gattermann, 'Die deutschen Fürsten auf der Reichsheerfahrt', i, 190 ff.

[35] The procedure was recorded in the famous *privilegium minus*; the newly elevated duke was granted the concession of being called up to serve in the imperial campaigns only in the immediate vicinity of Austria, see MGH DD F.I. no. 151, with references to research.   [36] *Sachsenspiegel Lehnrecht*, 4 § 1.

kings appears to contradict this, because it was taken for granted that tenants-in-chief were obliged to take part.[37] It was a different matter if the campaign was to be conducted beyond the borders of the Empire—in southern Italy, for example. In such cases there is evidence that the princes, by mutual consent, forced the operation to be abandoned, and that the emperor respected this decision.[38]

Tenants-in-chief always had to bear the cost of the journey themselves,[39] which, we can assume, led to the financial ruin of many a vassal during the Hohenstaufen period.[40] Thus in the long term, the Crown had no option but to call only on solvent vassals, or to keep the financial burden on them within reasonable bounds by itself paying a proportion of the costs incurred during the journey. The Hohenstaufen emperors appear to have opted for the second alternative. They increasingly supported vassals who took part in military campaigns by granting them *stipendia*, or investing them with fiefs.[41]

In order to assess the effectiveness of obligatory military service under feudal law, it is necessary to examine briefly

[37] Cf. Gattermann, 'Die deutschen Fürsten auf der Reichsheerfahrt', i. 190 ff.; Krieger, *Lehnshoheit*, 420. Compare also the so-called 'constitutio de expeditione Romana', MGH Const. i, 661–3, art. 3, which similarly rests on the principle that all tenants-in-chief are also under obligation to take part in an Italian campaign: 'Cuicumque autem secundum hanc legem eadem expeditio imperetur, si ad curiam Gallorum, hoc est in campum, qui vulgo Rungalle dicitur, dominum suum non comitetur et ibi cum militari apparatu non representetur, feodo, preter hos qui cum gratia dominorum suorum remanserint, in conspectu nostro absque spe recuperationis privetur.'

[38] After Frederick I's coronation as emperor in Rome (1155), the princes rallied against the planned campaign to South Italy, with the result that the expedition was subsequently abandoned. See Otto of Freising, *Gesta Friderici I imperatoris*, ed. G. Waitz and B. v. Simson, 3rd edn. (MGH SS rer. Germ.; Hanover and Leipzig, 1912), ii. chs. 37–8, 145. This was in principle also respected by Emperor Frederick, who, in a written summons of March 1157, promised Otto of Freising and the princes that the planned expedition against Lombardy would not extend further than the Apennine mountains; see ibid., ii. ch. 52, 158 (= MGH DD F.I. no. 163). Cf. also F. Opll, *Friedrich Barbarossa* (Darmstadt, 1990), 226 ff.; O. Engels, *Die Staufer* (5th edn., Stuttgart, 1993), 64.

[39] See Krieger, *Lehnshoheit*, 418, with references to research.

[40] To raise finances, vassals often had no alternative but to pawn substantial amounts; see the evidence given by Gattermann, 'Die deutschen Fürsten auf der Reichsheerfahrt', i. 198 ff.

[41] See the evidence given ibid., i. 200, 203, and K.-H. Spieß, 'Die Staufer und ihre Helfer', *Lebendiges Rheinland-Pfalz*, 21 (1984), 115.

the sanctions which the king could use against defaulting
vassals. In theory, the position was clear. Provided that the
call to arms in an imperial campaign was issued in good time,
and that the princes had sworn their support for the campaign, a vassal who disobeyed without any excuse was in
danger of forfeiting his fief or regalia to the king or to his
immediate lord.[42] In practice, however, the situation was
different. As a rule, a formal trial according to feudal law had
to be held by members of the same Estate before the king
could proceed against the accused.[43] It is true that Otto of
Freising reports that Emperor Frederick Barbarossa tried
to set a precedent in 1154 by stripping the Archbishop of
Bremen, the Bishop of Halberstadt, and several (unfortunately unidentified) secular tenants-in-chief of their regalia
or imperial fiefs because they did not appear for the Italian
military campaign which had been announced.[44] There are,
however, no further reports of the emperor taking such
action against defaulting vassals—including, presumably, the
unruly Archbishop of Salzburg who, despite all the emperor's warnings and threats, could not in the end be made
to fulfil his military obligations.[45]

It was even more difficult for the king to assert his right to
military service from the sub-vassals, as they were answerable

[42] MGH DD F.I. no. 242 (feudal law of 1158) and MGH Const. i. 661 ff.
('constitutio de expeditione Romana'), Art. 3.

[43] Compare K.-F. Krieger, 'Die königliche Lehnsgerichtsbarkeit im Zeitalter der
Staufer', *Deutsches Archiv für die Erforschung des Mittelalters*, 26 (1970), 400 ff. and
Krieger, *Lehnshoheit*, 492 ff.

[44] See Otto of Freising, *Gesta Friderici I imperatoris*, ii. ch. 12, as well as *Helmolds
Slavenchronik*, ed. B. Schmeidler, 3rd edn. (MGH SS rer. Germ.; Hanover, 1937),
ch. 83, 158: 'eo quod archiepiscopus omisisset Italicam expedicionem transgressor
iuramenti essetque reus maiestatis. Unde etiam legatus imperatoris veniens
Bremam occupavit omnes curtes episcopales et quaecumque reperisset addidit fisci
iuribus. Idem factum est Othelrico Halverstadensi episcopo.' Cf. also B. Töpfer,
'Kaiser Friedrich I. Barbarossa und der deutsche Reichsepiskopat', 422 f.

[45] The sources for this are familiar to us through the *Admonter Briefsammlung*; on
this point see also G. Hödl, 'Die Admonter Briefsammlung 1158–1162 (cap. 629)',
Deutsches Archiv für die Erforschung des Mittelalters, 25 (1969), 347–470 and 26
(1970), 150–99. On the political background see W. Schmidt, 'Die Stellung der
Erzbischöfe und des Erzstiftes von Salzburg zu Kirche und Reich unter Kaiser
Friedrich I. bis zum Frieden von Venedig (1177)', *Archiv für österreichische Geschichte*,
34 (1865), 28 ff., and G. Hödl, 'Das Erzstift Salzburg und das Reich unter Kaiser
Friedrich Barbarossa', *Mitteilungen der Gesellschaft für Salzburger Landeskunde*, 114
(1974), 37 ff., esp. 41 ff.

only to their immediate lords.[46] Here, the king was limited to supporting the claims of tenants-in-chief against their own vassals, either—as in Italy—by appropriate legislation,[47] or by individual proclamations and judgements which strengthened the position of the tenants-in-chief against their vassals.[48]

In addition to feudal law, the *ius ministerialium* was also a possible legal basis for military service.[49] Since the turn of the tenth century, temporal and ecclesiastical princes as well as the king had increasingly entrusted serfs from their *familia* with relatively high-status duties, such as affairs of court, administration and war. As Karl Bosl has shown,[50] the Salian and Hohenstaufen emperors in particular tried to use these *ministeriales imperii* as a personal alternative to imperial vassalage, with the aim of creating the basis for a general imperial administration in the future. The advantage for the king lay in this group's legal lack of freedom, which seemed to provide a guarantee of long-term service. It was also, in principle, much easier to enlist these *ministeriales* for military service than the free vassals. Especially in the Hohenstaufen

[46] Krieger, *Lehnshoheit*, 557, provides general information and references to further research on this point.

[47] See the feudal laws passed by Conrad II in 1037 (MGH Const. i, no. 45), Lothar III in 1136 (ibid., no. 120), and Frederick I in 1154 (ibid., no. 148, = MGH DD F.I. no. 91) and in 1158 (MGH Const. i, no. 177 = MGH DD F.I. no. 242); see also K.-H. Spieß, 'Lehnsgesetze', *Handwörterbuch zur deutschen Rechtsgeschichte*, ii (1978), 1717–21; Krieger, *Lehnshoheit*, 486ff., H. Patze, 'Friedrich Barbarossa und die deutschen Fürsten', *Die Zeit der Staufer: Geschichte—Kunst—Kultur*, v, ed. R. Haussherr and C. Väterlein (Stuttgart, 1979), 50ff.

[48] See the examples cited by Gattermann, 'Die deutschen Fürsten auf der Reichsheerfahrt', i. 234–5 as well as in MGH Const. ii, no. 369 (1254).

[49] For general remarks, compare Conrad, *Deutsche Rechtsgeschichte*, i. 297–8, with accounts of previous research, 307; K. Bosl, 'Das ius ministerialium. Dienstrecht und Lehnrecht im deutschen Mittelalter', *Studien zum mittelalterlichen Lehnswesen: Vorträge gehalten in Lindau am 10.–13. Oktober 1956* (Vorträge und Forschungen, 5; Lindau and Constance, 1960), 51–94; Krieger, *Lehnshoheit*, 176ff.; Spieß, 'Die Staufer und ihre Helfer', 115ff.

[50] K. Bosl, *Die Reichsministerialität der Salier und Staufer: Ein Beitrag zur Geschichte des hochmittelalterlichen deutschen Volkes, Staates und Reiches*, 2 vols. (Schriften der MGH, 10; Stuttgart 1950); K. Bosl, 'Die Reichsministerialität als Element der mittelalterlichen deutschen Staatsverfassung im Zeitalter der Salier und Staufer', id., *Frühformen der Gesellschaft im mittelalterlichen Europa* (Munich and Vienna, 1964), 329ff.; K. Bosl, *Die Grundlagen der modernen Gesellschaft im Mittelalter: Eine deutsche Gesellschaftsgeschichte des Mittelalters* (Monographien zur Geschichte des Mittelalters, 4; Stuttgart, 1972), ii. 268–9.

period, this meant that the *ministeriales* provided a considerable proportion of the troops in each military campaign.[51]

However, the fact that they were restricted to higher forms of service, and above all, their acquisition of knightly status, paved the way for the early social rise of the *ministeriales*. As knights, they were gradually assimilated into the group of free vassals.[52] By the end of the twelfth century, the results of this transition were already becoming obvious. In their role as overlords, kings could not prevent their *ministeriales* from accepting fiefs from other lords in accordance with feudal law. Thus the *ministeriales* succeeded in entering the feudal hierarchy, which had until then been the preserve of freemen alone. Moreover, recognition of their status within the feudal system called into question the power of the king himself as an employer. The oft-cited example of the imperial *ministerialis* Werner of Bolanden, who in addition to holding a fief from the king as his feudal overlord, held fiefs from forty-four other feudal lords, shows how much the tradition of service had already been eroded by the end of the twelfth century.[53] Clearly, neither Frederick Barbarossa nor Henry VI succeeded in making their *ministeriales* give absolute priority to the feudal relationship with their royal master above the liege homage due to other overlords. The *ministerialis* had become a vassal like any other.

In addition to feudal law and the *ius ministerialium*, two other possible legal bases for military service must briefly be mentioned at this point. The *Sachsenspiegel* obviously assumed that under the terms of general territorial law (*Landrecht*), all able-bodied men were obliged to defend the country and, if the need arose, could be called upon to do

---

[51] See Waitz, *Deutsche Verfassungsgeschichte*, viii, 123–4.

[52] Cf. Krieger's summary in *Lehnshoheit*, 177 ff., and B. Arnold, *German Knighthood 1050–1300* (Oxford, 1985).

[53] This is evident from the feudal book which Werner II of Bolanden started around 1250–60, but can probably be traced back to a document from the very end of the 12th cent.: *Die ältesten Lehnbücher der Herrschaft Bolanden*, ed. W. Sauer (Wiesbaden, 1882), 17 ff.; on the dating see A. Eckhardt, 'Das älteste Bolander Lehnbuch', *Archiv für Diplomatik*, 22 (1976), 317 ff.; also of interest is O. Engels, 'Bolanden, Herren von', *Lexikon des Mittelalters*, ii (1983), 356–7; Arnold, *German Knighthood*, 103.

so.[54] At no time during the Hohenstaufen period, however, not even during the Mongol invasion of 1241, are any cases known of the king using his right to demand military service under this type of law.[55]

Finally, the power that the king possessed over towns which lay outside his feudal and territorial jurisdiction also provided a legal basis for obligatory military service. Thus Emperor Frederick Barbarossa enlisted the Italian communes for military service.[56] In this case obligatory military service was specifically included in the oath of fealty which the consuls, as representatives of their communes, were obliged to swear to the emperor.[57] As this involved promising loyalty to the emperor not as a feudal lord, but in his capacity as *dominus et imperator*, the oath was not a feudal oath in the legal sense. However, its substantive provisions were influenced by feudal law, which meant that military service was to be rendered regularly, *contra omnes homines*, in the spirit of liege feudal relationships.[58]

It is only for the period after the disputed succession in 1198 that there is evidence of German towns being summoned to participate in imperial military campaigns in Germany. Thus Philip of Swabia's military expeditions were

---

[54] *Sachsenspiegel Landrecht*, ed. K. A. Eckhardt, 2nd edn. (MGH Fontes iuris Germanici antiqui, n.s. 1, 1; Göttingen, 1955), iii. 78, 2 ff.; see also Ficker, *Vom Reichsfürstenstande*, ii, pt. 1, 287.

[55] Compare Gattermann, 'Die deutschen Fürsten auf der Reichsheerfahrt', ii. p. xxxiii, n. 19a.

[56] See A. Haverkamp, *Herrschaftsformen der Frühstaufer in Reichsitalien*, 2 vols. (Monographien zur Geschichte des Mittelalters, 1; Stuttgart, 1971), 349 ff. On the enlistment of the communes by imperial vassals see also the letter from Count Guido Guerra II to the town of Modigliana demanding the presence of forty knights and as many foot-soldiers with the imperial army in Roncaglia; cf. H. Wieruszowski, 'A Twelfth-Century "Ars dictaminis" in the Barbarini Collection of the Vatican Library', id., *Politics and Culture in Medieval Spain and Italy* (Rome, 1971), 342, no. 12.

[57] See e.g. Emperor Frederick I's detailed charter for Pisa, of 1162 (MGH Const., i, pt 2, no. 205 = MGH DD F.I. no. 356) and the comments on this by G. Rauch, *Die Bündnisse deutscher Herrscher mit Reichsangehörigen vom Regierungsantritt Friedrich Barbarossas bis zum Tod Rudolfs von Habsburg* (Untersuchungen zur deutschen Staats- und Rechtsgeschichte, n.s. 5; Aalen, 1966), 12 ff.; see also MGH Const., i, no. 333, 476 (1191) and no. 337, 482 (1191) as well as Haverkamp, *Herrschaftsformen der Frühstaufer*, 349 ff.

[58] See above, p. 156.

manned by citizens from the towns of Goslar, Magdeburg, Hildesheim, and Erfurt.[59] Similarly, townsmen from Brunswick[60] and Cologne[61] fought beside Otto IV in 1204 and 1206. It seems that Emperor Frederick II preferred to receive financial contributions (*praecaria*) from his towns and villages in Germany in lieu of military service.[62] Only after the interregnum were royal or imperial towns regularly called upon for imperial military campaigns.[63]

We shall now turn to the second set of questions posed at the beginning of this chapter. What was the legal basis upon which mercenaries were hired? What advantages and disadvantages did this practice bring the Crown? In this case the legal basis was generally the contract in which the mercenary undertook to perform military service for a specific period in return for a certain wage. When examining the advantages and disadvantages of this form of service for the Crown, it is helpful to differentiate between two types of individuals with whom the Crown concluded contracts for mercenary service, that is, between those who were already legally bound to render military service to the king, and those who were not.

The second group consisted of those whom the king could not, according to common law, enlist for military campaigns. The Brabançons (mentioned at the beginning of this chapter) signed up by Frederick Barbarossa in 1166 fall into this category.[64] Although some at least of these troops must have

---

[59] Cf. the evidence provided by K. Lindt, *Beiträge zur Geschichte des deutschen Kriegswesens in der staufischen Zeit im Anschluß an die Kämpfe zwischen Philipp von Schwaben und Otto IV.* (diss. University of Freiburg; Tübingen, 1881), 29–30.

[60] Ibid. 28–9; Gattermann, 'Die deutschen Fürsten auf der Reichsheerfahrt', i. 131.

[61] Cf. Lindt, *Beiträge zur Geschichte des deutschen Kriegswesens,* 28; Gattermann, 'Die deutschen Fürsten auf der Reichsheerfahrt', i. 133.

[62] Thus, on the occasion of the military expedition against Lombardy in 1238, Emperor Frederick II wrote to the Archbishop of Mainz challenging him: 'quatinus cum civitatibus nostris et opidis per totam Alemanniam precariam imponi mandaverimus pro militibus inde ad nostra servicia conducendis, circa festinam collectionem tam militum quam precarie omnem quam poteris opem et operam sollicite studeas adhibere', E. Winkelmann, *Acta imperii inedita saeculi XIII et XIV,* vol. i (Innsbruck, 1880; reissue, 1964), no. 348, 310.

[63] Cf. H. Fischer, *Die Theilnahme der Reichsstädte an der Reichsheerfahrt vom Interregnum bis zum Ausgang Kaiser Karls IV.* (diss. University of Leipzig; Leipzig, 1883).

[64] See above, p. 151.

been subjects of the Empire,[65] they were unlikely to have had a direct feudal relationship with the emperor, or to have been under any obligation to serve him. The same applies to the mercenaries whom Henry VI paid out of the ransom he received for the release from prison of King Richard I of England,[66] and to the Flemish, English, and even Egyptian contingents who fought for Frederick II before the walls of Brescia in 1238.[67]

It is difficult to say what proportion of the forces in imperial military campaigns were mercenaries during the Hohenstaufen period. No mercenaries' contracts from this time have survived, and mercenaries do not appear as witnesses to imperial documents. All we have is a number of more or less incidental references in contemporary chronicles. As early as Barbarossa's time, vassals in Italy at least could be discharged from their feudal duty by paying an appropriate sum of money.[68] This fact alone suggests that the Hohenstaufen king depended on mercenaries to fill the gaps which this left in the feudal army. We can therefore assume that especially in Italy, a considerable proportion of the forces enlisted by the Empire consisted of mercenaries. This system of recruitment gave the king access, at short notice, to a high-calibre military force without incurring long-term obligations by bestowing fiefs or estates. On the other hand, the disadvantages of this system were far from negligible. Above all, it cost money, which first had to be obtained. In addition, recruiting this type of soldier, who had a bad repu-

---

[65] Cf. Grundmann, 'Rotten und Brabanzonen', 445 ff.

[66] See T. Toeche, *Kaiser Heinrich VI.* (Jahrbücher der deutschen Geschichte; Leipzig 1867; reissue 1965), 282 ff., 331; Gattermann, 'Die deutschen Fürsten auf der Reichsheerfahrt', i, 119, and on the political background P. Csendes, *Heinrich VI.* (Darmstadt, 1993), 123 ff.

[67] Cf. J. F. Böhmer and J. Ficker, *Regesta Imperii, v: Die Regesten des Kaierreichs unter Philipp, Otto IV., Friedrich II., Wilhelm und Richard 1198–1272* (Innsbruck, 1881–2; reissue 1971), no. 2375 a, and Gattermann, 'Die deutschen Fürsten auf der Reichsheerfahrt', i. 230–1

[68] Cf. above, p. 157. On Frederick Barbarossa's view of the emergent money economy cf. J. Fried, 'Die Wirtschaftspolitik Friedrich Barbarossas in Deutschland', *Blätter für deutsche Landesgeschichte*, 120 (1984), 195 ff., and U. Dirlmeier, 'Friedrich Barbarossa—auch ein Wirtschaftspolitiker,' in A. Haverkamp (ed.), *Friedrich Barbarossa. Handlungsspielräume und Wirkungsweisen des staufischen Kaisers* (Vorträge und Forschungen, 40; Sigmaringen, 1992), 509 ff.

tation,[69] produced specific problems of loyalty which the Crown later tried to overcome by converting the contract into a feudal relationship with an appropriate oath of fealty.[70]

The participation of mercenaries in campaigns, as described here, did not call into question or restrict obligatory military service in general. However, this is not necessarily true of cases in which the Crown entered into contracts with individuals who, for whatever reason, were already legally bound to offer military service. The existence of such a practice suggests that the king was no longer able to enforce his right to obligatory military service.

Not every contract which entailed the king offering some reward in return for service cast doubt on obligatory service. This was the case only when the king's offer appears to have formed the legal basis for service, that is, when he could no longer legally demand service from his subjects, and found it necessary instead to negotiate terms on an individual basis. As G. Rauch has shown,[71] however, we have evidence of such contracts only after the controversy over the imperial succession in 1198, when the two pretenders to the throne, whose kingship was not universally recognized, needed to purchase armed support. The introduction of this practice was to have important consequences for the following period. The king's original freedom to decide whether, and to what extent, he should contribute financially to campaigns was gradually transformed into a legal obligation to pay the participants for their service. This development was complete by the beginning of the fourteenth century.[72]

This brings us to our final question. What does the existence of mercenaries alongside obligatory military service suggest about the status of the military constitution of the Holy Roman Empire? We shall sum up by discussing five points under this heading.

1. During the Hohenstaufen period the imperial military constitution was still essentially based on obligatory military

---

[69] Cf. Grundmann, 'Rotten und Brabanzonen', 419 ff.
[70] Cf. Krieger, *Lehnshoheit*, 418, n. 153; 420, n. 166, with the evidence cited.
[71] Rauch, *Die Bündnisse deutscher Herrscher*, 48 ff., 174–5.
[72] Cf. Krieger, *Lehnshoheit*, 418, 420–1.

service according to feudal law. This meant that the potential for defence could only partially be tapped, for the *regnum Teutonicum* contained considerable amounts of allodial property,[73] whose holders did not, as a rule, owe the king obligatory military service.[74] The Crown's policy of feudalization, as demonstrated by the elevation of magnates to princely status (Namur, 1184; Braunschweig-Lüneburg, 1235; Hesse, 1292, etc.)[75] can be seen as an attempt to remedy this situation.

Nor did the Crown have access to the whole of the Imperial Church. Considerable parts of it, such as nunneries and churches whose priests, even if directly answerable to the empire, had not been invested with regalia by the king (including Cistercian houses and the papal monasteries) were not subject to military service.

2. The Crown failed to ensure that the loyalty of all its tenants-in-chief to itself took absolute precedence over all other feudal ties, such as liege homage relationships. If duties came into conflict, as happened above all in the case of non-princely tenants-in-chief, there was a danger that tenants-in-chief would refuse to participate in imperial campaigns.

3. The Salian and Hohenstaufen monarchies failed in their attempt to assert their rights as lords over the unfree imperial *ministeriales*. The emancipation of the *ministeriales* from the authority of their royal overlords was largely achieved during the Hohenstaufen period and had major and far-reaching consequences for the imperial military constitution. With the erosion of the Crown's legal right to military service, the personal basis for the establishment of a general imperial administration also collapsed. Thus

---

[73] Ibid. 79 ff., 89 ff., 577 ff.

[74] This explains the fact that the counts and barons of Guelders, Jülich, Cleves, Bar, Lützelburg, Namur (before their elevation to the princely estate), and Katzenelnbogen, Heiligenberg, Nellenburg, Werdenberg, Zimmern, are rarely recorded as taking part in Hohenstaufen imperial campaigns; cf. the compilation made by Gattermann, 'Die deutschen Fürsten auf der Reichsheerfahrt', ii. (62)–(216).

[75] Cf. G. Engelbert, 'Die Erhebungen in den Reichsfürstenstand bis zum Ausgang des Mittelalters' (diss. University of Marburg, 1948); Krieger, *Lehnshoheit*, 170–3, 199–215, 232, 577 ff.; K. Heinemeyer, 'König und Reichsfürsten in der späten Salier- und frühen Stauferzeit', *Vom Reichsfürstenstande*, ed. by W. Heinemeyer (Cologne and Ulm, 1987), 35 ff.

it was no longer possible to collect and administer rationally the payments into which military service had been commuted.

4. The Crown's difficulties in enforcing obligatory military service by means of sanctions were also attributable to causes external to the feudal system itself. A king in the Hohenstaufen period not only lacked an imperial administration, but also had little or no access to written records such as feudal books or registers of feudal documents. This deprived him of any effective means of checking vassals and their terms of service.

5. None the less, the mere existence of mercenary contracts does not mean that obligatory military service could no longer be enforced. Mercenary contracts with individuals who were not under an obligation to render military service did not affect vassalage as such. But it was a different matter when the king concluded contracts with individuals who were already under an obligation to provide military service. The Crown's practice of paying tenants-in-chief to render the military service which they were bound to provide in any case dates from the period of the disputed imperial succession (1198). Neither this, nor the development of a legal obligation to pay the participants in a campaign, left the imperial military constitution untouched. Even if obligatory military service itself was not undermined, the feudal army was gradually transformed into a mercenary force.

Part III

CHRISTIANS AND NON-CHRISTIANS

The Jews: Political and Social Contexts

7

The Jews in Medieval England, 1066–1290

Paul R. Hyams

The history of the Jews in medieval England, or Germany for that matter, is no simple matter. All Jews, even in the Middle Ages, felt themselves part of a supranational community linked together by religion, language, and culture. This community is, unfortunately, poorly documented. There are relatively few Hebrew chronicles and martyrologies. In compensation, the English Jewry is well defined in time, somewhat less so in place. The omnipresent possibility of fruitful juxtapositions of Jewish and non-Jewish source material positively draws one on to cross the invisible lines between political, economic, and religious history. We may well know more about the extrascholarly life of Rabbi Elijah of London than of any other medieval scholar in the West.[1] To exploit this potential to the full a scholar requires formidable skills of language and historical imagination. He needs to move comfortably through the sources of western Christendom as well as Jewish materials and the whole range of evidence for English history. Such men are rare, which is why the subject still awaits its great book.[2]

The continuous Jewish presence in medieval England be-

This essay dates from July 1987 with minor additions in square brackets.

[1] C. Roth, 'Elijah of London', *Transactions of the Jewish Historical Society of England*, 15 (1943), 29–62.

[2] The reader is referred to my earlier survey, 'The Jews as an Immigrant Minority, 1066–1290', *Journal of Jewish Studies*, 25 (1974), 270–93, aimed like this essay at a general historical audience, for references to the basic literature. To date Cecil Roth has come closest to the needed combination of skills for all the defects in his *A History of the Jews in England*, 3rd edn. (Oxford, 1964). The studies of Brand, Dobson, and Stacey noted below prove that non-Hebraists (amongst whom I too number) remain capable of serious and original contributions. [Stacey's forthcoming book on English Jews in the Middle Ages will certainly mark a substantial advance in our understanding.]

gan in the wake of the Norman Conquest. In the years after 1066, Jews were among the many minor francophone dependants to follow the new French rulers across the Channel. Their settlement, apparently confined for the first years to London, followed the widening ripples of French colonization, but always remained concentrated in towns, usually close to both castle and market-place. Castle, because they were from the first closely dependent on royal support for protection and status, hence also open to royal exploitation. Market-place, no doubt for their perennial core activity of moneylending.

Once established beyond London, from, say, the 1130s,[3] the Jewry was exposed to outside pressure from two quarters. Jews were in England, as elsewhere, subject to scrutiny from the Church, whose official policy towards them may be summarized in a word as containment. Jewish bodies were to be preserved towards their eventual conversion, as a prelude to the Last Days. In the meantime, they had to be repressed, wherever possible kept apart from ordinary believers, their freedom of action restrained for fear of the harm they might otherwise do in sowing doubts, by mockery or all-too-informed argument. Popular mistrust, shared by many individual churchmen, went further. It had three main roots. In part it stemmed from the religious identification of medieval Jews with the New Testament killers of Jesus. (How this affected their relationship with the Hebrews of the Old Testament remains less clear, and very much worthy of study.) A second major root was xenophobic, fear of the strange. Jews suffered alongside other alien groupings such as the Flemings, though their exclusion from social groupings that assumed Church membership and awareness of Jews' distant links (with Languedoc, even with Palestine and the East) intensified the reaction in their case. Probably also, their moneylending labelled them for some already in the twelfth century as predators on the economically

---

[3] The press announcement on 6 July 1987, right after the conference on which this volume is based, of the discovery of a ritual bath in Bristol may change this received chronology. R. W. Vaughan, 'Jacobs Well Rediscovered', *Temple Local History Group Newsletter*, 3 (1987), 7–15 is a preliminary publication. A date around 1100 is not at present to be excluded; if confirmed, this would raise interesting questions about other Jewish centres.

distressed.[4] This confusion of symptom (loans) with the real causes of financial distress is very widespread in Jewish history.

Beyond these preliminary points, recent historiography is largely and idiosyncratically dominated by the perceived need to explain the Expulsion of 1290. Received explanations come mainly in terms of the Jews' economic role or the authority of a centralized monarchy, or some combination of both. They stress popular opposition, especially after the Church had codified its own position in a reform context at the Fourth Lateran Council of 1215. Continuing royal favour and protection, however, restrained this popular anti-Judaism.[5] The Jewry's potential of royal revenue unrestrained by any need for noble consent proved increasingly attractive in the early thirteenth century. So much so that the 'Jewish Milch-Cow'[6] was close to exhaustion by the time of the political disturbances in the latter years of Henry III's reign (1258–67). Jewish finance was by then firmly associated with corruption at the royal court, where powerful and hated foreigners like the Lusignans were only the most visible of those attracted to the Crown's impressive central concentration of wealth and patronage.

By the accession of Edward I (1272), the Jewry's utility to the Crown had demonstrably decreased; its grasp on royal protection therefore weakened. Without the king's personal conversion to the notion of Expulsion (not a new notion in itself), none of this would have been decisive. Edward was profoundly affected by memories of his own political educa-

---

[4] Although H. G. Richardson rightly insisted in his *The English Jewry under Angevin Kings* (London, 1960), 141 that even in the 12th cent. Jews were not the *only* such lenders, the fact remains that no one gained in popularity by this activity. Richardson's study, though often distorted and sometimes perverse, is also learned, clever and—in a word—indispensable. He made strict professional standards of scholarship and analysis standard in the field.

[5] G. I. Langmuir, 'Anti-Judaism as the Necessary Preparation for Anti-Semitism', *Viator*, 2 (1971), 383–9 and id., 'Medieval Anti-Semitism', *The Holocaust: Ideology, Bureaucracy and Genocide*, ed. H. Friedlander and S. Milton (Milton, NY, 1980), 27–36 argues for a medieval transition between anti-Judaism and anti-Semitism. These papers are now collected as G. I. Langmuir, *Towards a Definition of Antisemitism* (Los Angeles, 1990), chs. 3 and 13. English historians might well adopt this terminology. I prefer here to conflate all hostility as anti-Jewish, and thus avoid begging questions that cannot be resolved in a brief survey.

[6] Roth, *History*, ch. 3.

tion during the disturbances after 1258. These experiences gave him his notion of political rectitude, a certain religious self-righteousness and an overweening acceptance of the expediency of concessions to critics of his self-seeking policies. Expropriation of the Jewry followed by Expulsion offered him a solution to pressing short-term needs. A 'dress-rehearsal' in Gascony dispelled any lingering suspicions that the rewards of Expulsion might not outweigh loss of the now much diminished incomes from a weakened Jewry. And that was the end of a Jewish presence in England until 1656.

Something like this represents recent received opinion about the Jews of medieval England. Revisionism is, however, in the wind and will gain force as, with painful slowness, the history of Jews gets drawn into the mainstream of historical research. Take as an instance the quite recent realization of English historians that our island is part of Europe. Since the 1960s, the reinterpretation of medieval political history in terms of a cross-Channel entity, an Anglo-Norman empire from the Conquest to the 1140s, as some would have it, has been a major historiographical theme.[7] This connection with Normandy remained especially strong even, though diminishingly so, after the 1154 accession of Henry of Anjou. These associations must have affected the Jewry more than most Jewish historians allow. The publication of a recent book by the American Hebraist Norman Golb on *Les juifs de Rouen au moyen age*[8] should fuel debate on the implications for Anglo-Jewish history.

Golb argues vociferously for the promotion of Rouen into one of the major European centres of medieval Jewish culture. His case—which we may note has failed to convince some of the most prominent of French historians of the Jews—rests essentially on two premises. First, he has re-examined many of the place-names in Hebrew MSS of medieval Jewish scholarly works. For the long-accepted readings

[7] J. Le Patourel, *The Norman Empire* (Oxford, 1975). R. W. Southern's trail-blazing 'England's First Entry into Europe', repr. in his *Medieval Humanism and Other Studies* (Oxford, 1970), ch. 8 originated in radio talks at the time of Britain's first abortive negotiations for Common Market membership in the early 1960s.

[8] N. Golb, *Les juifs de Rouen au moyen âge: portrait d'une culture oubliée* (Publications de l'université de Rouen, 66, 1985).

of 'RDWS' (Rodez) and 'DRWS' (Dreux) etc., he substitutes the reading 'RDWM', thereby staking a claim on Rouen's behalf to a large portion of the intellectual riches of medieval rabbinics. In 1976 there emerged from the earth beneath the Palais de Justice, as if divinely designed to support this bold hypothesis, the remains of a substantial Romanesque building on some of whose masonry could be descried graffiti in Hebrew. The site lay within the known bounds of the Jewry, and was identifiable with one described by a late medieval document as a 'schola judeorum'. Golb rejects in this instance the conventional translation of this as synagogue; a large synagogue is known to have existed elsewhere in the Jewry and this structure, he says, contravened contemporary rabbinic regulations for synagogues. It must therefore have been an actual school, the very 'Yeshivah' in which scholars, among them some of the greatest names of medieval rabbinics, taught, studied, and wrote.

Golb's book illustrates excellently the difficulty of this field. The wishful thinking and circular argument are obvious enough even to those as technically unqualified as myself, and are of a kind familiar to all students of the early medieval schools. Yet the cumulative effect is impressive; pending refutation, Rouen must be taken very seriously as a Jewish centre. If so, we can talk no longer merely of an Anglo-Jewry before 1204.[9] We have to deal perhaps with something considerably more involved and much closer to a single Anglo-Norman community, dominated intellectually from Rouen as politically from Westminster or the itinerant royal household, but very open to influences from such eastern neighbours as the Ile-de-France.[10]

The consensus in recent years to contrast the character of life within the Jewry during the first and the second centuries

[9] Cf. Richardson, *English Jewry*, 201: 'if not one community, two communities were closely allied'; also ibid. 110–11.

[10] For all the obvious political links with Anjou and Gascony, southern influences seem less important. It is perhaps appropriate to recall Count Geoffrey's deathbed warning (as reported by an Angevin chronicle) that his son, the future Henry II, should not mix the customs of England and Normandy with those of his other lands. Gascony needs bringing into the story. See Richardson, *English Jewry*, 77, n. 7, 294 for Henry II applying some legislation on Jewish pawns independently to England, Poitou, and Gascony.

of its existence owes much to the late H. G. Richardson, who chose 1210 as his 'turning-point' between a freer era and one of 'declining prosperity and mounting hardship' for the Jews. Royal exploitation was indeed so intense during this year on both sides of the Channel that many Jews are said to have left England and France for 'aliyah' (emigration) to Palestine.[11] It might thus serve as a plausible hinge for the kind of opposition once fashionable between an 'open' twelfth and a 'closed' thirteenth century.

No competent scholar can accept such a judgement without pausing to take note of the quantum leap in the volume of evidence for the successive periods. Peaceful, even friendly co-existence of Jews and gentiles is quite as well documented for thirteenth-century England as intercommunity hostility.[12] Much of what we know on either score comes from royal records that do not exist before 1200. We must clearly be cautious before deducing much about the warmth of the Jews' reception within English society from silence in the sources. The apparent contrast needs testing.

Richardson did somewhat romanticize Jewish life in the twelfth century, quite largely on the thin ground that Jews shared a common language (their second one) with the ruling class. But any hypothesis of cultural overlap must be firmly set into its ideological context, which means here anti-Jewish ideas. It is very much arguable that the Anglo-Norman Jewry experienced anti-Judaism in much the same way and at a comparable pace as its cousins elsewhere on the Continent. One can, no doubt, dispute the reality of seeing the First Crusade as the instant watershed sometimes presented by Jewish historians fixated by events in the Rhineland. One must recognize too that there still remains much we do not understand about the mechanisms by which feeling about Jews fluctuated. But enough evidence exists to permit serious doubts about Richardson's abstraction of Anglo-Norman Jewry from that unbroken process of ideological development during the twelfth and subsequent centuries posited for Western Europe as a whole.

[11] Richardson, *English Jewry*, 167–71.
[12] I made a good deal of this in my earlier paper, 'The Jews as an Immigrant Minority', esp. 273 ff.

The fact is that what holds for north-western Europe as a whole more or less has to apply to Normandy and England too. The incidents at the crusaders' departure from Rouen in 1096 were reported in English chronicles. England's known links to the Rhineland ensure that the horrific events there soon afterwards also left their mark.[13] Neither Jews nor gentiles could easily have ignored any new trends that resulted. Although the dearth of English materials from the early twelfth century makes one wary of speculation, two exceptional creative testimonies to the Jewish presence in East Anglia during the second half of the century establish a prima-facie case for the unexceptional character of English Jewry.

Substantial Jewish settlement in eastern England probably began only under Stephen. Communities at Bungay and Thetford proved particularly impermanent.[14] Norwich, the durable exception,[15] remains notorious in the annals of European Jewry as the location for the first reported Jewish blood libel, which we owe to the pen of the monk Thomas of Monmouth. The most recent study of his work concludes that its 'accusation of cruel murder by the Jews' lacking at this stage any substantial ritual context, was most probably Thomas's own 'historiographical creation'.[16] True as this may be in a certain sense, his originality is not to be exaggerated. The nasty false accusation of cruel murder against Jews at Würzburg in 1147 made in the context of forced baptisms and the like during crusading preparations, followed so soon after the Norwich affair that our accounts (one of them

[13] Roth, *History*, 5–6; cf. L. Poliakov, *The History of Anti-Semitism*, vol. i, trans. R. Howard (London, 1965), ch. 4 and Golb, *Les juifs de Rouen*, 77–91, 101–2, with whose material one might juxtapose the nuanced case made by M. Chibnall, *The World of Orderic Vitalis* (Oxford, 1984), 152–61 for a gentler transition in Normandy before *c.* 1171.

[14] Richardson, *English Jewry*, 13 notes that both were, unusually for England, under the private lordship of Hugh Bigod.

[15] V. D. Lipman, *The Jews of Medieval Norwich* (London, 1967).

[16] G. I. Langmuir, 'Thomas of Monmouth: Detector of ritual Murder', *Speculum*, 59 (1984), 820–46; id., 'Historiographic Crucifixion', *Les juifs au regard de l'histoire: mélanges en l'honneur de Bernhard Blumenkranz*, ed. G. Dahan (Paris, 1985), 109–26 = *Towards a Definition of Antisemitism*, chs. 9 and 12. On the influence of Thomas's *vita*, see further R. Finucane, *Miracles and Pilgrims: Popular Beliefs in Medieval England* (London, 1977), 118–21, 161–2 and B. Ward, *Miracles and the Medieval Mind* (Oxford, 1982), 68–76, 128.

Hebrew) are almost certainly independent of Thomas.[17] Elements of the later synthesis were clearly circulating already before the tragic incidents took place at Norwich. Peter the Venerable was, for example, aware at about this time that some of the rumours concerning a 'rex judeorum' placed him not at Narbonne (as Thomas had done) but at Rouen.[18] Roth's supposition that the fine on London Jews in 1130 for murdering a sick man belongs in some way to the same context thus has some plausibility,[19] and scholarly attention now needs to turn to the role of St William's cult as a stimulus to future allegations. Here certainly is no reason to see English conditions for Jewish settlement as better than elsewhere.

The other artefact, the Cloisters Cross, is more spectacular still, one of the most beautiful and striking objects I have ever seen. The 108 figures, nine complex pictorial scenes and— no less exciting—more than sixty inscriptions carried by this heavily carved cross not two feet high by fourteen inches across may amount to a fully meditated programme of anti-Jewish polemic. A full explication of the many learned allusions, textual and iconographic, when available, will fill important gaps in our understanding of where anti-Judaism fits into the network of positive spirituality and secular culture in twelfth-century England.[20] To demonstrate something of its value, I shall pursue here the unproven as-

[17] See *Annales Herbipolenses*, ed. H. G. Pertz (MGH SS rer. Germ., 16; Hanover, 1859, repr. 1963), 3–4; S. Eidelberg, *The Jews and the Crusades* (Madison, 1977), 127. Langmuir, 'Historiographic Crucifixion', 113–14 notes the absence of any allegation of crucifixion.

[18] Golb, *Les juifs de Rouen*, 130ff.

[19] *Pipe Roll 31 Henry I*, ed. J. Hunter (repr. London, 1929), 149; Roth, *History*, 8–9.

[20] The basic initial publication of the cross, 'The Bury St Edmunds Cross', *Bulletin of the Metropolitan Museum of Art*, n.s. 22 (1964), 316–40 was by T. P. F. Hoving, whose *King of the Confessors* (London, 1981) may be recommended as a rollicking good yarn about the emergence of the cross into the light of scholarly day. Among a growing literature, the following have been particularly stimulating: S. Longland, 'A Literary Aspect of the Bury St Edmunds Cross', *Metropolitan Museum Journal*, 2 (1969), 45–74; E. C. Parker, 'Master Hugo as Sculptor: A Source for the Style of the Bury Bible', *Gesta*, 20 (1981), 99–109 and N. Scarfe, *Suffolk in the Middle Ages* (London, 1986), ch. 7. I hope to examine the cross and its surrounding problems more fully after Professor Parker has published the results of her further art historical researches. [See now E. C. Parker and C. T. Little, *The Cloisters Cross: Its Art and Meaning* (New York, 1994).]

sumption that it originated during the third quarter of the century at the Benedictine monastery of Bury St Edmunds. This would coincide nicely with scenes depicted by the house's famous chronicler, Jocelin of Brakelond, writing only a little later, of Jewish creditors passing freely in and out of the cloister, even inside the abbey church where they might well have seen the cross. That it might have been designed to draw their Jewish sensibilities towards thoughts of conversion, as has been suggested, is not quite inconceivable. But it is more likely to have inflamed Christian minds, all too ready to attribute the abbey's debt problems to the overly free rein allowed to local Jews. Awareness of the supposed martyrdom of St William at Bury is traceable from the 1150s, and surely contributed to a 'copycat' blood libel in 1181.[21] The riot of 1190 in which fifty-seven Jews died, though part of the national wave of pogroms that followed the coronation of the crusader king Richard the Lionheart, nevertheless gained for Abbot Samson the Jews' expulsion from Bury.

Whether or not in the end Bury be adjudged its rightful place of origin, the cross's incandescent combination of breathtaking beauty and poisonous message imposes itself on one in a fashion unmatched by any other object of my personal experience. After meditating before it, one feels much less inclined towards Richardson's benevolent view of twelfth-century England as a home for a Jewry.[22]

I turn now to consider the condition of the Jews under the English monarchy. The most convenient starting-point for study of their early legal status is the well-known text from the *Leges Edwardi Confessoris*, a private treatise of the mid-twelfth century whose French associations may need empha-

[21] Langmuir, 'Historiographic Crucifixion', 113 notes the specific resemblance to 1144.

[22] One promising area for research lies in papal decretals directed to England in the later 12th cent., as many of the surviving examples were. W. Pakter, '*De His Qui Foris Sunt*: The Teaching of the Medieval Canon and Civil Lawyers Concerning the Jews' (Ph. D. thesis, Johns Hopkins University, 1974; University Microfilms, Ann Arbor, 1976) displays the range of material, of which *Decretales Ineditae Saeculi VII*, ed. S. Chodorow and C. Duggan (Monumenta Iuris Canonici, Ser. B, Corpus Collectionum, 4; Vatican, 1982), no. 20 may serve as an example.

sis. Its message of strict subjection to the king tempts one to associate it with ecclesiastical assertions that Jews as Christ-killers ought to serve Christians, and to find in it an antici-pation of such later phenomena as the 'Servi Camerae' under Frederick II. This should probably be resisted. The text represents Jews as so narrowly subjected to the king that he can seek their recovery 'tanquam suum proprium' from those who detained them against him, 'si uult et potest'.[23] The text's message depends on an analogy with ownership, drawn in a way familiar from royal protections and privileges to burgesses and other favoured grantees.[24] A chattel-owner-ship reading of this is an anachronism, even if English legal culture comprehended a clear conception of property in the mid-twelfth century, which some have doubted.[25] Possessives like 'mine', 'his', 'the king's' denote in the first instance relationships not property or possession. We may perhaps best treat this text, and the similar language in the royal charter of 1201, as a strong expression of the rights of profit-able royal lordship against the competition of private lords, in the way Langmuir has taught us to view comparable evi-dence from twelfth-century France.[26]

Human 'assets' can in any case be favoured and protected as well as exploited. Royal charters granted or secured privi-lege to the Jews as a community. The first known of these (though no longer extant) was issued by Henry II probably

[23] F. Liebermann, *Die Gesetze der Angelsachsen*, 3 vols. (Halle, 1903–16), i. 650.

[24] See examples of protections using 'sicut' or 'tanquam' phrases of monks, nuns and their property in *Early Yorkshire Charters*, ed. W. Farrer and C. T. Clay (Edin-burgh and Wakefield, 1914–64), i. 178, 365; ii. 730; iii. 1363, 1462; v. 240; viii. 31 (1138/47), all but the last from the second half of Henry II. The borough privilege cited by Langmuir (n. 26) is also easily matched.

[25] Thus Robert C. Palmer, 'The Origins of Property in England', *Law and History Review*, 3 (1985). He and others, in their concentration on common law doctrine concerning real property, overlook various earlier manifestations of the idea in the context of chattels etc.

[26] G. I. Langmuir, '*Tanquam Servi*: The Change in Jewish Status in French Law about 1200', *Les juifs dans l'histoire de France*, ed. M. Yardeni (Leiden, 1980) [= *Toward a Definition of Antisemitism*, ch. 7], esp. 34–6. After some hesitation, I am persuaded by the stress on a liege lordship which only 'requirat [strengthened in the later recension to 'perquirat'] . . . si uult et potest' Jews detained by others to follow Langmuir's dismissal of 'quia ipsi Iudei et omnia sua regis sunt'. See further the next note and Prof. Patschovsky's different view, which rightly stresses the common Carolingian context behind material from both sides of the Channel, elsewhere in this volume.

quite soon after his accession. It accorded rights of residence and a substantial degree of autonomy to Jews in both England and Normandy. Later royal charters differed only in detail.[27] Comparison of the whole group with similar successive grants made to urban and other favoured communities indicates one noteworthy feature of the Jewry charters. Despite being granted initially to a single leading family, they guaranteed to *all* the Jews in England and Normandy the same kind of rights enjoyed outside the Angevin domains only by privileged groups of Jews.

Such grants of liberties to specially favoured groups and individuals were at their zenith during the twelfth century, though they continued to be sought and received. They were, however, increasingly overtaken as indices of political development by legislation addressed to some or all of the king's 'subjects'. Despite a fair amount of known twelfth-century legislation including the Angevin 'assizes' and the certainty of substantial losses, it remains reasonable to see in Magna Carta the symbol of an important transition from liber*ties* as favours to liberty in a more general sense. Vulnerability to arbitrary treatment was the penalty meted out to social groups who failed to make this transition. Those villagers, for example, who missed their chance to claim new rights at common law, found themselves cut off from their neighbours as 'villeins' condemned by royal law to unfreedom.[28]

The special Angevin arrangements for the administration of the Jewry perhaps ensured in the medium term that Jews suffered a similar depression in standing. This was probably not the original intention, which assumed an *internal* organization of the Jewry for whose functioning there is almost no English evidence apart from some uninformative references to 'chapters of the Jews'. For *external* relations with the king, the leader was an officer nominated by the king but apparently also empowered from within by the Jews themselves. He was entitled 'arch-priest', conceivably from some connection

[27] To the analysis of the royal charters in Richardson, *English Jewry*, 109–10 should now be added Golb, *Les juifs de Rouen*, 135–42.
[28] See on this my *King, Lords and Peasants in Medieval England* (Oxford, 1980), esp. ch. 13.

with the 'chapters' just mentioned. Richardson's suggestion that this most obscure office emerged from a group of internal Jewish arrangements hinted at by French 'surnames' such as 'priest' and 'bishop' would then offer us a tiny glimpse of internal autonomy.[29]

Late in Henry II's reign, at about the time the archpriest emerges into light, the royal Exchequer began habitually to hive off disputes over Jewish revenues and other matters to an institution later known as the 'Exchequer of Jews'. This innovation probably coincided with the Crown's adoption of Jewish taxation among its routine revenue sources. The separate recording and administration of particularly fruitful revenue sources from the main body was a quite normal practice under the Angevins.[30] The Jewish 'chapters', which must presumably be rabbinic tribunals, may be compared to the courts in which burgesses and other privileged groups were entitled to settle their affairs within their own community. Where the Jews were unique was in being assigned a special royal court for external relations, and especially to settle disputes between Jews and Christians.[31] This innovation predated by some years the separation out from the Exchequer of the legal functions of the *curia regis* into the Bench, the origin of the later court of Common Pleas.[32]

[29] Richardson, *English Jewry*, 120–31. One hopes for analogues or other illumination from some Continental (perhaps German) source. On archpriests presiding over *capitula*, see my 'Deans and their Doings: The Norwich Inquiry of 1286', *Proceedings International Congress of Medieval Canon Law, Berkeley 1980* (Monumenta Iuris Canonici, Ser. C., Subsidia, 7; Vatican, 1985), 628 ff.

[30] Richardson, *English Jewry*, 52, 115–20.

[31] Cf. M. T. Clanchy, *From Memory to Written Record* (2nd edn., London, 1990), 71, 307. The jurisdiction of the Jewish Exchequer, though comprehensive, was not exclusive. One can find cases involving Jews on the rolls of other courts, including those of the 'great' exchequer and the court *coram rege* (the king's bench). I have examined the particular value of this material in an unpublished paper, 'The English Statutes of Jewry, 1269–1275'.

[32] B. Kemp, 'Exchequer and Bench in the Later Twelfth Century—Separate or Identical Tribunals?', *English Historical Review*, 88 (1973). Richardson's brief discussion, *English Jewry*, 149–53 does not see legal business as part of the original functions. Richardson, *English Jewry*, 203, and Golb, *Les juifs de Rouen*, 269–70 find little indication of any Norman Exchequer of Jews. See R. Chazan, *Medieval Jewry in Northern France* (Baltimore, 1973), 63–99, and J. Baldwin, *The Government of Philip Augustus* (Berkeley, Los Angeles, 1986), 160, 230 ff. for French administrative practice of the time. [And see now W. C. Jordan, *The French Monarchy and the Jews: From Philip August to the Last Capetians* (Philadelphia, 1989).]

The Jewish Exchequer combined legal with fiscal business in an even more wholehearted way than its parent, the Great Exchequer. It must owe this distinctive feature as much to the timing of its birth as to the more obvious governmental interest in keeping track of potential revenues, which certainly coloured all later activities. From 1194, slightly later than these first special arrangements, the Crown instituted registration of Jewish loans within sealed chests ('archae') in six or seven towns. This archaic, almost Carolingian instrument of market control remained, with some improvements, basic to royal exploitation of the Jews throughout the thirteenth century.

The diversion of the Jewry down this archaic corridor of exploitation goes far to explain the near-impossibility of extracting from the sources the kind of clear statement of Jewish legal status a Continental scholar might expect. Civil rights in anything like a modern sense were hardly an issue before Magna Carta secured to all free men their 'lex terrae'. The kind of 'lex' Jews possessed by their charters was not the same as that enjoyed their gentile neighbours; it clearly did not constitute 'lex terrae'. Until late in Henry III's reign, Jewish condition was special and not too burdensome. Their privileged methods of proof single them out as special. True, they were unable to draw external disputants into their own internal courts, as townsmen did. But they themselves could normally be sued only before the Justices of Jews in the Jewish Exchequer and are found from time to time suing in various normal royal and local courts.[33] They could certainly buy and sell land apparently in much the same commercial manner practised by gentiles, and seem little troubled by the theoretical basis of feudal tenure in 'fidelitas'.[34] They seldom chose to hold in demesne anyway, since like most active dealers in land their priority was liquidity and rents rather than any prestige of tenure. One may assume in general that they were until the 1270s legally free to enter any activity or

[33] One may doubt the assertion of Richardson, *English Jewry*, 112–14 that there were no distinctions between Jews and Christians before the law. They did, of course, share their exemption from the old ordeals and their claim to special mixed juries with other special groups. A Becket supporter had complained in the 1170s of the Church's lack of basic privileges enjoyed by Jews and townsmen.

[34] See, however, below, n. 50 and text.

group from which their religion did not bar them, almost anything in other words, except marriage, religion or (and importantly) membership of urban gilds.[35]

One may easily object here that civil rights are all very well but money is what matters, financial resources not social status. Let me revert therefore briefly to economics, commencing in the twelfth century.

A particular kind of economic argument has dominated recent interpretations of the fifty years preceding Magna Carta. It sees the Angevin monarchy forced by confrontation with its fundamentally richer Capetian rival into attempts at administrative restructuring and increasingly desperate fiscal measures. That is not how the Angevins looked to their neighbours at the time, as John Gillingham has pointed out with some force. The view's proponents have nevertheless persisted in a version of the argument reinforced by convenient economic support, in the shape of a case for a 'great inflation' between 1180 and 1220.[36] This thesis has its problems; my admittedly crude calculations suggest that the year-on-year rate of inflation approximated more closely to West German experience in the 1970s and 1980s than to that of the UK! That, in other words, the actual rate is low enough for us to call upon the economists to spell out the supposed consequences much more carefully than hitherto. The period none the less exhibits indisputable signs of tighter government attitudes towards finance, including some revenue-raising devices singled out for censure in Magna Carta. One Angevin innovation that escaped proscription there was the Jewish tallage.

This tightening of the squeeze came at a bad time for the Jews if inflation was indeed so serious a shock as we are told.[37]

[35] D. Keene, *Survey of Medieval Winchester*, 2 vols. (Winchester Studies, 2; Oxford, 1985), 76–8 explains away the single, known admission of a Jew to a gild merchant.

[36] Compare Southern's 'England's First Entry into Europe' and P. D. A. Harvey, 'The English Inflation of 1180–1220', *Past and Present*, 61 (1973), 3–30 with J. C. Holt, 'The Loss of Normandy and Royal Finances', *War and Government in the Middle Ages: Essays in Honour of J. O. Prestwich*, ed. J. C. Holt and J. Gillingham (Cambridge, 1984), 92–105.

[37] Inflation 'was the influence that began the Jews' financial weakness', Harvey, 'The English Inflation of 1180–1220', 25. Cf. R. B. Dobson, 'The Decline and Expulsion of the Medieval Jews of York', *Transactions of the Jewish Historical Society of England*, 26 (1979), 34–52 at 39.

Jews lost out in two mutually reinforcing ways. Their essential working capital decreased in real terms. Meanwhile, the real interest they received also fell, while at the same time appearing quite as visible and burdensome as ever to those taught that usury was an unmitigated evil, to all, that is, but the most sophisticated borrowers. The non-Jew who understood something of 'real' returns in the money market and consequently felt able to demand hefty discounts on his redemption of Jewish loans that came into their possession was still the exception. If 'professionals' of this kind were on the increase, intensified competition might present further problems. Jews certainly now faced increasing hostility and insecurity, a lower probability of repayment, and pressure on their profit margins, all at the same time.

Analysis of royal exploitation and Jewish finance suggests some kind of thirteenth-century watershed in the Jewish condition. Just when to place this, and whether the shift it produced in the relationship between English Jews and gentiles was in any way irreversible are questions much harder to answer. The case for 1210 now looks rather less compelling than it did to Richardson, and the hunt for a watershed must move on towards 1290.

Professor Robert Stacey has put in his bid for the 1240s and 1250s.[38] Writing from a deep understanding of Henry III's governmental practice and its economic effects, he was able to show that the levels of 'corrosive tallage' in the period from 1241 to 1255 were three times higher than those of the preceding decades, and that they were collected much as they were assessed, apparently in cash rather than bonds as in the past. This made the Jews 'cash poor', desperately short of working liquidity, and heading for 'a kind of spiral of collapse'. It also forced them directly to harass their debtors,

[38] Professor Stacey's paper, '1240–1260: A Watershed in Anglo-Jewish Relations?', *Historical Research*, 61 (1988), 135–50, was presented a mile or so across London to the Anglo-American Conference of Historians on the same day as I read this paper. I am very glad to have been afforded a sight of this in draft and to have been able to exchange preliminary thoughts with him in advance of both meetings. His earlier study, R. C. Stacey, 'Royal Taxation and the Social Structure of Medieval Anglo-Jewry: the Tallages of 1229–1242', *Hebrew Union College Annual*, 66 (1985), 175–249 and his book *Politics, Policy and Finance under Henry III, 1216–1245* (Oxford, 1987) place his arguments on a foundation of solid and original archival research.

on whom the impact may have been almost as serious. Stacey believes that the Justices of Jews were increasingly less prepared to allow debtors time to pay by instalment plans initiated by writs of extent. In this harsher climate, debtors attempted to reconcile their desperate will to retain possession of land with the Jew's need for cash revenue by means of perpetual fee-rents. It was all too easy to represent the resulting relationships as the unnatural and scandalous perpetual servitude of Christians to servile Jews. Accelerating participation by gentile financiers in the market in debt bonds, notably men from the hated group at the royal court, Walter de Merton as well as the queen's Lusignan relatives, also becomes, he feels, ever more noticeable. The new level of royal demands brought about the passing of a generation of dominant Jewish magnates, and no doubt materially also increased tensions within the Jewish communities.[39] Some otherwise unexplained internal disputes, such as the one that led to Edward I's somewhat surprising enforcement of a Jewish *herem* (excommunication) in 1275, must reflect squabbles over the incidence of tallage obligations.[40]

The 1250s saw enough other significant developments for some to proffer the dramatic events of 1255 as 'a genuine divide'.[41] A statute of 1253 was as notable for the key matters it omitted (tallages, the bond market, and the Church's claims to jurisdiction over Jews) as for its concession to a great deal of the Church's anti-Jewish programme.[42] An

---

[39] Stacey, 'Watershed', 141–2. Prof. Stacey would be the first to agree that each of his contentions needs careful consideration within a longer time-scale. They are likely to receive this in his forthcoming book. Among various candidates for magnate status after this period, for example, are Bonamy of York (for whom see Dobson, 'Decline and Expulsion', 45) and Benedict (f. Abraham) of Winchester, hanged for coinage offences 1279 (on whom see Keene, *Survey of Medieval Winchester*, 76–8). The whole 'magnate class' cries out for proper analysis and definition.

[40] See *Select Pleas, Starrs and Other Records from the Rolls of the Exchequer of Jews*, ed. J. M. Rigg (Selden Soc., 15, 1901), 87–8 and F. D. Logan, 'Thirteen London Jews and Conversion to Christianity: Problems of Apostasy in the 1280s', *Historical Research*, 45 (1972), 224 for the 1275 episode, which I still hope to discuss more fully on another occasion.

[41] Dobson, 'Decline and Expulsion', 36. Cf. G. I. Langmuir, 'The Knight's Tale of Young Hugh of Lincoln', *Speculum*, 47 (1973), 459–82 = *Toward a Definition of Antisemitism*, ch. 10; Stacey, 'Watershed', 142, 147–8.

[42] Richardson, *English Jewry*, 293 ff.; cf. ibid. 177 for a warning about lost legislation. I note the later emergence of missing topics in my unpublished paper on 'The English Statutes of Jewry, 1269–1275'. Logan, 'Thirteen London Jews', 225–6

alleged gold glut may by lowering the real price of gold have wreaked further havoc on Jewish financial strength through their preference for storing capital in the form of gold.[43] Possibly there was even some restatement of an ideology of Jewish malice in such a way as to encourage anti-Jewish action.[44]

The upshot was that reform of the Jewry became 'one of the desiderata' of the reforming party in the coup of 1258. The basic link doubtless derived from indebtedness, less I suspect from some supposed 'crisis in the knightly classes'[45] than through the manifest links with a hated and corrupt court group.[46] The way that the period of Montfortian ascendancy in 1263–4 released the royal brakes on popular anti-Jewish violence is well known.

The more interesting question is, however, why Jewish recovery and reconstruction was so restricted during the inevitable royalist reaction after 1267.[47] The issues raised by the reformers of 1258 did not all disappear. The information gathered by the special general eyre inquiries in the following years remained in some measure available to influence reconstruction after the political disturbances and very probably also the form of Edward I's further inquiries after 1274. Many even of the solutions of 1259 and later resurfaced in 1267 with the Statute of Marlborough.

Examination of the might-have-beens of the decade between, say, 1267 and Edward I's successful Welsh campaign, counsels a cautious attitude towards the claims for a water-

instances some Christian excommunications of Jews which royal officials were expected to enforce.

[43] Stacey, 'Watershed', 140 based on the interesting speculations of D. Carpenter, 'The Gold Treasure of Henry III', *Thirteenth Century England*, i, ed. P. R. Coss and S. D. Lloyd (Woodbridge, 1986), 77–82.

[44] So Stacey, 'Watershed', 148–50 based entirely on a survey of Matthew Paris. There is need for a full study of Paris in a wider ideological context. See e.g., J. B. Russell, *Lucifer: the Devil in the Middle Ages* (Ithaca, NY, 1984), 192 ff.

[45] D. Carpenter, 'Was there a Crisis of the Knightly Class in the Thirteenth Century? The Oxfordshire Evidence', *English Historical Review*, 95 (1980), 721–52 found the case unproven.

[46] Stacey, 'Watershed', 142–4, 147.

[47] C. H. Knowles, 'The Resettlement of England after the Barons' War 1264–7', *Transactions of the Royal Historical Society*, 5th ser. 32 (1982) has unfortunately nothing to say on the matter. [J. R. Maddicott, 'Edward I and the Lessons of Baronial Reform, 1258–80', *Thirteenth Century England*, i (1986), 1–30, esp. 5, 17–18, is a little more forthcoming.]

shed in the previous decades. Nothing that had happened to the Jewry by 1267 seems really irreversible. The special administrative arrangements which governed Jewry retained their positive value to Jewish autonomy into the 1260s but little further.[48] Demand among the gentry for Jewish capital seems also to have survived the political disturbances for a while. Jewish urban property remained more or less intact as the economic sheet-anchor it had always been until the 1270s. It remains an open question whether native Christian moneylending competitors emerged in substantial numbers from the urban patriciate and elsewhere before the last twenty years or so of the settlement.[49] The key withdrawal of royal support for everyday Jewish activities came through successive legislative enactments on the Jewry in the years between 1269 and 1275. One might also claim a certain watershed status for the adverse consequences of this shift from charters of liberties to general legislation.

The 1271 statute ending the Jews' right to hold land in fee should be read, for example, as a powerful symbol of exclusion from full civil rights as I have described them.[50] Even more symbolically, the 1275 Statute of Jewry terminated the

[48] A telling indication of this comes from the Jewish Exchequer, where the arch-presbyter had apparently kept his own counter-roll into the 1240s (*Close Rolls, 1234–1237*, 408; *1242–1247*, 51), possibly in Hebrew, like documented royal rolls of the 1250s and before (*Close Rolls, 1251–1253*, 164, 271; *The Cartulary of Boxgrove Priory*, ed. L. Fleming, Sussex Record Soc., 59, 1960, 44). There are no similar references after 1259. I owe this information and a great deal else to Dr Paul Brand and his two unpublished drafts on the Exchequer of Jews, 1265–1290, covering its personnel and its function and place within the machinery of government.

[49] These examples all come from Dobson, 'Decline and Expulsion', 39–43. The last question, of Christian financial competition is a crucial one. Richardson, Stacey, and others each raise the spectre of a significant Christian alternative to Jewish finance at different periods of the settlement. The decision between their largely impressionistic judgements should make a major impact on general English economic history, a field whose literature has yet to integrate the Jewish material to any substantial effect. Comparable studies of Jews in other town communities would also help, if as well done as Dobson's. Keene, *Survey of Medieval Winchester*, 324, 384–7 displays some of the potential.

[50] But how much more than a symbol? I am struck by the extreme rarity of grants *in fee* by Jews before 1271. *A Cartulary of the Hospital of St John the Baptist*, ii, ed. H. E. Salter (Oxford Historical Soc., 68, 1915), nos. 524–6 document a 1262–3 house sale 'in perpetuum' to a Jew, who passed it on to the hospital *c.* 1270; the group contains no grant *from* the Jew. One begins to wonder if the enactment might not have been basically declaratory. I survey the legislative group briefly in my unpublished paper.

Jews' licence to take open interest on loans, and made the underlying message quite explicit by exhorting Jews (just conceivably from sincere bigotry) to live in future from honest labour and commerce. Alongside were a whole group of anti-Jewish measures (such as the wearing of a Jewish badge) long pressed by the Church but not previously afforded secular enforcement.

Though no novelty in themselves, the measures constituted a direct threat to the Jews' livelihood.[51] The real question at the time must have been to know how far and on what terms the king intended to enforce them. The Jewish community's petition against the 1275 statute and its reception by deaf ears are good indicators of contemporary attitudes. There remained, as always with medieval legislation, the possibility of purchasing individual dispensations. Some are indeed known, but far too few to counter the impression of some genuine royal will behind the 1275 statute. Edward had never appeared very keen on the reconstruction of the Jewry. And what were in the last years of his father's reign decisions he was relatively free to make either way[52] later looked more nearly mandatory to an ex-crusader as his political options narrowed. The squeeze on Jewish financial activity progressively eliminated any hope of their economic revival. Here the 1278–9 coining prosecutions look potentially pivotal.[53] Meanwhile, anti-Judaism, now under royal patronage, ruled out any idea of reversion to the policy ways of Henry III by raising the political price out of sight. The ban on Jewish usury and the coming-together of popular anti-Jewish feeling with Edward I's personal inclinations and self-interest both date from the 1270s. The changed set-up looks increasingly irreversible.

By the 1280s the preconditions of survival no longer existed for a substantial Jewish community like that of the halcyon days. The revived consideration of Expulsion in 1290 should have come as no great surprise to Jews or gentiles. Yet even now Edward retained some room for

[51] Richardson, *English Jewry*, 178, 186, 190–1 chronicles earlier efforts.
[52] Keene, *Survey of Medieval Winchester*, 76–8 may be read to suggest that it took a 1273–4 coup within the urban patriciate to depress the Jews' fate there.
[53] Richardson, *English Jewry*, 217–25.

manœuvre. He might still have chosen to retain a small group of financial experts.[54] Thus the short-term events of 1290 themselves form the final watershed.

This survey of the relationship between the Jewry and the gentile majority under the English Crown, over the two centuries of Jewish settlement in medieval England, has developed into a study of periodization, the different ways in which one might divide up that history. The exercise has led me to question simple contrasts between the twelfth and thirteenth centuries, and to highlight continuing elements of archaism in a period, unified by the ideology of the majority Christian community. Interpretations of the essential developments in the relationship between this majority community and its Jews will differ, most specifically as to whether one should treat the sporadic but recurrent outbreaks of violence as symptoms of or stimuli to the underlying secular trends. Only a fully nuanced narrative history of the Jewry will enable one to surpass the bewildering vista of 'possible turning-points at which no turn was made'.[55] My own expectation here leans towards a punctuationist view rather than one of unidirectional cumulative evolution.[56] Richardson's periodization appears most plausible from the standpoint of power, of the king, and his government. Before Henry II's reign, questions about the Crown's relationship with the Jewry hardly arose. The Anglo-Norman Jewry was small in both scale and impact this side of the Channel. Assistance with the Crown's financial needs, first through loans then taxation, was the fatal cement that bound the parties together. Because of this as much as anything else, the Jewry failed to pass from twelfth century privilege into the freedom of thirteenth-century permanence.

[54] Cf. Dobson, 'Decline and Expulsion', 46. The accounts of Richardson, *English Jewry*, 213–33 and M. Prestwich, *Edward I* (London, 1988), 343–6 show that full integration of the Expulsion into the Edwardian historiographical mainstream remains a challenge. This coming synthesis will need to take into account the data offered by P. Binski, *The Painted Chamber at Westminster* (The Society of Antiquaries of London. Occasional Papers, new series, ix, London, 1986), ch. 3.

[55] Dobson, 'Decline and Expulsion', 36.

[56] I take the helpful biological images from Stephen Jay Gould, *The Panda's Thumb* (New York, 1980) and Richard Dawkins, *The Blind Watchmaker* (Oxford, 1986).

8

The Relationship between the Jews of Germany and the King (11th–14th centuries). A European Comparison

ALEXANDER PATSCHOVSKY

I

On 5 February 1343, Emperor Louis the Bavarian released Count John of Nuremberg from all debts he owed to Jewish creditors. To the Jews who were deprived of their property he gave as legal justification: 'because your body and your property belong to us and our realm, and we can do with you and it whatever we like.'[1] This event reveals that (i) the Jews were serfs (*Leibeigene*); (ii) the Jews were serfs of the king/emperor; and (iii) the emperor made brutal use of his 'right'. This had not always been the case, but it character-ized the final stage in the long history of relations between the German king and the Jews in his realm.

'Final stage' here refers to the judicial nature of this rela-tionship; it does not mean that things could not get worse. Louis the Bavarian merely defrauded the Nuremberg count's creditors, thus threatening their livelihood. But in at least one case, that of Nuremberg, Louis's successor, Charles

[1] *Monumenta Zolleriana*, iii, ed. R. von Stillfried and T. Märcker (Berlin, 1857), no. 110. The footnotes in the English version of this essay have been kept to a minimum. Nothing has been changed since 1993. A detailed discussion of the various problems touched upon here can be found in the expanded German version published as 'Das Rechtsverhältnis der Juden zum deutschen König (9.–14. Jahrhundert). Ein europäischer Vergleich', *Zeitschrift der Savigny-Stiftung für Rechtsgeschichte, Germanistische Abteilung*, 110 (1993), 331–71. I should like to thank all who discussed with me the many questions which this essay raises, and especially those who offered linguistic advice, namely Timothy Reuter, Christoph Cluse, Angela Davies, Steve Lake, and Caroline Mähl.

IV, agreed to the destruction of a whole Jewish community during the persecutions at the time of the Great Plague in 1349.[2] This, of course, created a new quality in relations between the German Jews and the king, and also between the Jews and all governmental powers beneath the king, namely the barons and the political representatives of the cities and towns, who were *de facto* responsible for the safety of the Jews living under their dominion, and had nothing better to do than to kill 'their' Jews with or without legal procedures, with or without the king's consent.[3] But the persecution at the time of the Great Plague was only in a factual sense the *ne plus ultra* of relations between Jews and the king, who was their supreme worldly authority. In principle, the legal argument quoted above omits nothing which might lower the status of the Jews. They were serfs, subject to the will of the king, their master—and he made use of his 'right'.

From the endpoint of this development we shall move back to its beginning in Carolingian times, when the sources allow us to distinguish between three groups of Jews:[4]

1. Non-privileged merchants living outside, but trading inside, the Carolingian Empire. Such merchants appear in the customs regulations of Raffelstetten dating from *c.*903–

---

[2] Basic for the Nuremberg events is W. von Stromer, 'Die Metropole im Aufstand gegen König Karl IV.', *Mitteilungen des Vereins für die Geschichte der Stadt Nürnberg*, 65 (1978), 55–90; see also A. Haverkamp, 'Die Judenverfolgungen zur Zeit des Schwarzen Todes im Gesellschaftsgefüge deutscher Städte', *Zur Geschichte der Juden im Deutschland des späten Mittelalters und der frühen Neuzeit*, ed. A. Haverkamp (Monographien zur Geschichte des Mittelalters, 24; Stuttgart, 1981), 71 ff., 87 ff., and F. Graus, *Pest—Geißler—Judenmorde: Das 14. Jahrhundert als Krisenzeit* (Veröffentlichungen des Max Planck-Instituts für Geschichte, 86; Göttingen, 1987), 208 ff.

[3] The fact that the governmental authorities themselves (and not any *misera plebs*) were responsible for the killings was stressed by Graus, *Pest—Geißler—Judenmorde*, esp. 215 ff.

[4] The following discussion is largely based on B. Blumenkranz, *Juifs et chrétiens dans le monde occidental, 430–1096* (Paris and La Haye, 1960), esp. 13 ff., 295 ff. The authoritative work on the legal status of the Jews is still G. Kisch, *Forschungen zur Rechts- und Sozialgeschichte der Juden in Deutschland während des Mittelalters nebst Bibliographien*, 2nd edn. (Ausgewählte Schriften, 1; Sigmaringen, 1978). The more I disagree, in certain respects, with him, the more I should like to emphasize my debt to him.

6.[5] Further examples are the learned Jewish geographer, Ibrahim ibn Jaqub, resident in Muslim Spain, whose travel journal dates from around 965,[6] and the Persian geographer Ibn Khordadbeh, whose famous Radanites date from about one century earlier.[7] These merchants travelled over wide distances between Baghdad and Aix-la-Chapelle, between Cordoba and the realm of the Chazars on the Caspian Sea, and even much further, to India and China. Their main occupation was conveying precious merchandise, especially slaves, between the Islamic Orient and the Christian Occident. These merchants had to pay duties at Frankish customs stations, but they enjoyed the protection which Carolingian rulers could grant to foreign merchants. There was no closer relationship than that between these itinerant Jewish merchants and the Carolingian kings.

2. The second group was that of the privileged merchants, regardless of whether they lived inside or outside the Carolingian Empire. As soon as they were granted a privilege by the Frankish king, a special relationship was established. The Jews asked for and received a number of favours facilitating their business and making it (at least legally) more secure.[8] These included exemption from customs duties and other fiscal obligations; full power of disposition over their property; guaranteed ownership of non-baptized slaves and the right to employ Christian servants; the right to live ac-

[5] MGH Capit. ii, no. 253 §9: 'Mercatores, id est Iudei et ceteri mercatores, undecunque venerint de ista patria vel de aliis patriis, iustum theloneum solvant tam de mancipiis, quam de aliis rebus, sicut semper in prioribus temporibus regum fuit.'

[6] The most recent edn. is by T. Kowalski, *Relatio Ibrahim ibn Ja'kub de itinere Slavico, quae traditur apud al-Bekri* (Monumenta Poloniae Historica, n.s. 1; Cracow, 1946); on Jewish merchants whom Ibrahim met on his journey, ibid. 146. Cf. E. Ashtor, *The Jews of Muslim Spain*, i (Philadelphia, 1973), 344 ff., esp. 349.

[7] *Kitâb al-masâlik wa'l-mamâlik (Liber viarum et regnorum) auctore Abu'l-Kâsim Obaidallah ibn Abdallah ibn Khordâdhbeh*, ed. M. J. de Goeje (Bibliotheca geographorum Arabicorum, 6; Leiden, 1889), 153–4 (Arab.), 114–15 (French trans.). For date and author see T. Lewicki, 'Les commerçants juifs dans l'Orient islamique non méditerranéen au IX[c]–XI[c] siècles', *Gli ebrei nell'alto medioevo: 30 marzo–5 aprile 1978* (Settimane di studio del Centro italiano di studi sull'alto medioevo, 26; Spoleto, 1980), 375–99, here 381 ff. with n. 27.

[8] The main source material is several privileges of Emperor Louis the Pious, transmitted to us as formularies, ed. K. Zeumer, MGH Formulae (1886), nos. 30, 31, 52; cf. Kisch, *Forschungen*, 47 ff.

cording to their religious law; the right to appeal to the king's court whose representative at the local level, the count, was the only judicial official to handle lawsuits between Jews and Christians; and favourable regulations concerning testimonies (in essence, equality between Jews and Christians). The king also defended these Jews (*tuitio, mundeburdium*). They were thus protected against many threats, but at the same time they became dependent on the king (a relation which will be dealt with later). This dependency can be seen in the fact that the penalty for killing a Jew under the protection of the king (10 pounds of gold) was to be paid to the royal chamber, not to the family of the killed person.[9] The service owed to the king by such privileged persons is not quite clearly defined as service to the royal chamber, as other merchants rendered it.[10] This service is assumed to be something like purveying merchandise from abroad to the royal household;[11] but it could also have involved making regular payments to the royal chamber, comparable with a tax as we know it from later times. The fact that Emperor Otto II left the city of Merseburg with all its appurtenances—including tolls, merchants, and Jews—to Archbishop Gisiler of Magdeburg in 974,[12] suggests that by that date at the latest, the Jews could be expected to provide regular fiscal income.

3. The third group of Jews was, numerically, the largest. This group lived within the Frankish realm, but was not privileged. Its members were found mainly (but not exclusively) in the large Jewish communities of southern France and the valley of the Rhone, where Jews had lived uninterruptedly since the days of the Roman Empire.[13] Given the

[9] MGH Formulae no. 30, 310.

[10] MGH Formulae no. 31, 310 lines 17–18: 'liceat eis sub mundeburdo et defensione nostra quiete vivere et partibus palatii nostri fideliter deservire'. Cf. the so-called *Praeceptum negotiatorum*, ibid. no. 37, 315 lines 3 ff.: 'ad nostrum veniant palatium, atque ad cameram nostram fideliter unusquisque ex suo negocio ac nostro deservire studeat ... sed liceat eis, sicut Iudeis [*read*: diximus; Kisch, *Forschungen*, 49, n. 20], partibus palatii nostri fideliter deservire.'

[11] Kisch, *Forschungen*, 51.

[12] Thietmar of Merseburg, *Chronicon*, Bk. iii, 1 and Bk. iv, 16, MGH SS n.s. ix, 98–9, 294–5.

[13] Blumenkranz, *Juifs et chrétiens*, 22 ff.; B. Blumenkranz, 'Les premières implantations de Juifs en France: du Ier au début du Ve s.', *Comptes rendues de l'Académie des*

personal principle of early medieval law, it is difficult to say
what law they lived under, and the sources do not provide an
explicit answer. It can be assumed that—apart from matters
of religious law—they lived according to Roman vulgar law,[14]
that is, according to the law of the Roman Christian population as in the period of the early Germanic kingdoms. No
special relationship between the king and this main group of
the Jewish population in the Frankish realm is discernible;
nor is it likely to have existed.

To sum up: in the Frankish realm there was a small group
of Jews, limited to a few individuals known by name, who had
acquired by privilege a special relationship with the king.
Neither this small group nor the majority of Jews (not to
mention the itinerant merchants from abroad) had the
status of serfs in the Frankish Empire. This can be demonstrated despite the meagreness of the sources at our disposal.
The Carolingian privileges for Jews from the time of Louis
the Pious excluded Jews both from the ordeal—the test typically used for serfs in judicial cases—and from the punishment of whipping, which was unthinkable for free men.[15]
Similarly, a capitulary promulgated by Charles the Bald
(Pîtres 864) forbidding the alloying of gold and silver contains penalties differentiating between free men, serfs, and
Jews. Free men were to pay the king's ban (60s.), serfs
(*colonus vel servus*) were to be whipped, and Jews were to pay
the same penalty as free men.[16]

II

This may serve to set the scene and introduce the question
which this chapter addresses. How and why did the free and
highly respected Jews of Carolingian times, who enjoyed the
king's legal protection as a precious favour, become 'serfs

Inscriptions et Belles-Lettres (1969), 162–74; Blumenkranz, *Histoire des Juifs en France*
(Toulouse, 1972), 14 ff. See also R. Chazan, *Mediaeval Jewry in Northern France: A
Political and Social History* (Baltimore and London, 1973), 10 ff.

[14] Kisch, *Forschungen*, 52; Blumenkranz, *Juifs et chrétiens*, 299 ff., 353–4.

[15] MGH Formulae nos. 30, 31, p. 310, lines 3 ff., 34–5. Cf. Kisch, *Forschungen*, 54–
5; Blumenkranz, *Juifs et chrétiens*, 360 ff.

[16] MGH Capit. ii no. 273 c. 23.

of the royal chamber' by the later Middle Ages, unfree and without rights? (This is denying that the arbitrariness of kings such as Louis the Bavarian or Charles IV was compatible with anything that could be called a 'right'.)

In principle, this is a problem in all the empires which followed the Carolingian Empire: France, Norman England, and Germany, as I shall call the main territory of the Roman Empire ruled by the king or emperor from one of the many dynasties which, in the course of history, succeeded to the throne. We will not be able to avoid crossing the borders between individual European countries, but this chapter will concentrate mainly on Germany and relations between the German king and the German Jews. This limitation is justified, as developments in Germany were broadly similar and yet quite different from those in neighbouring countries.

During the Saxon and Salian dynasties, significant information about relations between the Jews and the king starts with Emperor Henry IV. I refer to the well-known privileges granted to the Jews of Worms and Speyer (1090), and presumably—the privilege is known only as a *deperditum*—to the Jews of Regensburg.[17] In meaning and content, these privileges are almost identical with their Carolingian predecessors. They differ only on matters of detail. For example, the much disputed Jewish 'fencing-right' (*Hehlerrecht*)[18] appears for the first time in the Henrician *diplomata*. This is the legal principle that if stolen goods are bought in good faith from a thief, the real owner must reimburse the buyer in order to recover his property. (Nowadays the credulous buyer would be the loser.) The emperor also felt obliged to protect the Jews from forced conversions, for example, by fixing a compulsory delay of three days between a neophyte's decision to convert and his baptism. This was intended to ensure that the wish to convert had been arrived at freely.[19] The emperor also gave a warning that those who left the law of their fathers

---

[17] MGH DD H.IV. nos. 411 (Speyer, 19 Feb. 1090), 412 (Worms, deperditum), 509 (Regensburg, deperditum, presumably 1097); for textual tradition etc. see A. Gawlik, ibid., xliv–xlv, 742–3 and 697–8. See also Kisch, *Forschungen*, 52 ff.

[18] See Kisch, *Forschungen*, 107 ff.

[19] MGH D. H.IV. no. 411, 546–7: 'Si autem aliqui eorum sponte baptizari velint, triduo reserventur, ut integre cognoscatur, si vere christiane religionis causa aut aliqua illata iniuria legem suam abnegent.'

lost the right to inherit from their fathers, in other words, those who converted to Christianity should be aware that they would incur financial disadvantages.[20] This is a remarkable statement for the official *defensor Christianae fidei* to have made! It is well known that it was not merely rhetorical. In 1096, shortly after Henry had granted his privileges, the pogroms of the First Crusade destroyed many Jewish communities in Germany, and the emperor allowed the Jews who had avoided death by forced conversion to return to the faith of their fathers.[21] According to canon law this was a questionable decision. None other than the emperor's 'own' pope, Clement III, criticized it severely.[22]

It is possible that both the 'fencing-right' and the protection against forced conversion reflected recent developments in relations between Jews and Christians. In substance, however, Henry's privileges were an almost perfect continuation of the Carolingian tradition. These privileges were the right of individual groups which could be precisely defined in terms of composition and location.[23] It is almost certain that the privileges for Worms, Speyer, and Regensburg were only a small part of what was once issued for Jewish communities. None the less, the mere fact that Henry IV appeared to be the first German emperor to grant privileges to certain Jewish communities in his empire suggests that before,

[20] Ibid.: 'et sicut patrum legem reliquerunt, ita eciam et possessionem eorum.' MGH D. H.IV no. 412, 549 (= MGH D. F.I. no. 166, 285): 'et sicut legem patrum suorum relinquerunt, ita eciam relinquant hereditatem.'

[21] Evidence exists that this happened in Regensburg 1097: Frutolf of Michelsberg, *Chronica*, in *Frutolfs und Ekkehards Chroniken und die anonyme Kaiserchronik*, ed. F.-J. Schmale and I. Schmale-Ott (Ausgewählte Quellen zur deutschen Geschichte des Mittelalters, 15; Darmstadt, 1972), 108: 'Heinricus imperator ab Italia rediens Ratisponam, Baioarie urbem venit ibique aliquamdiu moratus Iudeis, qui baptizari coacti sunt, legibus suis uti, ut fertur, concessit.' The text was adapted by Ekkehard of Aura (ibid. 126: 'iudaizandi ritum concessit') and the Annalista Saxo, MGH SS vi, 730; Kisch, *Forschungen*, 57.

[22] P. Jaffé, *Regesta pontificum Romanorum*, 2 vols., 2nd edn. (Leipzig, 1885–88), no. 5336. The text is reproduced in: Codex Udalrici no. 90, ed. Ph. Jaffé, *Monumenta Bambergensia* (Bibliotheca rerum Germanicarum, 5; Berlin, 1969), 175; see J. Ziese, *Wibert von Ravenna: Der Gegenpapst Clemens III. (1084–1100)* (Päpste und Papsttum, 20; Stuttgart, 1982), 241.

[23] The privileges of Emperor Henry IV were formally received by individuals, who seem to have represented all Jews in their area. This can be concluded from the fact that the Speyer privilege was petitioned not only by three people known by name, but also by their *sodales*, MGH D. H.IV. no. 411, 546. See also Kisch, *Forschungen*, 53.

during, and after Henry's reign there were communities who
enjoyed no royal privileges whatsoever, and who consequently had no special relationship with the king. It is difficult to establish what law these non-privileged Jews lived
under. In contrast to the situation in southern France during
the Carolingian period, we must assume that on the right
bank of the Rhine and even in Lorraine there were no Jewish
communities within a Celtic-Roman population, or at least
none which had existed continuously from the late Roman
period. It seems that since the ninth and tenth centuries
Jewish merchants and their families had gradually settled as
merchants in the main centres of trade.[24] It is not quite clear
which law within the ordinary law these Jews lived by. We may
assume that they lived under the same law as ordinary merchants, perhaps slightly modified to make it suitable for their
different religion.

Another much praised action by Henry IV points in this
direction. In 1103 he included all the Jews in his realm,
together with churches, clerics, monks, women in danger of
rape, *and merchants* as defenceless institutions or persons, in
the first common *treuga dei (Landfriede)* guaranteed by the
German king.[25] It is significant that before 1100 the terms
'Jew' and 'merchants' were used almost synonymously in
German sources.[26] We can therefore be sure that until that
time the legal status of the two groups was completely
identical, apart from the differences caused by religious
prescriptions.

In other words, until the end of Emperor Henry IV's reign,
the Jews of Germany lived as they had done in Carolingian
times. They were highly esteemed, and a certain number
of them enjoyed the king's special protection. In both
cases they were free, that is, neither bond men, serfs, nor
slaves.

[24] Cf. e.g. I. Elbogen in the introduction to *Germania Iudaica*, i, 2nd edn.
(Tübingen, 1963), xviii–xix.
[25] MGH Const. i, no. 74, 125: 'iuraverunt [*sc.* filius regis et primates totius regni],
dico, pacem aecclesiis, clericis, monachis, laicis: mercatoribus, mulieribus ne vi
rapiantur, Iudeis.' Cf. Kisch, *Forschungen*, 56 ff.
[26] Cf. Kisch, *Forschungen*, 54. Sources: MGH D. O.I. no. 300 (9 July 965) and
MGH D. O.II. no. 198 (979), both for Magdeburg; see also the text by Thietmar
quoted above, n. 12, for Merseburg.

III

One century later, the situation had completely changed. In July 1236, Emperor Frederick II granted his famous privilege to all Jews of Germany, extending the special privilege given by his grandfather Frederick Barbarossa to the Jews of Worms to apply to all the Jews in the German Empire.[27] In this privilege, however, which the Jews had requested and which the emperor had granted to please them, the ominous term 'Jewish chamber-serfdom' crops up for the first time. As if it were nothing special at all but legally quite self-evident, the emperor spoke of the German Jews as *servi nostri, servi camere nostre, ad cameram nostram immediate spectantes*. At much the same time, in a letter to Pope Gregory IX, Frederick stressed the direct nature of the relationship between himself and the Jews in the Roman Empire and in his Sicilian realm.[28] In a privilege granted to the Jews of Vienna in 1238, he referred to them, in the same self-evident manner, as *servi camere nostre*.[29] In 1237, when Frederick gave his city charter to Vienna, which *inter alia* in the tradition of Roman and canon law prohibited Jews from exercising rights of government over Christians, he justified the concept of the *servitus Iudaeorum* by pointing out that it was based on an imperial decision made in ancient times as a punishment for the classical 'Jewish crime', the murder of Christ.[30]

---

[27] MGH Const. ii, no. 204.

[28] J. F. Boehmer, *Fontes rerum Germanicarum*, 4 vols. (Stuttgart, 1843–86), no. 2197 of 20 Sept. 1236. Text: *Historia diplomatica Friderici Secundi*, ed. J. L. A. Huillard-Bréholles, iv, pt. 2 (Paris, 1855), 912: 'Iudaeos autem, etsi tam in imperio quam in regno nobis communi iure immediate subiaceant, a nulla tamen ecclesia illos abstulimus que super eis ius speciale pretenderet, quod communi iuri nostro merito preferretur.'

[29] Text in: *Die Rechtsquellen der Stadt Wien*, ed. P. Csendes (Fontes rerum Austricarum, 3. Abt. 9; Wien, 1986), no. 7, 47: 'notum fieri volumus universis, quod nos Iudeos Wienne, servos camere nostre, sub nostra et imperiali proteccione recipimus et favore.'

[30] Cf. P. Csendes, 'Die Stadtrechtsprivilegien Kaiser Friedrichs II. für Wien', *Deutsches Archiv für Erforschung des Mittelalters*, 43 (1987), 110–34, here 129–30, §3: 'Ad hec katholici principis potestates [*variant*: partes] fideliter exequentes ab officiorum prefectura Iudeos excipimus, ne sub pretextu prefecture opprimant Christianos, cum imperialis auctoritas a priscis temporibus ad perpetrati Iudaici sceleris ulcionem eisdem Iudeis indixerit [perpetuam, *missed in the main MS*] servitutem.'

Guido Kisch has traced this concept, which politically and legally goes back to Innocent III, who first transferred the notion of Jews as the serfs of Christendom from the realm of theology to secular policy.[31] The imperial decision of ancient times which Frederick was quoting, however, is no more than a literary reminiscence. The *Vindicta Salvatoris*, which form part of the apocryphal literature, relate that both Pilate and the Jews were appropriately punished for their misdeeds. Pilate was sentenced to death and the Jews were punished by Vespasianus and Titus. Some were killed, while others were sold as slaves—thirty Jews for a penny, according to some versions of the *Vindicta Salvatoris*, in a clear reference to the 'Jewish crime'.[32]

In the section of his *Sachsenspiegel* dealing with the common law (*Landrecht*), Eike of Repgow found a conciliatory end to the story, which at the same time reflected the legal reality of his days. According to the tradition of the *Vindicta Salvatoris*, the Jews sold as slaves on the free market by Vespasianus and Titus had not yet managed to become protégés of the emperor. Yet Frederick II decided to act as protector of the Jews legitimized by imperial tradition, and it was this state of things which Eike of Repgow noted as the legal reality of his days. How could the difficulty be resolved? 'The Jews are part of the king's peace,' said Eike. (He meant not the common peace, but the special peace which the Jews had acquired by royal privilege.)[33] The Jewish historian Flavius Josephus had asked for this peace from Titus who granted it because Flavius Josephus had healed him from the gout.[34] This is a nice story (especially for historians, to whom

[31] Kisch, *Forschungen*, 62 ff.

[32] Cf. L. Weiland, 'Niederdeutsche Pilatuslegende', *Zeitschrift für deutsches Altertum und deutsche Literatur*, 17 (1874), 147–60, esp. 154–7. A. Linder (Jerusalem) is preparing a comprehensive study on this subject.

[33] For the peace of the king as common peace of the country, cf. Kisch, *Forschungen*, 16 ff. But Eike is speaking of the special peace granted by privilege to specified people under the king's protection; cf. E. Kaufmann, 'Königsfrieden', *Handwörterbuch zur deutschen Rechtsgeschichte*, ii (1978), 1032.

[34] Eike von Repgow, *Sachsenspiegel Landrecht*, ed. K. A. Eckhardt, 2nd edn. (MGH Fontes iuris, n.s. 1, pt. 1; 1955), iii 7 §3: 'Sleit ok de kerstene man enen joden, men richtet over ene dorch des koninges vrede, den he an eme gebroken hevet, oder dut he en ungerichte an eme. Dissen vrede <den> irwarf ene Josaphus weder den koning Vaspasianum, do he sinem sonen Titus gesunt makede van der icht.' Cf. Kisch, *Forschungen*, 72 ff.

miracles are not often attributed) but, like Frederick's justification for the *servus Iudaeorum*, it is merely an attempt to
justify *ex post facto* a state of affairs which had long been
well known, but was none the less felt to need special
explanation.

The state of affairs regarded as quite normal in Frederick
II's time was that Jews were *servi*, that is, serfs, without exception. As such they were under the immediate dominion of
the king/emperor, and thus under his protection. In the
wide field of royal/imperial power, they were attached to
one financial institution in particular—to the chamber.

IV

Neither Frederick himself nor his immediate successors
seem to have drawn any far-reaching conclusions from this
concept of royal/imperial chamber-serfdom.[35] Rudolf of
Habsburg was the first German king to transform the merely
theoretical legal principle of Jewish chamber-serfdom into
an instrument of real menace to the Jews of his realm. When
a large number of the Jews of Germany (including the most
famous rabbinical authority of his time, Rabbi Meïr of
Rothenburg) left for Palestine in 1286, full of messianic
hopes, King Rudolf put them into prison and confiscated
their property.[36] His justification was that they had tried to
leave his realm without his permission. As serfs of his chamber, over whose person and property he, as king, had a
special right, they were not permitted to do this.[37] Only now

---

[35] At least, no documents which suggest this have been found.

[36] The facts are dealt with in detail by I. A. Agus, *Rabbi Meir of Rothenburg: His Life
and his Works as Sources for the Religious, Legal, and Social History of the Jews of Germany
in the Thirteenth Century*, 2 vols (Philadelphia, 1947), esp. i. 125–55.

[37] Rudolf of Habsburg, *Mandatum primum super profugis Iudaeis* of 6 Dec. 1286,
MGH Const. iii, no. 388, 368–9: 'Cum universi et singuli Iudei utpote camere
nostre servi cum personis et rebus suis omnibus specialiter nobis attineant vel illis
principibus, quibus iidem Iudei a nobis et imperio in feodum sunt concessi, dignum
et iustum est ac utique consonum racioni, ut si aliqui Iudeorum huiusmodi facti
profugi sine nostra sive domini sui speciali licencia et consensu se ultra mare
transtulerint, ut se a vero dominio [*variant:* domino] alienent, de illorum
possessionibus, rebus et bonis omnibus tam mobilibus quam inmobilibus,
ubicunque ea reperiri contigerit, nos vel domini, quibus attinent, licite intromittere
debeamus ac ea non inmerito nostre attrahere potestati.'

did the Jews become aware of what serfdom to the royal chamber could mean in practice. Alluding to the well-known talmudic principle: 'The king's right is right' (*dina d^emalkuta dina*), Rabbi Meïr, describing this new kind of right added: 'but not his wrong' (*g^esilah*)![38]

It is remarkable that while Jewish chamber-serfdom was well known in Germany, even by name, at least from the time of Frederick II's general privilege for the Jews, those who were primarily affected by it, the Jews themselves, seem to have been unaware of it. In a responsum Rabbi Meïr of Rothenburg (1220–1293) could write: 'The legal status of the Jews in this country is that of a free landowner who has lost his land, but not his personal freedom. In its ordinary behaviour towards the Jews the government relies on this definition of their legal status.'[39] Legal practice must have accorded with Rabbi Meïr's statement, but legal theory was a different matter, and had been for a long time. In 1286, practice began to catch up with theory, and the Jews experienced a sad awakening. The fate of Rabbi Meïr is a good example. He was not ready to accept the new legal reality, and died in 1293 as the king's prisoner after a long period of custody in one of the king's castles (presumably Ensisheim).[40]

Rabbi Meïr could not foresee that the consequences drawn by Louis the Bavarian and Charles IV, Rudolf's successors, from the fact that the Jews had the status of serfs would be even worse than in his day. But he could have known that precisely those things which provoked his protest against the German rulers were everyday realities for his co-

[38] This phrase is often used by Rabbi Meïr; cf. Agus, *Rabbi Meir of Rothenburg*, ii. 499–500 no. 547; 520–1 no. 570; 540 no. 581, 552–3 no. 594. See also ibid. i. 140 ff. with other similar examples mostly of the 12th-cent. *responsa* literature. Of special interest in this respect is a statement by Rabbi Isaac of Dampierre (Ri) protesting against the way in which Philip Augustus of France had treated 'his' Jews in 1182. He had confiscated their property and forbidden them to leave his territories as they liked. Rabbi Ri claimed for the Jews the right of free choice to settle as the right of free seigneurs (*baalim*). This had been the situation in France, but was already changing at the time of Philip Augustus. Cf. E. E. Urbach, *The Tosaphists: Their History, Writings, and Methods*, 2 vols., 4th edn. (Jerusalem, 1980), i. 227–53, esp. 240–1. See also below, n. 41, the quotation from the *Milhemet Mitzvah* of Rabbi Meïr ben Simeon of Narbonne.

[39] Agus, *Rabbi Meir of Rothenburg*, ii. 553 no. 594; cf. Kisch, *Forschungen*, 59 with n. 43.

[40] Agus, *Rabbi Meir of Rothenburg*, i. 151–5.

religionists in the western monarchies, especially as his elder rabbinical colleague, Meïr ben Simeon of Narbonne, eloquently testified to this fact.[41] In a brilliant article, Gavin Langmuir shows that in France at the time of Philip Augustus arrangements between king and barons, and from 1198 on between the barons themselves, severely restricted the ability of Jews to move from the territory of one feudal lord to another.[42] The French feudal lords assured each other that they would not accept 'another's' Jews. In 1223 and 1230, these arrangements were cast in the form of royal ordinances, confirmed by oath by some members of the nobility.[43] Their observance was guaranteed by the king. Thus the enforcement of each baron's right to 'his' Jews became an instrument for the centralization of power in the hands of the French king.

Unlike the German king, the king of France neither had nor demanded an exclusive right over the Jews in his realm. But for the French Jews this meant only that each baron was their 'king', whose territory they were not allowed to leave without permission, and who regarded himself as the supreme owner of their property. That was serfdom *in praxi*. In France, the term 'serf' itself, however, was adopted rather late. It was used for the first time by King Louis IX in his ordinance of 1230, when he conceded his barons the right to seize a Jew of theirs *tanquam proprium servum* if he was found in the territory of another baron.[44] This was precisely

---

[41] In this context, the quotation from Rabbi Meïr's *Milhemet Mitzvah* as given by K. R. Stow, 'Servi camerae nostrae', *Dictionary of the Middle Ages*, xi (1988), 211 may suffice: 'We are his slaves [*Avadim*] . . . and our property is his to do with us as he pleases.' The historical context has been surveyed by R. Chazan, 'Anti-Usury Efforts in Thirteenth Century Narbonne and the Jewish Response', *Proceedings of the American Academy for Jewish Research*, 41/2 (1973/4), 45–57; see also Chazan, 'Archbishop Guy Fulcodi of Narbonne and his Jews', *Revue des études juives*, 132 (1973), 587–94. I am grateful to Israel Yuval (Jerusalem) for bringing these articles to my attention, and also for providing me with the full text of the quotation.

[42] G. I. Langmuir, ' "Iudei nostri" and the Beginning of Capetian Legislation', *Traditio*, 16 (1960), 203–39.

[43] Cf. the relevant texts in *Layettes du Trésor des Chartes*, ed. A. Teulet, vol ii (Paris, 1866), no. 1610; see also no. 2083.

[44] *Layettes*, ii no. 2083: 'statuimus quod nos et barones nostri Iudeis nulla debita de cetero contrahenda faciemus haberi, nec aliquis in toto regno nostro poterit retinere Iudeum alterius domini, et, ubicumque aliquis inveniet Iudeum suum, ipsum licite poterit capere *tamquam proprium servum*, quantumcumque moram fecerit Iudeus sub alterius dominio vel in alio regno.'

the situation which arose in the early history of medieval urbanization, when bond men left their lords to begin a new life of greater freedom in one of the rapidly developing urban communities.[45] The principle of Jewish serfdom, in

The appropriate use of the modern terms 'possession', 'ownership', 'property', etc. to describe relations between objects and people, and between people of different status in medieval times is always a problem, the more so as this relationship seems to be in a state of transition in the 12th and early 13th cents. I can accept the cautious definition given by Langmuir, ' "Iudei nostri" and the beginning of Capetian Legislation', 204 n. 4: ' "Possessory rights over Jews" should be stated more accurately as possession and exercise of numerous and extensive rights over *particular* Jews . . . I do not, however, wish to imply by this language that I equate the status of Jews in medieval law either with that of things in medieval law [= chattel] or with that of slaves in classical Roman law, although the right to capture Jews for purposes of extortion approaches a concept of physical possession.' But I cannot agree with his latest statements in id., '*Tamquam servi*: The Change in Jewish Status in French Law about 1200', *Les Juifs dans l'histoire de France: Premier colloque international de Haïfa*, ed. M. Yardeni (Leiden, 1980), 24–54, where he argues that terms such as 'servi' or 'servi camere' were merely metaphors and analogies, if not legal fictions (esp. p. 52). Such statements are surely wrong, as is demonstrated by the consequences, cited above, drawn by kings such as Louis the Bavarian and Rudolf of Habsburg, from the doctrine of chamber-serfdom.

In my opinion Langmuir's extreme position has a fundamental weakness. Here I shall stress only one point. Terms such as 'tamquam' and 'sicut' in conjunction with 'servus' and the like do not universally, or even generally, mean a mere comparison (p. 35), or draw an analogy. But in many cases—especially in the language of law—they do refer to the assigned thing itself. I shall give only two examples: (*a*) The city of Monza requests a privilege from Frederick Barbarossa in 1159, confirming that its citizens 'nullum dampnum vel gravamen ab aliqua civitate vel loco vel persona sustineant *tamquam liberi homines* nostri ad coronam et cameram nostram spetiali privilegio pertinentes' (MGH D. F.I. no. 253). As the whole purpose of the privilege was to gain guarantees from the emperor that the citizens of Monza and their possessions 'in eternum libertate et pace fruantur', it would be absurd to assume that they were referred to as free only as a legal metaphor or fiction, and not as a legal reality. (*b*) On 6 July 1415 Jan Hus was condemned as a heretic by the Council of Constance and burnt at the stake. The relevant passages of the *sententia condempnationis* contain the words 'Idcirco . . . praefatum Ioannem Huss haereticum fuisse haec sancta synodus pronunciat et *tamquam* haereticum iudicandum et condemnandum fore iudicat et condemnat per praesentem', *Corpus Oecumenicorum Decreta*, ed. G. Alberigo *et al.*, 3rd edn. (Bologna, 1973), 428. The text need not be commented upon. If Hus 'tamquam haereticus' was a heretic merely in legal fiction, his burning certainly was a fact.

In Louis IX's ordinance the non-existence of the Jews' right to move freely and the right of their masters to use the riches of 'their' Jews as they liked, clearly indicate their unfree status. The question of the place which Jews occupied on the broad scale of serfdom (*Unfreiheit*) is posed, but not answered, by reference to their unfree status.

[45] This connection is also considered by Langmuir, '*Tamquam servi*', 43–4, but he does not draw the necessary conclusions. Good examples are provided by T. Evergates, *Feudal Society in the Bailliage of Troyes under the Counts of Champagne*, 1152–

contrast to freedom of movement (which provoked Meïr of Rothenburg into resistance) was defined in France before the time of Frederick II.[46]

Compared with Germany, the status of Jews in France took a similar, yet distinctly different turn. In Germany, for a long time 'Jewish serfdom' existed only as a concept. Not until later was it put into practice. While according to legal theory the king remained the overlord of the Jews in his realm, he gave them as a pledge or in fief to the lords of the emerging territories, especially after the Interregnum, and thus ceased to be the real lord of 'his' Jews.[47] In France, therefore, the king was master of the Jews in fact, but not in name; in Germany he was called the Jews' master, but this was not always true. In France the Jews were serfs early in practice, later in name; in Germany it was the other way round.

One of the great vassals of the king of France was the English king, and French customs concerning the status of the Jews found their way to England together with the Jews migrating from Normandy at the end of the eleventh and the beginning of the twelfth centuries.[48] In the middle of the twelfth century they appear in the so-called *Leges Edwardi*.[49] According to this document the Jews of England were under the protection (*tutela, defensio*) of the king, who arrogated to

1284 (Baltimore and London, 1975), esp. 22–37. For evidence of the Jews' obligation to pay taille, a payment typically made by serfs in addition to formariage and mainmorte, see ibid. 19–20 with 217, n. 33 (dated 1222).

[46] See Langmuir, '"Iudei nostri" and the Beginning of Capetian Legislation', 226–7 with n. 92, rightly correcting Kisch, who tends to limit the problem of chamber serfdom to Frederick II's legislation.

[47] See e.g. G. Landwehr, *Die Verpfändung der deutschen Reichsstädte im Mittelalter* (Forschungen zur deutschen Rechtsgeschichte, 5; Cologne and Graz, 1967), 14 (Henry Raspe), 17 (Adolf of Nassau), 20 (Frederick the Fair), 26 (Louis the Bavarian), 31–2 (Charles IV), 33 (Wenzel), 34 (Ruprecht), 37 (Sigismund), 38 (Albrecht II), 146; see also A. Haverkamp, 'Die Judenverfolgungen zur Zeit des Schwarzen Todes', 77 ff.

[48] See e.g. P. Hyams, 'The Jewish Minority in Medieval England, 1066–1290', *Journal of Jewish Studies*, 25 (1974), 270–93, and his article in this volume.

[49] Leges Edwardi confessoris §25, ed. F. Liebermann, *Die Gesetze der Angelsachsen*, i (1903), 650: 'Sciendum est, quia omnes Iudei, quocumque regno sint, sub tutela et defensione regis ligie debent esse; neque aliquis eorum potest se subdere alicui diviti sine licentia regis, quia ipsi Iudei et omnia sua regis sunt. Quodsi aliquis detinuerit eos vel pecuniam eorum, requirat rex tanquam suum proprium, si vult et potest.' Concerning the date ('last years of Henry I' d. 1135), see C. Gross and E. B. Graves, *A Bibliography of English History to 1485* (Oxford, 1975), no. 2185.

himself an exclusive right to dispose of the Jews of his realm. In particular, he regarded their property as his own (*tanquam suum proprium*). This was the precise legal equivalent to the concept of chamber-serfdom as formulated by Frederick II.[50]

The *Leges Edwardi*, however, contain an important hint on the origin of the idea of *servitus Iudaeorum* in the king's service. They describe the special relationship between the English Jews and the king as *ligie*,[51] using the usual term for the direct relationship between the king and his feudal vassals. In relation to the Jews, the term *ligesse* certainly refers only to the direct relationship with the Jews in his realms which Frederick II claimed in his letter to Gregory IX. The origin of the term in feudal law is revealing. In substance, a feudal relationship is characterized by the protection of the lord on one side, and the service of the vassal based on fidelity on the other side. In other words, it is a relationship between partners, albeit of differing status.[52] It is well known that in time, the dependence of the vassal upon his lord became merely formal, and that the terms 'vassal' and 'lord' were no longer contradictions *in re*.[53] But for the Jews in England and on the Continent this relationship developed in another direction. Dependence on protection led, in the case of the Jews, to serfdom. In Germany, this was the exact opposite of the development of the *ministeriales*. The *ministeriales* in royal service were originally serfs, and through

[50] For another view, cf. Paul Hyams, above, pp. 181–2, with notes 24–6, who, following G. Langmuir, '*Tamquam servi*', 33 ff., interprets this passage on royal ownership as a mere analogy and rejects the idea of 'chattel-ownership' as anachronistic. Perhaps the term 'chattel-ownership' may indeed be misleading, at least at this time. But I think this passage expresses more than legal fiction or analogy. The Jews are not free in the choice of their protector, and the king can make claims on them as people, and on their property. However, the relationship between king and Jews may be defined in modern terms of legal property, it is more than the mere expression of an exclusive right of the king in respect to others. Astonishingly similar views of the status of the Jews in the kingdom of Bohemia around 1100 are expressed in the chronicle of Cosmas of Prague, Bk. ii, 45 and Bk. iii, 5, MGH SS rer. Germ., n.s. ii, 151–2 and 166.

[51] See above, n. 49.

[52] Cf. e. g. O. Brunner, *Land und Herrschaft*, 4th edn. (Wiesbaden, 1959), 262–3.

[53] For the late Middle Ages, see esp. K.-F. Krieger, *Die Lehnshoheit der deutschen Könige im Spätmittelalter (ca. 1200–1437)* (Untersuchungen zur deutschen Staats- und Rechtsgeschichte, n.s. 23; Aalen, 1979), esp. 22 ff. ('Lehnsherrschaft'), 176 ff. ('Dienstmannen').

royal service became free men, if not nobles. The Jews were free when they acquired royal protection, and thus became serfs.

V

How and when did this happen, and what was the decisive factor? According to Guido Kisch,[54] in Germany Frederick II's privilege of 1236 was responsible. The inclusion of the Jews in the *treuga dei* of 1103 provided a chance that Jews might become citizens among citizens, equals among equals in a common law to which all inhabitants of the country were subject in the same way. But the privilege of 1236 singled out the Jews, this time permanently, and put them under a special law. This might have been favourable for the moment, but because the king was the only one who granted this privilege, the Jews could not legally claim their right of protection. I doubt, however, whether the *treuga dei* legislation by the German rulers had the significance for the birth of a common 'civic' law which Kisch suggests. But this question would take us too far away from our topic here.[55] It seems more interesting to me that Frederick II's privilege did not have the fundamental importance for the development of the status of the Jews which Kisch claims. Frederick did not create a fundamentally new law. As was often the case, he merely made legal what had long been common practice.

Even the term 'serf', *servus*, for the Jews under royal protection was not invented by Frederick, as Kisch implies.[56] The first uses of this term of which I am aware come from the Iberian peninsula, a fact which is surprising, given the pros-

---

[54] Kisch, *Forschungen*, 47–61.

[55] This opinion could already be rejected on the grounds of the questionable importance of the *royal treuga dei*. The main reason why Jews ceased to appear in documents of royal *treuga dei* was that the *treuga dei* itself disappeared in the first half of the 14th cent. Frederick II's *treuga dei* of 1236 was, incidentally, not the last to mention Jews. At least one later example can be cited: King Albrecht I in his *treuga dei* of 17 Nov. 1298: *Nürnberger Urkundenbuch* (Quellen und Forschungen zur Geschichte der Stadt Nürnberg, 1; Nuremberg, 1959), no. 964.

[56] Kisch, *Forschungen*, 45, 66, 70–1. Kisch is justly contradicted by Langmuir, '"Judei nostri" and the beginning of Capetian legislation', 227 with n. 92, and Langmuir, '*Tamquam servi*', 28.

perity and the influential position in public life enjoyed by the Jews there.[57] As early as 1176 the *fuero* of the Aragonese town Teruel spoke of the town's Jews as 'serfs of the king' (*servi regis*), 'always belonging to the royal fisc' (*semper fisco regio deputati*). This text was adapted almost verbatim by the *fueroes* of Cuenca and Albarracín.[58] And Roger of Howden, writing around 1192, referring to the Jews in Portuguese Lisbon, tells us that they and the 'pagans' (that is, the Muslims), were *servi regis*.[59] The fact that Jews and Muslims are mentioned together in this quotation suggests the origins of Jewish serfdom in the Spanish realms. It appears to be a consequence of the *reconquista,* and is based simply on the right of the conqueror. The Christians of the reconquered cities and towns were freed, while Jews remained in serfdom, and Muslims were given this status in relation to the king. They were dependent on the conquering ruler's grace.[60]

[57] The standard work on the history of the Jews in Spain is F. Baer, *Studien zur Geschichte der Juden im Königreich Aragonien während des 13. und 14. Jahrhunderts* (Historische Studien, 106; Berlin, 1913); Baer, *A History of the Jews in Christian Spain,* 2 vols. (Philadelphia, 1961).

[58] See *Forum Turolii,* ed. F. Aznar y Navarro (Colecciòn de documentos para el estudio de la historia de Aragón, 9; Saragossa, 1905), 228 §425: 'Set est sciendum, quod Iudeus non habet partem in sua calumpnia, sive sit percussionis sivi homicidii, quia est domini regis tota. *Nam Iudei servi regis sunt et semper fisco regio deputati.* Similiter iudex in calumpnia Iudei novenum non accipiat nec habeat, cum nullum sudorem in illam habeat exigendam.' Fuero de Cuenca, ed. F. de Urena y Smenjaud (Madrid, 1935), 632 (Latin), 633 (Castilian: 'los judios sieruos son del rrey et son de su tesoro'). Fuero de Albarracín (Aragon), ed. A. and I. González Palencia, *Anuario de historia del derecho español,* 8 (1931), 484: 'Nam Iudei servi Domini sunt et semper fisco dominico deputati.'

[59] Roger of Howden's 'first version' under the name of Benedict of Peterborough ed. W. Stubbs, *Gesta Henrici.II* (Rolls Series, 49, 1867), ii. 119 [= 'second version', ed. W. Stubbs (Rolls Series, 51, 1868–71), iii. 45]. Complaining about the British crusaders making their way to the Holy Land via the Iberian peninsula and stopping in Lisbon, the chronicler says: 'Qui etiam exuentes de navibus suis in civitatem Ulixisbonae ascenderunt, et per vias et vicos incedentes superbe locuti sunt cum populo civitatis, et cum mulieribus et filiabus civium per vim coinquinati sunt, et *Iudaeos et paganos, qui erant ibi servi regis,* a civitate fugaverunt, et diripientes bona eorum domos eorum combusserunt.' For date and authorship cf. D. M. Stenton, 'Roger of Howden and "Benedict"', *English Historical Review,* 68 (1953), 574–82; Gross and Graves, *Bibliography,* no. 2903; recently D. Corner, 'The earliest surviving manuscripts of Roger of Howden's "Chronica"', *English Historical Review,* 98 (1983), 297–310, who argues for 1199–1201 as a date for the whole work.

[60] Cf. R. I. Burns, *Islam under the Crusaders: Colonial Survival in the Thirteenth-Century Kingdom of Valencia* (Princeton, 1973), 117–38, concerning the Muslims' conditions of surrender; ibid. 250 n. 4 the illuminating quotation of the *Fori Aragonum* of 1247: 'corpus ipsius Sarraceni sit domini regis'. This passage deals with 'free' Muslims, not 'serfs'!

Outside Spain, no such clear-cut situation existed. Therefore it was necessary to go back to *ligesse*, Augustine, and Titus in order to justify the status of Jews as serfs.[61]

We do not know how far the example of Spain influenced other parts of Europe. But it is not actually necessary to ask this question because the term was obviously first used in Spain for something that had long been a reality in the realms succeeding the Carolingian empire. If the chamber-serfdom of the Jews was not new in Europe when it was asserted by Frederick II, however, a crucial question arises. When did the privileged and the non-privileged—those specially protected by the king, and the other Jews and Jewish communities at the time of Henry IV—indiscriminately become serfs of the royal chamber in Germany?

This happened at the time of Frederick Barbarossa, as part of his systematic regalia policy. Space does not permit a detailed discussion here of the essence of, and the problems associated with, the term 'regalia policy'.[62] In brief, it was Frederick Barbarossa's policy to force everyone within his sphere of power to acknowledge the principle that there was no lordship which did not originate from the king.[63] It is well known that he mainly tried to enforce this principle in Italy. But the idea of deriving all seigneurial rights from royal power, just as a modern political system derives sovereignty from one single source, suffused his entire policy. In the context of this policy he redefined the status of the Jews by levelling the hitherto different legal statuses of individual Jews and Jewish communities, and by relating them all without distinction to the king. Kisch's suggestion[64] that Henry IV's privilege for the Jews of Worms already expressed

---

[61] The relationship between king and Jews/Muslims, however, has sometimes been expressed in feudal terms ('vasallus', 'homagium', 'fidelitas'); cf. Burns, *Islam under the Crusaders*, 280 ff., with many examples.

[62] See J. Fried, 'Der Regalienbegriff im 11. und 12. Jahrhundert', *Deutsches Archiv für Erforschung des Mittelalters*, 29 (1973), 450–528, esp. 453 ff. The standard work on Barbarossa's regalia policy is A. Haverkamp, *Herrschaftsformen der Frühstaufer in Reichsitalien*, 2 parts (Monographien zur Geschichte des Mittelalters, vol. 1; Stuttgart 1970), esp. i. 85–311.

[63] See esp. Haverkamp, *Herrschaftsformen*, i. 286–7, summarizing his research ('*Herrschaftsmonopol*').

[64] Kisch, *Forschungen*, 46, 54; ibid. 58, comments correctly that Barbarossa's Rhenish *treuga dei* of 1179 first mentions the Jews as people 'qui ad fiscum imperatoris pertinent' (MGH Const. i. 381).

the principle that all Jews belong to the royal chamber is not correct.[65] This expression was coined in Frederick Barbarossa's chancellery, and was frequently used in royal charters, not only in charters for Jews. Appurtenance to the royal chamber—other terms are *fiscus*, or even *corona*, and I once came across the pair *camera et corona*[66]—was claimed for the city of Die in the realm of Burgundy,[67] as well as for the Burgundian royal vassal Raimond d'Agoult.[68] The Bishop of Marseille acquired for himself and his church appurtenance to the royal chamber as a special grace,[69] and the privilege for the minters of Worms mentions minting and money-changing as appurtenances of the royal chamber,[70] while the cities (or *burgi*) of Monza, Sarzano, Cremona, and—outside Italy—Besançon,[71] were described simply as royal demesne (*Kammergut*, that is, in Latin, *camera*).

The precise judicial idea behind the claim of appurten-ance to the royal chamber in all these cases cannot be dis-cussed here. But I should like to suggest that this formula might not have been mere rhetoric, nothing more than an emphatic way of expressing merely a direct relation-ship to the Crown without any intermediary powers (*Reichsunmittelbarkeit*).[72] Only a comprehensive study of the chamber of the German king, also looking at how institu-tions of state in other European countries developed at that time, could provide a concrete answer. There can be no doubt, however, that declaring an appurtenance of persons

[65] It might suffice here to state that the following phrase in Frederick Barbarossa's charter for Worms (D. F.I. no. 166), 'presertim cum ad cameram nostram attineant', has no parallel in Henry IV's charter for Speyer (D. H.IV. no. 411) and, furthermore, that Henry's chancellery never used the expression cham-ber appurtenance.

[66] *Fiscus*: D. F.I. no. 774 (*treuga dei* of 18 Feb. 1179); *corona*: no. 743 (Bishop Robert of Die), no. 749 (Raimond d'Agoult); *camera et corona*: no. 253 (Monza). Haverkamp, *Herrschaftsformen*, i. 293, n. 14, points out that even *sedes* might be used as a synonym for 'chamber'.

[67] D. F.I. no. 743 (30 July 1178).

[68] D. F.I. no. 749 (6 Aug. 1178).

[69] D. F.I. no. 437 (17 Apr. 1164).

[70] D. F.I. no. 491 (24 Sept. 1165).

[71] Monza: D. F.I. no. 253 (*corona et camera*); Sarzano: no. 405; Cremona: no. 261; Besançon: no. 472.

[72] In this sense Haverkamp, *Herrschaftsformen*, i. 289 ff., esp. 292.

and institutions to the royal chamber was intended to express an immediate relation to the king.

Frederick Barbarossa thus brought the Jews into line with the above-mentioned illustrious appurtenances of the royal chamber. When he granted privileges to Jews or disposed of Jews (I am aware of about eight cases in Germany and Burgundy),[73] he almost always stressed the appurtenance to his chamber, but did not use the word 'serf' for Jews in his charters. Once, in his privilege for the Jews of Regensburg, he even gives a special reason for this appurtenance.[74] The Jews, that is, all the Jews of his realm belong to the imperial chamber because of a special prerogative originating in the imperial dignity.

Leaving aside the difference between 'imperial' and 'royal', which is more linguistic than real, we should emphasize that the emperor here openly states what otherwise must remain conjecture. He claims the right to defend the Jews and, as a consequence, the funds to finance this defence, as his *prerogative*. This is precisely the legal position which, in a different context, is described as the basis of his regalia policy.[75] This declaration of his power over the Jews is addressed to potential rivals, that is, the nascent territorial nobility and the ecclesiastical prelates, who were making themselves independent.[76] The Jews were merely the objects

[73] D. F.I. no. 166 (Jews of Worms, 6 Apr. 1157); no. 436 (Archbishop Raymond of Arles, 16 Apr. 1164); no. 437 (Bishop Peter of Marseille, 17 Apr. 1164); no. 491 (minters of Worms, 24 Sept. 1165); no. 746 (Archbishop Raymond of Arles, 4 Aug. 1178); no. 747 (Bishop Pontius of Avignon, 5 Aug. 1178); no. 774 (*treuga dei*, 18 Feb. 1179); no. 833 (Jews of Regensburg, probably late Sept. 1182).

[74] D. F.I. no. 833, probably dating from late Sept. 1182: 'Eapropter notum facimus universis imperii fidelibus praesentibus et futuris, quod nos solerter curam gerentes *omnium Iudeorum in imperio nostro degentium, qui spetiali praerogativa dignitatis nostrae ad imperialem cameram dinoscuntur pertinere*, Iudaeis nostris Ratisponensibus bonas consuetudines suas . . . concedimus', etc.

[75] Haverkamp, *Herrschaftsformen*, i. 85–102, 286 ff.

[76] I cannot accept the idea that Frederick Barbarossa, in emphasizing the royal/imperial prerogative, had the Pope in mind. Yet this argument is broached in S. W. Baron, ' "Plenitude of Apostolic Powers" and Medieval "Jewish Serfdom" ', *Yitzhak F. Baer Jubilee Volume* (Jerusalem, 1960), 102–24 (Hebr., with English summary). Undoubtedly the Pope—at least since the doctrine of *plenitudo potestatis* had been fully developed, i.e. since Innocent III—had also claimed supreme authority over the Jews, cf. for instance Innocent IV's commentary on 'Quod super', quoted in emended form by B. I. Kedar, 'Canon Law and the Burning of the Talmud', *Bulletin of Medieval Canon Law*, n.s. 9 (1979), 79–82. But I know of no case where Pope and

of this policy, and what they personally did or did not do had little bearing on what happened to them. The consequences of this policy, which resulted in a decisive change in Jewish status, emerged only slowly. They did not become fully apparent until the reign of King Rudolf of Habsburg. The Jewish communities which had possessed privileges before the time of Frederick Barbarossa, and those who were granted new privileges, or whose privileges were confirmed by the emperor, had to pay for their protection in the same way and to the same real protectors at the time of Frederick Barbarossa as before and after.[77] There is little evidence that the claim of royal overlordship over Jews led to real changes in propriety over Jews. In other words, the same emerging territorial lords or prelates who had protected the Jews within their area, and were paid for it, until the time of Frederick Barbarossa, did so thereafter. But they felt obliged (at least in general) to ask the king for permission to do so, for example, by way of enfeoffment. The extent to which the prerogative claimed by Barbarossa was accepted is clearly demonstrated by the large numbers of Jews given away by the Crown as fief or pledge in the period after the Interregnum. After all, nobody can dispose of things he does not possess, or whose right of ownership is not accepted by the recipient of the gift.

Frederick Barbarossa, therefore, was the first to assert and establish the principle that all Jews of his realm were related to him by the obligation to defend them on his side, and by appurtenance to his chamber, that is, the obligation to pay certain taxes, on the part of the Jews, regardless of whether a particular Jewish community had a special privilege or not. However, this action neither decided, nor even posed the question of Jewish status, that is, whether the Jews of the royal chamber were free or serfs. It seems that this question was never discussed, and I believe that there was no real reason to do so. The protection of the king, requested freely

Emperor disagreed because of legal claims raised on the basis of Jewish chamber appurtenance.

[77] This becomes quite clear when considering the privileges granted to Archbishop Raymond of Arles and Bishop Pontius of Avignon, where the claim for supreme royal/imperial superiority over the Jews led to nothing but confirmation of episcopal dominion over them (DD F.I. nos. 746, 747). It cannot be said that these privileges led to any real change for the Jews.

by the privileged and granted as a favour, existed as long as its basis in defence and fidelity remained. Barbarossa's vindication of the royal prerogative meant that it applied indiscriminately to all Jews, and that nobody was free to leave henceforth. It is clear that for people in such a cage, even if it seemed at first to be a golden one, the idea of serfdom must inevitably have grown of its own accord, the more so as it was a phenomenon common to Europe as a whole.

Frederick II's 1236 privilege for the Jews, therefore, was innovative only to the extent that it standardized hitherto differing regulations applying to the Jewish communities in Germany. On the main issue of Jewish status, Frederick II merely gave formal expression to what, since Barbarossa's time, had become an established legal belief, namely that all Jews had the same legal relationship with the king, and that this was not a relationship between king and vassal, tied by the bonds of lordship and fidelity, but one between master and serf.

VI

It should now be clear that the development of the status of the Jews in Germany can be understood only within an over-all European context. It is, however, also necessary to avoid a further inadmissible narrowing of perspective, that is, the consideration of Jewish status in isolation. The fact that the Jews could gradually become the property of their lords throughout Europe must have been related in some way to the general development of concepts of proprietary right in Europe. On this point a lively debate has recently been initiated, the end of which is not yet in sight. In England, Robert C. Palmer,[78] working on ideas originally put forward by S. F. C. Milsom,[79] has refuted the dominant school of thought established by the great legal historian Frederick

[78] R. C. Palmer, 'The Origins of Property in England', *Law and History Review*, 3 (1985), 1–50.
[79] On the problem of property rights see above all S. F. C. Milsom, *The Legal Framework of English Feudalism* (Cambridge, 1976), particularly 36ff. Cf. the review by P. Hyams, in EHR, 93 (1978), 856–61, and John Hudson, 'Milsom's Legal Structure: Interpreting Twelfth Century Law', *Tijdschrift voor rechtsgeschiedenis*, 59 (1991), 47–66, particularly 62ff.

William Maitland.[80] Palmer argues that around 1200 proprietary right passed beyond the idea of a relationship determined purely by personal appurtenance—'relative servility'
is the central concept coined by Maitland—and entered the
sphere in which property relationships are regulated in accordance with general principles. This was achieved not by
an act of will on the part of rulers, but by a gradual process
of expanding state control in the sense of Max Weber's
model of bureaucratization. According to this model, over-
lapping individual relationships which were originally determined personally are, at all levels of society, transformed into
a system functioning in line with rules which are absolutely
rational and abstract, and at the same time, suprapersonally
objective and universally valid.[81] In our context this would
mean that Jews as a group of dependants formerly attached
to the king alone in respect of proprietary right in the sense
of an appurtenance now acquired the status of serfs as a
general legal quality. Bracton's famous definition of the
Jews: 'Iudaeus vero nihil proprium habere potest, quia
quicquid adquirit non sibi acquirit sed regi, quia non vivunt
sibi ipsis sed aliis et sic aliis acquirunt et non sibi ipsis'[82] can
be understood in this sense. The revealing expression used
in the English sources for jurisdiction over material goods,
'catallum', is found around 1200 in a royal charter on the
Jews,[83] and the term 'serf' appears in Edward I's Statute on
the Jews of 1275.[84]

---

[80] Cf. F. Pollock and F. W. Maitland, *The History of English Law before the Time of Edward I*, 2nd edn. (Cambridge, 1898) i. 412–32 (The Unfree), 468–75 (The Jews). See also J. A. Watt, 'The Jews, the Law, and the Church: The Concept of Jewish Serfdom in Thirteenth-Century England', in *The Church and Sovereignty c. 590–1918. Essays in Honour of Michael Wilks*, ed. by Diana Wood (Studies in Church History, Subsidia 9; London, 1991), 156ff. Paul Hyams argues that Maitland's concept of 'relative servility', which is based on Bracton's work, is in practice found only sporadically. See his *Kings, Lords and Peasants in Medieval England: The Common Law of Villeinage in the Twelfth and Thirteenth Centuries* (Oxford, 1980), 82–124, 125.

[81] For a similar view see also Harold J. Berman, *Law and Revolution: The Formation of the Western Legal Tradition* (Cambridge, Mass., 1983), 237ff., 321f.

[82] Bracton, *De legibus et consuetudinibus Angliae*, ed. by George E. Woodbine. Trans., with revisions and notes, by Samuel E. Thorne, iv. 4 (Cambridge, Mass., 1977), 208 n. 3.

[83] See *Rotuli Chartarum*, ed. Thomas Duffus Hardy, i. pt 1. (Record Commission, London, 1837), 93 [King John, a charter from 1201].

[84] This point is emphasized by J. A. Watt, 156, 159f.

A far more complex picture is drawn by Dietmar Willoweit,[85] who places the whole question of property within the broader context of the reception of Roman law in the countries north of the Alps which followed Germanic law.[86] He emphasizes, correctly in my view, that this was an interactive process in which the conceptual world of Roman law was not simply accepted, but was transformed in accordance with interpretative patterns moulded by Germanic law. He demonstrates this by analysing changes in the semantic import of the two central concepts of proprietary right, 'dominium' and 'proprietas'; that is, the basic elements of a person's legal entitlement to goods as his property and to jurisdiction over them.

I do not wish to discuss further the details of Willoweit's research, to which Damian Hecker has made strong, but in my opinion substantially unjustified, objections.[87] I return instead to my topic: the development of the status of the Jews within the context of the overall development of proprietary rights. Space does not permit me, nor do I feel competent, to deal with this subject fully here, especially as the question of proprietary rights cannot be treated independently of the law on corporate bodies. There is an internal relationship between the increasing systematization of legal relations in the spheres of property and jurisdiction, and the building-up of a corporative network of individuals resulting in the standardization of their status. Here, too, the history of relations between the Jews and the German rulers is significant, as the contractual partners of the kings from Henry IV to Frederick II changed from individual, named Jews and their 'com-

[85] D. Willoweit, 'Dominium et Proprietas. Zur Entwicklung des Eigentums-begriffs in der mittelalterlichen und neuzeitlichen Rechtswissenschaft', *Historisches Jahrbuch*, 94 (1974), 131–56.

[86] P. H. Freedman, 'Catalan Lawyers and the Origins of Serfdom', *Medieval Studies*, 48 (1986), 288–314, makes similar observations on the interplay between Roman and domestic law in Catalonia resulting in an increasing tendency to systematize legal relationships, particularly in the law concerning persons. See esp. 289, 309.

[87] D. Hecker, *Eigentum als Sachherrschaft. Zur Genese und Kritik eines besonderen Herrschaftsanspruchs* (Rechts- und Staatswissenschaftliche Veröffentlichungen der Görres-Gesellschaft, N.F. 57; Paderborn etc., 1990), esp. 17–53. I wish to thank my colleague Rolf Köhn for this and other references in connection with the problem of proprietary rights.

panions', to whole communities, and, finally, to the Jewry of the entire empire.

With these hints at wide-ranging changes in the legal sphere and their profound impact on mentalities the matter must rest. This is, however, the only context in which the changing legal status of the Jews can be adequately described. For the proprietary relations of the Jews with the king, Louis the Bavarian's statement cited at the beginning of this chapter in any case marks the end of the development. This pronouncement can be regarded as a perfect example of the classic definition of property by the great Bolognese teacher of law, Bartolus. Bartolus defines 'dominium' as the full power of disposal over a thing,[88] that is, *chattel-ownership*. Can there be a more succinct expression of this than Louis the Bavarian's statement that the life and property of the Jews belonged to him and the empire, and that he had complete power to dispose of them as he desired?

[88] Ad lib. XLI Dig. tit. II De acquirenda possessione, 1.17 n. 6: 'Quid ergo est dominium? Responde: Est ius de re corporali perfecte disponendi, nisi lex prohibeat.'

The Crusading Movement

9

Preaching the Crusade in Wales

PETER W. EDBURY

In Lent 1188 Archbishop Baldwin of Canterbury toured Wales preaching the Third Crusade. He was accompanied in his travels by Gerald, Archdeacon of Brecon, the man whom posterity has dubbed 'Giraldus Cambrensis'. Gerald was a scholar of considerable literary ability, and he has left us a vivid narrative of their activities and experiences at that time. Moreover, he had completed the first version of his account, which he entitled the *Itinerarium Kambriae*, before the end of 1191, and so he was writing very soon after the events he described. The *Itinerarium* is a celebrated work, packed with entertaining anecdotes. It is a true forerunner of the modern *genre* of travel books replete with stories about the places visited on the way, information about natural history, tales of the supernatural, descriptions of the countryside and its inhabitants, and digressions to bring in further anecdotes on similar themes but from other parts of the world or from other ages. As a compendium of information about Wales in the late twelfth century it is outstanding, and its appeal remains so strong that a modern English translation is readily available.[1] But although the *Itinerarium* has been used extensively by historians of medieval Wales and the Welsh Marches, its connecting thread—the preaching of the crusade—has often been overlooked. Yet it is a unique example of a record of a preaching mission intended to attract volunteers. I want to begin by seeing what it has to tell us about recruiting men to join the expedition which was then, in the aftermath of the fall of Jerusalem in 1187, being organized to recover the Holy Places and what it has to say about the

---

[1] The standard Latin edn. of the *Itin[erarium Kambriae]* remains that of J. F. Dimock in *Giraldi Cambrensis Opera* (Rolls Series, 21, 1861–9), vi. 1–152. The English trans. is by L. Thorpe in Gerald of Wales, *The Journey through Wales and the Description of Wales* (Harmondsworth, 1978).

preaching of the Cross at that particular stage in the development of the crusading movement.

Wales at that time was divided between various native Welsh princes and the Anglo-Norman Marcher lords who for a century or more had occupied Usk valley up to and including Brecon and the whole of the south coast of Wales as far as Pembroke and Haverfordwest. In the early twelfth century King Henry I had kept a close hold on the territory under direct Norman rule and had succeeded in imposing his overlordship on the indigenous Welsh princes. But the equilibrium he had achieved broke down during the Anarchy, and it took his grandson, Henry II, about twenty years to restore the situation. In the early 1170s Henry managed to establish a *détente*. The Welsh rulers were confirmed in their gains at the expense of the Anglo-Norman lords, while the Marchers were guaranteed against further attacks; both groups were obliged to acknowledge the king's ultimate authority over the whole of Wales. In 1177 Henry demonstrated his dominance when at Oxford he took the fealty and liege homage of the two most powerful Welsh princes, Rhys ap Gruffydd of Deheubarth and Dafydd ab Owain of Gwynedd. At the same time the king apparently gave his approval to the suzerainty these two men had been asserting over the lesser Welsh lords. So by keeping the predatory instincts of the Marchers in check and by letting the Welsh princes attain at least some of their ambitions, Henry was able to secure an unwonted degree of peace which was to last throughout the latter part of his reign.[2]

In 1188, therefore, Archbishop Baldwin was able to move around without any difficulty. He and his party entered Wales from Hereford. After making contact with Rhys ap Gruffydd, they travelled to Brecon and then, keeping to the Anglo-Norman controlled areas, moved down the valley of the Usk and along the south coast to St Davids. Turning north, they entered Welsh Wales—the *pura Wallia* of the native princes—and were met by Rhys ap Gruffydd at Cardigan. He accompanied them as they made their way through his lands, bidding them farewell at his northern border, the

---

[2] R. R. Davies, *Conquest, Coexistence and Change: Wales 1063–1415* (Oxford, 1987), 290–2, cf. 53–5. See also W. L. Warren, *Henry II* (London, 1973), 159–69.

estuary of the River Dyfi. From there they hastened to Bangor, and, having made a brief excursion to the island of Anglesey, met the Prince of Gwynedd, Dafydd ab Owain, at Rhuddlan. After that they continued east to the Anglo-Norman city of Chester and thence south back to Hereford, pausing at Oswestry and Shrewsbury. The whole of this *laboriosum iter* had taken seven weeks.[3]

At suitable places the archbishop and members of his entourage preached to whoever had gathered to hear them. Presumably messengers had gone ahead to call the people together for the appointed day—in another of his works Gerald explicitly referred to a summons to hear the crusade preached at Haverfordwest[4]—and Baldwin clearly demanded that the rulers should attend. In the *Itinerarium* Gerald recorded one instance of a Welsh lord coming too late for the sermon and asking the archbishop's pardon for not having arrived on time. This man duly took the Cross, but Owain Cyfeiliog, the ruler of a part of Powys who alone of all the Welsh princes, so we are told, had made no attempt to come in person with his men to hear the archbishop, was excommunicated.[5] Coercive sanctions including the threat of anathema for those who refused to turn up to listen to the preaching of the Cross were part of the armoury of the preachers, and English evidence proves that these sanctions continued to be available far into the thirteenth century. On the other hand, the days when indulgences were offered as an inducement for people to attend the preaching of the Cross still lay in the future.[6]

In addition to the sermons that were preached at predetermined places and times, Archbishop Baldwin also signed people with the Cross following private interviews.[7] But it was clearly the public preaching that had the greatest impact.

---

[3] *Itin.*, 146. For a map and reconstruction of the chronology, see Thorpe, 30–6.

[4] *De rebus a se gestis*, ed. J. S. Brewer, *Giraldi Cambrensis Opera*, i. 74.

[5] *Itin.*, 48–9, 144. Having recorded Owain's excommunication, Gerald then, without any apparent sense of incongruity, gave his wisdom as a ruler a glowing accolade (144–5).

[6] For indulgences for hearing crusade sermons from the time of Pope Innocent III onwards, see J. A. Brundage, *Medieval Canon Law and the Crusader* (Madison, 1969), 154. For coercive powers to get people to attend in 13th-century England, see S. Lloyd, *English Society and the Crusade: 1216–1307* (Oxford, 1988).

[7] *Itin.*, 16, 48–9, 119.

The archbishop took the lead in speaking to the people, but frequently his sermons were supplemented by addresses from his colleagues. The Bishop of Llandaff preached at Usk, the Abbot of Strata Florida in Anglesey, and Gerald himself shared in the preaching at Haverfordwest, St Davids (where the archbishop left him to get on with it while he travelled ahead), and Shrewsbury. At Lampeter, after the archbishop had preached, there were sermons from Gerald and from the Cistercian abbots of Whitland and Strata Florida.[8] The role of the Cistercians is noteworthy and calls to mind the lead given by St Bernard at the time of the Second Crusade. Archbishop Baldwin was himself a Cistercian and had been Abbot of Ford Abbey in Somerset for a few years until 1180. In Wales the Cistercian Order had grown rapidly during the half century before 1188, especially in Deheubarth and the Marches, and had come to occupy a prominent position in monasticism there.

The preachers had a particular problem, that of language. The indigenous population spoke Welsh; the Marcher lords and their retinues would have conversed in French; in parts of the Marcher-controlled lands English would have been spoken. At Llandaff Gerald noted that the Welsh stood together on one side and the English on the other. At Haverfordwest he himself preached in Latin and French and then was amazed to see how many people who understood neither language flocked to take the Cross. Recalling this instance in a later work, he compared his experiences to those of St Bernard who, when preaching in French to the Germans before the Second Crusade, allegedly moved his audience to tears. On other occasions Alexander, Archdeacon of Bangor, interpreted the archbishop's exhortations into Welsh.[9]

It is unfortunate that Gerald gives no real indication as to what was actually said in the crusade sermons. Presumably the preachers concentrated on the loss of Jerusalem, the atrocities perpetrated by the Muslims, the heroism of earlier

---

[8] *Itin.*, 55, 82–3, 110, 119, 126, 144.

[9] *Itin.*, 55, 67, 83, 126; cf. 14; *De rebus a se gestis*, 76. It has been suggested that Gerald himself could not speak Welsh fluently. R. Bartlett, *Gerald of Wales 1146–1223* (Oxford, 1982), 14–15.

crusaders, and the indulgence and the assurance of salvation available to all who participated, but there would also have been *exempla*, tales of what might lie in store for those who remained deaf to the preachers' appeal and examples of how individual acts of devotion were rewarded. However, Gerald leaves us in no doubt that the preachers' appeal was strongly emotive and that the sermons ended with the insistence that men should come forward immediately to take the Cross in the sight of all. At Haverfordwest he split his own address into three parts, each of which ended with a call for people to take crusading vows there and then.[10] It would also seem that, where possible, prominent individuals were persuaded beforehand to take the lead in responding to the appeal. At Radnor, the first place in Wales at which the Cross was preached, Gerald himself and Peter, Bishop of St Davids, were the first to respond. Gerald admitted that he was acting on the king's instructions; it was only in a later recension of the *Itinerarium* that he added that he had acted of his own freewill to avenge the injuries inflicted upon the Cross of Christ. At Radnor Rhys ap Gruffydd was persuaded to particpate in the crusade, but it would seem that it was agreed that he should wait until the archbishop arrived in his own territory before taking the Cross. Presumably he would do so at a public ceremony designed to encourage as many of his men as possible to follow his example. However, by the time Baldwin's party reached his lands, he had changed his mind and decided not to go.[11]

Something of the flavour of the preachers' *exempla* as well as of the mentality of the age is doubtless preserved in some of the anecdotes Gerald recorded. The young men of Rhodri ab Owain's household in Anglesey who steadfastly refused to respond to the preaching were killed soon afterwards in a skirmish with brigands. A woman at Cardigan who forcibly prevented her husband from taking the Cross overlay her child in her sleep three nights later and so smothered him. On the other hand turf from the spot where the archbishop had stood at Haverfordwest restored a woman to sight and

---

[10] *De rebus a se gestis*, 75.   [11] *Itin.*, 14–15.

miracles were later performed at the place where he had preached at Cardigan.[12]

Responses varied. At Hay-on-Wye men came running to take the Cross, leaving their cloaks in the hands of wives or friends who were trying to hold them back. Einion, son of Einion Clud, sought permission from his father-in-law and suzerain, Rhys ap Gruffydd, before taking his vows. Rhys's own sons were even more circumspect. After some debate they agreed that one of them should go with the archbishop when he returned to the king to find out whether or not they were actually wanted. At Bangor Gerald recorded that Baldwin compelled rather than persuaded the local bishop to take the Cross and that this led to an outcry and loud expressions of grief from among his people.[13] Rhys ap Gruffydd was persuaded against going on crusade partly by his wife and partly by a kinsman, who himself was about to take the Cross, who commented that the worst thing that could happen to a crusader would be to come back alive. Clearly Rhys did not share this 'gung ho' attitude. The remark of course drew attention to a major consideration: as the First and Second Crusades had amply demonstrated, the chances of returning safe and sound were limited.[14] The likelihood of death on crusade as well as the expenses that participation entailed no doubt explains why the friends or relatives of would-be recruits tried to dissuade them from responding. The old woman at Cardigan who gave thanks to God that her only son had been deemed worthy in His sight to take crusading vows may indeed have been exceptional.[15]

There were other strands in crusade recruitment. At Whitland, Archbishop Baldwin obliged twelve archers from a nearby castle to take the Cross as a penance (*in poenam*) for the murder of a Welsh youth.[16] At Cruker a man raised the issue of a subsidy, apparently undertaking to join the crusade if he could have half his sustenance provided. The question

---

[12] *Itin.*, 83, 113, 126. Such stories can be compared with the miraculous anecdotes recorded by Caesarius of Heisterbach apropos the preaching of the Fifth Crusade in Germany. *Testimonia minora de Quinto Bello Sacro*, ed. R. Röhricht (Geneva, 1882), 162–8, 175–9.

[13] *Itin.*, 14–15, 20, 119, 125–6.   [14] *Itin.*, 15.

[15] *Itin.*, 113.   [16] *Itin.*, 82; cf. 55.

of subsidies for crusaders was important, and from the time of the Third Crusade it came to have a far greater prominence since it was now accepted that hardly anyone would be able to finance himself unaided.[17] At Swansea an old man offered a tithe of all he possessed in return for half the indulgence (*poenitentiae remissio*) available to the crusaders; then, when his offer was accepted, he offered a further tithe for the other half. Later that year, in May 1188, Pope Clement III allowed bishops in France and England to grant half the full crusade indulgence to non-crusaders who gave a tithe of their goods towards the costs of the expedition. It is interesting to find an example of this faculty being anticipated.[18] The practice of allowing people who wished to benefit from the indulgence but who had no intention of actually taking part in a crusade to take vows and then commute them was a feature of crusading which still lay in the future.

At Abergavenny the archbishop told a man who had said he wanted to discuss with his friends whether or not to take the Cross that he ought rather to ask his wife for her consent. Here Baldwin, who was evidently a canonist of some standing, was behaving with complete propriety by alerting the man to his wife's rights in the matter. The separation necessitated by going on crusade entailed the abrogation of marriage vows, and canon lawyers had long recognized that the wife was therefore entitled to give or withhold her agreement to her husband's absence. Indeed, as early as the First Crusade Pope Urban II had insisted that men should not set off without their wives' consent. It was only later, in a statement of 1201 which has been regarded as something of an aberration, that Pope Innocent III allowed that a man could take the Cross without his wife's permission.[19] What is significant about this incident, however, is the remaining part of Gerald's account of the conversation. The man replied to the archbishop's remark by saying that the crusade was an

---

[17] *Itin.*, 16.

[18] *Itin.*, 73–4. Ph. Jaffé, *Regesta pontificum Romanorum*, 2nd edn. (Leipzig, 1881–8), no. 16252; cf. Brundage, *Medieval Canon Law and the Crusader*, 154.

[19] *Itin.*, 49. See J. A. Brundage, 'The Crusader's Wife: A Canonistic Quandary', *Studia Gratiana*, 12 (1967), 428–42. For Baldwin as a canonist, see C. Duggan, *Twelfth-Century Decretal Collections and their Importance in English History* (London, 1963), 110–15.

issue for men and should not depend on the advice of women; thereupon he immediately took the Cross. Gerald recorded this exchange in a way which seems to show that he approved of the man's sentiments, and, as we have seen, elsewhere he made it clear that he was not sympathetic towards women who tried to obstruct their menfolk from joining the expedition. Perhaps unintentionally he managed to leave the impression that the archbishop, in accepting the vows of a man who on his own admission had not obtained his wife's consent, had connived at a breach of this rule. One wonders how generally crusade preachers let men who had not talked the matter over with their wives take crusading vows, or how often they bothered to enquire whether a recruit's wife had in fact been consulted.

It is time now to consider this preaching tour in its wider context. Why should Archbishop Baldwin go to Wales of all places to preach the crusade? The four dioceses which together comprised Wales were part of the province of Canterbury, but no archbishop had ever visited them or in fact was to do so again for about another century. It has frequently been suggested that Baldwin had an ulterior motive in going to Wales: preaching the crusade povided him with a pretext for asserting his ecclesiastical jurisdiction. Several years later Gerald was to champion the idea that the Welsh dioceses ought to form a separate province with an archbishop at St Davids—an office to which he himself aspired—but in the *Itinerarium* he made no direct mention of this issue.[20] Quite the contrary, he was careful to note in his account of the events of 1188 that Baldwin celebrated mass at the high altar of each of the four cathedrals in turn, and he also described how Baldwin ordered the local bishop to remove the body of Owain Gwynedd who had died excommunicate in 1170 from its place of burial in Bangor cathedral.[21] So the archbishop does seem to have used the opportunity afforded by the

---

[20] For Gerald's ambitions, see M. Richter, *Giraldus Cambrensis: The Growth of the Welsh Nation*, 2nd edn. (Aberystwyth, 1976). The allusion to the disputed rights of Canterbury over St Davids in *Itin.*, 15–16 is a later interpolation.

[21] *Itin.*, 67, 110, 125, 133, 137. Owain had been excommunicated by Archbishop Thomas Becket.

preparations for the crusade and by the political hegemony established in Wales by Henry II to give visible expression to Canterbury's rights in the Welsh dioceses. But it would be unwise to make too much of this point. As Gerald was later to note, Baldwin went to Wales because the king had sent him there. Moreover, Gerald himself seems to have accompanied Baldwin on Henry's orders.[22]

Gerald's role is readily understandable: he was a clerk in the king's service, and as a member of an Anglo-Norman family long-established in south Wales—and one moreover which had ties of blood with the key figure among the Welsh princes, Rhys ap Gruffydd of Deheubarth—he knew the country and could liaise with the local lords.[23] Baldwin too was a sensible choice, and not just because of his exalted status in the Church. He had had previous dealings with Rhys and in 1187 had conducted a legatine visitation which had brought him at least as far as the borders of Wales.[24] In addition, he must have been one of the very few people in England at the time who had some experience of crusade preaching. In 1185 he had preached the Cross with Eraclius, the Patriarch of Jerusalem, at Clerkenwell, and immediately before going to Wales in 1188 he had preached at the king's council at Geddington.[25] It is also possible that Baldwin was strongly motivated. Almost certainly it was to him that Peter of Blois addressed his appeal for crusade preaching to go ahead, and, as Richard of Devizes noted, he was one of only two English bishops who actually fulfilled their vows to go to the East.[26]

---

[22] *Itin.*, 14; *De rebus a se gestis*, 73; Giraldus Cambrensis, *Expugnatio Hibernica: The Conquest of Ireland*, ed. and trans. A. B. Scott and F. X. Martin (Dublin, 1978), 254. The wording in the *Expugnatio* can be understood to mean that it was Gerald who went at the king's instruction—this is the view of the editors—or that it was Baldwin.

[23] Bartlett, *Gerald of Wales*, 12–15; cf. 19–20.

[24] *De rebus a se gestis*, 57; *Epistolae Cantuarenses*, ed. W. Stubbs in *Chronicles and Memorials of the Reign of Richard I* (Rolls Series, 38, 1864–5), ii. 61, cf. 67, 76. Gervase of Canterbury, *Chronica*, in *The Chronicles of the Reigns of Stephen, Henry II and Richard I*, ed. W. Stubbs (Rolls Series, 73, 1879–80), i. 365.

[25] *Expugnatio Hibernica*, 203; *Gesta Regis Henrici Secundi Benedicti Abbatis*, ed. W. Stubbs (Rolls Series, 49, 1867), ii. 33.

[26] For Peter of Blois, see R. W. Southern, 'Peter of Blois and the Third Crusade', *Studies in Medieval History presented to R. H. C. Davis*, ed. H. Mayr-Harting and R. I. Moore (London and Ronceverte, 1985), 213–14. Richard of Devizes, *Chronicon de Tempore Regis Richardi Primi*, ed. J. T. Appleby (London, 1963), 15.

It is important to set Baldwin's tour of Wales in the context of King Henry's preparations for the crusade in England and France. Together with King Philip Augustus, Henry had taken the Cross at Gisors in January 1188. He had then immediately gone to Le Mans where he had decreed the famous tax known as the Saladin Tithe— a levy of one-tenth on all movable property to be paid by all who were not themselves participating in the expedition. After that the king crossed the Channel and moved rapidly to Geddington in Northamptonshire where at a council held in February the Saladin Tithe was imposed on England. The chroniclers agree that the response to the preaching of the Crusade at Gisors and at Geddington was considerable.[27] Roger of Howden noted that after the Council of Geddington priests and laymen were sent to collect the tithe in each county in England, and there is plenty of evidence for the resentment that this tax provoked.[28] But there is no evidence for any attempt to preach the crusade in each county in England. Gerald mentioned that Bishop Reiner of St Asaph had been preaching the Cross in his diocese in north Wales, but I am not aware of any other reference to the casual preaching of the crusade in England or Wales, or for that matter in Scotland.[29] The silence of the sources need not surprise us. No one, neither the king nor the Pope, wanted non-combatants taking the Cross and then getting in the way of the professional warriors. Indeed, burghers and peasants who took the Cross without their lord's permission were to be made to pay the tithe in full. The last thing Henry wanted was a Peter the Hermit or a Fulk of Neuilly taking the common people by storm. The preaching at Gisors and at Geddington had been addressed to the king's barons and

[27] *Gesta Regis*, ii. 29–33, 58–9; *Das Itinerarium peregrinorum*, ed. H. E. Mayer (Stuttgart, 1962), 276–8. For other references to the preaching at Geddington, see B. N. Siedschlag, *English Participation in the Crusades* (privately printed, 1939), 26; Warren, *Henry II*, 607.
[28] *Gesta Regis*, ii. 33. See S. K. Mitchell, *Taxation in Medieval England* (New Haven, 1951), 87, 119–22.
[29] *Itin.*, 142. I am indebted to Dr Simon Lloyd for confirming my suspicion that evidence for any systematic attempt to organize crusade-preaching in England is lacking. For Scotland, see A. Macquarrie, *Scotland and the Crusades, 1095–1560* (Edinburgh, 1985), 27–31 *passim*. Gervase of Canterbury, *Chronica*, i. 421 (cf. 426) refers to Baldwin's preaching in Wales in 1188.

retainers. Henry wanted the social and military élite to go on crusade accompanied by their men at arms. The civilian population was to make its contribution by paying the Saladin Tithe.

So if there was no attempt to send preachers the length and breadth of England to recruit men for the crusade, why did King Henry send Baldwin to preach the Cross in Wales? Why was Wales to be treated differently? Baldwin, Gerald, and their party set off almost as soon as the Council of Geddington was over. So while the tithe was being collected in England, they were making a systematic circuit of what was a rather backward and by twelfth-century Angevin standards uncentralized region. The fact was that Wales *was* different. Royal administration on the English model was unknown. Politically fragmented, Wales comprised a society of frontier lords and temporarily overawed but potentially hostile native princes. Of one thing Henry could be absolutely certain: neither the Marchers nor the Welsh princes would readily agree to the Saladin Tithe being collected from their people, and indeed the Marcher lords were to remain exempt from royal taxation for long afterwards.[30] If there was to be a Welsh contribution to the crusade at all, it would have to be in the form of warriors. In fact Henry may have been anxious to recruit archers from Wales for his expedition. He had frequently employed them in the past, and during the closing years of his reign they are found fighting for him in France in his conflict with the Capetians. In this connection it may be noted that the only recorded incident concerning a Welshman in the Holy Land during the Third Crusade is told to illustrate the man's prowess as an archer.[31]

It is also true that Wales was a potential trouble-spot. The Marcher lords and the Welsh princes were independently minded men whose propensity for engaging in private warfare was well known and whose capacity to use their power to

[30] Davies, *Conquest, Coexistence*, 286–7.
[31] For Welsh mercenaries in Henry II's service, see J. Boussard, 'Les mercenaires au XIIᶜ siècle: Henri II Plantagenêt et les origines de l'armée de métier', *Bibliothèque de l'école des Chartes*, 106 (1945/6), 193. For their use at the end of the reign, see *Gesta regis*, ii. 46, 50, 68. For the Welshman in the Holy Land, see Ambroise, *L'Estoire de le Guerre Sainte*, ed. G. Paris (Paris, 1897), lines 3731–70; *Das Itinerarium peregrinorum*, 344–5.

affect the political life of England remained potent long afterwards. It could well be that Henry hoped that the more who went on crusade the less likelihood there would be for conflict to break out while his own back was turned. Gerald himself later claimed that John, Count of Mortain (the future King John), upbraided him for emptying the earldom of Pembroke of all its strength, so great was the response to his own preaching at Haverfordwest. More to the point, the fragility of Henry's *détente* in Wales was laid bare when Rhys ap Gruffydd began attacking some Anglo-Norman strongholds in the south almost immediately after the king's death in 1189.[32]

Finally, what did Baldwin's preaching achieve? Gerald draws his account to a close by noting that he had signed about 3,000 men with the Cross, 'all of them skilled with the lance and the arrow and most warlike in their martial endeavours'.[33] But he was also aware of the delays that followed. Conflict in France and Henry's death prevented the main English expedition leaving until the spring of 1190. By then Wales was once again disturbed by warfare, and we may reasonably surmise that many of Baldwin's recruits never set sail. The one Welshman mentioned as participating in the siege of Acre must, if the incident recording his exploit is correctly located in the narrative, have travelled to the East ahead of the main army.[34] Towards the end of 1189 Gerald himself was absolved from the vow he took at the beginning of his tour. He preserved the notification issued by the papal legate which cited his poverty as the grounds for absolution, but perhaps the real reason for his withdrawal from the crusade was that King Richard wanted him back in Wales as part of his attempts to restore peace there.[35] But although Gerald never went to the East, he did not waver in his belief in the importance of the crusade. It is clear from his writings

[32] *De rebus a se gestis*, 76; Davies, *Conquest, Coexistence*, 292.
[33] *Itin.*, 147.
[34] For references, see n. 31. Someone called Simon 'de Wale' was drowned at Acre, *Gesta regis*, ii. 149.
[35] *De rebus a se gestis*, 84–5, cf. 80–1. See Bartlett, *Gerald of Wales*, 15. Richard of Devizes, *Chronicon*, 6, noted that the Pope allowed the king to release men from their crusading vows if he wanted them to remain in England in his service while he was away.

that towards the end of his life he became insistent on the idea that Henry II's refusal to respond to the pleas of Patriarch Eraclius when he visited England in 1185 was the turning-point in the king's career and precipitated his humiliation at the end of his reign.[36] Archbishop Baldwin, on the other hand, arrived in the East in the autumn of 1190 and died at the siege of Acre on 19 November.[37]

---

[36] Bartlett, *Gerald of Wales*, 67, 77–86; J. B. Gillingham, 'Roger of Howden on Crusade', *Medieval Historical Writing in the Christian and Islamic Worlds* (London, 1982), 60 and n. 60.

[37] Among studies bearing on Gerald and the preaching in Wales to have come to my attention after this paper was read, I should particularly like to note H. Pryce, 'Gerald's Journey through Wales', *Journal of Welsh Ecclesiastical History*, 6 (1989); C. Tyerman, *England and the Crusades 1095–1588* (Chicago and London, 1988); and P. J. Cole, *The Preaching of the Crusades to the Holy Land, 1095–1270* (Cambridge, Mass., 1991).

10

Kingship and Crusade in Twelfth-Century Germany

Rudolf Hiestand

The title of this essay may seem paradoxical. Otto of Freising's chronicle contains a well-known passage deploring that because of the schism, Urban II's proclamation at Clermont 'Francos orientales minus permovit'.[1] As for the Second Crusade, in which he had participated, he declares quite frankly that he will not discuss it at any length.[2] Most modern historians of the crusades accept his account. They describe the First Crusade as an enterprise in which no Germans except for Geoffrey of Bouillon and his men from Lorraine took part, and the crusading movement as a whole as 'Gesta Dei per Francos', to quote the title of Guibert of Nogent's chronicle.[3] Reporting a dispute held with a German in 1107 Guibert, bearing in mind his audience, condescendingly adds: 'dic mihi ad quos papa Urbanus contra Turcos praesidia contracturus divertit? Nonne ad Francos? Hi nisi praeissent et barbariem undecumque confluentium gentium vivaci industria et inpavidis viribus constrinxissent, Teutonicorum vestrorum, quorum ne nomen quidem ibi sonuit, auxilia nulla fuissent.'[4]

Indeed, Urban II, Raymond of St Gilles, Ademar of Le Puy,

---

[1] Otto of Freising, *Chronica sive Historia de duabus civitatibus* bk. vii, ch. 2, ed. A. Hofmeister, 2nd edn. (MGH SS rer. Germ., Hanover, 1912), 311: '[Orientales Francos] propter scisma, quod eo tempore inter regnum et sacerdotium fuit, haec expeditio minus permovit.'

[2] Otto of Freising, *Gesta Friderici*, ed. B. von Simson, 3rd edn. (MGH SS rer. Germ., Hanover, 1912), 65; also ed. F.-J. Schmale (Ausgewählte Quellen zur deutschen Geschichte des Mittelalters, 17; Darmstadt, 1964), 218: 'aliis vel alias hoc dicendum relinquimus'.

[3] Guibert of Nogent, *Gesta Dei per Francos* (Recueil des Historiens des Croisades: Historiens Occidentaux, 4; Paris, 1879), 113–263. But see now, for the title, R. B. C. Huygens, *La tradition manuscrite de Guibert de Nogent* (Steenburgis, 1991), 20–46. The correct form is 'Dei gesta per Francos'.

[4] Ibid. bk. ii, ch. 1, 136.

Fulk of Anjou, Guy of Lusignan, Raymond of Poitiers, and Rainald of Châtillon, were all French. So was Bernard of Clairvaux, the person with whom the twelfth-century crusading movement is most closely associated. Apart from Geoffrey of Bouillon, whom the Germans, the Belgians, and the French in a rather ridiculous dispute have each claimed as their own,[5] and leaving aside the rather disreputable figures of Walter Sansavoir and Emicho of Leiningen, only a single German name comes to mind in connection with the crusades: Frederick Barbarossa. The ideal of a fair knight and Christian monarch, Barbarossa went on a crusade as the last act of a long reign and died during it, like the French King Saint Louis in the thirteenth century.[6]

If the Germans had indeed remained aloof from the crusades as this *opinio communis* suggests, the main question which this essay addresses would be redundant. We would have had to ask instead what consequences its non-participation in the crusades had for German kingship. But this common interpretation needs to be questioned. A look at the chronicles of the First Crusade reveals that not even the assumptions on which it is based are sound. Ekkehard of Aura took part in the Crusade of 1101,[7] and his work later served as the main source for Otto of Freising's chronicle. According to Ekkehard's much more differentiated account, in the beginning ('in principio') the Germans did not hear of Urban II's speech because of the quarrel between pope and emperor. They therefore believed that the crusaders were moved by stupid folly, until they slowly became aware of their error and were also affected by the message.[8] Nor did Otto of Freising write 'non permovit' or

---

[5] See G. Waeger, *Gottfried von Bouillon in der Historiographie* (diss., Zürich, 1968).

[6] For the crusade of Frederick Barbarossa, see particularly E. Eickhoff, *Friedrich Barbarossa im Orient* (Tübingen, 1977) and R. Hiestand, '*precipua tocius christianismi columpna*. Barbarossa und der Kreuzzug', *Friedrich Barbarossa: Handlungsspielräume und Wirkungsweisen des staufischen Kaisers*, ed. A. Haverkamp (Vorträge und Forschungen, 40; Sigmaringen, 1991), 51–108.

[7] Ekkehard, *Chronica I*, in *Frutolfs und Ekkehards Chroniken und die anonyme Kaiserchronik*, ed. F.-J. Schmale (Ausgewählte Quellen zur deutschen Geschichte des Mittelalters, 15; Darmstadt, 1972), 140: 'hec bucina minime insonuit.'

[8] Ibid.: 'Inde est, quod omnis pene populus Theutonicus in principio profectionis huius causam ignorantes.' Here, Ekkehard often is understood wrongly as having said that the Germans had not taken part in the crusading movement at all.

the like, but 'minus permovit'—that is to say, less than other parts of the West.[9] Finally, both Ekkehard and Otto are speaking of the First Crusade and not of the crusading movement as a whole.

In fact, the usual view of the First Crusade is not correct. All reports mention Germans as taking part in the Peasants' Crusade, and as members of the main army. At least 15,000 Germans followed Peter the Hermit, exactly the same number as Frenchmen.[10] No doubt the majority of the crusaders were French, Provençal, or Norman, but there was also a large number of Germans. The real difference is that except for those from Lorraine, the Germans did not go to the crusade as a closed group under a single outstanding noble, and that among the leaders in the council, only Geoffrey of Bouillon was from the empire.[11]

I

This article will concentrate on participation by kings, and on the personal, political, and constitutional impact of the crusades on German history in the twelfth century. We shall start with a number of general observations. Henry IV did not, of course, take part in the First Crusade, not only because of the contemporary political situation, but also because of the original idea behind the crusade, and problems of logistics and protocol. The same is true of the Capetian and Anglo-Norman kings. Urban II's aim was not to set up an autonomous movement of Western Christians in the eastern Mediterranean, but to provide military support for the Byzantine Empire, in order at the same time to relieve southern France from the feudal strife that was disrupting it. The participation of kings would have led to political difficulties for which the late eleventh-century world was not prepared. It is enough to imagine the disruption caused by a large

---

[9] The trans. by A. Schmidt in Otto of Freising, *Chronik oder die Geschichte der zwei Staaten*, ed. W. Lammers (Ausgewählte Quellen zur deutschen Geschichte des Mittelalters, 16; Darmstadt, 1961), 503: 'fand [. . .] kein Echo' is not correct.

[10] Orderic Vitalis, *Historia ecclesiastica*, bk. ix, ch. 4, ed. M. Chibnall (Oxford, 1980), v. 28.

[11] Waeger, *Gottfried von Bouillon*.

military force passing through foreign countries, arousing suspicions, justified or not, about its real intentions. Similarly, there were difficulties involved in providing supplies for a king staying outside his own kingdom for many years, not to mention the problems caused by a king's long absence from states that were, on the whole, still organized around his person. Even for the German monarch it made a large difference whether he went on crusade or on a prolonged visit to Italy, where he was still in his own country and could convey his will over the Alps within a few weeks. On crusade in Hungary or Byzantium, let alone Anatolia, by contrast, such correspondence would not only take much longer but could easily be intercepted. Therefore the investiture dispute, Philip I of France's marital affair, and the domestic difficulties faced by William II Rufus of England have unquestionably been exaggerated as explanations for the kings' absence from the First Crusade.

We shall first examine German participation in each of the twelfth-century crusades in turn.[12] In 1101 there was a large German contingent under the leadership of Duke Welf IV of Bavaria. If we leave aside the Scandinavian expeditions of Erik of Denmark and Sigurd of Norway,[13] when Western kings first went to the East half a century after Clermont, the German king was among them. On the Third Crusade, Frederick Barbarossa—'as befits the emperor', to quote the *Itinerarium peregrinorum*[14]—was the first monarch to set out.

Nevertheless, modern historians usually also emphasize French participation in the Second Crusade, perhaps because Louis VII took the Cross spontaneously, while Conrad III was won over by Bernard of Clairvaux only after great hesitation. Another reason may be that the French king

[12] For the history of the crusades, see above all S. Runciman, *A History of the Crusades*, 3 vols. (London, 1951–4); *A History of the Crusades*, ed. K. M. Setton, vols. 1–2 (Madison, 1955–62); J. Prawer, *Histoire du royaume latin de Jérusalem*, 2 vols. (Paris, 1968–9); H. E. Mayer, *The Crusades*, 2nd edn. (Oxford, 1987).

[13] For Erik of Denmark cf. G. Meyer von Knonau, *Die Jahrbücher Heinrichs IV. und Heinrichs V.* (Leipzig, 1890–1909), v. 208; A. Fellmann, *Voyage en Orient du roi Erik Ejegod et sa mort à Paphos* (Helsingfors, 1938); for Sigurd cf. C. Riant, *Expéditions et pèlerinages scandinaves en Terre Sainte au temps des croisades* (Paris, 1865), 173–215.

[14] *Das Itinerarium peregrinorum*, ed. H. E. Mayer (Schriften der MGH, 18; Stuttgart, 1962), 280.

travelled farther across Anatolia, suffering great hardship, before he continued by ship for the shorter distance from Antalya to Antioch, rather than from Constantinople, where Conrad III had passed the winter of 1147-8, to Acre. But perhaps this general picture is simply based on the fact that the only detailed report, although incomplete, was written by a Frenchman, Odo of Deuil,[15] while Otto of Freising, as mentioned above, hardly described the crusade at all.[16] In military terms, Conrad III's contribution in 1147-8 certainly equalled that made by Louis VII. After Conrad arrived in the Holy Land, he was able to recruit a new army from among the pilgrims there, using the large sums of money and the military equipment given by Manuel Comnenos.[17]

This general picture also applies to the Third Crusade.[18] Barbarossa did not reach the Holy Land but died in Cilicia on 10 June 1190. After heavy losses in the following weeks, only a small remnant of the German army took part in the fighting around Acre in 1190-1, where Duke Frederick of Swabia died on 6 January 1191. The German crusade is therefore regarded as having been abortive. Yet the emphasis placed on the French role is not convincing. Philip II Augustus arrived in Acre in May 1191, but he returned home immediately after the fall of the town on a rather poor pretext, leaving the fight for Jerusalem to his rival and vassal, Richard the Lionheart. Admittedly, the Germans played a small part in the Fourth Crusade, because the competition between Philip of Swabia and Otto of Brunswick deterred the princes and many lesser people. But again, it would be mistaken to pass over such German participants as Abbot Martin of Pairis, or Bishop Conrad of Halberstadt.[19] Finally, there remains the crusade of 1197. Planned by Henry VI, executed

---

[15] Eudes de Deuil, *La croisade de Louis VII roi de France*, ed. H. Waquet (Documents relatifs à l'histoire des croisades, 3; Paris, 1949).

[16] See n. 2.

[17] R. Hiestand, ' "Kaiser" Konrad III., der zweite Kreuzzug und ein verlorenes Diplom für eine Abtei auf dem Berge Thabor', *Deutsches Archiv für die Erforschung des Mittelalters*, 35 (1979), 82–126.

[18] See Eickhoff, *Friedrich Barbarossa im Orient*, and Hiestand, '*precipua columpna*'.

[19] See the lists of participants in R. Röhricht, *Die Deutschen im hl. Lande* (Innsbruck, 1894), 91–4.

by German crusaders without the emperor, who was prevented from taking part by ill-health and political considerations, it was called the 'German Crusade'. Not surprisingly, however, it is excluded from the numbered series.

Returning to the question of what part the Germans played in the crusades, we could now go one step further and say that there was no crusade in the twelfth century without German participation, but one without French participation—the crusade of 1197.

II

In the rest of this essay I shall not concentrate on the individual crusades in which Germans took part, or on the special role which the German kings played in the Holy Land because of the imperial Crown. H. E. Mayer discussed this some years ago.[20] Instead, I shall reverse the question and ask what impact the crusades had on German kingship in the twelfth century. Even more generally, I shall examine to what extent crusades—merely planned or actually executed—influenced the course of German history. I shall therefore focus not on political and military events, but on their constitutional and social consequences. In an age of jet planes and political summits it is easily forgotten how extraordinary it was for a king to stay outside his own country in the Middle Ages, and what political and material difficulties, and problems of protocol this situation gave rise to. The Second Crusade was, in a way, the first official state visit abroad by a German king, and it provided the occasion for personal meetings between a yet uncrowned 'emperor' of the West and a *basileus*, as well as between an 'emperor' and a king of Jerusalem. The last meeting with a French king had been more than a century ago. A few decades later, on the Third Crusade, the—now crowned—Western emperor and the *basileus* both deliberately avoided meeting.

The crusades also helped to elevate the status of German

[20] H. E. Mayer, 'Kaiserrecht und Hl. Land', *Aus Reichsgeschichte und nordischer Geschichte*, ed. H. Fuhrmann, H. E. Mayer and K. Wriedt (Kieler Historische Forschungen, 14; Stuttgart, 1972), 193–208.

monarchs. While it remains a moot point whether a charter which Conrad III granted to an otherwise unknown monastery on Mount Tabor was the consequence of suzerainty over the Holy Land,[21] the words 'semper augustus' certainly became an important 'imperial' addition to Conrad's title as Roman king during the crusade—not during his stay in the Byzantine Empire, but in Palestine.[22] These words gave him a position similar to that achieved by Henry VI in 1186, when he was given the title of 'Caesar'. In 1184 the German emperor, together with the Pope and the kings of Western Europe, were installed to dispose of the crown of Jerusalem, when Baldwin IV's leprosy and the apparently poor health of his nephew Baldwin V had made the succession to the throne an urgent problem. And finally, by marrying the heiress of Jerusalem, Isabel of Brienne, in 1225 Frederick II acquired the title 'King of Jerusalem', which his grandson Conradin bore until his death as his sole legal royal title.

At a different level, the German emperor's temporary suzerainty over England was a result of the contest between Duke Leopold of Austria and Richard the Lionheart. Similarly, Henry VI's crusade gave him suzerainty over the Lusignan kingdom of Cyprus and the Armenian kingdom of Cilicia, as Antioch recognized Duke Frederick of Swabia as its legitimate lord in 1190. While feudal links with Cyprus and Armenia in the eastern Mediterranean concerned the emperor more than the German king, the ties forged between Germany and England after Richard's capture by Leopold of Austria and his extradition to Henry VI affected the German kingship.[23]

In a similar way, the Second Crusade strengthened the alliance with Byzantium, even if the Treaty of Salonica was less the basis of a new alliance than the confirmation of an earlier one, reinforced by a new project for matrimonial alliance, as Hanna Vollrath has recently sug-

---

[21] Hiestand, ' "Kaiser" Konrad III.', 98–112.

[22] Ibid. 113–26.

[23] H. Fichtenau, 'Zypern, Akkon und das Lösegeld für Richard Löwenherz', *Archiv für österreichische Geschichte*, 125 (1966), 11–32; R. Hiestand, 'Antiochia, Sizilien und das Reich am Ende des 12. Jahrhunderts', *Quellen und Forschungen aus italienischen Archiven und Bibliotheken*, 73 (1993), 70–121.

gested.[24] Similarly Henry VI's relations with Armenia could build on his father's relationship with the Rupenide Levon, to whom Barbarossa had probably promised a royal crown. Furthermore, Barbarossa's reign had, for the first time in German history, also inaugurated intense diplomatic contacts with non-Christian powers. In other words, as far as we can speak of 'foreign policy' in the twelfth century, the crusades both reinforced the German Empire's international involvement in the Balkans and the eastern Mediterranean world and, quite unexpectedly, superimposed new ties with England, now at the level of kingship, over the older ones between Welfs and Angevins.

III

But the question of relations between crusade and German kingship can be put in yet another way. What was the personal attitude of the German kings to the crusade in the twelfth century? At this level, the answer seems quite easy. Only two kings, Conrad III and Frederick Barbarossa, actually took part in a crusade themselves, and only Conrad III reached a crusader's real goal, the Holy City. Barbarossa died in 1190 before entering Syria, while Henry VI did not even leave Sicily.

However, the crusade had begun to play an important role for the German monarchs long before 1145–6. As early as the turn of 1102–3, a project devised by Henry IV to leave the Empire to his son and go to Jerusalem himself was discussed at a diet in Mainz.[25] All that remains unclear is

---

[24] Most recently H. Vollrath, 'Konrad III. und Byzanz', *Archiv für Kulturgeschichte*, 59 (1977, publ. 1979), 321–65; see also J. P. Niederkorn, 'Die Mitgift der Kaiserin Irene. Anmerkungen zur byzantinischen Politik König Konrads III.', *Römische Historische Mitteilungen*, 28 (1986), 125–39. Still, I would insist that the confirmation of an existing treaty is also to be considered an important political and especially legal, act; we may therefore very well continue to speak of a 'treaty of Salonica'. See now R. Hiestand, '*Neptis tua* und *faustus Graecorum*. Zu den deutsch-byzantinischen Verhandlungen um 1150', *Deutsches Archiv für Erforschung des Mittelalters*, 49 (1993), 501–55.

[25] Ekkehard, *Chronica I*, 182: 'Henricus imperator nativitatem domini Mogontie celebrans filio suo Heinrico regi rerum summam dimissurum seque sepulchrum Domini visitaturum per Emehardum episcopum publice predicari fecit.' When

whether the emperor himself announced his intention, whether Bishop Emehard of Würzburg presented it in a sermon, or whether it was only rumoured among those present without being officially promulgated.[26] While some saw it as a real crusade, to others the emperor's plan seemed more an individual pilgrimage of penitence.[27] According to the anonymous *Kaiserchronik* the rumours spread 'suddenly and for no reason'.[28] However, as the chronicler wrote his text after the emperor's death, he was aware that the intention remained unfulfilled, and his account must be read in this light. Nevertheless, even the most cautious reports mention that other people prepared themselves to set out with the emperor.[29] And the monk of Jerusalem who, after Henry IV's exhumation at Liège which the Church had imposed, was the only person who prayed at his grave, might symbolize the dead Salian's late inclusion in the Crusade after he was unable to perform it himself.[30] In any case, there were crusading plans at the German court as early as 1102, even before the eastern expeditions of the Dane Erik and the Norwegian Sigurd.[31] It was not Capetian France, where in the

Ekkehard speaks of *predicare*, he is using the same expression which is employed for Urban II's speech at Clermont. Ekkehard gives Christmas as a date, the *Annales s. Albani Moguntini* differ: 'in epyphania imperator [*one MS adds:* quasi] corde compuncto Deo promittebat pro delictis suis Hierosolimam pergere [*the same MS adds:* sicque optimates regni decipiebat]'; cf. Meyer von Knonau, *Jahrbücher*, v. 173; U. Reuling, *Die Kur in Deutschland und Frankreich* (Göttingen, 1979), 134 for the election of Henry V; U. Schmidt, *Königswahl und Thronfolge im 12. Jahrhundert* (Cologne and Vienna, 1987), 20 and n. 106.

[26] *Kaiserchronik*, in: *Frutolfs und Ekkehards Chroniken und die anonyme Kaiserchronik*, 224: 'subito rumor forte divulgatur imperatorem Heinrico filio suo rerum summam dimissurum seque sepulchrum Domini visitando pro peccatis suis Christo satisfacturum.'

[27] Ibid.

[28] Ibid.: 'subito [. . .] forte'.

[29] Ibid.: 'unde et nonnulli cum maximo favore [*ed., read:* fervore] ad ipsius se preparavere comitatum.' In the letter of Henry IV to abbot Hugh of Cluny the emperor adds the condition that his departure would not be until 'post confirmatam pacem': *Die Briefe Heinrichs IV.*, ed. C. Erdmann (MGH Deutsches Mittelalter, 1; Leipzig, 1937), 39 no. 31.

[30] Meyer von Knonau, *Jahrbücher*, v. 308.

[31] Ph. Jaffé, *Regesta pontificum Romanorum*, 2 vols., 2nd edn. (Leipzig, 1885–8), no. 5555, and C. Erdmann, *Die Entstehung des Kreuzzugsgedankens* (Stuttgart, 1935), 292 ff. I am deliberately excluding the Iberian peninsula here, as it is not yet clear whether the letters of Urban II and Paschal II imply similar projects at the time of the First Crusade or the crusade of 1100/1.

last years of his long reign Philip I was hardly fit to pursue domestic politics, nor the Anglo-Normans, but the German kings who first took account of the changed world situation after 15 July 1099 in their own political designs. Thus of all the western countries, Germany first took up the Crusade at the level of the monarchs.

Perhaps we should go even further back. Ekkehard of Aura reports that in 1101, on the death of King Conrad, Henry IV's son, signs of the cross were found on his arm.[32] Given the emotionally charged atmosphere of those years, this is an obvious allusion to the crusade, especially as Ekkehard had reported similar prodigies shortly before, among the signs preceding the large expedition of 1095.[33] None the less, it must remain open whether the signs on Conrad's arm were intended as signs of penitence (for the rebellion against his father) or as a confirmation of Conrad's deeply religious nature, which the chronicler constantly emphasizes. To be sure, almost fifty more years were to pass before a German king actually went to the Holy Land in person—Conrad III arrived there in 1148. However, it has long been overlooked that he was merely returning to places he knew well. Following a 'conversio morum suorum' after a lunar eclipse in spring 1124, Henry V's nephew had vowed to go to Jerusalem 'Christo militaturus'.[34] Of course, its biblical provenance suggests that the term 'militaturus' can be read figuratively and spiritually. It is more likely, however, that Conrad intended actually to spend a certain period as a *Gastritter*, that is, temporarily engaged to provide military service to the Holy

[32] Ekkehard, *Chronica I*, 162: 'Testari solent qui aderant in brachio corporis exanimi crucis signaculum subito exortum se vidisse'; cf. Meyer von Knonau, *Jahrbücher*, v. 148.

[33] Ibid. 142; cf. Fulcher of Chartres, *Historia Hierosolymitana*, bk. i, ch. 8, ed. H. Hagenmeyer (Heidelberg, 1913), 330.

[34] Ekkehard, *Chronica IV*, 364: 'perterritus Cunradus consobrinus imperatoris conversionem morem suorum professus Hierosolimam se profecturum ibidemque Christo militaturum devovit, indeque favorem non modicum ab omnibus, qui hoc audierant, acquisivit. Nonnulli quoque nequitie studiis antea dediti eidem se sociari profitentur comitatui.' Röhricht, *Die Deutschen im hl. Lande*, omitted Conrad from his list of crusaders between the First and the Second Crusades; W. von Giesebrecht, *Geschichte der deutschen Kaiserzeit* (Leipzig, 1881–95), iii. 980 left open whether Conrad did fulfil his vow.

Sepulchre.[35] Thus he put into practice what his grandfather Henry IV had intended to do in 1102–3 and Philip, first-born son of Louis VI and heir to the French throne, had announced as his intention, perhaps at the same time as Conrad.[36] In fact, Conrad was not present at the negotiations about Henry V's succession in 1125.[37] It is not clear, however, whether his departure was connected with Pope Calixtus II's call for a crusade in 1121–2, as Riley-Smith has recently suggested. Chronological reasons speak against this view.[38] The connection is more likely to have been the campaign for help initiated in 1123–4 by the brethren of the hospital of St John, and supported by Calixtus II. It seems to have affected the southern German regions in particular.[39] Thus Conrad III was in the Holy Land twice in his life, first in 1124–5, and then again in 1148. He was the only western monarch who visited Jerusalem twice. Frederick Barbarossa, too, had already been there when he decided to take the cross after the reports of the defeat at Hattin and the fall of Jerusalem in winter 1187–8. In 1147–9 he had accompanied his uncle Conrad III on the Second Crusade. Barbarossa had met Manuel Comnenos and had taken part in the siege of Damascus. His 1158 charter for the Hospitallers explicitly recalled his personal impressions of the Hospital's charitable works,[40] and his experiences during the Second Crusade certainly fed into his attempts to organize the crusaders' army more stringently in 1188–9.[41] Thus both Conrad III and Frederick Barbarossa had, when they took their crusading vow, already made a journey to Jerusalem. They were the only western monarchs who were

---

[35] For this typical military institution of the Holy Land, cf. R. S. Smail, *Crusading warfare 1095–1187* (Cambridge, 1956), 88 ff.

[36] Otto of Freising, *Gesta*, bk. i, ch. 36 (35), ed. Simson, 53; ed. Schmale, 200.

[37] See below, Sect. IX.

[38] On the crusade of the Venetians, cf. Andrea Dandolo, *Chronica*, ed. E. Pastorello (Rerum Italicarum Scriptores, 2nd edn., xii, pt. 1; Bologna [1958]), 232, and J. Riley-Smith, 'The Venetian Crusade of 1122–1124', *I comuni italiani nel regno di Gerusalemme*, ed. G. Airaldi and B. Z. Kedar (Genoa, 1986), 337–50.

[39] J. Delaville le Roulx, *Cartulaire général de l'ordre des Hospitaliers de St-Jean de Jérusalem*, i (Paris, 1894), 39 n. 47, and R. Hiestand, *Papsturkunden für Templer und Johanniter: Vorarbeiten zum Oriens Pontificius I* (Abhandlungen der Akademie der Wissenschaften in Göttingen, 3rd ser. 77; Göttingen, 1972), 424.

[40] MGH D. F[riderici] I. no. 152.

[41] See below, VII and nn. 82–3.

Hierosolymitae on ascending the throne and on their departure for the East.

Going beyond the twelfth century, we must fill in the gap between Henry VI and Frederick II. Philip of Swabia was involved in the Fourth Crusade, even if we reject the 'plot theory', which assumes that from the start, the Crusade was destined to conquer Constantinople, and perhaps to end there. Otto IV's crusading plans, hitherto neglected, have recently been re-examined on the basis of Walter von der Vogelweide's *Ottenton* and other evidence.[42] On the day of his coronation the Welf emperor, whose father had been in Jerusalem in 1172,[43] privately took the cross from the Bishop of Cambrai. At the diet of Würzburg at Whitsun 1209, the Abbot of Morimond had already demanded that as a penitence for his uncanonical betrothal with Beatrix of Swabia, he should not only found two monasteries, but also go on a crusade.[44] Thus even Otto IV could not separate himself from the crusading idea, even if he never drew up a concrete plan of departure. On his deathbed, the emperor remembered his non-fulfilled vow and left gifts to pay others to fight by proxy for the Holy Sepulchre.[45]

[42] Cf. the recent article by M. Nix, 'Der Kreuzzugsaufruf Walthers im Ottenton und der Kreuzzugsplan Kaiser Ottos IV.' *Germanisch-romanische Monatsschrift*, n.s. 34 (1984), 178–294, with reference to A. Hatto, 'Walther von der Vogelweide's Ottonian Poem: A new interpretation', *Speculum*, 24 (1949), 542–53 and E. Nellmann, 'Walthers unzeitgemäßer Ottenton', *Zeitschrift für deutsche Philologie*, 98 (1979), 22–60. For earlier works see E. Winkelmann, *Philipp von Schwaben und Otto IV. von Braunschweig* (Jahrbücher der deutschen Geschichte, Leipzig, 1873–8), ii. 159, 205ff., 292; D. Rüdebusch, *Der Anteil Niedersachsens an den Kreuzzügen* (Hildesheim, 1972), 41–6 adds nothing new.

[43] On the pilgrimage of Henry the Lion, most recently H. E. Mayer, 'Die Stiftung Herzog Heinrichs des Löwen für das Hl. Grab', *Heinrich der Löwe*, ed. W.-D. Mohrmann (Göttingen, 1980), 307–30.

[44] Cf. Winkelmann, *Otto IV.*, ii. 159, based on Otto of St Blasien, *Chronica* 51, ed. A. Hofmeister (MGH SS rer. Germ.; Hanover, 1912), 86f. and B. U. Hucker, *Otto IV.* (Hanover, 1990). Wilbrand of Oldenburg's journey is to be connected with this crusading plan, ed. J. M. C. Laurent, *Peregrinatores medii aevi quatuor* (Leipzig, 1873), 159–91.

[45] Cf. the *Narratio de morte Ottonis IV imperatoris*, ed. E. Martène and U. Durand, *Thesaurus novus anecdotorum*, iii (Paris, 1717), 1375: 'Postquam divina ordinatione in imperium electus, et a domino papa consecratus sum, pro tanto beneficio accepto ignorans, quid in recompensationem Deo offerrem, corpus et animam ei obtuli, qui pro me crucem sustinuit. Et exiens civitate Roma post consecrationem, assumpto in partem episcopo Camern, crucem accepi ab ipso, quam usque hodiernum diem in collo tuli, et ab hominibus occultavi, expectans

To sum up, only three out of the thirteen German kings between 1095 and 1245, to our knowledge, had no direct connection with the crusade: Henry V, Lothair III,[46] and Henry (VII), first-born son of Frederick II.

IV

As the medieval state in our period was always centred on individuals (*Personenverbandsstaat*), we must ask whether and to what extent the crusade influenced monarchs personally. Frederick Barbarossa's death was the most spectacular incident, and has already been mentioned. However, this does not constitute an adequate reply to the question. Conrad III and Frederick II certainly returned alive. Yet, in 1149–50 Wibald of Stavelot commented that on his return the king was a different person from the one who had left for the East two years earlier.[47] The medical assistance given to him by his imperial brother, Manuel I Comnenos, had cured Conrad of his grave illness in autumn 1147, but he was marked by it until the end of his life. His early death in 1152 removed the basis of a further matrimonial alliance, as agreed in Salonica, and of the negotiations between the two empires. For the Byzantines this project made sense only if the future husband of a Byzantine princess was king and emperor in the West. This would have been the only way to find a solution to the problem of southern Italy that was acceptable to both sides.[48] When Conrad III died in 1152, his second son Frederick of Rotenburg was a 7-year-old child. His father had not considered his succession possible, and therefore had not designated him. Thus on the one hand Conrad III's

opportunitatem, ut illam peregrinationem exequerer, prout deceret imperialem maiestatem, ad laudem et gloriam crucifixi, et recuperationem Terrae sanctae. Sed propositi executionem hactenus praepedivit diabolus.' Italian chroniclers like Malaspini would have Otto IV take part in the crusade of Damietta, cf. S. Borsari, 'L'espansione economica fiorentina nell 'Oriente cristiano', *Rivista storica italiana*, 70 (1958), 478 n. 5.

[46] The index to the *Diplomata* edition of Lothair III does not even have an entry 'Jerusalem'!

[47] *Wibaldi epistolae*, ed. Ph. Jaffé (Bibliotheca rerum Germanicarum, 1; Berlin, 1864), 314, no. 195.

[48] See Vollrath, 'Konrad III. und Byzanz'.

illness and early death as a consequence of his participation in the Second Crusade opened the way to the throne for Frederick Barbarossa; on the other hand, the alliance between Staufen and Comnenes was severely jeopardized and the old problem of the two emperors (*Zweikaiserproblem*) reopened.

It is easily overlooked how decisively the Third Crusade influenced the German kingship. When Barbarossa died in the River Saleph, Henry VI immediately had to take over both the succession in the empire and in Italy, and had to fight for his Sicilian rights and to secure his position as German king and emperor. But even more crucial was the death of the emperor's third son—who in the case of Henry VI's early death would have been the next Staufen claimant to the throne—Duke Frederick of Swabia, at Acre in 1191. When Conrad of Burgundy died in 1195, the Staufen party had to put forward Philip of Swabia as a candidate in 1198 when the rights of the child Frederick II could not be upheld.[49] Thus a new element entered the scene. As Philip had originally been designated for a clerical career until Henry VI recalled him in 1195, his candidature needed a special dispensation by the Church, and opened up the possibility of political claims and counterclaims. The *clericus* Philip seriously aggravated the situation for the Staufen party after 1197. If Duke Frederick had succeeded, this would not have entered the discussions. To be sure, this is not to suggest that there would have been no opposition at all to a Staufen succession in 1197–8, but circumstances strongly favoured the opposing party.

V

Immediately after Urban II's speech, the emperor was confronted with another aspect of the crusading phenomenon,

---

[49] For the events of 1197 now see A. Haverkamp in *Handbuch der europäischen Geschichte*, ed. T. Schieder, ii (Stuttgart, 1987), 336–72; still important is Winkelmann, *Philipp von Schwaben und Otto IV. von Braunschweig*, i. 1 ff.; H. Stehkämper, 'Erzbischof Adolf von Altena und die deutsche Königswahl 1195–205', *Historische Zeitschrift, Beiheft* 2 (Munich, 1973), 5–83; Hucker, *Otto IV.*, and below, Sect. IX.

the persecution of the Jews. In 1095–6 Henry IV was in Italy. The first reports of the crusading movement seem to have found little or no echo at the court. Henry IV did not interrupt his stay, as he evidently did not see any challenge to his royal authority. But the situation changed with the persecutions perpetrated by the groups led by Folkmar and Emicho, in a number of Rhenish towns such as Cologne, Worms, Speyer, Neuss, and Mainz, etc. Questions relating to the Jews are treated by Alexander Patschovsky elsewhere in this volume,[50] but they cannot be completely excluded from the problems of the crusades and the king's attitude towards them. At first the crusaders seem to have been looking mainly for booty and money; when there was no more money to be extorted, their aim clearly became to annihilate the Jews. Right from the start, the misguided religious idea that before an expedition to distant countries, the Christian world itself should first be 'cleansed', played a part.[51] The emperor was completely unprepared for what happened. Except for a written order to the bishops and counts, we have no record of an adequate response until very late, although the royal authority was concerned in its most intimate duty as guarantor of peace and provider of protection. The Jews were people of the king and they were under his special protection for which they had to pay him annual tributes. It is characteristic that individual Jewish communities immediately appealed to the king for help. Henry IV seems to have expected that an energetic appeal to the local authorities might restore order. On the other side, a Hebrew chronicle alleges that in a proclamation, Geoffrey of Bouillon stated that he wished to avenge the death of Christ by punishing the Jews.[52] This is, however, untenable, as the same chronicle

[50] See above.

[51] See also A. Waas, 'Volk Gottes und Militia Christi—Juden und Kreuzfahrer', *Judentum im Mittelalter*, ed. P. Wilpert (Miscellanea Mediaevalia, 4; Berlin, 1966), 410–34; D. Mertens, 'Christen und Juden zur Zeit des ersten Kreuzzuges', *Die Juden als Minderheit in der Geschichte*, ed. B. Martin and E. Schulin (Munich, 1981), 46–67; A. M. Shapiro, 'Jews and Christians in the period of the Crusades', *Journal of Ecumenical Studies*, 9 (1972), 725–49; A. H. Bredero, 'Het antijoods gevoelen van de middeleeuwse samenleving', *Nederlands Archief voor Kerkgeschiedenis*, 64 (1984), 1–38.

[52] *Hebräische Berichte über die Judenverfolgungen während der Kreuzzüge*, ed. A. Neubauer and M. Stern (Berlin, 1892), and S. Eidelberg, *The Jews and the Crusaders:*

immediately afterwards states that the duke had declared his intention to protect the Jews as ordered by the emperor's mandate.[53]

From both the Jewish and the Christian reports it is clear that the bishops, in their capacity as town lords, on royal orders initially tried to protect the Jews, but were in many cases unsuccessful. Nor could the distant king offer any effective help.[54] In a second phase even bishops in some places began to lay their hands on Jewish property.[55] Henry IV did not react to the offences until his return from Italy in 1097, when he granted the Jews in Regensburg and elsewhere who had been forcibly baptized the right to return to Mosaic law, thus pitting himself against the crusaders and their intense, but ill-directed religious feeling.[56] Thus he did not limit himself to issuing declarations against the culprits. Archbishop Ruthard of Mainz, for example, who had refused to punish his own men and who was, a little later, accused by Pope Clement III of having stolen a chalice of Jewish provenance, was forced to leave the town for many years.[57]

In addition to its religious implications, the persecution of the Jews also had a strong anarchic element. For the first time, we witness a clash between popular religious feeling and public order, a conflict between royal authority and the crusading movement from below. But the impression remains not only that the king saw these excesses as an attack

The Hebrew Chronicles of the First and Second Crusades (Madison, 1977); for the First Crusade in particular the report by Salomo bar Simeon, ed. Neubauer, 81–152; ed. Eidelberg, 21–72, and cf. the recent publication by R. Chazan, European Jewry and the First Crusade (Berkeley, Los Angeles and London, 1987).

[53] J. Aronius, Regesten zur Geschichte der Juden im fränkischen und deutschen Reich bis zum Jahre 1273 (Berlin, 1887); i. 87f. no. 178, and Monumenta Judaica: 2000 Jahre Geschichte und Kultur der Juden am Rhein, ii (Cologne, 1963), passim.

[54] Aronius, Regesten; E. Roth, 'Die jüdischen Gemeinden am Rhein im Mittelalter', Monumenta Judaica, ii. 60–130.

[55] Cf. Waas, 'Volk Gottes', 416.

[56] Ekkehard, Chronica I, 126; Frutolf, Chronica, 108; Kaiserchronik, 216. See also G. Kisch, Forschungen zur Rechts- und Sozialgeschichte der Juden in Deutschland während des Mittelalters (Zürich, 1955), 57 with bibliography. The anonymous chronicler from Darmstadt claims that the protection given by Bishop John of Speyer was the result of a special mandate from Henry IV (Neubauer and Stern), or of the king's aid (Eidelberg). This is impossible for chronological reasons: cf. Neubauer, Hebräische Berichte, 171; Eidelberg, The Jews and the Crusaders, 101.

[57] Roth, 'Die jüdischen Gemeinden am Rhein', 124 n. 22; Aronius, Regesten, 95 ff., 207.

on his rights, but that they also provided a welcome opportunity to move against towns and their lords.[58] At Mainz
Henry IV razed the town walls and for a certain period
diverted all the episcopal revenues to the royal treasury,
which gained far more than had been retained by the archbishop, or what the goods destroyed were worth.[59]

The beginning of the Second Crusade was again marked
by savage persecutions, led by the French monk Radulph,
whom Bernard of Clairvaux rebuked sharply.[60] Again, the
royal government was taken completely unawares and exercised its authority only late and inadequately.[61] But as the
king was in Germany this time, the persecutions did not
reach the scale of those of 1096, remaining rather isolated
outbreaks. However, no sooner had King Conrad III set out
when new persecutions began at Bacharach in the Rhine
valley, where the Jews explicitly complained about the king's
absence abroad.

Warned by these earlier experiences, Barbarossa gave
the Jews his protection publicly and in advance in 1187–8,
with the result that we hear of almost no persecutions.[62]
At the 'Curia Jesu Christi', the emperor threatened death
as the punishment for killing a Jew.[63] According to Hebrew
chronicles, the crusade did no serious damage to the
Jewish communities. The emperor is said to have required
'only little money' from them, but to have strictly
ordered the monks and clergy not to preach against the

---

[58] Frutolf, *Chronica*, 110; Ekkehard, *Chronica I*, 126 f.; Aronius, *Regesten*, 94 f., and
Meyer von Knonau, *Jahrbücher*, v. 29 n. 11.

[59] *Kaiserchronik*, 216.

[60] Cf. W. Bernhardi, *Konrad III*. (Jahrbücher der deutschen Geschichte; Leipzig,
1883), 523 ff.; *The Chronicles of Rabbi Joseph ben Joshua ben Meir the Sephardi*, trans. C.
H. F. Bialloblotzky, i (London, 1835), 119 ff. = F. Wilken, *Geschichte der Kreuzzüge*,
iii, pt. 1 (Leipzig, 1817), App. I, 1–17; Otto of Freising, *Gesta*, bk. i, ch. 39 (38), ed.
Simson, 58; ed. Schmale, 206 ff. does not mention the protection granted to the
Jews at Nuremberg.

[61] Ephraim bar Jakob, trans. Neubauer, *Hebräische Berichte*, 192; Eidelberg, *The
Jews and the Crusaders*, 125: 'At that time there was no king to protect Israel from the
errant ones, for king Conrad had [. . .] set out for Jerusalem.'

[62] For the Jews at the time of the Third Crusade, see Aronius, *Regesten*, 145; Roth,
'Die jüdischen Gemeinden am Rhein', 67; W. von Giesebrecht and B. von Simson,
Geschichte der deutschen Kaiserzeit, vi (Leipzig, 1895), 185 and 678; Waas, 'Volk
Gottes', 414; R. Chazan, 'Emperor Frederick I, the Third Crusade, and the Jews',
Viator, 8 (1977), 83–93.

[63] Aronius, *Regesten*, 13, 45, 123.

Jews.[64] In contrast to the situation at the end of the eleventh century, the king's authorities were now able to prevent large-scale disorders.[65] Under Henry VI persecutions were similarly suppressed right from the start. In addition to imposing fines which could amount to 500 silver marks, the emperor forced the culprits to rebuild the Jews' houses and synagogues, thus granting real reparations for the first time.[66]

In sum, it is clear that through the persecution of the Jews which they set off, the crusades represented a serious challenge to the king's authority. The king was only gradually able to fulfil his duty of protection to the extent required. To be sure, neither under Barbarossa nor under Henry VI were these interventions disinterested. The heavy fines Barbarossa imposed demonstrate that fiscal reasons played a part and show how welcome additional revenues were, given the imminent crusade. These revenues came from both sides, from persecutors and their victims alike.

Although the persecutions of the Jews had found the royal government unprepared, almost from the start they proved to be a force for securing internal peace on a large scale, just as establishing peace in the West had been one of Urban II's aims in proclaiming the crusade. It is not pure coincidence that in the first public peace set up by a German king for the whole kingdom, the edict of 1103 promulgated by Henry IV for a period of four years, the Jews were included *expressis verbis* among those to be protected.[67] It must be pointed out that this happened at the same diet at which rumours were circulating that the emperor was planning a journey to Jerusalem.[68] Similarly, before the Second and the Third Crusades, there were attempts to impose far-reaching

---

[64] Ephraim bar Jakob, trans. Neubauer, *Hebräische Berichte*, 209: 'Er schützte sie mit seiner ganzen Kraft'; similarly Elasar bar Juda, ibid. 218: 'Blos[s] der alte Kaiser und sein Sohn, der junge Kaiser, die lange leben mögen, waren den Juden gewogen.' Elasar continues to report that more than 10,000 crusaders intended to attack the Jews but the emperor intervened and his marshal dispersed them by force, on 26 March 1189. On 29 March, a proclamation of peace was made and the bishops revoked the crusade indulgence for those who offended against the Jews.

[65] The report of Elasar bar Juda, ibid. 214ff. bears quite a different tenor.

[66] Ephraim bar Jakob, ibid. 212; for a similar incident at Boppard, cf. ibid. 214.

[67] MGH Const. i, no. 74.

[68] Fulcher, *Historia Hierosolymitana*, bk. i, ch. 2, 123.

regulations for peace. On its own behalf the kingship now took up the peace movement earlier promoted by the Church, and began to transfer it into the public sphere. This was almost a logical consequence of what Urban II had intended.

VI

We must now return to the constitutional impact of the crusades on German politics. It is significant that neither Conrad III nor Barbarossa went on their first journey to the East as the designated and elected heir to the throne. In 1124 there was still hope that Henry V would have a son. The future Conrad III was only the second-born of the emperor's nephews and grandsons of Henry IV; in 1147 the presumptive heir, as elected and crowned King of the Romans, was Conrad's son Henry (VI).

On the other hand, on setting out for the crusade both Conrad III and Frederick Barbarossa left their eldest sons and presumptive successors at home, not only in order to guarantee an orderly administration. Since 1101 it had become evident to everyone that a crusade was too perilous to allow it to put dynastic continuity at risk. After all, even Duke Frederick I of Swabia had complained angrily that Conrad III had allowed his eldest son Frederick, the future emperor, whom he had designated for the succession to the duchy, to go on the crusade.[69] For the same reason, Henry VI remained at home in 1189, against Gregory VIII's original wishes.[70] Similarly, Henry VI never considered allowing his son to go on crusade, for we see the young Frederick on his way to Germany for his coronation at Aix-la-Chapelle when

---

[69] Otto of Freising, *Gesta*, bk, i, ch. 42 (41), ed. Simson, 59; ed. Schmale, 208–10: 'acrem in mente [. . .] indignationem gerens, quod filium suum Fredericum, quem ipse tamquam primogenitum ac nobilissime prioris comparis sue filium unicum [. . .] totius terre sue heredem fecerat, crucem permiserat accipere.'

[70] Eickhoff, *Friedrich Barbarossa im Orient*, 35 believes that Frederick could just as well have given the leadership of the crusade to Henry VI or Frederick of Swabia, but he overlooks the fact that Henry's own succession had not yet been secured (his marriage with Constance had not yet been blessed with a son), and that Frederick of Swabia could not rank as an adequate substitute. The emperor, for his part, had made a vow, which had to be fulfilled. Cf. now Hiestand, '*precipua columpna*'.

the crusaders' ships were setting off from Messina to the East on 1 September 1197. The same problems arose in France for Louis VII in 1147 and for Philip Augustus in 1190.

As it was uncertain whether the king would return safely or whether the succession to the throne might become acute during the crusade, everything had to be arranged as far as possible before the departure. Early fixing of the succession had been resisted since the time of the investiture contest because in the case of a vacancy arising, it limited the right of election to a merely formal act. None the less, three times in our period the German kings managed to obtain substantial concessions from the princes in view of an imminent crusade. Thus the crusade also become an instrument in the king's hand to be used against the elective principle, and in favour of dynastic right.

When Henry IV planned a crusade in 1102–3, the problem was not acute, as his son had been crowned since 1098. Yet significantly enough, Otto of Freising misunderstood Ekkehard's report that the emperor intended to give the regency to his son for the time of the crusade, and believed that he was acting to install his successor.[71] On the Second Crusade, Conrad III was able to have his son Henry (VI), only 10 years old at the time, elected and crowned.[72] The empire was conferred upon Henry for the length of Conrad's absence, with the explicit justification that 'ne post decessum eius regnum absque principe remaneret et aliqua perturbatione moveretur'.[73] Barbarossa had already secured the election of Henry VI in 1169, in view of his forthcoming negotiations with the Pope.[74] The 1188–9 crusade gave him

[71] Otto of Freising, *Chronica*, bk. vii, ch. 8, 510.

[72] Cf. Reuling, *Die Kur in Deutschland und Frankreich*, 182 ff; Schmidt, *Königswahl und Thronfolge*, 118 f.; according to F. Rörig, 'Geblütsrecht und freie Wahl', *Abhandlungen der Deutschen Akademie der Wissenschaften zu Berlin, Phil.-hist. Klasse* (1945/46) no. 6, 33, it was a concession to Conrad that he could designate his son, as he could not do so by existing law.

[73] Sigebert of Gembloux, *Chronica. Continuatio Gemblacensis*, MGH SS vi, 289. On the position of the Archbishop of Mainz, cf. King Henry's (VI) letter to Pope Eugenius III, ed. F. Hausmann, MGH D. H[enrici] (VI.) no. 9 (= *Wibaldi Epistolae* no. 116): 'ex antiquo suae ecclesiae et dignitatis privilegio sub absentia principis custos regni et procurator.'

[74] G. Baaken, 'Die Altersfolge der Söhne Friedrich Barbarossas und die Königserhebung Heinrichs VI.', *Deutsches Archiv für die Erforschung des Mittelalters*, 24 (1968), 46–78; E. Assmann, 'Friedrich Barbarossas Kinder', *Deutsches Archiv für die Erforschung des Mittelalters*, 33 (1977), 435–72.

the chance to obtain from the Pope the succession of Henry VI to the imperial crown in advance. Thus even at imperial level, the crusading vow militated against the time-lag between the death of one emperor and his successor's first Roman expedition and imperial coronation, which had until then been unavoidable. Finally, in Henry VI's time the crusading vow again proved to be an important factor in persuading the princes to elect the emperor's son, despite his tender age. Henry VI's early death, before Frederick II had been crowned at Aix, prevented this at a crucial turning-point in German history. The path towards hereditary and dynastic succession to the throne was blocked. Nevertheless, the crusade had been a strong and influential force in promoting the hereditary nature of the Crown. It should be stressed that in both cases—in 1147 and in 1196—a minor was to succeed, not an adult son.

VII

German monarchs and German participants played a crucial role in three crusades during the twelfth century. To look at the king or emperor is certainly not enough. A king never went on a crusade as an individual. He was always accompanied by a large number of followers and other crusaders. Of importance for the German kingdom was not only how many people went on crusade, but who exactly they were. We shall dismiss the often quite fantastic figures which the chronicles give for the earlier crusades,[75] and limit ourselves to verifiable facts. Each time, the list of participants was impressive.[76] To begin with the crusade of 1197, Henry VI's army was accompanied by the royal chancellor, Conrad of Hildesheim, Archbishop Conrad of Mainz, and the royal marshal, Henry of Kalden, who took over the leadership in place of the emperor, who did not embark in September

---

[75] I should just like to point out that, for the Second Crusade, the Byzantine Kinnamos, the French Eudes of Deuil, and Arabic writers all give almost equal figures of somewhat less than one million participants. No explanation of this has yet been given.

[76] Cf. Röhricht, *Die Deutschen im hl. Lande*, 9–21, 27–41, 52–81, 82–90.

1197, one archbishop, eight bishops, dukes, counts, and nobles, including Duke Frederick of Austria, the Landgrave of Thuringia, the Count Palatine Henry, etc.

In 1189 Barbarossa had with him his younger son, Duke Frederick of Swabia, his former chancellor Geoffrey, now Bishop of Würzburg, ten other bishops, and innumerable secular magnates, such as twenty-eight counts. At the diet of Strasbourg on 1 December 1187, several hundred knights took the cross even before the emperor himself made the vow.[77] The list of participants fills no less than five pages in the *Historia de expeditione*, attributed to one Ansbert.[78] In 1147 Conrad III was accompanied by his nephew and future successor, Frederick Barbarossa, by his stepbrother, Otto of Freising, by Duke Henry Jasomirgott, and by bishops and nobles.

The participation of the princes of the empire was not fortuitous. A king's official crusading vow was not a private act, but an act of state that was preceded by consultations and which bound the princes as well. A diet had been the forum for the announcement of Henry IV's crusading plan. Conrad III took the cross at Christmas 1146, at a diet in Speyer, and Barbarossa, as is widely known, did so at the famous 'Curia Jesu Christi' in Mainz in 1188. The official announcement of Henry VI's crusade (the emperor himself did not take the cross publicly) was made at a diet in Gelnhausen in 1195, and the vows of the princes followed at a series of subsequent diets in 1195–6.

The king generally wished to be accompanied by the princes—in 1188 Barbarossa delayed his decision until he was sure that enough princes would join him. The example of young Frederick Barbarossa in 1147, however, shows that the princes were not totally free in making their decision.[79] Before they could take part, they needed the agreement of the king, who could grant permission or withhold it. Even Geoffrey of Bouillon had to ask for Henry IV's permission

[77] According to the *Historia peregrinorum*, ed. A. Chroust, *Quellen zur Geschichte des Kreuzzugs Kaiser Friedrichs I.* (MGH SS rer. Germ. n.s., 5; Hanover, 1928), 124, Frederick Barbarossa is said to have personally decided to take the cross as early as in Strasbourg.

[78] *Historia de expeditione Frederici imperatoris*, ibid. 18–23.

[79] Cf. above, VI and n. 69.

before leaving in 1096,[80] a further illustration of the German king's involvement in the First Crusade. The crusade did not break feudal and public ties. In fact, in many ways it reinforced them. Many non-fulfilled vows and deferred departures can be explained by political implications of this sort. During the twelfth century, the majority of archbishops stayed at home. Only after 1180 did a considerable number of bishops come from the North. The crusade, and in particular the number of crusaders, demonstrated the power of the king. The fact that at *Laetare Jerusalem* in 1188 virtually the whole empire had gathered at Mainz reflected the unchallenged position of Barbarossa at that moment.

The crusading army needed firm leadership if heavy losses were to be avoided. As early as the Second Crusade, we know of a special law that was imposed on crusaders going by sea,[81] and Barbarossa issued strict regulations before the crusaders crossed the borders of the empire at Pressburg.[82] This special law of war for the crusade gave the king much greater authority over all participants, both high and low, than he could claim at home. The most important difference was that here his absolute power, including that over life and death, lasted not only for the duration of a short campaign, but perhaps for years, and that it applied to everybody without exception. The first to suffer under it were not humble crusaders, but nobles caught red-handed, stealing and robbing, who were put to death without pardon.[83] Similarly, Henry VI's crusaders had to swear absolute obedience to the leaders appointed by the emperor, and to stay with the army for at least one year.[84]

A crusade consisted not only of those who had taken the cross for purely religious motives and of their own free will. In all crusades we have an effect similar to that observed in

[80] Frutolf, *Chronica*, 108, and Ekkehard, *Chronica I*, 126.

[81] H. Conrad, 'Gottesfrieden und Heeresverfassung in der Zeit der Kreuzzüge: Ein Beitrag zur Geschichte des Heeresstrafrechts im Mittelalter', *Zeitschrift der Savigny-Stiftung für Rechtsgeschichte, Germ. Abt.*, 61 (1941), 71–126.

[82] Only the first words are reported in the *Historia de expeditione*, 24; cf. also Giesebrecht and v. Simson, *Geschichte*, vi. 218 and 692.

[83] Arnold of Lübeck, *Chronica Slavorum*, ed. J. M. Lappenberg (MGH SS rer. Germ.; Hanover, 1868), 128 f.

[84] MGH Const. i, no. 365.

medieval elections. The authority of the king persuaded great magnates and lesser nobles to join him. Thus the crusade was itself a sort of mobilization. The Second Crusade already displayed the beginnings of planning that aimed to limit participation to those who were well prepared to fight, in accordance with Urban II's original intentions of 1095. After his personal experience in 1147–9, Frederick Barbarossa went one step further and imposed strict rules governing how participants were to equip themselves.[85] Yet so long as overland routes were chosen, effective control of departures was impossible. A change was brought about by the German crusade of 1197. Henry VI, who had promised to send 1,500 knights and 1,500 sergeants together with 3,000 minor soldiers at his own expense, insisted that the whole army, and not only one group (as in 1147 and 1187–9) went by sea. This made it possible to control departures efficiently.

Once a monarch had taken a crusading vow, his first followers were his regular retinue. In our case this meant in particular the Hohenstaufen *ministeriales*. The same holds true for a number of princes of the empire. But the king also had to ensure that his absence did not leave the kingdom open to potential enemies, notwithstanding the special papal protection given to every crusader since Urban II.[86] The king therefore had a special interest in taking them with him, or neutralizing them for the time of the crusade. A well-known instance of this is the choice which Barbarossa gave Henry the Lion in 1188: either to join the crusade, or to go into exile a second time.[87] The Welf duke chose the latter—but

[85] *Historia peregrinorum*, 126, and *Annales Marbacenses*, ed. H. Bloch (MGH SS rer. Germ.; Hanover and Leipzig, 1907), 60: for two years; Otto of St Blasien, *Chronica*, ed. A. Hofmeister (MGH SS rer. Germ.; Hanover and Leipzig, 1912), 44: three silver marks for personal needs, which could hardly have been intended to cover the overall costs, if an English knight of the same period earned 2 s. per day; *Itinerarium peregrinorum*, 290: sufficient means for one year; see now Hiestand, '*precipua columpna*', 86–90 and id., 'Die Kriegskasse des Kaisers? Gedanken zum "Barbarossa-Fund" aus historischer Sicht', *Vierteljahrschrift für Sozial- und Wirtschaftsgeschichte*, 78 (1991), 190–7. For the recruitment in Lower Saxony, cf. Rüdebusch, *Der Anteil Niedersachsens an den Kreuzzügen*; for Westphalia, see H. Lahrkamp, 'Mittelalterliche Jerusalemfahrten und Orientreisen westfälischer Pilger und Kreuzritter', *Westdeutsche Zeitschrift*, 106 (1956), 269–346.
[86] Cf. J. A. Brundage, *Medieval Canon Law and the Crusader* (Madison, 1969).
[87] Arnold of Lübeck, *Chronica Slavorum*, 128.

did not fulfil his promise. Similarly, during the Second Crusade, some of the king's *ministeriales* began to break the peace in Saxony, which reached the ears of the king even in Jerusalem.[88]

This last incident shows clearly that even placing the regency in the hands of a crowned son still constituted a serious weakening of royal authority. In 1147–9 Wibald advised Henry (VI) to stay in Regensburg as much as possible,[89] in order to avoid any hostile designs on the part of the magnates. The fate of young Henry IV might still have been remembered. Significantly, in 1147–9 the regency could not influence the episcopal elections in the north, where the real leader of the empire, Abbot Wibald of Stavelot, was defeated at Bremen-Hamburg. Nor could the young king intervene in the election at Verden. The monarch's increased prestige as a result of his crusading vow was precariously balanced by a loss of authority at home.

For the sake of completeness, we must ask not only who went on crusade, but also who returned, or rather, who did not. The lists of German pilgrims and crusaders compiled by R. Röhricht are impressive. For a large number of them, he has to add that they did not come home, just as many medieval sources say of returnees, '*feliciter* revertit'.[90]

After 1095 and 1101, as well as after 1147 and 1189, thousands, if not tens of thousands, never came back. In 1101 Duke Welf of Bavaria died in Cyprus, many of his companions, a Count Bernard and the Burgrave of Regensburg, lost their lives in Anatolia, and Archbishop Thiemo of Salzburg and the Marchioness Ida were captured and never seen again. On the Second Crusade the German army suffered the catastrophe of Choirobakchoi in the Balkans. This destroyed mainly the crusaders' goods, but from Anatolia only a few safely reached the Aegean coast. Among the victims were the Bishop of Passau, Count Bernard of Plötzkau, and the Abbot of Zwiefalten. On the Third Crusade, losses were particularly heavy after the psychological shock of Barbarossa's death. Exhaustion and the climate

[88] *Wibaldi epistolae* no. 90 = MGH D. C[onradi] III. no. 196.
[89] *Wibaldi epistolae* no. 88.
[90] Cf. Röhricht, *Die Deutschen im Hl. Lande,* passim.

killed many, first in Antioch, then during the siege of Acre: Duke Frederick, Bishop Geoffrey of Würzburg, the Bishops of Meissen, Passau, Basle, Osnabrück, and Toul. Others died soon after their return, so that a connection with the crusade can legitimately be assumed. The one exception is the crusade of 1197–8. As no serious military engagement took place and travelling by sea was much easier now, losses were small. The Bishop of Toul, and the Abbots of Werth and Michaelbeuern died on the way to the Holy Land, but most of the losses were the result of a shipwreck in September 1197.

Given the structure of the empire, we do not need to stress what the gaps in the episcopate meant for the administration of royal *regalia*. The same applies to the counts of the royal demesne. But an important group is hardly remembered in the sources, although it suffered heavy losses. A large number of crusaders on the Second and Third Crusades as well as in 1197 were Hohenstaufen *ministeriales*. This meant that the losses affected the Hohenstaufen party in particular.[91]

We still lack specific research on the impact of these losses. Among the nobles they could have quite different effects. Benefices became vacant on the death of vassals, and where no heir remained, or legal obstacles prevented hereditary succession, there would be welcome escheats. The Hohenstaufen were able to increase their demesne considerably during the twelfth century, for example, by gaining the Welf and the Pfullendorfer inheritances. But this did not happen on a large scale. In 1190–1 Henry VI could not touch Thuringia. To illustrate the possible impact of such cases, we refer to the most spectacular case outside the German Empire: the death of Alphonse of Poitiers in 1270 at the siege of Tunis, leading to the union of the Midi and the French royal demesne.

On the other hand, the death of vassals could lead to a weakening of the basis of the kingship, not so much in terms of benefices, but through the loss of men—in other words,

[91] Cf. K. Bosl, *Die Reichsministerialität der Salier und Staufer: ein Beitrag zur Geschichte des hochmittelalterlichen Volkes, Staates und Reiches*, 2 vols. (Schriften der MGH, 10; Stuttgart, 1950–1).

by changing the relations between the king's followers and those of his enemies. Where the king could impose his will on the nobility and retain vacant benefices, the death of crown vassals favoured him and the royal demesne could increase. The opposite case, as in the twofold haemorrhage of the German king's followers on the Second and Third Crusades, had negative effects. Moreover, the German kingship could no longer gain anything substantial upon the death of ecclesiastical princes except for the *spolia*, and perhaps some influence over the election. Any territorial gain was precluded in these cases, as there could not be an escheat of ecclesiastical crown benefices.

VIII

The crusades were wasteful of both men and money. In Western Europe the crusade was one of the famous *quatre cas* for which kings had the right to be financially supported by their vassals and subjects.[92] In Germany no such law seems to have been in force, which raises the question of how the single German expedition was financed. The main corps of Henry VI's crusade was in the emperor's pay.[93] The money might have come largely from the Sicilian treasury, from what remained of Richard Lionheart's ransom payments, and above all from the Byzantine tributes of 1195–6.[94] But the Greek sources suggest that these more or less extorted payments amounted to no more than 20,000 ounces a year, while the knights and sergeants engaged by Henry VI alone cost 60,000 ounces.[95]

On the Second Crusade, by and large, the participants had had to look after themselves. The catastrophe of Chorobakchoi therefore forced many of them to return home. After his defeat in Asia Minor, Conrad III himself was dependent on the gifts of the *basileus* to allow him to con-

[92] Cf. F.-L. Ganshof, *Was ist das Lehnswesen?* (Darmstadt, 1961), 96f.

[93] MGH Const. i, no. 365; cf. *Chronica regia Coloniensis*, ed. G. Waitz (MGH SS rer. Germ.; Hanover, 1880), 137.

[94] For the *Alamanikon*, cf. Niketas Choniates, *Historia*, ed. J. van Dieten (Corpus fontium Historiae Byzantinae; Berlin, 1975), 476.

[95] MGH Const. i, no. 365.

tinue in a suitable style and to raise a new army at Acre. His uncle, Otto of Freising, did not even have a pair of shoes when he arrived at Constantinople.[96]

For the Third Crusade, Barbarossa issued precise regulations in Mainz governing the minimum amount of money each crusader had to be provided with, although the sources differ somewhat on the sum prescribed. Yet this reveals nothing about the problem of supplying the emperor, who not only had to maintain his own retinue, but also had to keep with him what could be called a general reserve for ceremonial and political needs. The Jewish communities made contributions, as they had probably already done in 1147, although the amounts cannot be estimated. Yet the question of how Barbarossa raised his money remains. The English chronicler Radulph Niger stresses that Barbarossa's procedure differed greatly from that adopted by the kings of Western Europe. Frederick Barbarossa, he writes, did not ask his subjects to pay special taxes, but financed the crusade by imposing what later came to be called a hearth-tax.[97] If this is true, the Hohenstaufen demesne and the public treasury would have had to pay. The English and French kings, by contrast, tried to spare the state's treasuries as much as possible and looked to their subjects for additional funds. In modern economic terms this constitutes the difference between increasing the public debt, as in the case of the empire, and increasing the quota of taxes, as in Western Europe. In fact, we have no evidence so far of any Saladin tithe or similar contribution in Germany before the year 1200, nor of extra taxes paid by vassals and magnates who remained at home. Of course, Frederick I did not have the necessary cash in hand. If the arguments put forward here are correct, he relied heavily on twelfth-century 'European high finance', investigated by W. von Stromer.[98] According to medieval attitudes it certainly befitted a 'good king' to pay the army for the liberation of the Holy Sepulchre out of his

---

[96] Cf. Gerhoch of Reichersberg, *De investigatione Antichristi*, MGH LdL iii, 143.

[97] Radulfus Niger, *Chronica*, ed. H. Krause (Berne, 1985), 288.

[98] See W. Stromer von Reichenbach, 'Bernardus Teutonicus und die Geschäftsbeziehungen zwischen den deutschen Ostalpen und Venedig vor Gründung des Fondaco dei Tedeschi', *Grazer Forschungen zur Wirtschafts- und Sozialgeschichte*, 3 (1978), 1–15.

own pocket, but in the long term such liberality was at the expense of the state. It once again prevented the development of a new instrument that was to be decisive for the formation of a strong modern state. For a crusade, the psychological barrier against 'taxes' could probably have been overcome, even in Germany, because in theory these sums went to the Holy Sepulchre and did not imply personal servitude to the king. In other words, the German kingship once again missed its chance. Soon, in the thirteenth century, this had significant and visible consequences. It is well known that in Germany, the kingship never succeeded in creating a powerful and effective financial administration.

IX

Finally, we shall return to the highest level of public life. In the history of the elections of the German kings, the year 1125 was a turning-point. Contrary to the law based on kinship, the crown was not given to Duke Frederick I of Swabia, the nephew of Henry V. Instead, after long negotiations, the princes elected Lothair of Supplingenburg, Duke of Saxony.[99] Recent research tends to neglect two points that earlier works at least alluded to. In addition to questions of principles and power, personal problems were also at stake in 1125. As his nickname 'Monoculus'—known since the mid-twelfth century[100]—shows, Frederick of Swabia suffered from a handicap which, in the medieval mind, prevented him from being eligible for the throne and placed him among the *inutiles*. The election of his younger brother Conrad, although he would have been the next candidate in this situation, was impossible because he was absent. As al-

---

[99] Merely hinted at in Meyer von Knonau, *Jahrbücher*, vii, 327 n. 28, and W. v. Bernhardi, *Lothar von Supplinburg* (Jahrbücher der deutschen Geschichte; Leipzig, 1879), 4 n. 10. For the events of 1125, now see Schmidt, *Königswahl und Thronfolge*, 34–9.

[100] First mentioned by Johannes Kinnamos, *Epitome Historiae*, ii, ed. A. Meinecke (Bonn, 1836), 89, in the West by Burkard of Ursperg, *Chronicon*, ed. O. Holder-Egger and B. von Simson, 2nd edn. (MGH SS rer. Germ.; Hanover, 1916), 8 ('quem a quibusdam audivimus denominari monoculum'), and *Annales Spirenses*, MGH SS xvii, 87. Otto of Freising's silence is certainly not surprising. Bernhardi, *Konrad III.*, 3 only hints at the fact.

ready mentioned, Conrad had decided to go to Jerusalem in 1124.[101] He was obviously not back by the time of Henry V's death. This explains why the sources never mention the younger of the Hohenstaufen brothers during the events of 1125.[102] He probably returned to the West in 1126, and is referred to again in June 1127, when he unsuccessfully tried to oppose Lothair. He did not definitely regain the royal crown for the Salian-Hohenstaufen family until 1138.

It should be pointed out in this context that Conrad's absence on his journey to Jerusalem had a twofold consequence for the elections of 1125. First, he could not intervene in favour of his brother Frederick, and secondly, the uncertainty as to whether and when he would return precluded serious consideration of his own candidature from the start. Not until 150 years later, in 1272, was an heir to the throne, though absent on crusade, acknowledged without difficulty on the death of his father: the Angevin Edward I.

In 1125 a potential candidate's absence in the Holy Land influenced the consultations, while at the end of the century it was the absence not of the candidate, but of the electors that interfered with the course of events.[103] In late 1197, when the death of Henry VI became known in Germany, many princes, most of them belonging to the Hohenstaufen party, were in Syria. Here the news initially found little response, but when rumours of the conflicts at home began to circulate in early 1198, princes and other participants returned at the first opportunity.

Among the princes in the east was Archbishop Conrad of Mainz. His role in an election would have been of considerable importance, especially because procedural difficulties had arisen. Before his departure, he had handed over his public duties to the second man in the German episcopate, the Archbishop of Cologne. At that time, this was purely a matter of customary law, not of political choice. But the implications were to become serious in the situation of 1197–8. Mainz, with rather pro-Hohenstaufen attitudes,

---

[101] See above, III and n. 34.
[102] Briefly mentioned by Meyer von Knonau, *Jahrbücher*, vii, 327 n. 28, and Bernhardi, *Lothar von Supplinburg*, 4 and n. 10.
[103] For the crisis of 1197–8 see the references in n. 49 above.

would normally have presided over the elections. Now Adolf of Altena, certainly not a Hohenstaufen supporter, not only had the presidency but also had two votes, his own and that of Mainz. Even if we no longer regard him as the man behind the Welf candidature, he certainly did not promote the rights of the young Frederick, or of Philip.

Also absent in 1197–8 were the German chancellor, Conrad of Hildesheim, and with him a large number of bishops who had taken the crusading vow. During the deliberations in the winter of 1197–8 and in 1198, the Hohenstaufen party was therefore weakened even more than in 1125. Its most influential men were abroad. When they came back in summer 1198 the main decisions had been taken. Otto IV had been elected and the Hohenstaufen party had responded by electing Philip of Swabia. The crusade had once again had a decisive impact on events within the empire.

To sum up: this brief survey of the history of German kingship in the twelfth century shows what a profound impact the crusades had on its development. Our overview also suggests that it would be misleading merely to take at face value the words of the chroniclers of the First Crusade. Their accounts were exaggerated from the start and, at least from the crusade of 1101, completely out of date. We should not take them as general conclusions about the relations between the German kingship and the crusade. 'Gesta Dei per Francos'? The personal part played by the German kings in the crusades should not be underestimated. But beyond this, the crusades had an important influence on the course of German and European history in general. The crusades had no less of an impact on public affairs in Germany than in France and England, but it was doubtless quite different.

Part IV

URBAN AND RURAL SOCIAL DEVELOPMENTS IN THE HIGH MIDDLE AGES

Urban Communities

11

English Towns

SUSAN REYNOLDS

The period between 900 and 1300, or thereabouts, which may be taken to cover the high Middle Ages, has not been an area of great activity among English urban historians of late. More interest has been focused on the early Middle Ages, where archaeology has been so profitable and important, and on the later Middle Ages, where traditional discussions of oligarchies and crafts have been diversified by a newer interest in what is generally called the decay or decline of late medieval towns. Decline and decay have, maybe, a peculiar fascination for the late twentieth-century British—the fascination of supposed recognition.[1] In all these fields much new information has been produced, though a captious critic can maintain that its interpretation would profit from more rigorous reasoning and, in particular, more criticism of traditional categories. The words 'decline' and 'decay', for instance, represent very unclear concepts, while the archaeologists' use of the word *burh* and of expressions like 'middle Saxon', 'late Saxon', and 'medieval'—the last to indicate a period which begins only in 1066—suggests that their findings are being set into an insular and outmoded framework of history.[2] Some of the best recent work has come from the increasingly expert integration of archaeological and documentary sources, most notably on the history of Winchester and London. Until recently little serious work had been done for some time on the history of medieval London in our period, probably because historians had been discouraged by the mass of apparently unrewarding property deeds

[1] Archaeological surveys: J. Schofield and R. Leech (eds.), *Urban Archaeology in Britain* (Council of British Archaeology Research Report 61, 1987); *Medieval Archaeology* (1957–) contains annual notices of excavations.

[2] I have discussed these problems in 'The Writing of Medieval Urban History in England', *Theoretische Geschiedenis*, 19 (1992), 43–57.

surviving from the twelfth and thirteenth centuries. Now, however, it has been notably advanced by the work of Derek Keene and his assistants. During the brief period for which they were funded they produced a great deal of critically assessed information on London before 1666, primarily on the topography of the city but also on many other subjects as well.[3]

Archaeology has not, of course, been important only for the early Middle Ages. Important discoveries have been made on our period too: among many others one may note the excavation of the Franciscan church which played such an important part in the formation of the university at Oxford, and thus in the history of the town.[4] Other topographical work, for instance on the formation of urban parishes, has also been illuminating, and the first three volumes of the British *Atlas of Historic Towns* have appeared.[5] It may be worth noticing that even on the later Middle Ages, where there has been more work on different aspects, there has not generally been so much emphasis on urban history in its regional setting as has come from the German tradition of *Landesgeschichte*. That is growing, however, notably on the economic side. On our period, however, as on the earlier and later Middle Ages, the most vital gap to be filled is an intellectual rather than a topical one. Medieval urban historians need, in my view, to give far more critical thought to the implications of the words they use and the difference between what the words mean to us and what they may have meant to people who used them, or words related to them, in

[3] M. Biddle (ed.), *Winchester in the Early Middle Ages* (Oxford, 1976); D. J. Keene, *Survey of Medieval Winchester* (Oxford, 1985); id., 'A New Survey of London before the Great Fire', *Urban History Yearbook, 1984*, 11–21; cf. id. and V. Harding, *Survey of Documentary Sources for Property Holding in London before the Great Fire* (London Record Society, 22, 1985).

[4] T. Hassall and others, 'Excavations in St Ebbe's, Oxford, 1967–1976', *Oxoniensia.* liv (1989), 71–277, includes the final report on the friary site.

[5] On parishes see e.g. the works cited in Reynolds, *Introduction to the History of English Medieval Towns* (Oxford, 1977); the first volume of the atlas appeared under the title *Historic Towns*, ed. M. D. Lobel (London, 1969); the second as *Atlas of Historic Towns*, ed. M. D. Lobel and W. H. Johns (London, 1975). The third as *The British Atlas of Historic Towns: The City of London from Prehistoric Times to c. 1520*, ed. M. D. Lobel (Oxford, 1990).

the past. The serious study of medieval towns started in the nineteenth century, and its preoccupation ever since with the attainment of corporate status; with oligarchy and democracy, closed patriciates and craft guilds; and with controversies between free trade and protection or about the right of association, reflect the preoccupations of the nineteenth and twentieth centuries more closely than they do any climate of ideas that seems to be detectable in medieval sources. This, if it is not presumptuous to say so when I know so much less about German towns, appears to be the case with some at least of the work that is still being done on them too.[6]

To start with, there is the very idea of the 'town community'—the *Stadtgemeinde.* I maintain that we shall not make sense of town government and the winning of liberties and autonomy, of whatever degree, so long as we underestimate the collective activity that formed an essential part of all medieval government. Charters and liberties were not necessary for collective action, only for greater freedom of collective action. Most 'town communities'—*Stadtgemeinden*—were not formed as part of a deliberate drive towards independence, let alone as part of a 'communal revolution' in the twelfth century: in so far as towns were communities, most of them were communities already, much as were villages and counties and all other units of government. Although towns as such had particular characteristics which particularly promoted feelings of solidarity and the development of local custom, their ability and right to act collectively was in principle, so far as I understand the sources, no different from that of any other group. Most of the towns that won liberties in the twelfth century and later did so because they were already capable of acting collectively to negotiate for themselves. That is clear in England, where the first surviving document one could reasonably call a charter of urban liber-

---

[6] Some of my doubts in the English context are expressed in 'Medieval Urban History and the History of Political Thought', *Urban History Yearbook, 1982,* 14–23, and on western European towns in general in *Kingdoms and Communities in Western Europe, 900–1300* (Oxford, 1984), 34–6, 59–64 (on the concept of the corporation), 67–78 (on the nature of guilds and their relation to crafts), 168–214 (on urban government and politics).

ties—made by a local lord to a quite insignificant market-town—does not come before the very end of the eleventh century,[7] but where London seems to have had some kind of common fund by the end of the tenth century;[8] where town law (*burhriht*) is referred to quite early in the eleventh century, implying the existence of more or less separate town assemblies which had developed more or less distinctive customs;[9] and where Domesday Book is full of references to the collective responsibilities of townspeople and to arrangements which some towns seem to have negotiated collectively with the king before 1066 about their military obligations and dues.[10] Incidentally, some of the discussions of the first appearance of the Latin word *burgensis* look rather less significant in the light of the English record of vernacular terms like *burgwara* or *portmenn* (as well as the Latin *urbani*) even before 900.[11]

However that may be, if, according to this argument, charters and liberties did not generally create communities which for the first time became capable of collective activity, then most of the learned arguments about the definition of 'borough status' and the achievement of 'corporate status' lose most of their significance. In my view they derive from anachronistic legal categories. Anachronism has been an

[7] R. H. Gretton (ed.), *Burford Records* (Oxford, 1920), 301–2; cf. R. B. Patterson (ed.), *Earldom of Glucester Charters* (Oxford, 1973), no. 43.

[8] F. Liebermann (ed.), *Die Gesetze der Angelsachsen* (Halle, 1903–16), i. 234 (IV Ethelred, 4.2, and, though less clearly, 3.2). For the date: P. Wormald, 'Aethelred the Lawmaker', in D. Hill (ed.), *Ethelred the Unready* (Brit. Archaeol. Reps. 59, 1978), 47–80.

[9] Liebermann, *Gesetze*, i. 477 (Episcopus, c. 6).

[10] Some are noted in S. Reynolds, 'Towns in Domesday Book', in J. C. Holt (ed.), *Domesday Studies* (London, 1987), 295–309. Much work on Domesday was done in connection with the celebrations of 1986, including that connected with the facsimile edn. produced by Alecto Historical Editions: see A. Williams and R. W. H. Erskine (eds.), *Domesday Book Studies* (London, 1987). On towns: G. H. Martin, 'Domesday Book and the Boroughs', in P. H. Sawyer (ed.), *Domesday Book: A Reassessment* (London, 1985), 143–63; C. Dyer, 'Towns and Cottages in Eleventh-Century England', in H. Mayr-Harting and R. I. Moore (eds.), *Studies in Medieval History presented to R. H. C. Davis* (London, 1985), 91–106.

[11] e.g. W. de G. Birch (ed.), *Cartularium Saxonicum* (London, 1885–93), nos. 248, 449, 515, and for other references see A. di P. Healey and R. L. Venezky, *Microfiche Concordance to Old English* (Toronto, 1980), e.g. *sub burgawara, burgliod, byrhwara, burhwita, ceastregewara, portmenn*: this point is discussed briefly, with some reference to discussions elsewhere, in *Kingdoms and Communities*, 161, 163.

inevitable result of the traditional procedures of legal history, at least in England: that is, of tracing the origins of modern categories through finding similar terminology in the past and then assuming that words were always used with the same, and invariably exact and consistent, meanings. To turn the words of one of the nineteenth-century fathers of legal anthropology against the nineteenth-century tradition of legal history: 'The distinctions of the later jurists are appropriate only to the later jurisprudence.'[12] If we can try to forget modern categories and think of tenth- and eleventh-century conditions and ideas, we shall find little or no reason to suppose that the Latin word *burgus*, or the vernacular *byrig* and its variants,[13] then had any particular legal or constitutional connotation. There was none for it to have, and the nature of the legal system would have prevented usage from being consistent if there had been. When people at the time referred to a *byrig* or *ceastre*, or a *port* or *wic*, they presumably did so because they were referring to places which seemed distinctive and therefore were often—though not always—described by a distinctive word. Since people then—even the scribes of Great and Little Domesday—probably used language in the way everyone except parliamentary draftsmen and modern legal historians generally use it, they may not have thought much about the words they used, probably sometimes used words inconsistently and interchangeably, and were certainly not thinking in the exact legal categories of the later jurists. Even after 1100, consistent legal and constitutional connotations accumulated less quickly and consistently than traditional legal teleology suggests.

Anachronistic legal categories—the distinctions of the later jurists—are also responsible for the distortions imparted to medieval urban history, both in England and elsewhere, by the idea that towns needed to achieve something we can usefully call 'corporate status' and that the use of the

---

[12] H. S. Maine, *Ancient Law* (London, 1905 edn.), 230 (in ch. 8).

[13] The form *burh* is so commonly used by historians and archaeologists, sometimes with the curious plural *burhs*, as to have acquired a spurious technicality, but it was not apparently the most common in surviving OE sources: Healey and Venezky, *Microfiche Concordance to Old English*.

word 'commune' (in one of its various medieval forms) is somehow connected with this. In the legal system of the time, however, no one had yet needed to consider the difference between groups and individuals. Groups were as a matter of course allowed to act at law like individuals, provided that, like individuals, they did not act subversively or infringe the rights of others. In this climate of thought the modern legal distinction between corporate and non-corporate groups would have been meaningless. As Henry III of England remarked in 1254, the law and custom of the kingdom allowed *villate et communitates villarum* to prosecute lawsuits through three or four of their members as well as through their lord.[14] That being so, many of the anomalies and problems about medieval corporate activity that have exercised legal and urban historians since the time of Gierke derive from the interpolation into the Middle Ages of nineteenth-century concerns about individuals, collectivities, and 'legal personality' that have no place there.

As in most of northern Europe, English towns began to acquire new, formal, but varying measures of autonomy in the twelfth century. This was partly the result of conflicts with external authorities but partly the result of developments in government in general, including the evolution of new and profitable methods of delegating authority. England has been made to look unduly different, partly because some English historians have wanted to distance twelfth-century English towns from what they thought shockingly unconstitutional goings-on across the Channel, and partly because of their love of arcane pseudo-technical terms like 'borough farm'. There certainly does not seem to have been anything in twelfth-century England like the events at Laon in 1109–12 (though thirteenth-century London saw some quite exciting and revolutionary episodes) but then those events were exceptional in France. In England there is plenty of evidence that towns were anxious to run their own affairs, and the occasional use of the word 'commune', together with the

[14] H. M. Cam, *Law-Finders and Law-Makers* (London, 1962), 79–80, quoting the entry from *Close Rolls of Henry III, 1254–6*, 173.

reactions it evoked, suggests that the 'French connection' involved aspirations that kings and clergy saw as subversive. On the other hand, the strength of royal authority in England forced urban politics into a genuinely different mould. There was less opportunity here for towns to revolt and less need for them to do so in order to protect themselves and their members against the dangers of anarchy. Meanwhile, however, royal authority promoted some degree of collective action: municipal institutions were stimulated and conditioned by the need to collect and pay over both lump sums (the *firma burgi*) and other taxes. At a time, for instance, when Henry II had not formally allowed the Londoners to elect their own sheriffs, the city was none the less responsible for assessing and collecting some of its taxes and also seems to have had final responsibility for each year's debt.[15] Once a measure of autonomy was achieved, moreover, the maintenance and development of royal authority (at a time when it was in difficulties in Germany) kept all municipal gains precarious. Charters could be, and were, suspended or withdrawn. From the thirteenth century it became customary for towns to get—and pay for—confirmations of past charters at the beginning of each reign, while some apparently new liberties, like 'return of writs', conveyed nothing but old rights in a new, expensive, and sometimes restricted form.[16] Royal power and the growing influence of the common law also imposed some degree of uniformity: the usual untidiness of medieval procedures made it only relative, but 'families' of English towns and their law cannot be mapped in the way that German ones can. All this reflects real differences in the political conditions in which towns lived, but they should not be exaggerated or assumed to derive from significantly different social and economic conditions, let alone from some kind of inherited and permanent 'national character'. When municipal records begin many similarities between

[15] S. Reynolds, 'The Rulers of London in the Twelfth Century', *History*, 57 (1972), 343 and 'The Farm and Taxation of London, 1154–1216', *Guildhall Studies in London History*, i (1975), 219–20, 224–5.
[16] M. T. Clanchy, 'The Franchise of Return of Writs', *Transactions of the Royal Historical Society*, ser. 5, xvii (1967), 59–82.

towns in England and towns elsewhere, including Germany, become more obvious. Of course there are also differences: it is no good simply applying models derived from one country or one town to another. For anyone who is willing to try to break through the traditional terminology, comparisons can, however, be exciting and illuminating to both sides.

Another relic of nineteenth-century ideas about medieval history that still hampers our understanding concerns guilds and the primarily economic purposes that, despite much evidence to the contrary, historians often attribute to them whenever they find them in towns. At least in the earlier— and, in England, the high—Middle Ages, groups described as guilds, whether urban or not, seem to have normally been voluntary clubs, of which the primary function seems to have been drinking, together with the performance of some religious ceremonies, especially burials. Beyond that they could be turned, like any other human association, especially a voluntary association, to any other purpose, selfish or unselfish, which the members might choose.[17] Townsmen naturally found the bond of this kind of association useful for mutual protection when they travelled. A guild—whether called a guild of merchants or a guild of burgesses—could also provide a forum for collective activity in a town where seigniorial officials loomed over the normal and official governing assembly, though it seems clear that some towns managed to organize themselves and negotiate liberties well enough without one. At the time no one seems to have bothered about the distinction between guild and town, while the rules of membership in both seem to our way of thinking to have been hopelessly unclear. London, which apparently never had a guild merchant *eo nomine*, has probably been calling its town hall 'the Guildhall' ever since the early twelfth century.[18] As Geoffrey Martin has put it, 'guilds

---

[17] E. Coornaert, 'Les Ghildes médiévales', *Revue Historique*, 199 (1948), 22–55, 206–43; O. G. Oexle, 'Die mittelalterlichen Gilden: ihre Selbstdeutung und ihr Beitrag zur Formung sozialer Strukturen', in A. Zimmermann (ed.), *Soziale Ordnungen im Selbstverständnis des Mittelalters* (*Misc. Mediaevalia*, 12, 1979), 203–26; G. Rosser, 'Going to the fraternity feast', *Journal of British Studies*, 33 (1994), 430–46.

[18] F. M. Stenton, 'Norman London', in G. Barraclough (ed.), *Social Life in Early England* (London, 1960), 198.

were a form of association as unself-conscious and ubiqui-
tous as the committee is today'.[19] It is therefore not surprising that towns spawned sectional guilds as well as guilds
which represented the whole community. Members of the
same craft within a town might often choose to form a guild
of their own and might go on to use it, whether licitly or
illicitly, as a forum in which to organize themselves to further
their political or economic interests. Weavers in a number of
English towns did this, for instance, in the twelfth century.
When municipal governments became established, however,
they normally frowned on independent guilds of craftsmen.
The regulation of individual crafts, like the regulation of the
economy as a whole, was a matter for the government as a
whole. It might be delegated to appointed (or even freely
elected) masters or wardens of a craft (who might have a
guild of their own), but there is still an essential difference of
principle between an independent guild of craftsmen and
a craft association whose authority is delegated from the
municipal authority.[20] As the centuries passed some guilds
became more established and independent in the management of their crafts, and some of their religious functions
disappeared in the sixteenth century, so that the distinction
became increasingly obscured. As Weber admitted when he
drew attention to it, it is anyway one of polarities which must
always be relative in its empirical application.[21] It may also be
difficult to detect in the records. None the less it was recognized by at least some rulers of towns in England and elsewhere in the twelfth and thirteenth centuries. All tried to
keep crafts under municipal control and some regarded
sectional guilds—whether connected with crafts or not—as

[19] G. H. Martin, 'The English Borough in the Thirteenth Century', *Transactions of
the Royal Historical Society*, ser. 5, xiii (1963), 123–44.

[20] In *Kingdoms and Communities*, 334, I said that the distinction between voluntary
and imposed associations was not always significant in medieval terms. I stand by
that, but craft organizations, to judge from some of the conflicts about them, were
one of the exceptions. For the prohibition of sectional associations see e.g. C. Gross,
The Gild Merchant (Oxford, 1890), i. 227, and cf. the information cited on pp. 113–
15 on relations between town governments and crafts (which Gross sometimes calls
'craft guilds'). On the quashing of independent weavers' guilds see also E. M. Carus-
Wilson, *Medieval Merchant Venturers* (London, 1954), 225–7.

[21] M. Weber, *Theory of Social and Economic Organization* (New York, 1947), 148–52
(= *Wirtschaft und Gesellschaft*, I, c. 1, §13–15).

divisive and thus potentially subversive. Historians who translate words like *officia* or *ministeria* as 'guild' or 'craft-guild' not only by implication ignore the vast number of guilds that have no craft connection at all, but conceal what may be a real difference among craft associations, so as to make the mixtures of purposes and motives in them even harder to understand than they are already. The official purpose of craft organizations in the high Middle Ages was the promotion of the interests of the whole community, which were assumed to be capable of harmonization but were not supposed to involve equality. Some of the conflicts between municipal governments and crafts, or between different crafts, were due to the corruption and greed of individuals but some were also due to the difficulty of reconciling a number of conflicting interests—interests that we, unlike medieval people, may think were irreconcilable. If the terminology of the sources had been followed in more of the published work on English towns in the high Middle Ages, we would be in a better position to interpret the policies of urban governments and their critics—and indeed to decide whether the distinction between guilds and crafts which is suggested here is in fact a significant one.

The final anachronism I want to attack is that involved in thinking of town governments in terms of oligarchy and democracy. Neither word was used in medieval England—or perhaps in medieval Germany?—in connection with town government and both suggest an entirely foreign set of political ideas. I have yet to find any evidence of serious and widespread discontent with the general structure of government in English medieval towns, even in the fourteenth century, when such evidence can be found in the countryside.[22] For several years in the thirteenth century London was governed by a mayor who was alleged to have more or less ignored the aldermen in favour of riotous open meetings, while at the same time another chronicler describes the oppression of governors in other cities and towns by a

[22] The use of the term 'oligarchy' is defended by S. Rigby, 'Urban "Oligarchy" in Late Medieval England' in J. A. F. Thomson (ed.), *Towns and Townspeople in the Fifteenth Century* (Gloucester, 1988), 62–86.

confederacy (*conjuratio*[23]) of ribalds calling themselves bach-
elors.[24] There may have been ideas of real political revolution
around at this time, but it is not clear that the policies of the
apparently revolutionary mayor of London involved social or
economic revolution. What is clear is that in most of the
conflicts of 1258–65, and in all the others of which I have
found evidence in nineteen other towns in the twelfth and
thirteenth centuries, the accusations were of injustice and
oppression. The most common form these took was of unfair
assessment of taxes and engrossment or forestalling of
trade—all practices that were universally reckoned as abuses
of the existing system. All the evidence found so far suggests
that most burgesses, and most outside authorities to whom
the oppressed appealed, disapproved of government by narrow cliques just as they did of government by the mob: town
governments sometimes behaved like oligarchies but they
were not supposed to be democracies. They were supposed
to be more like what Aristotle called aristocracies. When
established rulers behaved like oligarchs rather than aristocracies the answer was generally to elaborate accounting
procedures and require wider consultation on important
matters.

Whether understanding is promoted by describing town
governments as patriciates or their members as patricians is
another question. Again it is not a word that was used at the
time and it is one which invites one to look for closed groups
and family links at a time when such genealogies as can be
constructed often appeal only to the eye of faith. A good
many of the supposed 'patriciates' in English towns—and I
suspect elsewhere—are the creations of modern investiga-
tors who define their 'patricians' variously and then find
what they are looking for.[25] Once again we are looking at
medieval towns through lenses prepared by those nineteenth-century urban historians who saw them as the origin

[23] I see no reason to suppose that this had any technical meaning, let alone that
it was synonymous with *communia, communio* etc. Many associations, including pious
and unrebellious guilds, were bound by oath.
[24] *Annales Monastici* (Rolls Series 36, 1864–9), iv. 138.
[25] Reynolds, *English Medieval Towns*, 68, 78–80. On the origins of the expression:
ead., *Kingdoms and Communities*, 204.

of forces important to their own time. In England that generally meant either seeing towns as nurseries of popular
government and standard-bearers of democracy against aristocratic oppression, or presuming that they had always been
as corrupt and oligarchic as the Municipal Corporations
Commission thought them to be in 1835. Either interpretation distorts our view of medieval conditions and ideas.

This essay was meant to survey the present position of work
on English 'town communities'—that is, in effect, on urban
history—in the central Middle Ages. It seems to have turned
into an attack on what has been done and a demand, which
may seem arrogant, for it to be done differently. Despite the
apparent arrogance the demand may be justified in so far as
we already know a fair amount about English towns at this
period and, since new written sources are not likely to turn
up, are not likely to discover very much more except through
the work of archaeologists. We can, however, still try to refine
our interpretations of our knowledge. Even if some or all of
my suggestions towards that are mistaken they may stimulate
others to do better. I hope, too, that they may make it easier
to compare medieval towns in England with towns elsewhere—and particularly with German towns.

12

Aspects of Urban Social History in Salian and Staufen Germany

HERMANN JAKOBS

German scholarship[1] has been much concerned with urban development during the 'communal movement', both in close detail and in its European context.

1. All over Europe, towns which were already in existence, whether as episcopal *civitates* or urban settlements attached to castles, abbeys, or other great churches, took part in that movement. Even before it began, however, they were already communities and had some municipal institutions in the form of town courts, parishes, and wards or quarters. The court represented both the ruler of the town and its community, whose members enjoyed the privileges won for the town by its ruler.

Bishops' sees were founded at different times: with the revival of towns in the area of Roman *civitates*, and with new foundations of the time of Boniface, and in the reigns of Charlemagne, Louis the Pious, Otto the Great, and Henry II

Translated by S. Reynolds: I should like to thank my English colleague for her helpfulness and expertise, to which this assay owes a number of clarifications and improvements. J. Weis, MA (Heidelberg), assisted with editorial work and checking the footnotes. This survey excludes Italy, Burgundy, and Bohemia, which constituted separate *regna* within the Salian and Staufen Empire, but it includes those areas which then formed part of the kingdom of Germany though they are no longer within modern Germany. Full evidence for most of the events and dates mentioned in this essay is given in H. Jakobs, 'Stadtgemeinde und Bürgertum um 1100', *Beiträge* . . . (1) (see n. 1), 14–45

[1] In order to make my survey reasonably intelligible I have provided a note of more recent work at the end (Sect. 13), and given a select bibliography for each section in footnotes. Some general collections of articles by various authors, however, will be more frequently cited below and details are given here: (1) *Beiträge zum hochmittelalterlichen Städtewesen*, ed. B. Diestelkamp (Cologne and Vienna, 1982). (2) *Bischofs- und Kathedralstädte des Mittelalters und der frühen Neuzeit*, ed. F. Petri (Cologne and Vienna, 1976). (3) *Vor- und Frühformen der europäischen Stadt im Mittelalter*, ed. H. Jankuhn, W. Schlesinger, and H. Steuer (2 vols., Göttingen, 1973–4). (4) *Köln, das Reich und Europa*, ed. H. Stehkämper (Cologne, 1971). (5) *Stadt und*

in the rest of the country. By the time of the Saxon and Salian kings, however, the cathedral cities seem to have been constitutionally homogeneous and it was only in the new cities founded or refounded east of the Elbe in the twelfth century that town government was not entrusted to the bishops.

In Germany the cathedral cities[2] provided the model for the formation of urban constitutions. The exempt jurisdiction of the urban *districtus*; the participation by the community of the municipal court in the regalian privileges held by the bishop as lord of the town and the attainment of membership of that community through the ownership of plots for building houses (*areae*); the building of town walls; the shaping of the 'holy place' topography of the cathedral city by continuous new building; the formation of lesser communities, and especially parishes, within them; the development of markets; and the reinforcement of a city's function as the secular centre of the surrounding area by the way it met liturgical and religious needs—all these were fundamental and seminal features of German urban history.

Urban development elsewhere, at seaports (for example, Emden and Hamburg), in the vicinity of many royal abbeys and collegiate churches (for example, Gandersheim, Quedlinburg, and Aachen), and at royal estates or palaces (about ten between Nimwegen and Zurich) were obviously of considerable economic importance, but these towns were less complex in terms of 'topographical duality', constitution, and social structure. Until the twelfth century the proliferation of smaller markets continued to be almost entirely

Herrschaft: Römische Kaiserzeit und Hohes Mittelalter, ed. F. Vittinghoff (Munich, 1982). (6) *Stadt und Stadtbürgertum in der deutschen Geschichte des 13. Jh.*, ed. B. Töpfer (Berlin, 1976). (7) *Die Stadt: Gestalt und Wandel bis zum industriellen Zeitalter* (2nd edn.; Cologne and Vienna, 1985). (8) *Untersuchungen zu Handel und Verkehr der frühgeschichtlichen Zeit in Mittel- und Nordeuropa*, pt. 3: *Der Handel des frühen Mittelalters*, ed. K. Düwell, H. Jankuhn and W. Siems (Göttingen, 1985). (9) *Südwestdeutsche Städte im Zeitalter der Staufer*, ed. E. Maschke and J. Sydow (Stadt in der Geschichte, 6; Sigmaringen, 1980). (10) *Gilden und Zünfte: Kaufmännische und gewerbliche Genossenschaften im frühen und hohen Mittelalter*, ed. B. Schwineköper (Vorträge und Forschungen, 29; Sigmaringen, 1985).

[2] H. Jakobs, 'Vescovi e città in Germania', *I poteri temporali dei vescovi in Italia e Germania nel Medioevo*, ed. C. G. Mor and H. Schmidinger (Bologna, 1979), 283–328.

confined to the estates of royal churches, like the markets of the Abbot of Lorsch at Brumath, Oppenheim, Zullestein, Bensheim, Weinheim, and Wiesloch.

2. *Mercatores publici*, who included aliens—traders from the Middle East, Jews, Norsemen, Frisians, among others— pursued their international *consuetudo negotiandi* under royal protection. We may assume that this became integrated with local market law, to the benefit of local traders, and that the *mercatores publici* were brought under local market law. Yet how it happened is not entirely clear.

Before 900 there was no concept of royal control of markets and even after that date only in the East Frankish and Ottonian kingdom. The king guaranteed the peace and protection of markets as an ecclesiastical immunity and gave his consent to minting and tolls. The charters to this effect, except for three by Otto III, were granted exclusively to imperial churches. The royal monopoly was broken for the first time in 1075 by the Abbot of Reichenau's charter to Allensbach.

Mercantile liberties in this period came only from the king or from bishops as lords of towns. Customary mercantile law (see Alpertus Mettensis on Tiel) was different from *púrgréht* (see Notker the German), but both came to be moulded by the privileges granted by ecclesiastical lords of towns, who were less interested in merchants with their own special privileges than in their own *homines ecclesie*. Town lords therefore promoted the social and legal assimilation of merchants as local inhabitants. Merchants who settled in certain places secured favourable privileges, such as, for instance, in Naumburg in 1033 and in Halberstadt on several occasions, but in other cases, conflicts broke out. There were troubles in Worms in 1025 about judicial duels in suits for debt, and in Cologne in 1074 about the seigneurial requisitioning of a ship.[3]

3. Like the peace movement of which it formed part, the communal movement constituted a reaction to social condi-

---

[3] Sect. 2: G. Dilcher, 'Marktrecht und Kaufmannsrecht im Frühmittelalter', *Untersuchungen* . . . (8), 392–417; K. Kroeschell, 'Bemerkungen zum "Kaufmannsrecht" in den ottonisch-salischen Markturkunden', ibid. (8), 418–30; G. Althoff, 'Warum erhielt Graf Bertold im Jahre 999 ein Marktprivileg für Villingen?', *Die*

tions and the growing legal insecurities of the time. These were partly a consequence of social changes in sections of society which were assuming new importance: new demands for legal rights were being made by knights in the courts of their lords, by peasants in villages and other rural communities, and by burgesses in towns.

The only disturbances in the kingdom of Germany which might be comparable to those of the *coniurationes* of northern France were those in Cambrai in 1077 and 1107, when a peace association was established under pressure from Henry V. The troubles in Cologne in 1074, 1105, and 1114, like those in Trier and Mainz in the 1130s and 1150s, were to a very considerable degree determined by political tensions in the world outside. Similarly, the *Pax Sigewini* made in Cologne in 1083 is not a document of urban history so much as a unique source for the social history of the archbishopric.[4]

4. During the communal movement urban communities underwent structural changes that are revealed in the weakening—not the overthrow—of seigneurial jurisdiction: in the legal activities of sworn associations; in demands for the election of parish priests; and in the emergence of associations and groups distinct from the official courts. These newly emergent associations were active chiefly in financial and economic affairs.

The first privileges granted to towns rather than to their lords illustrate the way in which legal rights were being extended to new groupings. In 1066 the Bishop of Liège, as Lord of Huy, granted *libertas villae* to the *burgenses* of Huy in return for services to the Church, gave them jurisdiction within the town, and made it a place of asylum. There followed charters from Henry V to Speyer in 1111, to Worms in 1114 (though this was subsequently altered, at the very

Zähringer (Veröffentlichungen zur Zähringer-Ausstellung iii; Sigmaringen, 1990), 269–74; G. Köbler, '*Burgreht* und *diotreht* im Lichte der Interferenzforschung', *Sprache und Recht. Festschrift für R. Schmidt-Wiegand*, ed. K. Hauck *et al.*, i (Berlin and New York, 1986), 416–54.

[4] Sect. 3: A. Vermeesch, *Essai sur les origines et la signification de la commune dans le nord de la France* (Heule, 1966); H. Keller, 'Der Übergang zur Kommune', *Beiträge . . .* (1), 55–72; H. Stehkämper, 'Die Stadt Köln in der Salierzeit', *Die Salier und das Reich*, ed. S. Weinfurter, iii (Sigmaringen, 1991), 75–152.

least), and from Lothar III to the *fideles cives* of Strasbourg in 1129. Jurisdictions developed in many different ways but there was a general tendency to secure the promise of suitable judges and *Schöffen*.[5] Ecclesiastical immunities and the legal standing within the town of ecclesiastical *familiae* soon became a problem (for example, Speyer 1101; the Metz document of 1069 is interpolated) that grew as they constantly made new demands (*privilegium fori*, freedom from taxes). Guilds influenced the life of town communities indirectly through the model of fraternal togetherness presented by their internal organization (O. G. Oexle) rather than directly through participation in town government. Certainly their influence was in general less than that of the Charité of Valenciennes before 1070. The first craft associations (*Innungen*) appear both under the patronage of town lords (charter for twenty-three fishmongers at Worms, 1106), and as voluntary associations approved by the burgesses, like the bedlinen-weavers of Cologne who received a sealed charter from the city in 1149. The burgesses of Cologne made treaties about tolls and judicial procedures with the burgesses of Trier in 1149 and with those of Verdun in 1178. Although town councils[6] formally come into existence only after 1200, when they appear first in the episcopal towns of the Upper Rhine, they had their roots in the earlier groups of episcopal counsellors (*consilium episcopi*) as well as in the consulates of north Italian cities. The disputed succession to the Crown in 1198 proved a turning-point above all for the episcopal towns and resulted in considerable polarization between lords and urban communities.[7]

[5] Latin *scabini* (French *échevins*): the local panels of judgement-finders who appear as part of early municipal governments in some Frankish and Saxon areas; at Cologne in the 12th cent. they also called themselves *senatores*. Cf. the London aldermen (translator's note).

[6] *Stadträte* (Latin *consiliares*, *consules*) (translator's note).

[7] Sect. 4: E. Ennen, 'Europäische Züge der mittelalterlichen Stadtgeschichte', *Köln, das Reich und Europa* (4), 1–47; B. Diestelkamp, 'König und Städte in salischer und staufischer Zeit—Regnum Teutonicum', *Stadt und Herrschaft* (5), 248–97; D. Kurze, *Pfarrerwahlen im Mittelalter* (Cologne and Graz, 1966); E. Maschke, 'Stadt und Herrschaft in Deutschland und Reichsitalien (Salier- und Stauferzeit)', *Stadt und Herrschaft* (5), 299–331; P. Michaud-Quantin, *Universitas: Expressions du mouvement communautaire dans le Moyen Age latin* (Paris, 1970); H. Grafen, 'Die Speyerer im 11. Jahrhundert: Zur Formierung eines städtischen Selbstverständnisses in der Salierzeit', in H. W. Böhme (ed.), *Siedlungen und Landesausbau*, ii (Sigmaringen,

5. From the start new towns were constituted as communes of a new kind with liberties that took little account of existing liberties, especially those of the Church. They were designed to attract new settlers.

Over a thousand new towns were founded in Germany in the twelfth and thirteenth centuries, including those in the new settlements east of the Elbe. This great expansion produced a new hierarchy of local and regional centres in which the markets and industries of traditional and new centres had to compete against each other. After the middle of the twelfth century this competition between towns—because it also involved rivalries between princes—rapidly undermined the previously straightforward coinage system. The more important old towns profited from the general economic vitality while many of the new towns remained mere peasant communities.[8] Forerunners of the new foundations can be found in cases where lords created planned settlements of merchants (as in 1033 in Naumburg) and of Jews (1084 in Speyer), in non-royal grants of markets (Allensbach, Radolfzell, and indeed, Freiburg im Breisgau in 1120), and also in some planned but unchartered settlements, such as, for instance, those laid out beside the monastery of Schaffhausen in the 1080s, and in Zurich in the 1090s. The king gradually lost his prerogative control of markets and fortifications, as is shown by the fact that the Archbishop of Mainz fortified Aschaffenburg without royal permission in 1122. Princes used the foundation of new towns as a means of extending their territorial authority, though it was only after 1200 that the potential of towns as fortresses was seriously exploited. New towns, including those in Slav territory, were often established on or near the site of earlier settlements: Freiburg im Breisgau, a Zähringer foundation of 1120, Lübeck (Schauenburger in 1143, Welf in 1159, royal in 1180), Grosswusterwitz (Archbishop of Magdeburg in

1991), 97–152; D. Demandt, *Stadtherrschaft und Stadtfreiheit im Spannungsfeld von Geistlichkeit und Bürgerschaft in Mainz (11.–15. Jh.)* (Wiesbaden, 1977); B. Töpfer, 'Stellung und Aktivitäten der Bürgerschaft von Bischofsstädten während des staufisch-welfischen Thronstreits', *Stadt und Stadtbürgertum* (6), 13–62.

[8] *Ackerbürgerstädte*, i.e. in the terminology of Max Weber, settlements with quasi-urban liberties and constitutions but with predominantly agricultural economies (translator's note).

1159), and Hagenau (Staufer in 1164) are examples which have long been cited by constitutional and social historians. The liberties which the Duke of Zähringen and the *coniuratores fori* of Freiburg swore to uphold, with their provision for the election of advocate and priest, were more generous than was customary under the Staufen system, in which royal or seigneurial *ministeriales* dominated the towns. 'Families' of interrelated town constitutions began to develop as early as the twelfth century. These relationships were part of a general development of the right both to settle in towns and villages, and to make clearances of land outside them. In northern areas we have a significant mixture of rural and urban rights of settlement in the *Weichbild*,[9] of which the first grant was made in 1178 by the Bishop of Münster.[10]

6. There was no direct relationship between the legal rights of the inhabitant of a town and the autonomy of the community as a whole, but towns made a point of supporting the attempts of their burgesses to win and secure their individual rights. Legal rights in a town, which would be given

---

[9] A grant of *Weichbild* (*Weich* = vic; *bild* = bill) resembled an English grant of a borough or free borough, since it conveyed much the same as burgage tenure (that is, freedom of inheritance and alienation, fixed money rents, and freedom from various dues seen as servile or arbitrary). It might include more extensive liberties but did not necessarily do so. Like the word 'borough', *Weichbild* could also be used in a geographical sense for the privileged area, but *ius quod vulgo wicbilede dicitur* could be granted to rural as well as to urban communities (translator's note).

[10] Sect. 5: N. Kamp, 'Probleme des Münzrechts und der Münzprägung in salischer Zeit', *Beiträge*...(1), 94–110; E. Nau, 'Staufische Münzpolitik', *Südwestdeutsche Städte* (9), 49–67; W. Schlesinger, 'Der Markt als Frühform der deutschen Stadt', *Vor- und Frühformen* (3), 262–93; H. Stoob, 'Die hochmittelalterliche Städtebildung im Okzident', *Die Stadt* (7), 125–50; H. Wiessner, 'Die Anfänge der Stadt Naumburg an der Saale und ihre Entwicklung im Mittelalter', *Blätter für Deutsche Landesgeschichte*, 127 (1991), 115–43; H. Keller, 'Die Zähringer und die Entwicklung Freiburgs zur Stadt', *Die Zähringer: Eine Tradition und ihre Erforschung*, ed. K. Schmid (Sigmaringen, 1986), 17–29; B. Diestelkamp, 'Welfische Stadtgründungen und Stadtrechte des 12. Jh.', *Zeitschrift der Savigny-Stiftung für Rechtsgeschichte, Germ. Abt.*, 81 (1964), 164–224; B. am Ende, *Studien zur Verfassungsgeschichte Lübecks im 12. und 13. Jh.* (Lübeck, 1975); H. Stoob, 'Über Formen und Wandel staufischen Verhaltens zum Städtewesen'; id., *Forschungen zum Städtewesen in Europa*, i (Cologne and Vienna, 1970), 51–72; G. Wegener, 'Zur Verbreitung des Kölner Stadtrechts', *Köln, das Reich und Europa* (4), 173–212; K. Kroeschell, *Weichbild: Untersuchungen zu Struktur und Entstehung der mittelalterlichen Stadtgemeinde in Westfalen* (Cologne and Graz, 1960); H. K. Schulze, 'Kaufmannsgilde und Stadtentstehung im mitteldeutschen Raum', *Gilden und Zünfte* (10), 377–412.

and guaranteed to anyone who acquired and owned a
hereditas there, gave access to the town court, which corre-
sponded to the court held by a count elsewhere. The paying
of ground rents in towns did not in itself involve any loss of
personal freedom such as was involved in the payments owed
by those known as *censuales.*

All burgesses automatically had the right to plead in their
town court, while servants or dependants, although they
could not participate in the internal political life of the town,
shared in the privileges which the community as a whole had
in relation to the outside world. Jews formed separate communities with their own law. From the earliest grants (Speyer
1084, Worms 1090) this involved separation from the Christian communities and, after pogroms began, protection
from them.

Various types of dues represented different levels of personal freedom: in many towns, like Regensburg, for instance,
most of the burgesses were *censuales* owing rent to one or
other of the city churches. In the twelfth century municipal
courts received demands for fugitive serfs, probably quite
frequently, from lords outside. In 1118–19 the Archbishop
of Mainz granted the *habitantes infra ambitum muri* the right
to plead only at their town court. Very soon afterwards
Conrad of Zähringen gave the same privilege to Freiburg,
while the first royal grant was that of 1129 for Strasbourg. In
general it would be wrong not to include *ministeriales* and all
the other seigneurial officials who lived in a town among its
burgesses. On the other hand, their right to go either to the
town court, with burgesses as judgement-finders, or to their
lord's court, with *pares* as judgement-finders, as best suited
them, must have been advantageous to them and promoted
their social mobility.

Public records of the burgesses' legal business began to be
kept in the parishes of Cologne in 1130, including deeds
concerning the conveyance and inheritance of property and
contracts of loans and sales. Bishop Bertram of Metz, who
came from Cologne, introduced this system of parish chests
(*Schreinsgerichtsbarkeit*)[11] to his cathedral city in 1197. Other-

---

[11] The records are called *Schreinskarten* and *Schreinsbücher* from the *Schreine* (Latin
scrinia, chests) in which they were kept (translator's note).

wise it is only from the later thirteenth century that municipal registers of various kinds survive in any number.[12]

7. The part played by people of noble rank (*Altfreie*) in
urban development varied from region to region but is generally obscure north of the Alps. The urban upper classes,
being *divites*, were also *potentes*, and were thus assumed to
bear responsibility in the community, so that they needed no
special legitimation to take control. They strengthened their
position by serving as seigneurial officials and by forming
their own exclusive associations.

As early as 1074 Lampert of Hersfeld saw the qualifications
of the *primores civitatis* in terms of wealth, family connections,
boldness, and high worth (*merita*). In 1171 the Archbishop
of Cologne declared frankly that choosing *Schöffen* at
Andernach *ex humilioribus et pauperioribus* had been a mistake,
because a poor man was liable to be *formidolosus ad . . . minas
potentis*. The monopoly of court, parish, and fraternity offices
by the rich did not apparently create many problems in the
twelfth century. It was the establishment of a council at Cologne after the dynastic crisis of 1198 which constituted the
first attack on the domination of towns by great families, in
this case by the families of the *Richerzeche*.[13] Cologne seems to

---

[12] Sect. 6: G. Droege, 'Der Einfluß der mittelalterlichen Freiheitsbewegung auf
die frühe Stadt', *Civitatum Communitas: Festschrift H. Stoob*, ed. H. Jäger, F. Petri, and
H. Quirin, i (Cologne and Vienna, 1984), 56–70; H. Jakobs, 'Verfassungstopo-
graphische Studien zur Kölner Stadtgeschichte des 10. bis 12. Jh.', *Köln, das Reich
und Europa* (4), 49–123; *Germania Judaica*, i, ed. I. Elbogen, A. Freimann, and H.
Tykocinski (Breslau, 1917/34; repr. Tübingen, 1965), ii, ed. Z. Avneri (Tübingen,
1968); H. Fischer, *Die verfassungsrechtliche Stellung der Juden in den deutschen
Städten während des 13. Jh.* (Breslau, 1931; repr. 1969); F. Graus, 'Judenfeindschaft
im Mittelalter', *Antisemitismus*, ed. H. A. Strauss and N. Kampe (Schriftenreihe
der Bundeszentrale für politische Bildung, 213, 1984), 29–46 (ed. Frankfurt am
Main and New York, 1985); K. Bosl, *Die Sozialstruktur der mittelalterlichen Residenz-
und Fernhandelsstadt Regensburg* (Munich, 1966); B. Diestelkamp, 'Gründerleihe',
Handwörterbuch zur deutschen Rechtsgeschichte, i (1971), 1821–3; K. Schulz 'Zensualität
und Stadtentwicklung im 11./12. Jh.', *Beiträge . . .* (1), 73–93; K. Schulz,
Ministerialität und Bürgertum in Trier (Bonn, 1968); J. Fleckenstein, 'Ministerialität
und Stadtherrschaft: Ein Beitrag zu ihrem Verhältnis am Beispiel von Hildesheim
und Braunschweig', *Festschrift H. Beumann*, ed. K. U. Jäschke and R. Wenskus
(Sigmaringen, 1977), 349–64; M. Groten, 'Die Anfänge des Kölner
Schreinswesens', *Jahrbuch des Kölnischen Geschichtsvereins*, 56 (1985), 1–21; H. Patze,
'Stadtgründung und Stadtrecht', *Recht und Schrift im Mittelalter*, ed. P. Classen
(Vorträge und Forschungen, 23; Sigmaringen, 1977), 163–96.

[13] The name of the dominant association of Cologne: literally, the guild or club
of the rich (translator's note).

have been unique in that as early as the twelfth century all officials were appointed by fraternity-like collegiate groups which themselves recruited their members by co-option. The chief *Schöffe* (*magister scabinorum*) was chosen by the college of *Schöffen*, which was bound to the archbishop as lord of the city by the oaths of its members. The *Bürgermeister* (*magistri civium*) of the parishes were the serving masters of the colleges or fraternities of officers in each parish, while the two *Bürgermeister* of the whole city led the *Richerzeche*, with one of them also holding office as *Schöffe*. In the thirteenth century the newly established council followed the same pattern, co-opting its members as if it were a fraternity.

8. The spirit of the Church reforms of the eleventh century affected towns by stimulating demands for elections, benefactions to churches (including parish churches) over which the community claimed rights, and the spread of fraternal charities, including the first craft associations and guilds. Women were admitted to some of the associations, like the *Drechslerzunft* of Cologne in 1180, and took part in their funeral ceremonies. Participation in collective activities and good works became a means by which new social strata won greater freedom.

Donations by burgesses for the welfare of their souls (*sêlingêrede*) are recorded from 1100. They were made to collegiate churches and monasteries both in the towns and outside. Quite often the donations were for hospitals through which the townspeople could make provisions for themselves both in this world and the next. The first lay overseer (*laicus provisor*) of a hospital appears in Cologne in 1142.[14]

---

[14] Sects. 7 and 8: E. Maschke, 'Bürgerliche und adlige Welt in den deutschen Städten der Stauferzeit', *Südwestdeutsche Städte* (9), 9–27; B. Berthold, 'Sozialökonomische Differenzierung und innerstädtische Auseinandersetzung in Köln im 13. Jh.', *Stadt und Stadtbürgertum* (6), 229–87; H. Jakobs, 'Bruderschaft und Gemeinde: Köln im 12. Jh.', *Gilden und Zünfte* (10), 281–309; M. Groten, 'Die Kölner Richerzeche im 12. Jh. Mit einer Bürgermeisterliste', *Rheinische Vierteljahresblätter*, 48 (1984), 34–111; W. Peters, 'Zum Alter der Kölner Richerzeche', *Jahrbuch des Kölnischen Geschichtsvereins*, 59 (1988), 1–18; K. Schulz, 'Patriziergesellschaften und Zünfte in den mittel- und oberrheinischen Bischofsstädten', *Gilden und Zünfte* (10), 311–35; S. Reicke, *Das deutsche Spital und sein Recht im Mittelalter* (2 vols., Stuttgart, 1932).

9. Latin and vernacular usage included various words for townspeople, including the term *burgensis*, which seems to have originated in France. It was first used in England in 1086 and crossed the Rhine in 1120, though the quality of the evidence here is not at all comparable with that from England. It is not clear whether the use of the word implied any new privileges. Although the total content of burgess privileges at one time or place was never specified, they included freedom from manorial obligations; collective freedom from military service and from providing lodging for the lord and his followers; tax and toll privileges; the grant of jurisdiction to the town court and the appointment of its officers; the right of asylum; the rationalization of legal procedures; and freedom for new immigrants. No substantially new demands seem to have been made after 1150 and by about 1200 the characteristic urban *libertates* may have been absorbed into urban consciousness.[15]

10. Walls and towers from the beginning formed symbols of urban identity. From the twelfth century seals were used for the same purpose, while other symbolic objects are found in different areas.

The oldest town seals in Europe are attested in 1133–4 in Genoa, 1148 in Rome and a little later in the three metropolitan sees of the Rhineland. The Rhenish seals show the patron saints of their respective cities: that of Trier has Christ handing the key to St Peter and St Eucharius, scholar of St Peter and the first Bishop of Trier. The legends on the Mainz and Cologne seals call the one *specialis* and the other *fidelis filia s. Romanae ecclesiae* and show that city and church were regarded as constituting a single legal entity, respectively SANCTA COLONIA and AUREA MAGONTIA. The Trier legend on the other hand calls down a blessing on *urbs* and *plebs*. Other early seals describe the towns and their communities as *oppidum* (Soest, 1158), *communitas* (Metz, 1180), *gens*

---

[15] Sect. 9: H. Ammann, 'Vom Städtewesen Spaniens und Westfrankreichs im Mittelalter', *Studien zu den Anfängen des europäischen Städtewesens: Reichenau-Vorträge 1955–1956* (Vorträge und Forschungen, 4; Lindau and Konstanz, 1958; reprint Darmstadt, 1965), 104–50, with a map referring to the spread of *burgenses*; R. von Keller, *Freiheitsgarantien für Personen und Eigentum im Mittelalter* (Heidelberg, 1933).

(Worms, 1199), *burgenses civitatis* (Utrecht, 1196), *Confluentini* (Coblenz, 1198), *burgenses civitatis, urbs et plebs* (Strasbourg, 1201), *cives* (Speyer, 1212), *universitas* (Huy, 1215), *burgenses* (Lübeck, 1223), and *castrum* (Valenciennes, thirteenth century). Before the mid-thirteenth century seals depicted patron saints in their cities (Trier, Mainz, Cologne), or churches as representing the buildings of the town (Utrecht, Coblenz, Speyer), the perron or town cross (Huy), or a ship with a merchant and steersman (Lübeck). The Aachen seal, which shows Charlemagne enthroned, was originally (by 1134) not a town seal but belonged to the bench of *investiti* of the royal church of St Mary there and was *in custodia decani Aquensis ecclesiae*. Equestrian seals like those used by Italian cities from about 1155 are not found in any German towns before the end of the Staufen period. Who was in charge of town seals and authorized to use them in this earliest period is very uncertain.[16]

11. Towns were formally integrated into national politics only to a limited and variable extent.

Communes in Germany did not gain access to imperial or princely feudal courts. They did not become *seigneuries collectives*, nor could they be represented in a *curia* by their *iudices* or *consules*. In this connection, however, it should be noted that in Germany the electoral princes alone constituted the *Reichstag* until the end of the fifteenth century (P. Moraw). Until then, moreover, the relationship between the 'imperial cities'[17]—especially numerous in the formerly Staufen southwest—and the imperial government was neither uniform nor always harmonious. Lübeck and Vienna were the first towns to be formally raised to the position of *loci imperiales*. This was the act of Frederick II who normally, as in the *statutum* of 1231–2, sanctioned the efforts of the princes to integrate

---

[16] Sect. 10: T. Goerlitz, *Der Ursprung und die Bedeutung der Rolandsbilder* (Weimar, 1934); C. Römer, *Der Braunschweiger Löwe: Welfisches Wappentier und Denkmal* (Brunswick, 1982); H. Stehkämper, 'Imitatio Urbis - Altrömische Ämterbezeichnungen im Hochmittelalter in deutschen Städten', *Wallraf-Richartz Jahrbuch*, 47 (1986), 205 ff.; T. Diederich, *Rheinische Städtesiegel* (Neuss, 1984); H. Jakobs, 'Nochmals Eugen III. und die Anfänge europäischer Stadtsiegel', *Archiv für Diplomatik*, 39 (1993), 85–148.

[17] The traditional English trans. of *Reichsstädte*; not every *Reichsstadt* was a city in the sense of being a cathedral town (translator's note).

towns into their respective territories, allowing royal interests to take second place. The *statutum* also reveals the continuing importance of sworn associations within the towns by ordaining that they were all to be quashed or kept under control. Most towns now came under the authority of the rulers of the territories in which they lay, though some of the ancient episcopal cities managed to win their freedom, *de facto* though not *de iure*. Strasbourg was the first to achieve this, thanks to its victory over its bishop at the battle of Hausbergen (1261), followed by Cologne as a result of the battle of Worringen against its archbishop in 1288. Thus episcopal towns under episcopal rule which had developed autonomous governments may be classified as free cities.[18] In the history of urban mentalities 'free cities' and 'imperial free cities' have a distinctive and interesting place of their own.[19]

12. It is not possible to say very much about urban or 'bourgeois' culture in the Staufen period. The chivalric world clearly influenced the development of a courtly culture in towns, however, through the *ministeriales*. The first 'bourgeois' hero of an epic was *der gute Gerhard*. Rudolf of Ems took as his model for the character a merchant of Cologne, *dominus* Gerhard Ungemass (*immoderatus*), a *ministerialis* of the archbishop, who served as *Untervogt* (*subadvocatus*) in 1166–7 and toll-collector (*telonearius*) in 1169–96, held office in the *Richerzeche*, and became chief *Schöffe* and *Bürgermeister*. He died on 21 January 1197.

---

[18] The traditional English trans. of *Freistädte*, though see previous note (translator's note).

[19] Sect. 11: F. Opll, *Stadt und Reich im 12. Jh.* (Vienna, Cologne and Graz, 1986); V. Samanek, *Kronrat und Reichsherrschaft im 13. und 14. Jh.* (Berlin, 1910); H. Stehkämper, 'Über die rechtliche Absicherung der Stadt Köln gegen eine erzbischöfliche Landesherrschaft vor 1288', *Die Stadt in der europäischen Geschichte: Festschrift E. Ennen*, ed. W. Besch *et al.* (Bonn, 1972), 343–77; E. Voltmer, 'Von der Bischofsstadt zur Reichsstadt: Speyer im Hoch- und Spätmittelalter', *Geschichte der Stadt Speyer*, i, ed. W. Eger (Stuttgart, 1982), 249–368; W. von Groote, 'Die Angaben Galberts über Personen und Gremien des "öffentlichen Rechts" in Flandern 1127', *Handelingen der Maatschappij voor geschiedenis en oudheidkunde te Gent*, n.s. 34 (1980), 109–23; W. Goez, "Fürstenprivilegien", *Handwörterbuch zur deutschen Rechtsgeschichte*, i (1971), 1358–61; G. Möncke, 'Zur Problematik des Terminus 'Freie Stadt' im 14. und 15. Jh.', *Bischofs- und Kathedralstädte* (2), 84–94; R. Sprandel, *Mentalitäten und Systeme* (Stuttgart, 1972).

His robe of sable, ermine-lined,
All men admired, so too his belt,
With precious stones enclasped,
That cost him many a pound.[20]

13. Like historians elsewhere, those in Germany no
longer try to find a single origin for towns or for the municipal constitutions which were once seen as their defining
characteristic. During the nineteenth and twentieth centuries key factors were variously identified, including *Hofrecht*,
or more precisely the development of urban liberties out of
the government that bishops exercised over towns by delega-
tion from the king (K. W. Nitzsch); the community of the
mark and the rural neighbourhood (G. von Below); the law
of the market (S. Rietschel); the constitution of the court (G.
Seeliger); and the guild and *coniuratio* (H. Planitz). Max
Weber's influence on German scholarship has been much
stronger 'than all the footnotes suggest' (C. Haase). This is
partly because of the old convention of distinguishing
precommunal and communal stages, measured in terms of
freedom, in the development of European towns. But in
more recent German scholarship the boundary between free
and unfree towns has become very blurred: a great deal of
stress has been laid on the seigneurial contribution to medieval towns, notably by K. Bosl and W. Schlesinger. Studies of
ministeriales and *censuales* have lent support to this approach
(K. Schulz) and it certainly makes sense for the one thousand small towns and for the smaller episcopal towns, as well
as for towns under Staufen or princely control, though it
tends to ignore the great cities. Our recognition of the uni-
versality of the idea of freedom in the Middle Ages (J. Fried)
needs to be applied in urban history, to complement eco-

[20] Sect. 12: H. M. Klinkenberg, ' "Bürgerliche Bildung" im Mittelalter?', *Studien
zur deutschen Literatur des Mittelalters*, ed. R. Schützeichel (Bonn, 1979), 334–70; R.
Sprandel, *Gesellschaft und Literatur im Mittelalter* (UTB, 1218; Paderborn etc., 1982);
U. Peters, *Literatur in der Stadt: Studien zu den sozialen Voraussetzungen und kulturellen
Organisationsformen städtischer Literatur im 13. und 14. Jh.* (Tübingen, 1983); T. Zotz,
'Städtisches Rittertum und Bürgertum in Köln um 1200', *Institutionen, Kultur und
Gesellschaft im Mittelater. Festschrift für J. Fleckenstein zu seinem 65. Geburtstag*, ed. L.
Fenske *et al.* (Sigmaringen, 1984), 609–38; S. Zöller, *Kaiser, Kaufmann und die Macht
des Geldes: Gerhard Unmaze von Köln als Finanzier der Reichspolitik und der 'Gute Gerhard'
des Rudolf von Ems* (Munich, 1993).

nomic central-place theories, though these, of course, remain fruitful and have proved their value, particularly in regional history (A. Haverkamp). H. Keller's studies of north Italian communes form an outstanding example of the way that recent German work has moved outside national borders to find new European perspectives. So too does the work of Edith Ennen, the Grand Old Lady of German urban history, whose work stands serene above controversy, with its image of the town as a cradle of our modern civil rights.

Despite the *Elenchus Fontium* the provision of critical texts of German urban history has not advanced very far but more progress has been made with historical maps. Since 1972–3 excellent fascicules of the *Deutsche Städteatlas* have been published by the Münster Institut für vergleichende Städtegeschichte and of the *Rheinische Städteatlas* by the Bonn Institut für geschichtliche Landeskunde. Two rich and varied collections of essays which give a good view of West German work as well as of a wide range of international scholarship are *Beiträge zum hochmittelalterlichen Städtewesen*, edited by B. Diestelkamp (1982), and *Gilden und Zünfte*, edited by B. Schwineköper (1985). Yet O.G. Oexle, in *Coniuratio und Gilde*, and K. Schreiner in his study of the 'communal movement' and 'craft revolution' have still, even in Otto Brunner's country, had to show the scholarly world how much our historical categories have been shaped by the political and social assumptions of nineteenth-century historiography. Among East German scholars in our field, B. Töpfer, E. Werner, and E. Müller-Mertens have achieved international reputations.

There is still much to be learned from surviving written documents, even for the early and central Middle Ages, let alone for the later part of the period, on which most interest in Germany has focused during the last three decades. Topographical studies have developed increasingly refined methods, to which archaeology has made a notable contribution in some towns, as, for instance, for Lübeck at the time of its foundation. In several towns, including Cologne, place-names are recorded from the twelfth century or even earlier. By the twelfth century many of their original meanings had been lost but they can be traced through the Latinized forms of the charters or the paraphrases by which the scribes tried to make sense of the old forms. The history of names seems to me as promising a line of research, at least in some places, as the excavation of walls and artefacts. We need more information on the insignia of seals. The compilation of a *corpus sigillorum* of European towns in the period when seal-types were being formed (until about 1250–1300) would be a valuable international project, and not an impossibly ambitious one.[21]

[21] Sect. 13: K. Schreiner, 'Die mittelalterliche Stadt in Webers Analyse und die Deutung des okzidentalen Rationalismus: Typus, Legitimität, Kulturbedeutung', *Max Weber, der Historiker*, ed. J. Kocka (Göttingen, 1986), 119–50; K. Bosl (above, n. 12 to Sect. 6); W. Schlesinger (above, n. 10 to Sect. 5); K. Schulz (above, nn. 12, 14 to Sects. 6, 7–8); H. Keller (above, nn. 4, 10 to Sects. 3, 5); J. Fried, 'Über den Universalismus der Freiheit im Mittelalter', *Historische Zeitschrift*, 240 (1985), 313–61; *Die abendländische Freiheit vom 10. zum 14. Jahrhundert*, ed. J. Fried (Vorträge und Forschungen, 39; Sigmaringen, 1991); A. Haverkamp, 'Die "frühbürgerliche Welt" im hohen und späten Mittelalter: Landesgeschichte und Geschichte der städtischen Gesellschaft', *Historische Zeitschrift*, 221 (1975), 571–602; E. Ennen, *Die europäische Stadt des Mittelalters*, 4th edn. (Göttingen, 1987); *Beiträge . . .* (1); *Gilden und Zünfte* (10); O. G. Oexle, 'Conjuratio und Gilde im frühen Mittelalter: Ein Beitrag zum Problem der sozialgeschichtlichen Kontinuität zwischen Antike und Mittelalter', *Gilden und Zünfte* (10), 151–214; K. Schreiner, ' "Kommunebewegung" und "Zunftrevolution": Zur Gegenwart der mittelalterlichen Stadt im historisch-politischen Denken des 19. Jh.', *Stadtverfassung, Verfassungsstaat, Pressepolitik: Festschrift E. Naujoks*, ed. F. Quarthal and W. Setzler (Sigmaringen, 1980), 139–168; B. Töpfer, *Volk und Kirche zur Zeit der beginnenden Gottesfriedensbewegung in Frankreich* (Berlin, 1957); E. Werner, *Stadt und Geistesleben im Hochmittelalter, 11.–13. Jh.* (Weimar, 1980); E. Müller-Mertens, 'Bürgerlich-städtische Autonomie in der Feudalgesellschaft', *Zeitschrift für Geschichtswissenschaft*, 29 (1981), 205–25; P. Segl, 'Mittelalterforschung in der Geschichtswissenschaft der DDR', *Geschichtswissenschaft in der DDR*, ii, ed. A. Fischer and G. Heydemann (Berlin, 1990), 99–148; R. Hammel, 'Frühe Stadtgeschichte und Archäologie: Kritische Betrachtungen aus der Sicht eines Historikers', *Zeitschrift des Vereins für Lübeckische Geschichte und Altertumskunde*, 64 (1984), 9–38; H. Jakobs, 'Namenkundliches zum Kölner Stadtbild im Frühmittelalter', *Althochdeutsch*, ii (Heidelberg, 1987), 1433–54; T. Diederich, 'Prolegomena zu einer neuen Siegeltypologie', *Archiv für Diplomatik*, 29 (1983), 242–84.

The Manorial System

13

Lords, Peasants, and the Development of the Manor: England, 900–1280

Christopher Dyer

Historians who reconstruct long-term changes in medieval society are often tempted to visualize an 'ideal type' of early manor—a self-sufficient organization, provided with a large demesne on which goods, and especially food were produced by means of the heavy labour services of a numerous dependent peasantry, the whole unit being subject to the jurisdiction of the lord who drew his revenues from the combination of demesne produce and tenant dues. Changes in society can then be described in terms of either the growth or decline of this institution, and every variation from the ideal type can be explained as either a stage in the evolution of the pure manor, or a deterioration from its peak of development.

In England it was once believed that the manor was still developing throughout the period 900–1280, but since the 1950s, with the recognition that manorial forms existed as early as the seventh century, the manor can be seen as a mature institution containing seeds of decay at the time of Domesday Book, and could even be described as declining from the tenth century.[1]

We are perhaps wrong to attempt to reduce a complex story to simple unilinear trends. The manor was after all the means by which the aristocracy gained their living from the land. The aristocracy were immensely varied, being stratified

---

[1] T. H. Aston, 'The Origins of the Manor in England', with 'A Postscript', *Social Relations and Ideas*, ed. T. H. Aston, P. R. Coss, J. Thirsk, and C. Dyer (Cambridge, 1983), 1–43; T. H. Aston, 'The English Manor', *Past and Present*, 10 (1956), 6–14; E. A. Kosminsky, *Studies in the Agrarian History of England in the Thirteenth Century* (Oxford, 1956).

horizontally, split vertically between clergy and laity, and divided between different regional cultures; they changed and adapted constantly to new circumstances. Lords needed different types of revenue, and they were influenced in the exploitation of resources by the agrarian potential of the land, the development of the market, and the degree of independence of the local peasantry. Manors of one type might have been declining while others were growing; manorial structures were changed or renewed when manors passed from one type of lord to another. There were many routes to manorialization, and many paths of manorial decline, all occurring at different periods, and in different parts of the country. To use an analogy drawn from astronomy, it is perhaps more fruitful to think of manorial structures in a 'steady state', with new manors arising to replace those that decayed, rather than to assume a 'big bang' at an early date, perhaps in the seventh century, or the ninth, from which all subsequent developments flowed. In some regions the manor in even an approximation of the 'pure' form never existed. In northern pastoral areas, for example, the absence of a large arable demesne meant that the manorial centre did not become much more than a collection point for peasant dues, initially in kind but later in cash. Perhaps like all ideal types, the perfect manor is an intellectual construct, that never really existed anywhere, but still serves for us a useful conceptual purpose.

These preliminary remarks are by way of a preparation for an account of social development, in which generalization will be attempted, but where there will always be complications and contradictions. The period can conveniently be divided into three: 900–1086, 1086–1180, and 1180–1280.

900–1086

This period is one of contradictory tendencies, in which some types of manor declined and fragmented, while in some circumstances new, firmly based manors were created. At the end of the period Domesday Book provides an embarrassing wealth of evidence, but earlier centuries are relatively obscure, because England lacks any equivalent of the continental *polyptiques*. The sources that are available to us, charters, suggest that in the ninth, tenth, and eleventh centuries the large estates were breaking up into smaller parcels.[2] The fringes of the great land units that had dominated the country in the seventh and eighth centuries were being turned into relatively small holdings (covering a territory of 400 ha. or less), often in the hands of a lesser aristocracy of thegns. The internal structure of these manors is not revealed until 1086, when Domesday Book shows that some had relatively large demesnes, and were well supplied with slave labour, suggesting that the decreasing size of manorial units was associated with a greater intensity of exploitation of resources.[3] This was not universal, because small manors could tend towards the opposite extreme: some had looser forms of organization, and a few even lacked demesnes; in places they could appear to have been so small (notably in the south-west) that the term 'manor' seems too grand a term to describe them.[4]

The older land units still sometimes survived at the time of Domesday in the hands of the king or major churches. They could be very large (with an area in excess of 4000 ha.), often consisting of federations of dependent parcels called berewicks and sokelands, with demesnes of such small size that the bulk of their revenues must have come from peasant rents.[5] They are better described as centres for the collection of tribute, preserving premanorial forms. In eastern England, small units of land holding seem to have proliferated at an earlier stage, so that the new Benedictine monasteries founded or refounded after the Danish invasions acquired many parcels of land by gift or purchase and created large manors with demesnes by a process of amalgamation and consolidation.[6]

---

[2] M. Chibnall, *Anglo-Norman England, 1066–1166* (Oxford, 1986), 135–47.

[3] J. D. Hamshere, 'Domesday Book: Estate Structures in the West Midlands', *Domesday Studies*, ed. J. C. Holt (Woodbridge, 1987), 155–82.

[4] W. G. Hoskins, 'The Highland Zone in Domesday Book', in id., *Provincial England* (London, 1965), 15–52.

[5] G. R. J. Jones, 'Multiple Estates and Early Settlement', *Medieval Settlement*, ed. P. H. Sawyer (London, 1976), 15–40; N. Gregson, 'The Multiple Estate Model: Some Critical Questions', *Journal of Historical Geography*, 11 (1985), 339–51; F. M. Stenton, *Types of Manorial Structure in the Northern Danelaw* (Oxford, 1910); S. P. J. Harvey, 'The Extent and Profitability of Demesne Agriculture in England in the Later Eleventh Century', *Social Relations and Ideas*, 45–72.

[6] E. Miller, *The Abbey and Bishopric of Ely* (Cambridge, 1951), 16–25; J. A. Raftis, *The Estates of Ramsey Abbey* (Toronto, 1957), 6–19.

The economic background to these varied patterns of fragmentation, continuity, and formation of manors is now understood more clearly because of archaeological research into towns and the consequent reinterpretation of the documentary evidence. The tenth century is now recognized as an important period of urbanization: the numbers of towns grew, the town-dwelling population increased, and important economic activities, such as industrial production and marketing, were concentrated in urban settlements.[7]

This commercial development affected the manor in contradictory ways. First, presumably under the influence of a growing market for agricultural produce, peasants in Hampshire are recorded as paying cash rents (at a rate of 40d. per hide) as early as the year 900.[8] And by the time of Domesday, many *censarii* had as their primary obligation the payment of rent; we do not appreciate fully their importance because some were omitted from Domesday, and have to be discovered in other sources.[9] Thus the opportunity of commodity production released some peasants from manorial labour obligations. At the same time, lords and wealthier peasants must have been employing the thousands of smallholders, called bordars and cottars in Domesday, to do agricultural and craft work. Many people migrated, not least in order to take advantage of the new openings in the towns, and it can be argued that late Anglo-Saxon England saw heightened social as well as geographical mobility.[10] Evidently the beginnings of marketing weakened some features of manorial organization.

The lords also could take the opportunities provided by the market. It is true that some of them pursued a policy of self-sufficiency, exemplified by monasteries which organized their manors in rotas for the supply of food to the monks for

[7] C. Dyer, 'Recent Developments in Early Medieval Urban History and Archaeology in England', *Urban Historical Geography*, ed. D. Denecke and G. Shaw (Cambridge, 1988), 69–80.

[8] *The Agrarian History of England and Wales*, i, pt. 2, ed. H. P. R. Finberg (Cambridge, 1972), 452–3.

[9] J. F. R. Walmsley, 'The *Censarii* of Burton Abbey and the Domesday Population', *North Staffordshire Journal of Field Studies*, 8 (1968), 73–80.

[10] W. G. Runciman, 'Accelerating Social Mobility: The Case of Anglo-Saxon England', *Past and Present*, 104 (1984), 3–30; J. Campbell, 'Some Agents and Agencies of the late Anglo-Saxon State', *Domesday Studies*, 201–18.

a fixed number of weeks in each year. On the other hand, outlying manors, of which there were many because of the dispersed character of English aristocratic estates, could be exploited more effectively if they were required to produce cash revenues. Domesday hints at commodity production by its lists of demesne stock, showing that manors kept many more sheep, pigs, and cattle than even the most carnivorous household could eat.[11] Above all, Domesday assigns values to manors in cash—an estimation of potential revenues perhaps, but an impossible projection unless they were indeed generating a money income. Some had urban houses attached to them which could be used as venues for the sale of produce. Thus some demesnes were strengthened and stimulated as productive units. And there is evidence that while some peasants substituted cash payments for labour service, others were being settled on the demesne and required to work for their holdings. Slavery was declining in the eleventh century, often because lords gave the former slaves holdings, converting them to *bovarii* or bordars, who fed themselves from their parcels of land, but who were committed to onerous duties on the demesne.[12] Also the locally numerous boors or *geburs* (called *buri* and *coliberti* in Domesday) have been identified as a category of tenants settled on the demesne, restricted in their movements and often subjected to heavy labour services.[13] Although the bulk of the English peasants remained technically free, they were subjected to strong lordly control, including jurisdictional powers arising from the acquisition by major churches of local hundred courts. There is a still unresolved problem over the legal status of the peasants in this period: how can we reconcile the apparently free status of many peasants with the degree of close control to which they were subjected in such matters as inheritance and services?

The traditional view that the Norman Conquest strengthened (or even created) the manor no longer finds much

---

[11] P. H. Sawyer, 'The Wealth of England in the Eleventh Century', *Transactions of the Royal Historical Society*, 5th ser., 15 (1965), 145–64.

[12] M. M. Postan, *The Famulus* (*Economic History Review*, suppl. 2, 1954), 5–11.

[13] D. Pelteret, 'The *Coliberti* of Domesday Book', *Studies in Medieval Culture*, 12 (1976), 43–54; id., 'Two Old English Lists of Serfs', *Medieval Studies*, 48 (1986), 470–513.

support. Rather it is thought that the changing relations between lords and peasants can best be explained in terms of long-term shifts in land holding, the market, and jurisdiction. The political changes after 1066 had some influence on the manor, especially in some regions. In the east the more independent peasants were brought under tighter control, and Domesday reports complaints of excessively heavy demands on some manors.[14] In the north a radical change was possible when Norman lords made new manors in the areas previously devastated in William I's punitive raids, with the introduction of demesnes and regular labour services in a region that had previously been subject to a relatively light seignorial control.[15]

Finally, settlement historians have found, again using archaeological evidence, first that nucleated villages developed in England as late as the ninth to twelfth centuries, and secondly that many of them were laid out according to a regular plan, using standard units of measurement, with equal-sized house plots arranged in rows along a street or around a green.[16] These discoveries have many implications for manorial history. The simple reasoning that manors pre-date villages, and therefore that the lords must have planned and laid out the villages, may work for such areas as the north in its recovery from devastation, but it will not explain why single nucleated settlements developed in places divided among many lords, or why on some manors of powerful lords nucleation of settlement did not occur. Planned villages are closely linked with regular field systems, and both must have originated in circumstances of agrarian and ecological pressure which we still do not fully understand. Village communities, which were capable of taking on the management of manors as collective lessees in the eleventh century, may well have been involved in village reorganization.[17] In which case the regularly planned village is evidence not of close

[14] R. Welldon Finn, *Domesday Studies. The Eastern Counties* (London, 1967), 169–76, 186–208.

[15] W. E. Kapelle, *The Norman Conquest of the North* (London, 1979), 158–90.

[16] C. C. Taylor, *Village and Farmstead* (London, 1983), 107–50; B. K. Roberts, *The Making of the English Village* (London, 1987).

[17] R. S. Hoyt, 'Farm of the Manor and Community of the Vill in Domesday Book', *Speculum*, 30 (1955), 147–69.

seignorial control but of the limitations on the power of manorial lords, who had to deal with a strong and coherent village community.

1086–1180

In the twelfth century the greater abundance of evidence means that the trend toward the gradual decline of the manor can be recognized more clearly. Manors were reduced in size, because the large land units continued to be fragmented by social and political pressure. Fiefs were created for knights, and endowments for the new wave of monastic foundations. Manors were divided because of occasional partible inheritance, and in response to the growing market for land. The new manors were often irregular in structure. At one extreme the Cistercian Order created granges which consisted of demesnes worked by lay brothers and wage labour, without any tenant land. The Augustinian canons also managed the glebes that they were granted with parish churches as small demesnes with few or no tenants. Another new order, the Templars, at the other end of the spectrum of manorial types, often received small endowments of tenant lands from their benefactors, which lacked any demesne at all.[18]

On the more conventional manors on large church estates the demesnes shrank in size. This was a consistent small-scale movement, not a catastrophic collapse, and presumably continued a trend of the eleventh century.[19] Usually parcels of demesne were detached and granted to peasant tenants in return for cash rents.[20] The remainder of the demesnes that continued to be controlled by the lords were not directly exploited but leased or farmed out to middlemen—knights, clergy, officials, or peasants—who took over the demesne or the whole manor for a fixed term and paid an annual rent in

[18] Kosminsky, *Agrarian History of England*, 109–16; R. A. Donkin, *The Cistercians* (Toronto, 1978), 37–67.

[19] Harvey, 'Extent and Profitability', 69–72. For contrary views see A. R. Bridbury, 'The Farming Out of Manors', *Economic History Review*, 2nd ser., 31 (1978), 503–20; R. Faith, 'Demesne Resources and Labour Rent on the Manors of St Paul's Cathedral', *Economic History Review*, 47 (1994), 657–78.

[20] M. M. Postan, 'The Chronology of Labour Services', in id., *Essays on Medieval Agriculture and General Problems of the Medieval Economy* (Cambridge, 1973), 89–106.

cash or kind. This again continued a method of estate management that may well have been prevalent in earlier centuries. It was very convenient for the lord, because it removed from him a great deal of risk and trouble and assured him a steady income from the land. The farmers speculated on good years that would make a profit for them over and above the rent that they paid. They might have ambitions to gain long-term hereditary control, making the demesne part of their patrimony (as feudal tenants did with their fiefs), and lords had to be vigilant to prevent such a disastrous development.[21]

The core of the demesne labour supply came from the descendants of the freed slaves, who held tenements in 'base sergeantry' for specific and continuous agricultural work such as ploughing, carting, or shepherding. Seasonal tasks were still performed by peasants' labour services. The trend to commute labour services either partially or completely for cash rents must have increased the demand for wage labour, and there was no shortage of smallholders for employment. The numbers of peasants who owed cash rents, or who were only loosely connected to manors increased with internal colonization. Before 1100, newly colonized land was assimilated into the manor and the tenants of new land were absorbed into the system of dependent tenures owing labour service. Increasingly in the twelfth century assarts were regarded as a separate category of tenement, held as privileged free tenures for cash rents.[22] The assarting of woodlands tended to be piecemeal and individualistic, the result of peasant initiative, which lords were willing to encourage for the sake of the increased cash revenues.[23]

Historians have puzzled over the economic background to these twelfth-century developments. In many ways the advance of cash payments and the assarting movement look

[21] R. Lennard, *Rural England, 1086–1135* (Oxford, 1959), 105–212; E. Miller, 'England in the Twelfth and Thirteenth Centuries: An Economic Contrast?', *Economic History Review*, 2nd ser., 24 (1971), 1–14.
[22] *The Peasant Land Market in Medieval England*, ed. P. D. A. Harvey (Oxford, 1984), 7–19.
[23] B. K. Roberts, 'A Study of Medieval Colonisation in the Forest of Arden, Warwickshire', *Agricultural History Review*, 16 (1968), 101–13.

like the usual accompaniments of steady urbanization, growth of commerce, and population increase. If these were the main influences, why was it primarily the peasants who took advantage of the new circumstances, while the lords seem to have behaved more passively, and failed to use their demesnes to yield greater profits? Does the answer lie in the inertia of lords content with a stable income? Or did England really go through an economic malaise, perhaps associated with the troubles of Stephen's reign?

The decline should not be exaggerated, because most of the evidence comes from the records of large ancient church estates, those of Benedictine monasteries and bishoprics. Other landlords, such as the Cistercians, were more enterprising, and made a fortune from commodity production. The lesser lay landlords, the knights who were becoming more prominent in government at this time, relied on their demesnes under direct management to supply both their households and the market. They demonstrated their managerial skills by acting as farmers for the larger landlords, thus adding to their landed incomes.

Why did the twelfth century see the beginnings of a great extension of manorial documentation, which became even more abundant in the thirteenth century, and was associated with more precision in the definition of lands and services? One plausible suggestion is that peasant holdings had for centuries consisted of shares in the resources of their villages, and were not territorialized into specific strips of land until the twelfth century.[24] Perhaps more documents were written because of the increased sophistication and self-confidence of lords? Or were they compiled as a defensive move, because tenants were questioning their rents and services and leaving the manor? And lords had surely to maintain a constant vigilance to protect themselves from encroachments from rival lords and the officials of the Crown? A growth in the number of documents, once regarded as proof of the vigour of the manorial régime, may be a further indication of the manor's ill-health.

[24] *The Peasant Land Market*, 7–19.

1180–1280

The conventional explanation of the reversal of the twelfth-century trends is that a rapid inflation that began about 1180 disrupted the equilibrium of the system by which manors were farmed out to middlemen. Lords were frightened by rising prices, and disturbed by the loss of profits, and took their manors into direct management in the period 1180–1220. The price rise continued, probably because of an increase in population. The farmers were dismissed, and new careers opened up for administrators recruited from the clergy and the gentry, who were rewarded with payments in cash, and therefore represent an early group of clients bound to their lord by ties of 'bastard feudalism'. Training courses and textbooks imparted the necessary skills of accounting, auditing, and the holding of manorial courts. The hard task of running manors from day to day was left to peasant tenants compelled to serve as reeves as an obligation of servile tenure. This break in historical continuity has caused much anguished debate among historians. The evidence of a price rise is contained without doubt in the royal pipe rolls. Wheat and cattle were bought and sold in the early thirteenth century at double and treble their price in the 1170s.[25] The period of inflation can be compared in severity with that of the sixteenth century or the twentieth.

The most convincing explanation that has been offered to date has been that a great deal of silver flowed into the country, which derived ultimately from the new mine which was opened at Freiburg in 1168. The coins were sent in payment for large consignments of wool exported to Flanders, for which there is a good deal of independent evidence. The importance of the money supply seems to be confirmed by a rapid growth of mint output in England, especially in the 1180s.[26] Various alternative explanations for the price

[25] P. D. A. Harvey, 'The English Inflation of 1180–1220', *Peasants, Knights and Heretics*, ed. R. H. Hilton (Cambridge, 1976), 57–84; P. D. A. Harvey, 'The Pipe Rolls and the Adoption of Demesne Farming in England', *Economic History Review*, 2nd ser., 27 (1974), 345–59.

[26] T. H. Lloyd, *The English Wool Trade in the Middle Ages* (Cambridge, 1977), 1–13; N. J. Mayhew, 'Frappes de monnaies et hausse des prix en Angleterre de 1180 à 1220', *Etudes d'histoire monétaire*, ed. J. Day (Lille, 1984), 159–77; P. Spufford, *Money and its Use in Medieval Europe* (Cambridge, 1988), 109–31.

rise have been offered, none of them fully convincing. If a surge in population raised the demand for foodstuffs, there would have been a reduction in wages, but wages seem to have moved upwards with the price of goods. An ingenious legal historian has suggested that the reforms of the common law in the late twelfth century strengthened property rights, encouraged a lively land market, and so caused a build-up of inflationary pressure by increasing the velocity of monetary circulation. It seems unlikely that a land market could develop so suddenly, and on a sufficient scale, to have such a universal effect on prices.[27]

The inflation marked the beginning of a sustained commercial growth. The Crown licensed hundreds of markets, and lords created dozens of new seignorial boroughs during the thirteenth century.[28] Demesnes produced huge quantities of grain, wool, and meat for sale. The tradition of self-sufficiency was relaxed because it was so much more convenient to buy foodstuffs. Some monasteries later in the thirteenth century sold their demesne grain and bought their domestic supplies in local markets.

Controversy surrounds the new definition of serfdom that drew sharper distinctions between free and unfree in the decades around 1200. For legal historians this was a by-product of the extension of the Crown's jurisdictional powers, which needed a clear definition of those who were subject to the royal courts. Economic historians regard the chronology of the establishment of new law of villeinage as strangely coincidental with the financial pressures caused by the inflation. The Crown needed profits of justice and the aristocracy gained from an extension of their social control.[29]

Does this package of developments mark, as it is some-

[27] R. C. Palmer, 'The Economic and Cultural Impact of the Origins of Property: 1180–1220', *Law and History Review*, 3 (1987), 139–56.

[28] R. H. Britnell, 'The Proliferation of Markets in England, 1200–1349', *Economic History Review*, 2nd ser., 34 (1981), 209–21; M. W. Beresford and H. P. R. Finberg, *English Medieval Boroughs* (Newton Abbot, 1973), 39; R. H. Britnell, *The Commercialisation of English Society 1000–1500* (Cambridge, 1993), 79–151.

[29] R. H. Hilton, 'Freedom and Villeinage in England', *Peasants, Knights and Heretics*, 174–91; P. R. Hyams, *King, Lords, and Peasants in Medieval England* (Oxford, 1980), 221–65.

times alleged, a clear divergence of English social development from that of the continent? Some have gone so far as to compare the thirteenth-century English manor with the estates revealed in the ninth-century *polyptiques*, and others have plausibly suggested that English lords were forced back on to a more direct system of demesne exploitation because they lacked the profits of justice enjoyed by their Continental contemporaries.[30]

There were differences between the twelfth and thirteenth centuries but the break between them was not as sharp as first appears. First, beginning with seignorial agriculture, the area of land in demesne often remained stable or even shrank slightly in the thirteenth century.[31] Direct assarting by lords to extend the demesne was relatively uncommon. So the manorial managers were not as dedicated to increasing demesne production as is sometimes alleged. Lords bought land to build up their estates in the thirteenth century, but it was often used to add to rent income rather than demesne production. On many estates the profits of the demesne accounted for 40 per cent or less of the total estate revenues, and rents and other tenant payments provided very large sums. Nor was there much of a transformation in attitudes to estates. The mentality of the new breed of managers, judging from the writings of 'Walter of Henley' and his ilk, was cautious and conservative, and emphasized extraction of wealth rather than investment and improved production. Secondly, turning to the generation of income from the peasants, customary tenants continued to make a contribution to work on the demesne, but the growing population made available an abundance of cheap wage-labour, which was both more reliable and more productive than servile labour. The trend towards cash rents continued the process that had been apparent in the twelfth century and even earlier. In the late thirteenth century lords were negotiating with individual villeins to convert their tenures into lease-

[30] M. Bloch, *Seigneurie française et manoir anglais* (Cahiers des Annales, 16; Paris, 1967), 64–89.

[31] C. C. Dyer, *Lords and Peasants in a Changing Society* (Cambridge, 1980), 61–4, 79–82; Miller, *Ely*, 97; F. R. H. Du Boulay, *The Lordship of Canterbury* (London, 1966), 206–7.

holds paying cash only.[32] When servile tenants contested
their status in the royal courts in the thirteenth century, they
were usually disputing, not the level of labour services, but
the occasional cash payments such as marriage fines, heriots,
tolls, and tallage.[33] Serfs were valued by lords at least as much
as a source of cash as of labour.

Nor does the structure and management of the English
manor present a complete contrast to the *seigneurie* of the
Continent. In regions of England, such as parts of the north
and the north-west Midlands, the profits of justice and the
revenues from mills contributed a very high proportion of
lords' revenues, which gives the seignorial régimes of these
areas a Continental flavour.[34] There were also many exceptions to the rule that lords resumed active demesne management as a major feature of estate exploitation. Royal manors
continued to collect rents and tallages from tenants rather
than produce grain and wool. The royal administration
lacked either the will or the means to adopt the more
commercial policies of the aristocracy.[35] Eccentric manorial
forms, without demesnes for example, continued to prolifer-
ate in the hands of the gentry as lands were detached for sale
or developed by assarting in the woods and wastes. In such
regions as the south-west and the north-west, demesnes were
leased out to farmers throughout the thirteenth century, and
some manors had no demesnes at all.[36]

The expanding market of the thirteenth century had the
paradoxical effect of reviving manorialism on many English
estates. It was a strange form of manorial exploitation which
had emerged by the late thirteenth century, which can
scarcely be regarded as an 'ideal type' of manor in view of the
extensive use of wage-labour, nor can it be described as a
capitalist system because of the low levels of investment and
the widespread reliance on the profits of lordship. The gen-

[32] R. H. Hilton, *The English Peasantry in the Later Middle Ages* (Oxford, 1975),
139–60.
[33] R. H. Hilton, 'Peasant Movements in England before 1381', id., *Class Conflict
and the Crisis of Feudalism* (London, 1985), 122–38.
[34] Kosminsky, *Agrarian History of England*, 181–6; Hilton, *English Peasantry*, 231–7.
[35] M. K. McIntosh, *Autonomy and Community* (Cambridge, 1986), 13–49.
[36] e.g. J. Hatcher, 'Non-Manorialism in Medieval Cornwall', *Agricultural History
Review*, 18 (1970), 1–16.

try manors which were provided with large demesnes and few serfs, and which bore some resemblance to capitalist farms, often had a limited ability to make a killing on the market because the bulk of the produce was consumed in the household.[37]

The about-turn in the management of the English manor in the thirteenth century marked a temporary interruption in an extended decline. The restraints on the aristocracy from the state, the stubborn peasant resistance to lords' demands and the lords' own preference for steady incomes based on cash rents, all led to diminishing returns from the manorial system. As the power of the lords of manors was gradually reduced, tenants were able to reap the rewards. Peasants with large holdings, especially the wealthy stratum of freemen, were already taking advantage of the growth of the market in the thirteenth century. Even servile tenants with large holdings were able to buy land and extend the scale of their agriculture.[38] They were taking the economic initiative, especially in areas of weak manorialism and a highly developed market, such as East Anglia, while the manor continued its long decline into a somnolent rent-collecting agency.[39] Even the extension of literate government, which helped the lords to exploit their manors more thoroughly, benefited some peasants. Freeholders conveyed their land by charter, and villeins found that the written record of their tenures and customs in the lords' court rolls had some value. Their regard for the power of the written word is shown by their appeals to Domesday Book, which they hoped would contain evidence of their ancient freedom.[40]

The Importance of the Manor

Since the advances made in English manorial history in the 1930s and 1950s (I am thinking particularly of the outstand-

[37] R. H. Britnell, 'Minor Landlords in England and Medieval Agrarian Capitalism', *Landlords, Peasants and Politics in Medieval England*, ed. T. H. Aston (Cambridge, 1987), 227–46.

[38] J. Hatcher, 'English Serfdom and Villeinage: Towards a Reassessment', *Landlords, Peasants and Politics*, 247–84.

[39] B. M. S. Campbell, 'The Complexity of Manorial Structure in Medieval Norfolk: A Case Study', *Norfolk Archaeology*, 39 (1986), 225–61.

[40] E. M. Hallam, *Domesday Book through Nine Centuries* (London, 1986), 50–1.

ing contributions of Aston, Kosminsky, and Postan), interest in the subject has waned. Historical research in the pre-Conquest period has concentrated on the topography of estates rather than their economies. In later periods, the peasantry in their own right are studied, with research concentrating on such problems as social stratification, marriage and the family, the land market, and the cohesion of the village community. Some argue that the force behind medieval economic change was the shifting balance between population and the land, in which process the manor seems an institutional irrelevance. Yet there has been a continued interest in social relationships, and particularly in the struggle between lords and peasants, which was played out within the manorial arena. Some historians of the peasantry are prone to forget too readily the manor's continuing presence, which influenced and regulated many aspects of the life of the countryside. The manor cannot be neglected because all lines of research into medieval rural society have to be conducted through the medium of the records of manorial administration, which filtered and even distorted the information as it was written down. Eventually we will return fully to the manor and reinterpret its history in the light of the newly won knowledge of the structure and dynamics of medieval society.

14

The Decline of the Classic Manor in Germany during the High Middle Ages

Werner Rösener

In an informative outline of the history of German agriculture, Georg von Below stresses the importance of the transformation of the medieval manorial system. He considers the decline of the classic manor to have been 'the most significant event in the agrarian history of Germany during the high Middle Ages',[1] comparable to the colonization of the east. A totally different view was put forward by Alfons Dopsch. In his book *Herrschaft und Bauer* (1939), he completely rejected the notion of far-reaching change in the medieval manorial system. According to Dopsch, no such economic upheaval took place at all.[2] Before going on to examine this controversial issue in greater detail, it is necessary to clarify a number of fundamental terms.

In German agrarian historiography, the term *Villikations-verfassung* usually denotes a form of manorial organization which is known in French as the *régime domanial classique* and in English as the *classic manor*.[3] This manorial system was characteristically centred on the demesne of the lord of the manor, to which dependent peasant holdings were attached. The demesne, comprising arable land, meadowlands, and gardens, was either occupied and farmed by the lord himself, or run by an estate official, the *villicus, maior,* or *cellerarius*.

---

[1] G. von Below, *Geschichte der deutschen Landwirtschaft des Mittelalters in ihren Grundzügen* (2nd edn.; Quellen und Forschungen zur Agrargeschichte, 18; Stuttgart, 1966), 80.

[2] A. Dopsch, *Herrschaft und Bauer in der deutschen Kaiserzeit* (Jena, 1939), 135.

[3] Cf. H. K. Schulze, 'Grundherrschaft', *Handwörterbuch zur deutschen Rechtsgeschichte*, ii (1971), 1824–42; R. Kötzschke, *Allgemeine Wirtschaftsgeschichte des Mittelalters* (Jena, 1924), 227–42; G. Duby, *L'économie rurale et la vie des campagnes*

The *villicus* farmed the demesne with the aid of unfree farm labourers and peasants rendering compulsory labour services. He also collected dues in cash and kind from the dependent tenant farmers, and presided over the manorial court.

In direct contrast to the classic manor with its distinctive demesne economy was the *Rentengrundherrschaft* (the manor as an institution providing rent), in which manorial centres functioned solely as collection points for peasant dues, but not as manors in the true sense. Between these two poles of manorial organization there was a whole range of hybrid and transitional forms, such as, for example, the type of manorial estate on which the demesne lands were cultivated by tied farmhands or day labourers. The character of the manorial estates owned by the king, the nobility, and the Church was determined to varying degrees by different patterns of manorial organization. During the early Middle Ages the classic manor also developed in Imperial possessions and on the estates owned by the major bishoprics and Imperial abbeys. It doubtless represented the most common form of agricultural organization. To what extent the classic manor had also spread through the numerous landed possessions of the nobility is difficult to estimate, given the current state of research.

I

The transformation of the manorial system in Germany during the high Middle Ages was just one of a number of changes affecting the power structure, the economy, and

dans l'Occident médiéval, i (Paris, 1962), 97–100; B. H. Slicher van Bath, *The Agrarian History of Western Europe,* A.D. *500–1850* (London, 1966), 40–9; F. Lütge, *Geschichte der deutschen Agrarverfassung vom frühen Mittelalter bis zum 19. Jahrhundert* (2nd edn., Deutsche Agrargeschichte, 3; Stuttgart, 1967), 45–56; F. L. Ganshof and A. Verhulst, 'Medieval Agrarian Society in its Prime: France, The Low Countries, and Western Germany', *Cambridge Economic History of Europe,* i (Cambridge, 1966), 305–19; A. Verhulst, 'La Genèse du régime domanial classique en France au haut moyen âge', *Agricultura e mondo rurale in Occidente nell'alto medioevo* (Settimane di studio del Centro italiano di studi sull'alto medioevo, 13; Spoleto, 1966), 135–60; G. Fourquin, *Histoire économique de l'Occident médiéval* (2nd edn., Paris, 1979), 56–67; *Le Grand Domaine aux époques mérovingienne et carolingienne,* ed. A. Verhulst (Ghent, 1985); W. Rösener, *Bauern im Mittelalter* (Munich, 1985), 25–9.

society as a whole. It can only be briefly surveyed here. The economic upturn which took place from the eleventh to the thirteenth centuries was accompanied by an extraordinary population increase in all European countries.[4] This growth was sustained by a considerable rise in agricultural production—the result both of additional, newly cleared land coming under the plough, and of an improvement in the use of land.[5] Both factors—population increase and agricultural progress—were closely linked and interdependent. Increased agricultural production stimulated further growth in the population, while the rise in population encouraged cultivation of more land, especially in newly cleared areas. The demographic factor should not, therefore, be seen in isolation, but against the background of various forces underlying structural change during the high Middle Ages.

During this period population growth was also closely connected with a number of other trends. Towns began to flourish, and trade and communication networks developed and gave rise to a market economy based on money and the division of labour.[6] The increase in urban trade and the range of goods on offer in the markets affected the agricultural sector, leading to an increase in the financial requirements of landowners and the peasant population. Production for the market, the exchange of goods, and the circulation of money thus came to play an increasingly important role in the rural economy and gradually transformed the agricultural system. Any investigation of structural change in the high Middle Ages must, therefore, take account of the reciprocal connections between a number of factors: population growth, cultivation of the land and ad-

---

[4] J. C. Russel, 'Population in Europe, 500–1500', *The Fontana Economic History of Europe*, i: *The Middle Ages*, ed. C. M. Cipolla (London, 1972), 37–41; *Determinanten der Bevölkerungsentwicklung im Mittelalter*, ed. B. Herrmann and R. Sprandel (Weinheim, 1987).

[5] W. Abel, *Agrarkrisen und Agrarkonjunktur* (3rd edn., Hamburg, 1978), 27–43; id., *Geschichte der deutschen Landwirtschaft vom frühen Mittelalter bis zum 19. Jahrhundert* (3rd edn., Deutsche Agrargeschichte, 2; Stuttgart, 1978), 29–47.

[6] F.-W. Henning, *Das vorindustrielle Deutschland, 800 bis 1800*, i (Paderborn, 1974), 69–123; E. Ennen, *Die europäische Stadt des Mittelalters* (2nd edn., Göttingen, 1975), 73–104; H. Kellenbenz, *Deutsche Wirtschaftsgeschichte*, i (Munich, 1977), 105–38; J. Le Goff, 'The Town as an Agent of Civilisation 1200–1500', *The Fontana Economic History of Europe*, i. 71–106.

vances in the agrarian economy, and the growth of trade. These formed the basis for the prosperity of the towns and the rise of a market economy. Thus, according to Wilhelm Abel, the high Middle Ages marked a turning-point which 'separates the era of the (relatively) self-sufficient closed circuit of production and consumption from the era of the trading economy based on the division of labour'.[7]

During the twelfth and thirteenth centuries the fluctuations and general trends outlined above gradually led to the breakup of the traditional, classic manor. The basic structure of the manorial system was particularly suited to economic conditions in the early Middle Ages, when the market and the supply of money were at an early stage of development. At the beginning of the high Middle Ages, when trade and communications began to intensify, these underlying conditions no longer applied. The rise of the money economy transformed the basis of the manorial system.[8] The expansion of the market, the increase in the production of goods in the towns, and the first signs of a division of labour between town and country meant that the demesne lands progressively lost their former importance as suppliers to the households of the feudal lords. Basic necessities, especially articles produced by craftsmen, could now also be obtained at the markets which were being established all over the country. Although the classic manor of the early Middle Ages afforded feudal lords and their peasant tenants a high degree of economic independence and self-sufficiency, it also tied the tenants down and impeded growth in agricultural production. Furthermore, the crusades and increased contacts with the eastern Mediterranean created a demand for luxury consumer goods among noble and ecclesiastical landowners, which could be met only by raising the level of income from manorial estates.[9] This desire on the part of landowners to increase money income was matched by a desire on the part of the peasants for greater independ-

---

[7] Abel, *Geschichte der Landwirtschaft*, 55.

[8] H. Pirenne, *Sozial- und Wirtschaftsgeschichte Europas im Mittelalter* (3rd edn., Munich, 1974), 69–88.

[9] Lütge, *Agrarverfassung*, 83; F.-W. Henning, *Landwirtschaft und ländliche Gesellschaft in Deutschland*, i (Paderborn, 1979), 91–3.

ence. In particular, the peasants were eager to have greater freedom to dispose of their labour and to exploit the opportunities offered by the markets in the towns to sell their produce. The commutation of labour services into regular payments of money appeared to open up a practical means to this end, and to satisfy the interests of both sides.

II

In addition to these general trends and the need to adapt to the new economic situation, there were other specific causes of the decline of the classic manor during the high Middle Ages in Germany, and of the reduction in the number of landowners who managed their estates directly. The administration of feudal manors with their sophisticated legal and economic structures was a relatively complicated task. To supervise estate officials, ensure that the peasants fulfilled their labour obligations, and secure yields from the demesne farms required efficiency and organizational skills. The decline in direct management and the transition to a manorial system in which payment in cash and kind predominated made it possible to reduce high administrative costs.

In their studies of the causes of the decline of the classic manor, the American historians D. C. North and R. P. Thomas place particular emphasis on these administrative aspects of the system.[10] The rise of the market economy and economic expansion in the towns gave landowners the opportunity to abandon the practice of running their estates on the labour services owed to them by their peasants, and hence considerably to reduce 'transaction costs'.[11] Leasing

[10] D. C. North and R. P. Thomas, 'The Rise and Fall of the Manorial System: A Theoretical Model', *Journal of Economic History*, 31 (1971), 777–803.

[11] Ibid. 793: 'The development and extension of a market for goods altered the basic economic conditions to which the classic institution of the manor had been the efficient response. Continued reductions in the costs of using the market to exchange goods eventually eliminated the need to specify the consumption bundle if a contract were based on a fixed wage, a fixed rent, or a sharing of the output. Wages, rents, or a portion of the output, whether received in money or in kind, could now be exchanged via the market for the consumption bundle the individual desired. When this point was reached, the traditional labour-sharing arrangements no longer enjoyed a relative advantage in terms of transaction costs.'

manorial land to peasants in return for fixed payments in cash and kind doubtless required a significantly smaller administrative apparatus and lowered the cost of collecting peasant dues.

During the early high Middle Ages serious conflicts arose with estate officials, who demanded more independence while at the same time usurping the rights of the landowners.[12] For the most part these officials came from the manorial *familia* and, in the course of time, rose to form a qualified élite within manorial society. As their positions were strengthened by their important function in the administration of the manors, the stewards and cellarers sought to turn their offices into hereditary fiefs and to achieve noble status. Especially in large ecclesiastical manors, such as the episcopal church of Constance and the Imperial abbey of St Gallen, we find many cases in the twelfth and thirteenth centuries of estate officials who used their positions of authority within the manorial system as a stepping-stone to knightly status, and to acquiring stewardships and manors as fiefs.[13] Once in possession, they generally refused to hand over the produce of the manor in the customary way, preferring instead to perform military service as knights. The alienation of numerous manors and manorial rights by rising *ministeriales* was an inevitable consequence of this process of emancipation. The only effective means of preventing stewardships from becoming hereditary offices, of containing the social ambitions of the *villici*, and of averting the alienation of manorial estates which presented itself to many landowners was the radical dissolution of the manorial system, entailing in its turn the leasing of demesne lands to dependent peasants.

In addition to the unreliability of the *villici*, the growing unwillingness of the peasants to fulfil labour obligations was

---

[12] von Below, *Landwirtschaft*, 66–70; Lütge, *Agrarverfassung*, 83.

[13] K. H. Ganahl, *Studien zur Verfassungsgeschichte der Klosterherrschaft St. Gallen von den Anfängen bis ins hohe Mittelalter* (Innsbruck, 1931), 117–43; G. Bradler, *Studien zur Geschichte der Ministerialität im Allgäu und in Oberschwaben* (Göppingen, 1973), 106–14; *Continuatio Casuum sancti Galli*, ed. G. Meyer von Knonau (Mitteilungen zur Vaterländischen Geschichte, 17, 1879), 99–100: 'cellerarii ecclesiae jura villicationis in modum beneficiorum habere contendebant, et contra consuetudinem quidam ex ipsis more nobilium gladium cingebant.'

another important reason for the decline of the classic manor. The rise of the towns with their wide-ranging economic activities, and the attractive conditions of settlement available to peasants in newly colonized areas offered many dissatisfied dependants the opportunity to escape from the constraints of the manorial system and to create freer lives for themselves elsewhere.[14] The personal discharge of compulsory labour services on the manorial estates met with increasing resistance from peasants liable to such services, since these labour contributions reduced the amount of time and energy they could devote to the running of their own farms.[15] In 1117, when the Alsatian monastery of Maursmünster commuted the three-day labour services of its dependants into cash payments, the abbot justified this measure by referring to the increasing unwillingness of the peasants to discharge their labour obligations. The services in question had been badly, negligently, and reluctantly performed; commutation was, therefore, in the interest of both the peasants and the monastic landlords.[16] The improved condition of the peasants in the economy of the high Middle Ages and their growing self-confidence made them less and less willing to perform time-consuming labour services on manorial estates. On the other hand, the manorial economy's loss of labour services was more than offset by the increase in revenues. Thus many landowners who wished to retain responsibility for managing their own estates became more and more inclined to commute services into cash payments and to employ day labourers instead of relying on peasants liable to compulsory service.

[14] Cf. K.-H. Spieß, 'Zur Landflucht im Mittelalter', *Die Grundherrschaft im späten Mittelalter*, ed. H. Patze (Vorträge und Forschungen, 27; Sigmaringen, 1983), 163–4; Rösener, *Bauern*, 31–7.

[15] See Dopsch, *Herrschaft und Bauer*, 126.

[16] A. Hanauer, *Les Constitutions des campagnes de l'Alsace au Moyen-Age* (Paris, 1864), 51: 'Anno Verbi Incarnati circiter 1117, pie memorie abbas Adelo ex Gorzio, venerabili cenobio, ad Mauri gubernandum accitus monasterium, deliberato animo, communicato fratrum suorum consilio, pro inutilitate, pro incuria, pro torpore ac desidia curie servientium, hominum videlicet, ut dicebantur, dominicalium, triduanum commutavit servitium ea conditione, eo tenore, ut quantum in censu, tantum pro servitio redderetur, sicque tam illorum pudori seu inutilitati, quam nostre consuleretur sumptuositati.'

III

The specific mechanisms by which the classic manorial system was dismantled differed according to region and type of manor. Time-scales also varied. Three main forms of dissolution can be identified.[17]

1. The whole demesne could be leased to a single tenant in return for a fixed rent, or on a share-cropping basis. In such cases the demesne essentially remained intact and frequently continued to serve the landowner as a collection point for rents and as the seat of the manorial court.
2. The demesne lands could be divided up into a number of small, independent farmsteads.
3. The demesne lands could be split up into a large number of individual, dependent holdings.

In addition to these three main variants, a whole range of specifically local procedures for dividing up and renting out demesne lands can also be found. As landowners either withdrew from, or reduced their participation in, the running of their manorial estates, labour services were largely rendered superfluous and were generally commuted into cash payments. As a result, in many places these services were reduced to a few days a year, which meant that the burden on the peasant economy was minimal. In some regions manors went through an intermediate stage of dissolution in the twelfth century, when undivided manors were leased *in toto* to estate officials and knightly vassals in return for a share of the produce or for a fixed rent. After a time, however, even these manors were divided up, the demesne and peasant holdings were separated from one another, and rented out to peasant tenants on an individual basis. In most instances the dissolution of manors also meant

[17] J. Kühn, *Das Bauerngut der alten Grundherrschaft* (Leipzig, 1912), 5; Lütge, *Agrarverfassung*, 84–5; W. Rösener, *Grundherrschaft im Wandel. Untersuchungen zur Entwicklung geistlicher Grundherrschaften im südwestdeutschen Raum vom 9. bis 14. Jahrhundert* (Göttingen, 1991), 468–71.

that large numbers of unfree manorial serfs were released. Some became small farmers while others found employment, either as day labourers or in rural or urban crafts.

The transformation of the manorial system in the high Middle Ages did not, as has often been claimed, lead to the practice of direct management being totally abandoned. Large, middling, and small landowners continued to administer some of their estates in person. In particular, they often retained direct control of farms at the centre of the manorial complex in order to guarantee supplies of basic necessities.[18] All in all, however, the disintegration of the classic manorial system led to a considerable reduction in direct management by landowners. As a result, the economic interdependence of demesne and dependent tenant farms, which formed the nucleus of the manorial system in the early Middle Ages, largely came to an end. Labour services decreased significantly, and personal ties between dependent peasants and landowners were relaxed. In many regions peasants also gained greater freedom of movement, higher social status, and more rights over farms and other smaller leaseholdings. The phasing out of labour services strengthened the autonomy of the peasant economy and made the work of the peasants more effective and rewarding. As part of this development, peasant farms increasingly supplied the towns with agricultural produce. Progressive development of the land, the extra acreage devoted to agricultural use and, above all, the increase in grain production in the twelfth and thirteenth centuries guaranteed the expanding towns a relatively secure supply of basic foodstuffs. Thus the dissolution of the old manors and the general transformation of the agricultural order boosted peasant efficiency and stimulated agricultural production to meet the needs of the growing population.

In the nineteenth century Lamprecht and Inama-Sternegg argued that direct manorial management disappeared com-

---

[18] W. Rösener, 'Ritterliche Wirtschaftsverhältnisse und Turnier im sozialen Wandel des Hochmittelalters', *Das ritterliche Turnier im Mittelalter*, ed. J. Fleckenstein (Veröffentlichungen des Max-Planck-Instituts für Geschichte, 80; Göttingen, 1985), 327; id., *Grundherrschaft im Wandel*, 560–66.

pletely during the high Middle Ages.[19] Their views were rightly refuted by Dopsch, who cited examples showing that the practice was by no means universally abandoned.[20] More recent studies of agrarian history in the high and late Middle Ages have similarly confirmed that even after the breakup of the classic manorial system, a large number of landowners retained direct control of their demesnes.[21] However, there were fundamental differences between the classic manorial economy of the early Middle Ages and the kind of direct management practised by landowners in the late Middle Ages. In the later period demesne farms were chiefly culti-vated by free wage-earners and day labourers; in the earlier period by villeins and unfree serfs. The directly managed demesnes of the late Middle Ages also supplied considerable quantities of produce to the market, thus differing from their early medieval forerunners, who clearly tended towards economic autonomy. Although the earlier picture of the decline of the classic manor has been revised in a number of important ways, the radical changes that took place during the high Middle Ages were extremely significant. Dopsch's view[22] that no far-reaching transformation of the manorial system took place in the twelfth and thirteenth centuries and that it is therefore impossible to speak of a real decline of the classic manor, is not supported by more recent research on individual regions and manors.[23]

In some parts of the German Empire the process by which the manorial system disintegrated began in the eleventh century, accelerated during the twelfth century and came to an end in the thirteenth and fourteenth centuries.[24] It seems

[19] K. Lamprecht, *Deutsches Wirtschaftsleben im Mittelalter*, i, pt. 2 (Leipzig, 1886), 862–984; K. Th. von Inama-Sternegg, *Deutsche Wirtschaftsgeschichte*, ii (Leipzig, 1891), 148–9, 162–4.

[20] Dopsch, *Herrschaft und Bauer*, 132–64.

[21] *Die Grundherrschaft im späten Mittelalter*, ed. H. Patze (Vorträge und Forschungen, 27; Sigmaringen, 1983), *passim*.

[22] Dopsch, *Herrschaft und Bauer*, 129–64.

[23] Ch.-E. Perrin, 'La Société rurale allemande du Xe au XIIIe siècle d'après un ouvrage récent', *Revue historique de droit français et étranger*, 4th ser., 24 (1945), 82–102; Ph. Dollinger, *L'Évolution des classes rurales en Bavière depuis la fin de l'époque carolingienne jusqu'au milieu du XIIIe siècle* (Paris, 1949), 122–8; Rösener, *Grundherrschaft im Wandel*, 557–66.

[24] Cf. Dollinger, *L'Évolution des classes rurales en Bavière*, 122–8; Ch.-E. Perrin, 'Le Grand domaine en Allemagne', *Recueils de la Société Jean Bodin*, 3 (1949), 115–47;

to have started in Lorraine and in some western parts of the empire. Studies by Perrin have shown that by the eleventh and twelfth centuries it had already produced significant changes in the older manorial system.[25] The present writer's own investigations into neighbouring south-west Germany have demonstrated that the process of disintegration extended over a long period during the twelfth and thirteenth centuries, taking different forms at different times in individual manors.[26] In the manors owned by the old abbeys and Imperial churches, the old system disintegrated mainly in the twelfth century, whereas in manors belonging to the Benedictine monastic order, the transformation quite clearly began later and reached its culmination in the middle of the thirteenth century.

On leasehold farms, sharecropping was a transitional stage in the development of the late medieval leasehold system, and at the turn of the fourteenth century many traces of the classic manor remained. In the south-west these structural changes produced what was predominantly a system of rents and leaseholding which, however, was not as 'fossilized' as is often suggested.[27]

In the south-east region of Germany the decline of the classic manor began at about the same time as in the south-west, although in some areas the process took somewhat longer to be completed.[28] Developments in Bavaria during the high Middle Ages have been studied in detail by Dollinger.[29] In his view the classic manors in Bavaria went into decline mainly in the twelfth century. They were supplanted by a new agricultural infrastructure based on tenant

---

Lütge, *Agrarverfassung*, 83–94; Henning, *Landwirtschaft*, i. 93–6; E. Münch, 'Die Grundherrschaft des vollentfalteten Feudalismus im Prozeß des gesellschaftlichen Fortschritts', *Zeitschrift für Geschichtswissenschaft*, 27 (1979), 145–8.

[25] Ch.-E. Perrin, *Recherches sur la seigneurie rurale en Lorraine d'après les plus anciens censiers, IXe–XIIe siècle* (Paris, 1935), 626–59; Ganshof and Verhulst, *Medieval Agrarian Society*, 306–7

[26] Rösener, *Grundherrschaft im Wandel*, 557–66.

[27] W. Rösener, 'Die spätmittelalterliche Grundherrschaft im südwestdeutschen Raum als Problem der Sozialgeschichte', *Zeitschrift für die Geschichte des Oberrheins*, 127 (1979), 17–69.

[28] Dopsch, *Herrschaft und Bauer*, 60–78, 129–64.

[29] Ph. Dollinger, *L'Évolution des classes rurales en Bavière*, German trans.: *Der bayerische Bauernstand vom 9. bis zum 13. Jahrhundert* (Munich, 1982).

farms, in which the manorial estates were combined into *officia*. Dollinger insists that this transformation amounts to a 'veritable economic revolution'.[30] The close ties between peasant holdings and their administrative centres were relaxed, and the labour services which had become superfluous because of the division of demesne lands were generally superseded by money rents. Ultimately, Bavarian landowners ceased to play any active role in the administration of their possessions—they had become absentee landlords.

Although Werner Wittich's *Die Grundherrschaft in Nordwestdeutschland* (1896)[31] stimulated a number of important studies of the impact of structural change during the high Middle Ages on the manorial system in general, and on agriculture in north-west Germany in particular, the work was long overrated. More recent studies by Weigel, Achilles, and Last,[32] moreover, have shown that Wittich's main arguments about the disintegration of the classic manor in north-west Germany are untenable, especially those relating to the release of *lati*, the joining together of hides to form new *Meierhöfe* (estates leased to *villici*) and the emergence of a so-called 'pure form' of manorial organization following the disintegration of the classic manorial system in the thirteenth century. Despite these objections, no authoritative work on the actual process of change in the north-western part of Germany has yet been published. To fill this gap remains an essential task for historians.

In the northern Rhineland, manorial estates evidently began to adapt to the new conditions in the early twelfth cen-

[30] Dollinger, *L'Évolution des classes rurales en Bavière*, 122: 'En Bavière comme dans le reste de l'Allemagne, le système des villications, après être resté pendant trois siècles le type dominant de l'économie seigneuriale, est remplacé au cours du XIIe par un type nouveau, qu'on peut appeler le système de censives. Il se produit donc à ce moment une véritable révolution économique.'

[31] W. Wittich, *Die Grundherrschaft in Nordwestdeutschland* (Leipzig, 1896); id., 'Die Entstehung des Meierrechts und die Auflösung der Villikationen in Niedersachsen und Westfalen', *Zeitschrift für Social- und Wirthschaftsgeschichte*, 2 (1894), 1–61.

[32] H. Weigel, 'Studien zur Verfassung und Verwaltung des Grundbesitzes des Frauenstiftes Essen (852–1803)', *Beiträge zur Geschichte von Stadt und Stift Essen*, 76 (1960), 174–87; W. Achilles, 'Die Entstehung des niedersächsischen Meierrechts nach Werner Wittich', *Zeitschrift für Agrargeschichte und Agrarsoziologie*, 25 (1977), 145–69; M. Last, 'Villikationen geistlicher Grundherren in Nordwestdeutschland in der Zeit vom 12. bis zum 14. Jahrhundert (Diözesen Osnabrück, Bremen, Verden, Minden, Hildesheim)', *Die Grundherrschaft im späten Mittelalter*, i. 369–450.

tury.[33] Influenced by agricultural developments in the neighbouring Low Countries, in the Lower Rhine region the manorial system was abandoned at an early stage and replaced
—especially near the towns—by a distinctive system of fixed-
term leases for agricultural land. According to Irsigler, the
conversion of old demesne farms into fixed-term tenancies
took place around Cologne mainly in the thirteenth century,
while further north various forms of hereditary tenancy became the rule.[34]

IV

The fact that so much attention has been paid to the general
decline in the direct management of manorial possessions
during the high Middle Ages in Germany should by no
means encourage us to regard this process as having been
inevitable. The emergence of new forms of estate management on lands owned by some of the new monastic orders,
and developments in England should warn us against jump-
ing to conclusions. In the twelfth and thirteenth centuries
large numbers of new Cistercian and Praemonstratensian
monasteries managed their estates directly.[35] At a time when
many of the old Benedictine abbeys were abandoning direct
management, the new orders were developing methods of
exploiting their extensive possessions as fully as possible, by
farming the land themselves with the help of lay brothers

[33] B. Huppertz, *Räume und Schichten bäuerlicher Kulturformen in Deutschland* (Bonn,
1939), 101–9; F. Steinbach, 'Die rheinischen Agrarverhältnisse', *Collectanea Franz
Steinbach*, ed. F. Petri and G. Droege (Bonn, 1967), 416–25; F. Irsigler, 'Die
Auflösung der Villikationsverfassung und der Übergang zum Zeitpachtsystem im
Nahbereich niederrheinischer Städte während des 13./14. Jahrhunderts', *Die
Grundherrschaft im späten Mittelalter*, i. 295–310.

[34] Irsigler, 'Die Auflösung', 309–10.

[35] Cf. L. J. Lekai, *The Cistercians, Ideals and Reality* (Kent, 1977), 282–333; R. A.
Donkin, *The Cistercians: Studies in the Geography of Medieval England and Wales* (Toronto, 1978); C. Higounet, 'Le premier siècle de l'économie rurale cistercienne',
Atti della settima Settimana internazionale di studi medioevali Mendola, 1977 (Milan,
1980), 345–68; *L'Économie cistercienne: Troisième Journées internationales d'histoire*,
1981 (Flaran, 3; Auch, 1983); W. Rösener, 'Zur Wirtschaftstätigkeit der
Zisterzienser im Hochmittelalter', *Zeitschrift für Agrargeschichte und Agrarsoziologie*, 30
(1982), 117–48; D. Lohrmann, 'Die Wirtschaftshöfe der Prämonstratenser im
hohen und späten Mittelalter', *Grundherrschaft im späten Mittelalter*, i. 205–40.

and paid labourers, and also by participating actively in land development schemes. The Cistercians sold the abundant produce from their excellently managed granges at markets in neighbouring towns, thus making considerable profits. In contrast to Germany during the high Middle Ages, in England the process of commercialization that took place in the twelfth and thirteenth centuries did not lead to a marked decline in the direct management of manorial holdings which might have resulted in a fundamental transformation of the manorial system.[36] English landlords, faced with an increase in agricultural production and a rise in grain prices, sold the surpluses from demesnes under direct management at urban markets. In the high Middle Ages English landowners took advantage of the emerging market economy to make profits from the sale of their agricultural produce, whereas their French and German counterparts largely abandoned direct management and reverted to forms of ownership based predominantly on rents in cash and in kind.[37] An explanation of this astonishing difference will come to light only after further analysis and discussion.

[36] M. M. Postan, 'England', *Cambridge Economic History of Europe*, i (Cambridge, 1966), 548–632; J. Z. Titow, *English Rural Society, 1200–1350* (London, 1969), 60–2; E. Miller and J. Hatcher, *Medieval England: Rural Society and Economic Change 1086–1348* (London, 1978), 184–97, 213–24.

[37] Cf. Bloch, *Seigneurie française et manoir anglais* (2nd edn., Cahiers des Annales, 16; Paris, 1967).

Social Mobility

15

Some Observations on Social Mobility in England between the Norman Conquest and the Early Thirteenth Century

JOHN GILLINGHAM

It may be, as David Herlihy has asserted, that 'the reality and importance of social mobility in the Middle Ages are today unquestioned.' It may also be that no one any longer believes in the existence of a medieval society based upon 'a system of closed and stable estates in which social mobility was officially discouraged and rarely achieved'.[1] Unfortunately a very great deal depends on just what we mean by 'rarely'. Obviously this is an area in which our approach has to be as quantitative as possible. Particular examples of mobility may illuminate the kinds of process at work, but we are not entitled to use words like 'rarely' unless we know how common they were, both in their own period and compared with equivalent cases in other periods. One difficulty with particular examples is that they are often those which contemporary opinion found remarkable and contemporary opinion, an unreliable guide at the best of times, is especially so in those areas—like social mobility—where misconceptions and prejudices abound. In the twelfth century, as in other centuries, there was a strong current of opinion which disapproved of social mobility. The ideal ruler, like Duke Richard II of Normandy as portrayed in Benoit's *Chronique des ducs de Normandie*, was one who tolerated no 'vilains' at his court and whose officials, one and all, were 'gentil homme'.[2] As a com-

---

[1] D. Herlihy, 'Three Patterns of Social Mobility in Medieval Society', *Journal of Interdisciplinary History*, 3 (1973), 623–47.

[2] *Chronique des ducs de Normandie par Benoit*, ed. C. Fahlin (3 vols., Uppsala, 1951–67), lines 28,824–40.

ment which Gerald of Wales passed on King Dermot McMurrough implies, the ruler who was an 'erector humilium' was also easily thought of as a tyrant, a 'nobilium oppressor'.[3] No wonder Becket reacted heatedly to the charge that the king had raised him 'de exili'.[4] Statements relating to social mobility found in narrative or literary sources and made in a climate of opinion like this cannot safely be regarded as anything other than expressions of the author's own highly subjective stance: a famous example would be Orderic's comment on the men whom Henry I 'raised from the dust'.[5]

On the other hand, among medievalists, the student of English history is singularly fortunate in possessing a wide range of documentary sources capable of yielding quantitative information. Unfortunately not until the period of the manorial surveys and court rolls of the mid-thirteenth century and later do we begin to have the evidence to enable us to tackle the subject of patterns and rates of mobility in the population at large.[6] Before this date we can only skate on very thin ice, using the tentative conclusions of economic historians to draw still more tentative inferences. Undoubtedly the agricultural base of the economy was expanding, but whether there was more—or less—per capita wealth is a much harder question to answer. Even those historians who take an optimistic view of medieval agriculture and its capacity for progress are inclined to believe that greater productivity per unit area was gained at the expense of productivity per capita.[7] Undoubtedly there were more

---

[3] Giraldus Cambrensis, *Expugnatio Hibernica: The Conquest of Ireland*, ed. A. B. Scott and F. X. Martin (Dublin, 1978), 40, and cf. 24. This combination had, in Walter Map's opinion, been Aethelred the Unready's greatest failing – and Edmund Ironside's fatal mistake, Walter Map, *De Nugis Curialium*, ed. M. R. James, C. N. L. Brooke and R. A. B. Mynors (Oxford, 1983), 420–2, 428–30.

[4] *Materials for the History of Thomas Becket*, ed. J. C. Robertson, (Rolls Series, 67, 1875–85), v, 499.

[5] Orderic Vitalis, *Ecclesiastical History*, ed. M. Chibnall (6 vols.; Oxford, 1969–80), vi, 16.

[6] For a model of what can be done with these court rolls see Z. Razi, *Life, Marriage and Death in a Medieval Parish: Economy, Society and Demography in Halesowen, 1270–1400* (Cambridge, 1980), esp. 87–97 for 'a strong downwards social mobility' reinforced by a brisk land market.

[7] It occured therefore where labour was abundant, i. e. cheap where demesne managers were concerned; simply plentiful on the small-holdings of the peasantry,

towns, and larger towns, in England in 1250 than in 1050. But it is not easy to know whether or not England at the later date was more urbanized than earlier, or whether a higher proportion of the population was migrating from country into town. In this period therefore the student of social mobility is inevitably very largely, though not entirely, confined to the élite, to the subjects of mobility within it and recruitment to it. Within these limits in Domesday Book and the pipe rolls he has sources which, for the period, are remarkably susceptible of a statistical treatment, nowadays computer assisted.[8] Of course there are still problems. The twelfth century, like most centuries, had no clearly articulated system of social classification.[9] More difficult to get around are the familiar problems posed by a period of expansion. In absolute terms, both population and the level of documentation were rising.[10] So we know more about more people, particularly about the élite, those who made their mark. In these circumstances although social mobility undoubtedly appears to increase with the passage of time, it is always possible that appearances are deceptive. Indeed, considerations of this sort have allowed a historically minded sociologist to argue that this period actually witnessed a declining rate of social mobility, a reversal of the trend towards accelerating mobility which had, in his view, characterized late Anglo-Saxon society.[11]

Given the limited and problematic nature of the evidence it is thus hardly surprising that historians of the period should, until recently, have paid little attention to the subject

B. M. S. Campbell, 'Agricultural Progress in Medieval England: Some Evidence from Eastern Norfolk', *Economic History Review*, 2nd ser., 36 (1983), 26–46.

[8] e. g. J. Palmer, 'Domesday Book and the Computer', *Domesday Book: A Reassessment*, ed. P. H. Sawyer (London, 1985), 164–74; J. McDonald and G. D. Snooks, *Domesday Economy: A New Approach to Anglo-Norman History* (Oxford, 1986); J. McDonald and G. D. Snooks, 'How Artificial were the Tax Assessments of Domesday England? The Case of Essex', *Economic History Review*, 2nd ser., 38 (1985), 352–72; J. D. Hamshere, 'Domesday Book: Estate Structures in the North Midlands', *Domesday Studies*, ed. J. C. Holt (Woodbridge, 1987); and on the 1130 Pipe Roll, J. Green, *The Government of England under Henry I* (Cambridge, 1986), 220–7.

[9] Green, *The Government*, 136–8.

[10] On the proliferation of documentation see above all, M. T. Clanchy, *From Memory to Written Record: England 1066–1307* (London, 1979).

[11] W. G. Runciman, 'Accelerating Social Mobility: The Case of Anglo-Saxon England', *Past and Present*, 104 (1984), 3–30.

of social mobility.[12] They have not ignored it altogether, of course. They have commonly noted its existence, usually in the context of some particularly striking example of individual upward mobility, almost always an individual in Crown service.[13] Indeed, in company with the historians of most other periods, they are inclined to think of society in 'their' period as being 'fluid' rather than 'static'.[14]

This is doubtless partly because, like most sociologists, they tend to regard social mobility as a 'Good Thing'—and like to think of their own preferred period as being full of 'Good Things'—but also because they are inclined to compare the social order of their period with one that never existed, i.e. with the ideal type of a traditional social order within which the families of greater and lesser landlords, dependent tenants and labourers succeed one another in unvarying accordance with inherited custom.[15] Inevitably, by comparison with

[12] On the one hand there have been systematic studies of fairly well-defined and numerically small groups like magnates (a main thread in the essays now collected in C. W. Hollister, *Monarchy, Magnates and Institutions in the Anglo-Norman World*, London, 1988); royal servants (Green, *The Government*, 134–214, 226–81) and judges (R. V. Turner, *The English Judiciary in the Age of Glanvill and Bracton, c. 1176–1239*, Cambridge, 1985). At the other extreme Alexander Murray made the concept of 'social differentiation by movement' the determinative basis of his bold and wide-ranging *Reason and Society in the Middle Ages* (Oxford, 1978).

[13] e.g. William Marshal, described on the back cover of S. Painter, *William Marshal* (pb. edn. Baltimore, 1967) as achieving 'the extreme degree of social mobility possible in his age'. Or Geoffrey de Clinton and Bernard the Scribe, both made famous in Southern's seminal study of patronage in the early 12th century, reprinted in R. W. Southern, *Medieval Humanism* (Oxford, 1970), 214–17, 225–8; for further comment on Clinton's career, D. Crouch, 'Geoffrey de Clinton and Roger, Earl of Warwick: New Men and Magnates in the Reign of Henry I', *Historical Research*, 55 (1982), 113–23. In the 13th cent. there is Walter de Merton who became 'a multimillionaire' in Henry III's service, M. T. Clanchy, 'England in the Thirteenth Century: Power and Knowledge', *England in the 13th Century* ed. W. M. Ormrod (Woodbridge, 1986), 1–14. For Simon of Felsted, an example of a man who rose in the service of a lesser lord, in this case the Abbess of Caen, see M. Chibnall, *Anglo-Norman England, 1066–1166* (Oxford, 1986), 146–7. For some justified doubts about a method which relies upon 'the perfect example', see C. W. Hollister, 'Elite Prosopography in Saxon and Norman England', *Medieval Prosopography* 1 (1980), 12–14.

[14] e.g. A. L. Poole, *Obligations of Society in the XII and XIII Centuries* (Oxford, 1946), 8.

[15] I take this summary definition from Runciman, 'Accelerating Social Mobility', 3. The fact that I do so is an indication of my indebtedness to this article. Although I disagree with many of Runciman's conclusions I found his approach to the problem of how to assess social mobility in the absence of quantitative evidence extremely helpful.

this ideal type, all real societies are fluid, are to be likened, in Paul Hyams's phrase, to a handicap race, not to a layer cake.[16] Thus simply to point to the existence of some degree of social mobility in any given society is to state a truism which does not take us very far. In this essay I hope to avoid such unhelpful comparisons. On the other hand I must plead guilty at once to the charge of believing that this period of English history is unusually full of 'Good Things' for the student of social mobility. I begin by picking out five.

1. As a direct result of the Norman Conquest the decades after 1066 witnessed a faster rate of mobility within the ruling élite than any other period in the entire history of England. If ever there was a period that justified Pareto's famous description of history as 'the graveyard of aristocracies' it was this one.

2. The twelfth century witnessed the emergence of primogeniture, a system of inheritance which has hitherto bulked large in discussions of social mobility in England, on the grounds that it compels younger sons to move into other fields if they are to avoid the downward mobility for which their birth seems to destine them.[17]

3. This period saw the disappearance of one type of mobility which had been a feature of most earlier societies: mobility across the great divide between slavery and freedom.

4. As a consequence of the Gregorian and monastic reform movements there was a uniquely serious and sustained attempt to persude people to become celibate. Since differential fertility and replacement rates are generally considered to be critical factors in determining patterns of mobility, this lends this period a quality all of its own.

5. The emergence of schools and universities, institutions specializing in education, a development of some importance given the central role traditionally accorded education in most studies of élite recruitment.

---

[16] P. R. Hyams, *King, Lords, and Peasants in Medieval England* (Oxford, 1980), 268.
[17] Notably in the works of Lawrence Stone.

I take these five points in turn.

1. The impact of the Norman Conquest is, of course, writ large in the pages of Domesday Book. For the historian of social mobility Domesday is doubly remarkable. Not only is it a unique record in its almost complete coverage of England at two distinctly dated moments in time, the time of King Edward and 1086; it is also a record which reveals a situation unique, so far as can be seen, in English history: the more or less total overthrow of an established ruling class. By 1086 little more than 5 per cent of Domesday land values were still held by pre-Conquest tenants-in-chief.[18] And even those fortunate survivors tended to be, as Eleanor Searle has observed, Englishmen whose heirs were daughters married to Normans.[19] After 1070 Englishmen came to be systematically excluded from high ecclesiastical office.[20] In government few important positions were held by Englishmen after 1071. In the whole of English history no ruling élite ever suffered greater downward mobility than this. This overwhelming downward mobility necessarily created vacancies at an unprecedentedly high rate and, in consequence, a uniquely high rate of exchange mobility within the élite. Into the vacancies moved the newcomers, mostly Normans. Nearly all made enormous gains though on the whole it was not so much the Norman magnates as the younger sons and men of relatively obscure origin who gained most.[21] Most of William's sheriffs were new men whose fortunes had been made by the Conquest.[22] In this turbulent world it is the

[18] W. J. Corbett, 'The Development of the Duchy of Normandy and the Norman Conquest of England', *Cambridge Medieval History*, v (Cambridge, 1926), 508; F. M. Stenton, 'English Families and the Norman Conquest', *Transactions of the Royal Historical Society*, 4th ser., 26 (1944), 1–12. Against recent doubts Stenton's term 'a tenurial revolution' has been vindicated by R. Fleming, 'Domesday Book and the Tenurial Revolution', *Anglo-Norman Studies*, 9, ed. R. A. Brown (Woodbridge, 1987), 87–102.

[19] E. Searle, 'Women and the legitimization of succession at the Norman Conquest', *Anglo-Norman Studies*, 3, ed. R. A. Brown (Woodbridge, 1981), 159–70.

[20] F. Barlow, *The English Church 1066–1154* (London, 1979), 57–66.

[21] Orderic Vitalis, *Ecclesiastical History*, ii, 190; cf. Green, *The Government*, 143–4: 'The Norman Conquest of England had provided unparalleled opportunities for men of humble origins to win lands for themselves.'

[22] J. Green, 'The Sheriffs of William the Conqueror', *Anglo-Norman Studies*, 5 (Woodbridge, 1983), 129–45.

speed with which a man could rise to the highest rank in secular society which is remarkable. At other times men rose from relative obscurity to the rank of earl—Eadric Streona in Aethelred's reign or Geoffrey Fitz-Peter and Hubert de Burgh in the late twelfth and early thirteenth centuries.[23] But none surely rose as fast as Robert de Comines, created Earl of Northumbria in 1068—or, come to that, fell so fast, though the effect of the killing of De Comines in January 1069 was, of course, to create another vacancy almost at once.[24] England was a Norman colony, 'a land of enterprise . . . where young men usually of respectable origins but frequently of moderate means, could rise high in the social hierarchy through military, political or administrative service'.[25]

Although it is only the landholders whose fortunes after 1066 can, thanks to Domesday Book, be considered in quantitative terms, there can be little doubt that other groups felt the impact of the Norman Conquest. Builders and stonemasons, for example, must surely have been employed on an unprecedented scale in that orgy of demolition and rebuilding of all the major English churches that followed 1066. There was work for them too in the great surge of castle building—not all of which can have been carried out by forced labour—which was so crucial to the success of the Norman invasion. Another group to find new and greater opportunities were the interpreters—and the mere fact of their existence is itself an indicator of the greater gap, the greater social distance between the French-speaking élite and those who only spoke English.[26]

[23] S. Keynes, 'A Tale of Two Kings: Alfred the Great and Aethelred the Unready', *Transactions of the Royal Historical Society*, 5th ser. 36 (1986), 213–16. On Geoffrey Fitz-Peter's origins and early career see Turner, *The English Judiciary*, 93, 99. Geoffrey entered the ranks of the *curiales c.* 1182–3 and was made an earl in 1199; Hubert de Burgh belonged to a Norfolk gentry family, entered royal service in the late 1190s, and was created earl in 1227, for political and military services. On his family see C. Ellis, *Hubert de Burgh, A Study in Constancy* (London, 1952), app. 1.

[24] Simeon of Durham, *Historical Works*, ed. T. Arnold (Rolls Series, 75, 1182–5), i, 98–9.

[25] J. C. Holt, 'Feudal Society and the Family in Early Medieval England, i: The Revolution of 1066', *Transactions of the Royal Historical Society*, 5th ser., 32 (1982), 193–212, esp. 206.

[26] For an interpreter attached to the Abbot of Ramsey's household, J. A. Raftis, *The Estates of Ramsey Abbey* (Toronto, 1957), 51; for the embarrassment of an early

2. Primogeniture. In the first generation after the conquest almost nothing was inherited, virtually everything was
acquisition, and acquisition on a scale sufficient to satisfy the
ambitions of brothers and younger sons, sufficient to enable
them to escape the constraints of Duby's marriage pattern
with its inhibition on the marriages of younger sons.[27] But for
how long did this last? At what date do we first reach a
generation whose chances in life were unaffected by the
upheaval of 1066? There is no very clear or obvious answer to
this. To some extent the extraordinary post-Conquest situation was prolonged by a continuing flow of new acquisitions
caused by the succession wars of William II's, Henry I's, and
Stephen's reigns, i.e. by the ordinary accidents of medieval
politics.[28] On the other hand it has been observed that by the
time of Henry I land which had earlier been treated as
acquisition was increasingly being regarded as patrimony
and that those who managed to stay loyal to the king were
rewarded by being able to enjoy fairly secure inheritance.
Holt moreover has drawn attention to charters which begin,
once again, to speak the language of hereditary tenure.[29] At
this social level hereditary tenure increasingly meant primogeniture. Why this 'unnatural' law came to predominate still
remains something of a mystery. It may be that the circumstances of the Conquest lent greater weight to the interests of
lords, enabling lords, and in particular the lord king, to insist
on impartible succession, while the interests of the family
were at least able to ensure that if only one son were to
succeed then the eldest.[30] However this may be, it does at

12th-cent. Somerset parish priest who spoke only English and therefore had to
remain silent in the presence of bishop and archdeacon, John of Ford, *Vita Beati
Wulfrici anachoretae Haselbergiae*, ed. M. Bell (Somerset Record Soc., 47, 1932), 29;
cited by Barlow, *English Church*, 133. Naturally parish priests never became bishops,
though this was not a feature unique to this linguistically divided society.

[27] J. C. Holt, 'Feudal Society and the Family in Early Medieval England, iii:
Patronage and Politics', *Transactions of the Royal Historical Society*, 5th ser., 34 (1984),
15–16.

[28] Holt, 'The Revolution of 1066', 205.

[29] R. DeAragon, 'The Growth of Secure Inheritance in Anglo-Norman England',
Journal of Medieval History, 8 (1982), 381–91; J. C. Holt, 'Feudal Society and the
Family in Early Medieval England, ii: Notions of Patrimony', *Transactions of the Royal
Historical Society*, 5th ser. 33 (1983), 193–220, esp. 214–17.

[30] Pollock and Maitland, *The History of English Law*, reissued by S. F. C. Milsome,
2 vols (Cambridge, 1968), ii. 262–74; Chibnall, *Anglo-Norman England*, 174. It is

least seem clear that at some stage younger sons, after a generation or two in which they had enjoyed, and perhaps come to expect, increased opportunities, found their prospects diminishing. In these new circumstances what strategies could they, or their parents, adopt? Best of all perhaps would be to find a magic wand which would suddenly increase the number of available heiresses. And indeed they may have found such a wand in the shape of the *statutum decretum,* probably to be dated to the latter years of Henry I's reign, which laid down that, in the absence of a son, the inheritance was to be shared between the daughters instead of going, as hitherto, to a single female heiress.[31]

3. The ending of mobility across the boundary between freedom and slavery. Whether or not, as Runciman suggests, rates of enslavement and manumission were higher in the tenth and eleventh centuries than they had been earlier, it is clear that by the and of the twelfth century these rates had dropped to zero.[32] Exactly when and how this happened is something of a puzzle. To judge from the *Leges Henrici Primi,* in the early twelfth century movement into and out of slavery was still something to be reckoned with, a passage requiring the appropriate public rituals.[33] But after the reign of Henry I it is next to impossible to find any references either to penal slavery or to the slave trade within England. The 1102 Council of Westminster was not the first Church Council in England to prohibit the slave trade, but it was, significantly, the last.[34] According to William of Malmesbury the efforts of Wulfstan of Worcester had persuaded the men of Bristol to

possible that some form of impartible descent had become customary in England outside Kent before 1066; but if so it seems to have been a custom much modified by the capacity of some landholders to bequeathe property widely. This the social conventions of the Normans in England did not permit, Holt, 'The Revolution of 1066', 197–9.

[31] J. C. Holt, 'Feudal Society and the Family in Early Medieval England, iv: The Heiress and the Alien', *Transactions of the Royal Historical Society,* 5th ser., 35 (1985), 1–28, esp. 8–10.

[32] Runciman, 'Accelerating Social Mobility', 11. In Domesday slaves comprised over 10% of the recorded population, but they may have comprised a much smaller proportion of the actual population in 1086.

[33] *Leges Henrici Primi,* ed. L. J. Downer (Oxford, 1972), cc. 78, 1–78, 3. Cf. 76, 3 for an enumeration of the ways in which persons could become slaves; also 77, 1–77, 2a.

[34] Eadmer, *Historia Novorum in Anglia,* ed. M. Rule (Rolls Series, 81, 1884), 143.

give up the slave trade and they had then been an example throughout England. In this passage William's language suggests that he thought of the slave trade as a thing of the past.[35] Once there was no slave trade then the high cost of replacing slaves probably made other forms of labour a more attractive economic proposition. In these circumstances manumissions and the death and escape of slaves may have combined to render slavery extinct.[36]

Although it would obviously be wrong to attribute the end of slavery—a development common to northern Europe as a whole—to the insular experience of the Norman Conquest, it is none the less possible that the aftermath of 1066 may have contributed to the process. Slaves who took advantage of the turmoil of these years to run away may well have found many more people willing to help a fugitive than would have been the case before 1066. English resentment at the plight of the English people, the atmosphere of the *murdrum* fine, could well have come to the rescue of English slaves on the run from their newly installed French masters.[37] Indeed in an economic climate seemingly characterized by labour shortage, some English farmers and landholders may have seen protecting and providing for runaways as an attractive method of acquiring additional labour.

In one sense the runaway slave is no more than a special case of a general phenomenon: the ability of people to rise vertically in society as a direct result of moving horizontally. Even for the non-slave this was rarely an easy matter. Competition for labour seems to have meant that in the early period nearly all tenants were tied to their holdings, entitled to leave only with their lord's licence.[38] Those tenants who

---

[35] William of Malmesbury, *Vita Wulfstani*, ed. R. R. Darlington (Camden Soc., 40, 1928), 43–4. On Wales, R. R. Davies, *Conquest, Coexistence, and Change: Wales 1063–1415* (Oxford, 1987), 119–20. See *The Letters of John of Salisbury*, i. ed. W. J. Millor and H. E. Butler (London, 1955), 135. This may explain why Gerald gives the impression that slaves were still being imported into Ireland later in the century, *Expugnatio Hibernica*, 70.

[36] J. Hicks, *A Theory of Economic History* (Oxford, 1969), 124–32.

[37] Hyams, *King, Lords, and Peasants*, 251–3 for a discussion of the way in which English birth 'almost carried a presumption of servility', and cf. *Leges Henrici Primi*, c. 77, 2.

[38] On labour shortage and the flight, enticement and stealing of men see J. Hatcher, 'English Serfdom and Villeinage: Towards a Reassessment', *Past and*

could give, sell, or leave their lands without licence were highly privileged.[39] From Domesday it would appear that approximately three-quarters of the tenant population— *villani*, bordars, and cottars—were tied in ways which marked them off from the 14 per cent of tenants who were categorized as *liberi homines* or sokemen. In the case of the Westminster Abbey estates *villani*, bordars, and cottars comprised as much as 84 per cent of the enumerated population, with only 3.5 per cent being freemen and sokemen.[40] But by c. 1225, the date of the earliest surviving custumal of Westminster Abbey's manors, about 11 per cent of the tenants named were described as being free. Thus Barbara Harvey has suggested that the most striking change in the period after the Domesday survey was 'the rise of a class of free tenants', many of them descendants of men classified as *villani* in 1086. In her view proximity to towns helped some, usually the wealthier, tenants escape from dependence into freedom in the twelfth and thirteenth centuries, but more important still were local opportunities for assarting and colonization. Yet, she continues, every local breakthrough on this and all other estates might have been in vain had it not been for Henry II's 'vital juridical principle' that royal justice was available to every free tenant.[41] The notion that one of the king's responsibilities was to protect men against seigneurial excess, taken together with the range of remedies offered by the royal courts as a result of the measures taken during Henry II's reign, meant that from then on tenants who wished to loosen the ties that bound them to their lords had a potentially effective ally in the shape of the king's courts. This development could have put the Crown in the socially embarrassing position of appearing to help rustics

---

Present, 90 (1981), 3–39, esp. 26–32. See also Hyams's discussion in his chapter on the origins of common-law villeinage, *Kings, Lords, and Peasants*, 221–65.

[39] Thus in 1142 when 38 *rustici* whose holdings were needed for the foundation of Revesby Abbey were offered the choice of resettlement elsewhere on apparently identical terms or 'the liberty of going with all their goods wherever they wished' no less than 31 preferred to be landless but lordless; the example cited by Hatcher, 'English Serfdom', 31–2.

[40] B. Harvey, *Westminster Abbey and its Estates in the Middle Ages* (Oxford, 1977), 101–6.

[41] Ibid. 107–15.

against the *generosi* had it not been for the concomitant emergence of the new common-law doctrines of villeinage and freedom.[42] Thus by the late twelfth century there was a new legal boundary between freedom and unfreedom in place; and once again movement across this boundary could only take place with the lord's approval.[43] It was none the less a significant shift. By the time of 'Bracton' the unfree could not lawfully be killed or mutilated by their lords, whereas in the mind of the compiler of the *Leges Henrici Primi* a master who killed his slave was guilty of no more than a sin.[44]

4. Under the Normans the English Church continued to grow in size much as it had done before 1066. From the mid-twelfth century onwards the picture is in some respects a more static one. There were no new cathedrals after Carlisle (founded in 1133), and it was gradually becoming more difficult to create new parishes. None the less there still seems to have been a growing number of cathedral prebends and vicars, and a continuing proliferation of non-parish churches and altars. Moreover, what rigidities there were in the system were very largely the result of the activities of a growing number of canon lawyers.[45] But the old problem remains. In an age of overall population growth and growing, yet always inadequte, documentation, it is hard to know whether or not this meant that the Church was becoming proportionally more important as an avenue of social advance. It is at this point that the religious reform movements become so crucial. The most readily quantifiable measure of their success is to be found, as C. N. L. Brooke pointed out,

[42] Hyams, *King, Lords, and Peasants*, 240–50, and note Harvey's observation that many of the free tenants can not really be described as peasants, *Westminster Abbey*, 117.

[43] *The Treatise on the Laws and Customs of the Realm of England commonly called Glanvill*, ed. G. D. G. Hall (London, 1965), Bk. 5, ch. 5, including a reference to a former villein being made a knight. Richard Fitz-Nigel, *Dialogus de Scaccario*, ed. C. Johnson, corr. F. Carter and D. Greenway (Oxford, 1983), 53.

[44] *Leges Henrici Primi*, c. 75, 4; 'Bracton', *De Legibus et Consuetudinibus Angliae*, ed. S. E. Thorne (4 vols., London, 1968–77), ii. 37.

[45] On the continuing foundation of new churches, J. Blair, 'Local Churches in Domesday and Before', *Domesday Studies*, 265–78, esp. 271–3; the problems of the 'fossilization' of the mid-12th cent. and later are highlighted in Murray, *Reason and Society*, 307–8.

in the rise in the numbers of regular clergy in England in this period.[46] In 1066 there were some sixty religious houses and perhaps 1,000 monks and nuns; by 1216 there were approximately 700 houses and some 13,000 monks, nuns, regular canons and canonesses.[47] No matter what estimate we make of the overall population growth during the same period, what is beyond doubt is that there was a significant increase in the proportion of the population who adopted the monastic way of life. In these circumstances there is clearly a prima-facie case for accepting Knowles's contention that very few houses remained 'preserves of the aristocracy', and that during the course of the twelfth century recruits came increasingly from the children of all classes of free men. 'Every indication goes to show that in the reigns of Richard and John the monasteries were recruited almost entirely from what may be called, at the risk of anachronism, the middle class.'[48]

It is true, of course, that in many contexts the bald figures for numbers of religious houses could be profoundly misleading. Many of the 'new' communities may have been merely transformations of the old secular minsters which were such a prominent feature of the Anglo-Saxon church.[49] None the less in this context there is a significant difference. The old houses were populated by canons who could be, and presumably sometimes were, married. In the new 'regular' communities, however, marriage and children were, to say the least, frowned upon. Thus it is possible that one of the effects of the celibacy campaign was to put a brake on the fertility of the landholding class. Whether or not this could have been on a scale sufficient to form an exception to Herlihy's central principle, that those social strata which commanded the larger part of available resources consistently reared the greater number of children, it is impossible

[46] C. N. L. Brooke, 'Gregorian Reform in Action: Clerical Marriage in England, 1050–1200', _Cambridge Historical Journal_, 12 (1956), 1–21, esp. 7–8.

[47] D. Knowles and R. N. Hadcock, _Medieval Religious Houses: England and Wales_, 2nd edn. (Cambridge, 1971), 494.

[48] D. Knowles, _The Monastic Order in England_ (Cambridge, 1963), 424–5. And in the 13th cent. the mendicant orders would recruit more widely still.

[49] J. Blair, 'Secular Minster Churches in Domesday Book', _Domesday Book: A Reassessment_, 104–42.

to know.[50] This is to see things in terms of numbers, replacement rates, but in terms of the pattern of recruitment there is one other development which should be borne in mind: the great change in the monastic world of the twelfth century, the ending of the system of child oblates. This major shift in the timing of the moment of entry into the religious life meant that from now on individuals had a much wider and freer choice than ever before. In Southern's words, 'a conscript army was replaced by volunteers'.[51] Here surely was a profoundly important change in the pattern of social mobility, a widening of the opportunities for the exercise of choice.

If reform meant that twelfth-century houses were less and less self-repopulating communities, then it follows, of course, that they would, to an increasing extent, have to recruit from outside. Naturally the Gregorian campaign against clerical marriage tended to affect the secular clergy in a similar way, making the formation of clerical dynasties that much harder.[52] Although among the lower clergy marriage and hereditary succession to benefices remained common until the mid-thirteenth century at least, the higher clergy—the ecclesiastical élite—were distinctly more vulnerable to the pressure of reform. After the mid-twelfth century hereditary succession to prebends was no longer the norm within the cathedral chapter of Hereford, for example, even though as late as the early thirteenth century there were still some individual canons who were married.[53] The effect of this was to increase the rate at which the higher clergy had to be

[50] Herlihy's conclusion was that 'the more rapid expansion of the higher social strata tended to create a top-heavy social pyramid' and therefore 'the dominant direction of social mobility in medieval society had to be downward', 'Three Patterns of Social Mobility', 626–33, esp. 632. For discussion of some of the other problems associated with a high rate of 'upper-class celibacy', Murray, *Reason and Society*, 342 ff.

[51] R. W. Southern, *Western Society and the Church in the Middle Ages* (Harmondsworth, 1970).

[52] Moreover the monastic expansion may itself have had a direct impact since, as Barlow observed, 'the main way in which the custom of hereditary succession (to churches) was broken was by the impropriation of churches to monasteries and the provision of vicars', Barlow, *English Church*, 131–2.

[53] J. Barrow, 'Hereford Bishops and Married Clergy, *c.* 1130–1240', *Historical Research*, 60 (1987).

recruited anew in each generation, thus increasing the importance of the Church as a channel of vertical circulation.[54] But if clerical sons were no longer to succeed their clerical fathers, then how was the clergy to be recruited? Of course the clergy still had other male relatives, notably nephews, but how was a choice to be made between them? How was their suitability—and that of other candidates—for office to be assessed? In England the question was a particularly acute one for those who did not choose to demonstrate their enthusiasm for the Church by entering one of the regular orders; the secular world in which they chose to remain was a fiercely competitive one. In a kingdom where there were very few secular collegiate churches apart from cathedrals (and where half the cathedrals were monastic), prebends were in short supply. Moreover demand was almost certainly rising. As Julia Barrow has pointed out, one consequence of primogeniture was that 'because they could not inherit much property from their families, clerks who were the sons of knights and barons had only the advantage of birth, not the advantage of wealth as well, over clerks who were the sons of burgesses.'[55]

5. If another aspect of the Church reform movement, the campaign against simony, meant that respectable candidates could no longer buy ecclesiastical office, there was at any rate no prohibition against them buying education.[56] Here, it may be, is one of the pressures which brought about the dramatic expansion of education which is such a feature of the twelfth century. It is in this century that we find, for the first time, institutions specializing in education. Hitherto, as Nicholas Orme has emphasized, educational provision, no matter how excellent, had always been ancillary to the main business of the institutions which offered it, whether

[54] In Herlihy's opinion, 'this made the Church the most visible avenue of social advance in the medieval world', 'Three Pattterns of Social Mobility', 624.

[55] J. Barrow, 'Cathedrals, Provosts and Prebends: A Comparison of Twelfth-Century German and English Practice', *Journal of Ecclesiastical History*, 37 (1986), 536–64, esp. 563–4.

[56] On some of the implications for social mobility of the prohibition of simony see Murray, *Reason and Society*, 214–6.

they were religious houses or royal and aristocratic house-holds.[57] The establishment of numbers of public elementary schools, including some in quite small towns and villages, 'public' in the sense of being open to anyone who could afford to go there, was clearly the educational environment out of which the universities of Oxford and Cambridge developed in the late twelfth and early thirteenth centuries. Southern's view of this period is that 'there were greater opportunities for schools and teachers than ever before. Perhaps these opportunities never again rose so fast until the nineteenth century.'[58] To judge from a jaundiced comment made by Walter Map, the material advantages which education could bring were widely appreciated. In his *De Nugis Curialium*, a work which vividly reflects the anxieties of a secular clerk seeking patronage in a highly competitive court society, he complains that it was so that their children might get on in the world that the poor and the servile were keen to send them to school.[59]

For generations past the traditional way to get on in the world had been through service, and throughout this period it remained so. An ambitious Welshman was advised to enter the service of King Henry I. 'He will honour you and exalt you over your fellows; he will make all your kinsmen envious of you.'[60] The same applied to the service of lesser lords. Jocelin of Brakelond describes how, when Samson was elected Abbot of Bury, 'a great crowd of new kinsmen (*novorum parentum*) came to meet him, all desiring to be taken into his service.'[61] But merely to insist upon continuity here is to leave a number of questions unanswered, some of them, no doubt, unanswerable. For example, did the numbers of new opportunities tend to stagnate once new lord-

[57] N. Orme, *From Childhood to Chivalry: The Education of the English Kings and Aristocracy 1066–1530* (London, 1984), 48–67; id., *English Schools in the Middle Ages* (London, 1973), 59–60, 167–70.

[58] R. W. Southern, 'From Schools to University', *The History of the University of Oxford*, i, ed. J. I. Catto (Oxford, 1984), 1–36, esp. 1–2.

[59] Map, *De Nugis Curialium*, 12.

[60] *Brut Y Tywysogyon or The Chronicle of the Princes, Red Book of Hergest Version*, ed. T. Jones (Cardiff, 1955), 80–1.

[61] *The Chronicle of Jocelin of Brakelond*, ed. H. E. Butler (London, 1949), 24.

ships were no longer created at the phenomenally high rate characteristic of the decades after 1066? Or did, as is often asserted, the development of schools reflect a rising demand for educated officials as part and parcel of a general demand, from kings, bishops, monasteries, and all great landowners, for administrative servants of all kinds?[62] I shall devote the rest of this sketch to a brief consideration of these two questions.

First, if instead of limiting our view to England we also take the Celtic lands into account, then it is clear that a continuing process of conquest and colonization enabled new lordships to be created throughout the whole of this period.

In 1092 'King William went north to Carlisle with a large army and restored the town and built the castle. He drove out the former ruler of that district and garrisoned the castle with his men. Then he returned south, and sent thither very many peasants with their wives and livestock to settle there and till the soil.'[63] This entry from the *Anglo-Saxon Chronicle* summarizes a sequence of events that was to be followed time and time again, notably in Wales and Ireland, though not usually with such direct royal involvement. It seemed to the author of the *Gesta Stephani* that Henry I was turning Wales into a 'second England'; to the Welsh that he was planning to exterminate them completely or drive them into the sea'.[64] The pace of advance slowed down after Henry I's death; even so Wales remained a land of opportunity for conquerors and settlers throughout most of this period. Not, it may be, 'a land of easy opportunities or great rewards'—none the less attractive enough for those who were not already well established (e.g. younger sons) in England and Normandy and who were prepared to pay the price of continuing military effort and constant vigilance.[65] Further north, in Scotland,

---

[62] Southern, 'From Schools to University', 1.

[63] *The Peterborough Chronicle*, ed. C. Clark (Oxford, 1970), 19.

[64] *Gesta Stephani*, ed. K. R. Potter and R. H. C. Davis (Oxford, 1976), 16; *Brut Y Tywysogyon*, 78–81.

[65] Davies, *Conquest, Coexistence*, 85–6, and, for the settlement of colonists, 93–100. On the south-west of Wales in particular see I. W. Rowlands, 'The Making of the March: Aspects of the Norman Settlement in Dyfed', *Anglo-Norman Studies*, 3, ed. R. A. Brown (Woodbridge, 1981), 142–58.

opportunities came in a more peaceful form, particularly in the reign of David I (1124–53) when the eager adventurers found a welcome at the Scottish court and were rewarded with estates covering a vast area in southern Scotland.[66] Then, in the late 1160s, an entirely new field of enterprise was opened up, Ireland,—particularly useful at times when in Wales native political revivals made life awkward for the newcomers. At such times they turned a ready ear to the blandishments, the recruiting offers which came from further West. The early thirteenth-century *Song of Dermot* makes these very explicit.

> Whoever shall wish for land or pence
> Horses, armour or chargers
> Gold and silver, I shall give them
> Very ample livery.
> Whoever shall wish for land and pasture
> Richly shall I enfeoff them.[67]

The second question. Was the apparently growing demand for administrative services real or illusory, and if real, then how important? So far as the central government is concerned, we do have some genuine hope of being able to give relatively concrete answers to some of the relevant questions. For the first time in English history, in the shape of the twelfth-century pipe rolls, there survives the kind of evidence to encourage historians of this subject to adopt a quantitative approach. On the basis of the earliest surviving pipe roll, Judith Green has made a systematic analysis of the origins and careers of the 104 men—at least 96 of them laymen— who were involved in government during the exchequer year 1129–30. Of these 104, 51 came from landholding families; of these 51, 17 came from greater families, (which she defines as those who held more than 5 knights fees in chief from the Crown), and 34 from lesser landholding families.

---

[66] Modern summaries in A. A. M. Duncan, *Scotland: The Making of the Kingdom* (Edinburgh, 1975), 133–42; and G. W. S. Barrow, *Kingship and Unity: Scotland 1000–1306* (London, 1981), 29–36, 44–7.

[67] *The Song of Dermot and the Earl*, ed. G. H. Orpen (Oxford, 1892), 34–5. On the settlement of Ireland see R. Frame, *Colonial Ireland, 1169–1369* (Dublin, 1981), esp. chs. 2 and 4; J. F. Lydon, *The Lordship of Ireland in the Middle Ages* (Dublin, 1972), 84–102; *A New History of Ireland*, ii: *Medieval Ireland*, ed. A. Cosgrave (Oxford, 1987), 213–24.

The social origins of 53 of the 1130 group are obscure—and it seems reasonable to assume that they were also humble. Out of the total of 104, Green discovered 18 who made very substantial gains from royal patronage; of these fortunate 18, 8 emerged from obscurity—the most famous being Roger of Salisbury. On the other hand no less than 35 of the 53 obscure men seem to have made no gains at all. Morover out of the 17 who already belonged to the greater landholding families no less than 6 made substantial gains.[68] This, doubtless, is not surprising, but it should remind us of Orderic's other comment (i.e. not his one about men raised from the dust): King Henry 'honoured his magnates (*optimates*) generously, he bestowed on them riches and honours, and so by his accommodating policy he won their fidelity'.[69] Unfortunately we still await similarly systematic studies of the personnel of goverment based on later pipe rolls, but here at any rate there may be a way forward, a fruitful field for further research.[70]

Despite the lack of similar work on later records, there can be little doubt that the machinery of government continued to expand. The increasing output of royal documents implies a growing number of clerical staff.[71] William Fitz-Stephen claimed that as chancellor Thomas Becket had no less than fifty-two clerks in his own and in the king's service.[72] Indeed to all appearances the pace of bureaucratic development accelerated towards the end of the twelfth century, particularly during Hubert Walter's periods of office as justiciar and chancellor (1193–1205).[73] By 1200 indeed the expansion of government had reached a point at which, for the first time in English history, one can detect within it the emergence of a group of specialists: the king's judges, men

---

[68] Green, *The Governnent*, 283–4. On a closely related subject see S. L. Mooers, 'Patronage in the Pipe Roll of 1130', *Speculum*, 59 (1984), 282–307.

[69] Orderic Vitalis, *Ecclesiastical History*, v. 296.

[70] For a fine example of what can be done with the pipe rolls see T. K. Keefe, 'King Henry II and the Earls: the Pipe Roll Evidence', *Albion*, 13 (1981), 191–222.

[71] Clanchy, *From Memory to Written Record*, 29–59.

[72] *Materials for the History of Thomas Becket*, iii. 29.

[73] Clanchy, *From Memory to Written Record*, 48–53. Hubert Walter has been described as 'the son of an obscure East Anglian knight who wielded power over both the English church and secular government in a way not to be seen until Cardinal Wolsey', Turner, *Judiciary*, 292.

like Simon of Pattishall and Osbert Fitz-Harvey, no longer
the multi-purpose royal servants of old, but men whose
governmental activity was concentrated on the work of justice.[74] In part this development was presumably a consequence of the way in which law was becoming a learned
science, and the administration of the law therefore a matter
for the appropriately educated expert. But once this was so
then it was not just the judges who needed professional
training. In the royal courts of the same period we find, again
for the first time in English history, evidence for the existence of a small group of professional lawyers, men who act
on behalf of a number of clients and whom a client might
employ for just one piece of litigation. From the 1240s
we can find men similarly employed in the city courts of
London.[75]

As this London example suggests these developments were
not restricted to the sphere of royal government. Indeed,
they could not have been. The greater the output of government documents, the greater the number of individuals who
came into contact with them in one form or another. This
means, as James Campbell has pointed out, that in the
twelfth century 'not only was central government organised
in such a way that it could deal directly with more men and
institutions, there were also more men and institutions
whose status and knowledge were such that they were capable of dealing directly with the central government.'[76] Here
we have a two-way relationship which was itself the consequence of social changes: the increasing provision of education, the increasingly large proportion of the population
which participated in literacy.[77] Thus during the course of
the twelfth and thirteenth centuries we find more men and

[74] This is one of the main conclusions of Turner's study of the careers of forty-
nine justices in this period.
[75] P. A. Brand, 'The Origins of the English Legal Profession', *Law and History
Review*, 5 (1987), 31–50.
[76] J. Campbell, 'The Significance of the Anglo-Norman State in the Administrative History of Western Europe', *Histoire Comparée de l'administration*, ed. W.
Paravicini and K. F. Werner (Munich, 1980), repr. in *Essays in Anglo-Saxon History*
(London, 1987), 181.
[77] Clanchy, *From Memory to Written Record*, 56, has most barons 'using documents'
by 1200, knights by 1250, peasants by 1300.

institutions employing their own clerical staff.[78] The implications of these developments are beautifully illustrated by
Southern's comment on the silver embossed ivory writing-
case with silver inkhorn which Bernard and his brother
Nicholas, men of English descent and both of them scribes
in Henry I's chancery, presented to the church at Laun-
ceston. 'The church converted it into a reliquary. As the
instrument by which one English family had climbed back
into prosperity, it deserved to be held in honour.'[79]

These changes were then to play an important role in
shaping the ways in which lords responded to the crisis of
inflation which shook the economy in the years either side of
1200. Until the late twelfth century it appears to have been
normal for great landlords to farm out their estates so that
they had not only predictable incomes but also only a limited
number of individuals to deal with. The stability of the system
is indicated by the fact that long-term leases for several lives
were common and that these long-term grants had tended to
turn into hereditary tenures. Obviously the steep rise in
prices around 1200 created severe problems for any lord
who continued to live on fixed rents paid by hereditary
tenants. The landlords' solution, to take over the direct management of their estates, meant that they now required, and
had to deal with, a whole army of professional receivers,
treasurers, auditors, and bailiffs. 'In place of a single officer
with omnicompetent responsibilities, lords employed a variety of officials.'[80] It would have defeated the whole point of
the reorganization if these new officials had been rewarded
with newly created hereditary tenures. Thus even the highest
ranking of them could normally expect no more than some
form of life-grant, and usually in cash rather than in land.[81]
Whether or not there had ever before been a price rise as

[78] There is some dispute about the chronology of this development, ibid. 40–1.
[79] Southern, *Medieval Humanism*, 227.
[80] P. D. A. Harvey, 'The English Inflation of 1180–1220', *Past and Present*, 61
(1973), 3–30 and id., 'The Pipe Rolls and the Adoption of Demesne Farming
in England', *Economic History Review*, 27 (1974), 345–59. The quotation is from S.
L. Waugh, 'Tenure to Contract: Lordship and Clientage in Thirteenth-Century
England', *English Historical Review*, 101 (1986), 811–39, 815.
[81] Waugh, 'Tenure to Contract', 813–32. For a discussion of the officials of a 12th
cent. aristocratic household see D. Crouch, *The Beaumont Twins* (Cambridge, 1986),
139–55.

steep as this we cannot know; but what does seem certain is that earlier lords would not have been able to respond in this manner. The switch to direct management, the managerial revolution, was only possible in a society capable of producing numerate and literate men in sufficient numbers. And even Campbell, not a man to underestimate the achievement of centuries before the twelfth, implies that this would not have been possible earlier.[82] From the point of view of social mobility these were major developments. They meant not only that there was now employment for a vastly greater number of officials than ever before, but also that recruitment was more likely to be on the basis of professional competence rather than hereditary succession, though the two, of course, are not mutually exclusive.

Is it possible to draw any broad conclusions? Runciman argued that after the end of Anglo-Saxon England the rate of social mobility was bound to slow down because economically, ideologically, and politically there was little prospect of either innovation or disturbance.[83] Clearly this line of argument will not work. Inflation, the Church reform movements, and the Norman Conquest were developments which, economically, ideologically, and politically, had enormous consequences in the sphere of social mobility, consequences which—amongst other things—tended to increase the rate of mobility.

In the end, it seems to me, we cannot ignore the evidence which suggests that this was an age not merely of economic expansion, but also of economic intensification. Although the English economy clearly remained underdeveloped when compared with the economies of Flanders and North Italy, it was, none the less, becoming increasingly market-orientated, with more money and more goods in faster circulation than before. It has indeed been argued that a rise in horse-hauling in the twelfth and thirteenth centuries increased the velocity of goods transportation and, hence, the opposite flow of money to pay for them.[84] For these sorts of

---

[82] Campbell, 'Significance of the Anglo-Norman State', 180.

[83] Runciman, 'Accelerating Social Mobility', 28–30.

[84] J. Langdon, 'Horse Hauling: A Revolution in Vehicle Transport in Twelfth and Thirteenth Century England?', *Past and Present*, 103 (1984), 37–66. Moreover the evidence suggests that a great deal more coin was being put into circulation. The

reasons Barbara Harvey has suggested that it was probably in the twelfth century that peasant surpluses became important to the urban market.[85] In terms of social relationships and social mobility this means that we are not dealing with a steady state, or even a contracting universe which merely appears to be expanding. We are dealing with one which in many critical ways really was expanding. As economic activity intensified, as government became more complicated, so people were presented with more choices, more choices of occupations and—accentuated by the disappearance of both slavery and the system of child oblates—more chance of personal fulfilment.[86]

mint accounts for London and Canterbury in the reign of Henry III indicate an output of some 8 million pennies a year in the period up to 1247, whereas the current best guess for the currency of Aethelred and Cnut implies, on my arithmetic, an output of about 4 million a year, C. E. Blunt and J. D. Brand, 'Mint Output of Henry III', *British Numismatic Journal*, 39 (1970), 61–6; D. M. Metcalf, 'Continuity and Change in English Monetary History, *c.* 973–1086. Part 2', *British Numismatic Journal*, 51 (1981), 52–90, using Table 5 on p. 62. Moreover the effect of inflation *c.* 1200 should have been to make the silver penny a still more useful medium of exchange.

[85] Harvey, *Westminster*, 6.

[86] Cf. S. Reynolds, *Kingdoms and Communities in Western Europe 900–1300* (Oxford, 1984), 337–8. Haverkamp's conclusion that this period was for by far the greater part of the German population 'ein Zeitalter der Befreiung von persönlichen Abhängigkeiten oder deren Abschwächung', in A. Haverkamp, *Aufbruch und Gestaltung: Deutschland 1056–1273* (Munich, 1984), 308, is a reminder that many of the developments sketched above were the common experience of medieval Europe as a whole. What then were the peculiarly English variations on the theme? I suppose the more systematic application of primogeniture and the high rate of inflation *c.* 1200 (perhaps) and (certainly) the destruction of the old élite as a consequence of the Norman Conquest.

16

Forms of Social Mobility:
The Example of *Zensualität*

MICHAEL MATHEUS

The story of one Odegena, an Englishwoman, provides a
suitable starting-point for this essay because it is a good
example of social mobility.[1] Towards the end of the eleventh
century Odegena left the *regiones Anglicas* to settle at the
Benedictine abbey of St Trond, which belonged to the diocese of Liège. It is a case of rare good fortune that the one
surviving copy of a document dating from 1095 (a *traditio*)
not only tells us the name of this woman, who belonged
neither to the aristocracy nor the clergy, but also contains
information about the conditions under which this particular case of social mobility took place.

The occasion for the writing of the document was, as so
often, a dispute which involved not only Odegena but her
entire family, and in particular, her husband. Because of the
damaged state of the copy, his name is not known.[2] At a time
which can no longer be pinpointed, this *servus sancti Trudonis*
had left the dominion of his monastery. The document states
that for some time he lived in *regionibus Anglicis*, and adds
that his stay there was *benigne et honeste*. This brief hint, which
may derive from the man himself, gives the impression that
he had enjoyed a certain esteem in his new surroundings,
and that he had done quite well. Unfortunately we do not
learn why he returned to his place of birth (*ad natales fines*),

---

This essay examines the problems which German scholars associate with the term
Zensualität, and which are not widely known among English-speaking scholars. As I
am preparing a larger study on the subject, references in this article are kept to a
minimum.

[1] C. Piot (ed.), *Cartulaire de l'abbaye de Saint-Trond* (2 vols., Brussels, 1870–4), no.
XXI, 28f.

[2] Rijksarchief Hasselt. Abdij Sint-Truiden: Cartular no. 20, 206f. Even with a
quartz lamp, a faded note in the margin of the document is unreadable.

the *villa* Hamaal, a few kilometres south-west of St Trond. The text states further that during his absence the *servus* had married the said Odegena, who was *ingenua*, that is to say, freeborn. At the instigation of the Abbot of St Trond, whose name the source does not mention, the *servus* then persuaded his wife to take a step which was quite common both in the dominion of St Trond and in numerous other ecclesiastical institutions on the Continent. She made over herself and her children to the saint of the abbey. In practice, this meant that she bound herself to fulfil specific contractual obligations, namely to pay St Trudo—*de facto* the abbot and the monastery—annual taxes of one *denarius* on the feast of St Trudo, and twelve *denarii* in case of death. Furthermore, the abbot exercised a limited control over who she and her offspring could marry, and they were also subject to his jurisdiction.

The various kinds of sources which report such *traditiones* rarely yield more than this kind of information about payments and obligations. However, our document is unusual in another respect. It tells us that the family of the *servus* had been endowed with a certain amount of arable and grazing land which was part of the *cultura dominica* belonging to the *curtis* of the abbey at Halmaal. In return, an annual tax of 30 *solidi* had to be paid, unless the owners of the land rendered the abbey service *more militis*.

This part of the contract suggests that Odegena's husband was experienced in fighting on horseback and that the couple's children could also be expeced to render service *more militis*. The renowned Belgian historian, François-L. Ganshof, assumes that the *servus* had done many years of military service, and speculates that he may have been among the forces of William the Conqueror.[3] All we can say with certainty, however, is that he earned his living as a mercenary.

The political context of this case needs to be briefly explained. From the document itself we learn that Geoffrey of Bouillon, who had been Duke of Lower Lorraine since 1087,

---

[3] F. L. Ganshof, *Étude sur les ministeriales en Flandre et en Lotharingie* (Brussels, 1926), 172. See also E. Sabbe, 'Les relations économiques entre l'Angleterre et le continent au haut-moyen age', *Le Moyen Age*, 56 (1950), 169–93.

had initially refused to accept the contract. Statements by the witnesses present at the legal act eventually persuaded him to give up his resistance and to agree to a renewal of the contract (*literata pactione*), which previously may not even have been recorded. Although we find out nothing about Geoffrey's motives, his intervention points to a situation which was important for all those involved. Since the 1080s St Trond had been directly affected by the consequences of the investiture conflict. In particular, between 1083 and 1099 various candidates had vied for the position of abbot. These disputes were closely connected with territorial struggles between aristocratic families of the region, in which the stewards of the abbey played an important part. Duke Geoffrey was involved in these quarrels. In 1095, one year before he went to Jerusalem, he tried to make his own candidate abbot of St Trond.[4]

These political and religious struggles were likely to have had a lasting impact on Odegena's family. The long and arduous fighting around the investiture conflict was related to wider processes of economic and social change. The position of traditional bearers of authority was weakened, while opportunities opened up for those dependants who were experienced in the dangerous, risky business of fighting on horseback. During such crises it was frequently necessary to secure the support of potential fighters by making over to them tilled land belonging to ecclesiastical and aristocratic domains. Such fiefs (*Dienstlehen*) often became hereditary.

This sort of geographical and social movement of people is an example of what historians and social scientists have labelled social mobility. While scholars distinguish between vertical and horizontal mobility, they do not generally discuss the theoretical and methodological implications underlying the concept. As a rule, these terms are used in a sense

---

[4] See the bibliography *Monasticon Belge*, vi: *Province de Limbourg* (Liège, 1976), 15 ff.; E. Linck, *Sozialer Wandel in klösterlichen Grundherrschaften des 11. bis 13. Jahrhunderts. Studien zu den familiae von Gembloux, Stablo-Malmedy und St. Trond* (Veröffentlichungen des Max-Planck-Instituts für Geschichte 57; Göttingen, 1978); W. Peters, 'Die Beziehungen der Abtei St. Trond zum Papsttum im 12. Jahrhundert', *Revue Bénédictine*, 95 (1985), 130–45. The author of the present essay is preparing a study on the *Zensualität* of St Trond.

so vague that they mean no more than general geographical and social mobility, and movement between different social positions.

In recent years, a great deal of research has been done on forms of horizontal mobility. Because of the nature of the sources available, this research has concentrated mainly on the late Middle Ages. Here the concept of horizontal mobility covers geographical movements of people differing widely with respect to extent, duration, and destinations. To take only two examples, the term is used for the entire spectrum of 'being on the move', from temporary to permanent, relating both to individuals and groups, as well as for relocations, again both temporary and permanent. (The methods employed by the many social sciences which investigate modern migration processes are of limited use for our purposes.) Today, the interest of researchers extends far beyond travelling bearers of authority, the traditional subject of enquiry, to embrace various groups of newcomers, clerics and preachers, pilgrims and crusaders, mercenaries, traders and messengers, beggars, day labourers and seasonal workers, and finally, in the later Middle Ages, journeymen and scholars, to name only some of the most important groups.[5] Space does not permit me to deal with the variety of forms of horizontal mobility which this list hints at. Instead, I shall concentrate on two problem areas.

From the eleventh century onwards the roads filled with people.[6] This comment was made by Karl Bosl, who, more than any other recent German-speaking medievalist, has used the term 'social mobility' for the period from the

[5] Cf., e.g. the contributions by K. Schulz, L. Schmugge, J. Miethke, and F. Graus in P. Moraw (ed.), *Unterwegssein im Spätmittelalter* (Zeitschrift für Historische Forschung, Beiheft 1; Berlin, 1985).

[6] K. Bosl, 'Über soziale Mobilität in der mittelalterlichen "Gesellschaft". Dienst, Freiheit, Freizügigkeit als Motive sozialen Aufstiegs', *Vierteljahrschrift für Sozial- und Wirtschaftsgeschichte*, 47 (1960), 306–32. Reprint in K. Bosl, *Frühformen der Gesellschaft im mittelalterlichen Europa. Ausgewählte Beiträge zu einer Strukturanalyse der mittelalterlichen Welt* (Munich and Vienna 1964), 156–79; id., 'Soziale Mobilität in der mittelalterlichen Gesellschaft. Soziale Aufstiegsbewegungen im europäischen Mittelalter', in id., *Die Gesellschaft in der Geschichte des Mittelalters* (Göttingen 1966, 3rd expanded edn., 1975), 44–60; id., 'Die horizontale Mobilität der europäischen Gesellschaft im Mittelalter und ihre Kommunikationsmittel', *Zeitschrift für bayerische Landesgeschichte*, 35 (1972), 40–53, here 48.

eleventh to the fourteenth centuries. This assessment, however, does not take regional and temporal differences into account. His view is based mainly on additive phenomenological descriptions, for the most part vague, of various wandering groups, some of which did not appear until the high Middle Ages. The sources available do not permit the extent of geographical mobility to be measured with statistical accuracy. Even changes such as the emergence of begging and the use of mercenaries as mass phenomena in the late Middle Ages are virtually impossible to measure in earlier centuries. Ultimately, it may often prove impossible to make even cautious estimates of the size of the various geographical movements.

A dilemma remains. Where Bosl and others wanted to prevent horizontal mobility from being regarded as unimportant, or from being dismissed altogether, there is now another danger. Made more aware by the experiences of our own time, we may overestimate the extent and the possibilities inherent in geographical movements, and fail to take into account the legal, social, economic, and infrastructural factors that placed limits on them, and not least, the risks which they entailed.

At the beginning of the eleventh century horizontal mobility increased significantly in large areas of the Continent as ecclesiastical and secular authorities, including the new religious orders of the twelfth century, colonized both previously settled land and hitherto uninhabited areas. The expansion of existing towns, the founding of new ones, and the establishment of many rural settlements, all resulted in a considerable concentration of settlement. This development is closely related to demographic factors. Under changing social and economic conditions, the birth-rate rose. By the year 1300 the population had perhaps tripled in size. Together with other factors, for the most part regional, this population increase was an important prerequisite for migration. In settling the east, for example, people migrated over vast distances. Recent research suggests, however, that the extent of these migratory movements has for a long time been considerably overestimated. And despite impressive population growth rates in hitherto sparsely populated regions, marked differences remained. Only in the north-west of the empire, in Flanders, Brabant, and along the lower Rhine, was a density of settlement reached comparable to that in the south of the much smaller kingdom of England.

We now come to my second problem area. Not only in the case of Odegena's family does a change in place of residence appear to be the prerequisite for other types of changes. Our example illustrates two of these: a change in legal status, and the acceptance of a specific function. The way in which the freeborn Odegena tied herself to the Abbey of St Trond is by no means exceptional. In various regions of the empire, hundreds of surviving transfer notes and charters, whose number varies according to the period in question, document such transfers to saints, that is to say, to ecclesiastical institutions, an action which we find difficult to understand today. We have to bear in mind that many such events were not recorded in writing. As a document from Worms, dating from the first half of the eleventh century shows, such transactions involved not only persons who *sponte ex libertate se beato Petro tradiderunt*, but also those who *servitute liberati aliorum traditione venerunt*.[7] Liberation from servitude, quite often the result of buying freedom, and subsequent *traditio* to a saint also took place within the context of the *familia*. Thus in 1025 King Conrad II confirmed the actions of the Bishop of Speyer, who *ex servilibus personis censuales fecisset*.[8]

The groups of people concerned were often, but not always, termed *censuales*. German researchers generally use the collective term *Zensuale* to cover different variants such as *censuales, censarii, censuarii, cerocensuales,* and *tributarii*.[9] Some

[7] H. Boos (ed.), *Quellen zur Geschichte der Stadt Worms. 1. Theil: Urkundenbuch der Stadt Worms*, i (Berlin, 1886), no. 51, 46.

[8] MGH. DD. Konrad II., no. 41, 46 f. E. Voltmer, *Reichsstadt und Herrschaft. Zur Geschichte der Stadt Speyer im hohen und späten Mittelalter* (Trierer Historische Forschungen 1; Trier, 1981), 20 f.

[9] Cf. the works of Knut Schulz: K. Schulz, 'Zum Problem der Zensualität im Hochmittelalter', in id. (ed.), *Beiträge zur Wirtschafts- und Sozialgeschichte des Mittelalters. Festschrift für H. Helbig zum 65. Geburtstag* (Cologne and Vienna, 1976), 86–127; id., 'Zensualität und Stadtentwicklung im 11./12. Jahrhundert', in B. Diestelkamp (ed.), *Beiträge zum hochmittelalterlichen Städtewesen* (Städteforschung A 11; Cologne and Vienna, 1982), 73–93; K. Schulz, 'Stadtrecht und Zensualität am Niederrhein (12–14. Jahrhundert)', in E. Ennen and K. Flinck (eds.), *Soziale und*

French scholars call these groups *Tributaire*.[10] Significantly, however, other scholars prefer the term *Sainteur*.[11] This more strongly emphasizes the religious dimension and is used mainly for those who decided to submit themselves to the authority of the saint.

Common to all the different groups covered by the concept of *Zensualität* is the obligation to pay taxes. These could be paid in cash or kind (for example, beeswax) and varied considerably in amount. Depending on when and where the *Zensualen* lived, they could be liable for additional payments on marriage or death, and also subject to other legal obligations. In general, the annual taxes were tied to individuals, not to property such as land or houses. But this distinction cannot be drawn in every case in which the sources mention *censuales*. In addition, there is good reason to believe that orginally property taxes were understood as payments tied to people, while in the towns, for instance, the opposite could happen and poll taxes might be transformed into area and land taxes. None the less, we must retain, in principle, the distinction between property and personal taxes frequently indicated in the sources. If these taxes did not apply to property, they were compatible with various forms of horizontal mobility.

In the following, I shall make a number of points about the phenomenon of *Zensualität*, which was common in many areas of the Empire.

First, in recent studies, German scholars have tended to speak of *Zensualität* in cases involving poll taxes, death duties, and marriage dues either for individuals or groups, even if the work of Knut Schulz has made us more aware of the fact that these obligations varied considerably depending

---

wirtschaftliche Bindungen im Mittelalter am Niederrhein (Klever Archiv 3; Kleve, 1981), 13–36; K. Schulz, 'Freikauf in der Gesellschaft des Hochmittelalters. Dargestellt an bayerischen Quellen', in U. Bestmann, F. Irsigler, J. Schneider (eds.), *Hochfinanz, Wirtschaftsräume, Innovationen. Festschrift für W. von Stromer* (3 vols, Trier, 1987) 1197–1226.

[10] Cf. above all P. C. Boeren, *Etudes sur les tributaires d'église dans le comté de Flandre du IXᵉ au XIVᵉ siècle* (Amsterdam, 1936).

[11] Cf. e.g. L. Verriest, *Le servage dans le comté de Hainaut. Les sainteurs. Le meilleur catel* (Brussels, 1910); P. Duparc, 'La question des sainteurs ou hommes d'église', *Journal des savants*, (1972), 25–48.

on the period and the region. Generally there is a danger that the overall term of *Zensualität* obscures the variety of legal forms which existed, and some of which can be clearly defined. For example, the 1035 household law (*Hofrecht*) of Limburg provides a choice between labour service of one day per week, and an annual poll tax.[12] This points to the important area of taxes which provided release from corvées. However, only if such obligations are clearly distinguished from more favourable legal forms does a widespread process of fundamental importance become evident. Other groups within the *familia* gradually came to aspire to the comparatively favourable status of the *Zensualen*. Occasionally, it was usurped. Legal forms of *Zensualität* often served as a model for the many great changes taking place between 1000 and 1300 in the larger ecclesiastical manors. They could be granted as an incentive by ecclesiastical lords; at times they had to be conceded in situations of crisis.

Second, on the whole, the loosening of ties and the removal of corvées was a varied process that involved many groups both in the *familia* and outside it. Against the background of the general increase in population, more favourable legal forms provided opportunities in areas where new land was being cultivated, and where *hereditas* could be acquired in expanding or newly founded settlements.[13] Nevertheless, we cannot ignore the fact that many people tried to escape from their personal ties by running away.

Third, recent studies have justly emphasized the possibility of movement connected with legal forms of *Zensualität*. But they tend not to pay sufficient attention to the risks such movements involved. The protection which the *Zensualen* could expect from their lords decreased as the distance separating them from their patrons increased. Forgeries as well as other written records of legal procedures, especially from the twelfth century onwards, suggest that their status was endangered. On the other hand, legal ties gave lords certain

---

[12] MGH. DD. Konrad II., no. 216, 294 ff.

[13] F. Irsigler, 'Freiheit und Unfreiheit im Mittelalter. Formen und Wege sozialer Mobilität', *Westfälische Forschungen*, 28 (1976/77), 1–15; id., 'Urbanisierung und sozialer Wandel in Nordwesteuropa im 11. bis 14. Jahrhundert', in G. Dilcher, N. Horn (eds.), *Sozialwissenschaften im Studium des Rechts*, iv, *Rechtsgeschichte* (Munich, 1978), 109–23.

means of restricting or preventing attempts by *Zensualen* to gain independence.

Fourth, it is still a matter of dispute among scholars whether the legal status of the *Zensualen* can be distinguished from that of the *Ministerialen*. Recently Knut Schulz has suggested that there may have been a 'transition zone' (*Übergangszone*) between the two forms. However, he concludes that the status of *Zensuale* is clearly distinguished from that of the *Ministeriale*.[14] In fact, different status has been attested in some regions, especially from the twelfth century onwards. On the other hand, J. Fleckenstein has justly pointed out the danger of drawing an oversimplified picture, especially of the early *Ministerialität*, by putting together individual instances of service customs (*Dienstrechte*) which differ according to period and region.[15] This warning must also be taken into account when distinguishing the status of the *Ministeriale* from that of others. The example cited above of the *Zensualen* of St Trond fighting on horseback is relevant here.

Fifth, an oversimplified picture of the legal forms subsumed under the term *Zensualität* has perhaps also contributed to the fact that the religious dimension which was certainly attached to them has often been underestimated or ignored. Thus in the most recent study of St Trond, E. Linck concluded that there was no evidence of a religious element among the *Zensualen* as far as their status was concerned.[16] He overlooked the fact that most records of transfer explicitly mention the annual payment as due *super altare in calice* on the feast of the saint.[17] It is not only in this case that legal acts (*Rechtshandlungen*) within a religious framework are significant for the status of the group. Indeed, it is likely that an analysis of the forms in which annual payments were

[14] K. Schulz, 'Zensualität und Stadtentwicklung im 11./12. Jahrhundert' (as in note 10), 92.

[15] J. Fleckenstein, 'Die Entstehung des niederen Adels und das Rittertum', in id. (ed.), *Herrschaft und Stand. Untersuchungen zur Sozialgeschichte im 13. Jahrhundert* (Veröffentlichungen des Max-Planck-Instituts für Geschichte 51; Göttingen, 1979), 2nd edn., 17–39, here 24.

[16] E. Linck, *Sozialer Wandel in klösterlichen Grundherrschaften* (as in n. 5), 87.

[17] C. Piot, *Cartulaire de l'abbaye de Saint-Trond* (as in n. 2), vol. 1, no. XV, 19f. and others.

made, in this and other cases, could help both to describe, and to distinguish between, specific groups. It certainly made a difference whether *Zensualen* rendered their tribute personally on the feast of the saint or paid their dues via the administrative channels. The combination of ritual acts and individual emotional experiences may have been an important factor, both for the legal status and the self-image of the 'payers of tax to an altar' (*Altarzinser*), as I should like to call this group.

An example of urban *Zensualität* indicates the significance of such legal forms. It was again Knut Schulz who showed that the well-known twelfth-century imperial charters for Speyer and Worms were connected with the phenomenon of *Zensualität*. The population of these cities had received important privileges (*Vorrechte*) through these charters. They were released from various obligations, especially heriots, which Schulz interprets as a characteristic feature of *Zensualität*. Schulz thus deduced that most of the population of Worms and Speyer were subject to the obligations of the *Zensualen*. These obligations, he argues, were abolished in connection with the attempt to secure rights of property alienation and laws of inheritance.[18]

While this is an extremely interesting interpretation, I shall now turn to an aspect of this argument which has generally been neglected by scholars. The privileges of the Speyer charter, at least in the version that was engraved above the portal of the cathedral, were granted only on the following conditions.[19] All the inhabitants of the city, including those who would settle there in future, were obliged to participate in the festivities celebrating the anniversary of the death and burial of Henry IV (7 August). We may imagine a

[18] K. Schulz, 'Zensualität und Stadtentwicklung im 11./12 Jahrhundert' (as in n. 10), 79 ff.

[19] H. Hilgard-Villard (ed.), *Urkunden zur Geschichte der Stadt Speyer* (Strasburg, 1885), no. 4, 17 ff.: *concessimus et confirmavimus, ea tamen interposita condicione, ut in anniversario patris nostri sollempniter ad vigilias et ad missam omnes conveniant, candelas in manibus teneant et de singulis domibus panem unum pro elemosina dare et pauperibus erogare studeant*. In 1219, when Frederick II granted town status to the Palatine village of Annweiler, this was also connected with an anniversary: *ut cives predicti anniversarium obitus nostri diem solempni recolant frequentatione*. J. L. A. Huillard-Bréholles (ed.), *Historia diplomatica Friderici secundi . . . i*, pars 2 (Paris, 1852), 679 ff.

solemn procession of all the inhabitants of the city, each carrying a wax candle. Thus everyone was involved in commemorating the emperor's person at his grave in the cathedral. The building of the cathedral itself had stimulated trade and commerce in the city. The significance of the obligations relating to the celebration of the emperor's anniversary for creating an awareness of the special role of the city should not be underestimated. There are clear parallels with similar activities in the area of *Zensualität*. Until the late Middle Ages, one of the main reasons for dependants being transferred to churches was to ensure that they would save their former lord's soul by paying annual contributions, either in wax or money, to the church.[20] Although the 1111 charter granted important privileges, it did not abolish all the legal differences which existed between city-dwellers. Yet despite these continuing differences, all the inhabitants of Speyer were intended to be *Zensualen* within the framework of a *memoria* founded by the emperor against the background of the struggle between *regnum et sacerdotium*.[21]

Sixth, these few examples illustrate the great variety of social groups covered by the term *Zensualität*, which has become familiar to German medievalists. The fact that the sources mainly record changes in status connected with these legal forms may have contributed to the labelling of such processes as social or vertical mobility. In our context, however, these terms should be used only with great caution. Vertical mobility often seems to be associated with the concept of modern industrial class societies, whose complex

[20] M. Borgolte, 'Freigelassene im Dienste der Memoria. Kulttradition und Kultwandel zwischen Antike und Mittelalter', *Frühmittelalterliche Studien*, 7 (1983), 234–50.

[21] The corpse of the excommunicated emperor is said to have been worshipped in Liège even before it was transferred to Speyer. For the religious and political aspects of this see F. Graus, *Volk, Herrscher und Heiliger im Reich der Merowinger* (Prague, 1965), 328; P. R. Mathé, *Studien zum früh- und hochmittelalterlichen Königtum. Eine problemgeschichtliche Untersuchung über Königtum, Adel und Herrscherethik*, Ph.D. thesis (University of Berne, 1969), 78f.; J. L. Kupper, *Liège et l'église impériale XIe–XIIe siècles* (Bibliothèque de la Faculté de Philosophie et Lettres de l'université de Liège 228; Paris, 1981), 152, 479. For the relationship between Henry IV and Liège see W. Peters, 'Coniuratio facta est pro libertate. Zu den coniurationes in Mainz, Köln und Lüttich in den Jahren 1105/06', *Rheinische Vierteljahrsblätter*, 51 (1987), 303–12, here 309.

forms of organization and communication give them a relatively high degree of cohesion and homogeneity. Changes in the position of individuals or groups are assessed in the context of society as a whole and hence perceived as social advancement or decline. Such conditions were largely absent in the high Middle Ages. While a considerable degree of social advancement and decline existed, by no means all the phenomena subsumed under the term *Zensualität* can be connected with it.

It is impossible within the framework of the present work to discuss the schematic interpretations of society (*Deutungsschemata*) drawn up by literate élites, and their complex interconnections with social reality. These schemata have been the subject of renewed interest in recent years. Drafted by clerics and nobles, that is, by members of groups with relatively wide social connections, these schemata were certainly a factor in social interrelationships.[22] The intention behind drawing them up was not to describe a reality undergoing drastic changes, although they were, of course, influenced by these changes. Rather, their authors aimed to define the place of what from our present-day perspective look like very different social groups in a world determined by God.

All attempts so far systematically to classify the various forms of *Zensualität* have proved problematic. To the extent that German legal and constitutional historians of the old school looked at the *Zensualen* at all, they defined them as a class (*Klasse*) or estate (*Stand*), related to nineteenth- and twentieth-century categories such as 'peoples' (*Volk*) and 'nations' (*Nationalstaat*). Attempts to define the *Zensualen* within a consistent legal framework ignored the fact that the period itself lacked a standardized legal terminology. Thus in describing the legal status of *Zensualen*, contemporaries used a number of terms such as *condicio, ius, lex,* and *ordo,* which were also used in many other contexts.

In the 1960s and 1970s it was above all Karl Bosl who tried to define three larger groups or strata below the level of the

O. G. Oexle, 'Die funktionale Dreiteilung der Gesellschaft bei Adalbero von Laon. Deutungsschemata der sozialen Wirklichkeit im früheren Mittelalter', *Frühmittelalterliche Studien,* 12 (1978), 1–54, here 54.

noblility and the clergy. In his rather dubious terminology, these are the *Ministerialen,* the *Zensualen* and, finally, the great mass of dependants or serfs.[23] This attempt to create a tripartite hierarchy, which Bosl takes as an indicator of vertical mobility is, however, ultimately the product of modern notions of 'peoples' (*Volk*) and of 'society'. Thus *Zensualität* was declared a general social phenomenon, and its importance was considerably overrated. The fact that it is comparatively well documented in the archives of ecclesiastical institutions has also led to its significance being exaggerated.

The various legal forms of *Zensualität,* some of which, especially in the old settlement areas, have a long history, were restricted in their changing and varied regional manifestations to the areas under the control of monasteries and collegiate churches. This allowed them to penetrate many rural and urban spheres where they overlapped with other legal forms, or were displaced by them in a number of ways, depending on the time and place.

Inevitably, the financial situation of the various groups of *Zensualen* differed. Given the many changes that took place in the course of the high Middle Ages, *Zensualität* was attractive to both individuals and groups for a number of reasons. It offered many opportunities to secure material, legal, and religious existence. On the other hand, *Zensualität* also provided ecclesiastical institutions with a number of opportunities permanently to bind groups to them, for a variety of reasons. The status of the *Zensualen,* however, came under threat whenever they were affected by disputes between their patrons and the opponents of those patrons. The significance of *Zensualität* and the factors that determined it can perhaps be explained more satisfactorily by comparison with regions which lacked similar legal forms. Medieval England, which Odegena left almost 900 years ago, may well provide interesting information.

---

[23] Cf. e.g. K. Bosl, 'Kasten, Stände, Klassen im mittelalterlichen Deutschland. Zur Problematik soziologischer Begriffe und ihrer Anwendung auf die mittelalterliche Gesellschaft', *Zeitschrift für bayerische Landesgeschichte,* 32 (1969), 477–94. Most recently reprinted in id., *Die Gesellschaft in der Geschichte des Mittelalters* (as in n. 7).

Notes on Contributors

DAVID A. CARPENTER is a Reader in History at King's College London. He is the author of *The Battles of Lewes and Evesham 1264/65* (1987), *The Minority of Henry III* (1990), and numerous articles in books and learned journals.

CHRISTOPHER DYER is Professor of Medieval Social History in the University of Birmingham. He is the author of *Lords and Peasants in a Changing Society. The Estates of the Bishopric of Worcester 680–1540* (1980), and of *Standards of Living in the Later Middle Ages. Social Change in England, c.1200–1520* (1989). He has written many essays and articles on aspects of the social and economic history, and archaeology, of medieval England, and is currently editor of the *Economic History Review*.

PETER W. EDBURY is a Senior Lecturer in History at the University of Wales College of Cardiff. His main field of research is the internal history of the Crusader principalities in the Near East in the twelfth to fourteenth centuries, and he is currently working on a history of the Third Crusade and also on Jean d'Ibelin's legal treatise. Among his publications are The *Kingdom of Cyprus and the Crusades 1191–1374* (1991) and, in collaboration with John G. Rowe, *William of Tyre. Historian of the Latin East* (1988).

JOHN GILLINGHAM was educated at Oxford and Munich Universities and is now Professor of History at the London School of Economics. He has written on English, French, and German history; his publications include *Richard the Lionheart* (2nd edn., 1989), *The Wars of the Roses* (1981), and *Richard Coeur de Lion. Kingship, Chivalry and War in the Twelfth Century* (1994).

ALFRED HAVERKAMP is Professor of Medieval History at the University of Trier. He has published widely on the high and late Middle Ages, in particular, on German and Italian history. His publications include *Herrschaftsformen der Frühstaufer in Reichsitalien*, 2 vols. (1971), *Aufbruch und Gestaltung*, 2nd revised edn. (1993), and *Medieval Germany 1056–1273*, 2nd revised edn (1992). He has edited *Friedrich Barbarossa. Handlungsspielräume und Wirkungsweisen des staufischen Kaisers* (1992) and various other books, and is one of the co-editors of the *Journal of Medieval History*. He is the author of *Italien im hohen und späten Mittelalter 1056–1454*, published in the *Handbuch der europäischen Geschichte*, vol. 2, and of numerous articles on medieval and Jewish history. He is at present editing *Gebhardt, Handbuch der deutschen Geschichte*, vol. 1: *Deutsche Geschichte im Mittelalter.*

RUDOLF HIESTAND is Professor of Medieval History at the University of Düsseldorf. He has written widely on Western–Byzantine relations from the tenth to the thirteenth centuries and on the Papacy and the Crusades. He is Director of the project editing the *Regesta Pontificum Romanorum*, published by the Akademie der Wissenschaften in Göttingen and the Pius Stiftung. Among his publications are *Byzanz und das Regnum Italicum im 10. Jahrhundert* (1964), *Papsturkunden für Templer und Johanniter* (1972), *Papsturkunden für Templer und Johanniter. Neue Folge* (1984), and *Papsturkunden für Kirchen im Heiligen Land* (1985). Currently he is preparing the *Oriens Pontificius Latinus.*

PAUL R. HYAMS was a Fellow of Pembroke College, Oxford, until 1989 and remains an Emeritus Fellow. He is now Associate Professor of History at Cornell. As well as a book on *King, Lords and Peasants in Medieval England* (1980), he has published many articles on medieval law and society, on Jews, and even on Heinrich Mitteis and English Constitutional History. He is currently writing a book, *Rancor and Reconciliation: Violent Wrong and its Motivations in Medieval England*, which by applying Feud questions to England might facilitate some new comparisons with Germany.

HERMANN JAKOBS, Professor emeritus of History at the University of Heidelberg,   is contributing to the *Papstregestenwerk* being published by the Akademie der Wissenschaften in Göttingen (*Germania Pontificia IV*, 1978; vol. V in preparation; *Zu den Fuldaer Papsturkunden*, 1992). A co-editor of the Oldenbourg Grundriß der Geschichte, he is the author of *Kirchenreform und Hochmittelalter 1046–1215* (3rd edn., 1994) which forms part of this series, and of *Eugen III. und die Anfänge der europäischen Stadtsiegel* (1980). He has published widely on medieval constitutional and urban history.

KARL-FRIEDRICH KRIEGER is Professor of Medieval History at the University of Mannheim. His publications include *Ursprung und Wurzeln der Rôles d'Oléron* (1971), *Die Lehnshoheit der deutschen Könige im Spätmittelalter (ca. 1200–1437)* (1979), *Geschichte Englands von den Anfängen bis zum 15. Jahrhundert* (1990), *König, Reich und Reichsreform im Spätmittelalter* (1992), *Die Habsburger im Mittelalter. Von Rudolf I. bis Friedrich III.* (1994), and a number of articles on medieval history.

Notes on Contributors

373

KARL JOSEPH LEYSER († 1992) was Chichele Professor of Medieval History, Oxford University, and Fellow, All Souls College, Oxford, from 1984 to 1988. From 1948 to 1984 he was Official Fellow and Tutor in History, Magdalen College, Oxford. His publications include *Rule and Conflict in an Early Medieval Society: Ottonian Saxony* (1979), *Medieval Germany and its Neighbours 900–1250* (1982), and numerous articles in learned journals. These together with unpublished work have now been edited by Timothy Reuter and published in two volumes, *Communications and Power in Medieval Europe: The Carolingian and Ottonian Centuries* and *Communications and Power in Medieval Europe: The Gregorian Revolution and Beyond* (1994).

MICHAEL MATHEUS is Professor of History at the University of Mainz. His publications are mainly on the social, constitutional, and economic history of the high and late Middle Ages. Titles include *Trier am Ende des Mittelalters* (1984), and *Hafenkrane. Zur Geschichte einer mittelalterlichen Maschine* (1985). A major study, *Adelige als Zinser von Heiligen*, is in preparation.

NICHOLAS ORME is Professor of History at Exeter University, and has written widely on educational, religious, and cultural history in England up to the sixteenth century. His books include *English Schools in the Middle Ages* (1973), *From Childhood to Chivalry* (1984), *Education and Society in Medieval and Renaissance England* (1989), and *Nicholas Roscarrock's Lives of the Saints* (1992). His history of *The English Hospital 1070–1570* was published in 1995, and he is currently studying the history of childhood in medieval England.

ALEXANDER PATSCHOVSKY, who formerly worked at the Monumenta Germaniae Historica (Munich), is now Professor of Medieval History at the University of Constance. He has published widely on heretical movements, and recently, in the field of Jewish history. His publications include *Der Passauer Anonymus. Ein Sammelwerk über Ketzer, Juden, Antichrist aus der Mitte des 13. Jh.* (1968), *Die Anfänge einer ständigen Inquisition in Böhmen* (1975), and *Quellen zur böhmischen Inquisition im 14. Jh.* (1979).

J. O. PRESTWICH has been a Fellow of The Queen's College, Oxford, since 1937 and was elected to an Honorary Fellowship in 1990. His published work has been chiefly concerned with problems of war and government under the Norman and Angevin kings.

MICHAEL PRESTWICH is Professor of History in the University of Durham, where he is currently Pro-Vice-Chancellor. His main research interests lie in the military and political developments of the thirteenth and fourteenth centuries. His publications include *War, Politics and Finance under Edward I* (1972), *The Three Edwards* (1980), *Edward I* (1988), and *English Politics in the Thirteenth Century* (1990). He edited *Documents Illustrating the Crisis of 1297–98 in England* (1980), and has written numerous articles.

SUSAN REYNOLDS is an Emeritus Fellow of Lady Margaret Hall, Oxford, from which she retired in 1986. She now lives in London, where she is currently working on medieval and modern ideas about states and nations. She has written three books, all published by Oxford: *An Introduction to the History of English Medieval Towns* (1977), *Kingdoms and Communities in Western Europe, 900–1300* (1984), and *Fiefs and Vassals: the Medieval Evidence Reinterpreted* (1994), and a collection of earlier articles, *Ideas and Solidarities of the Medieval Laity: England and Western Europe* (1995).

WERNER RÖSENER is Professor of History at the University of Göttingen, and a Research Fellow at the Max Planck Institute for History. He has published numerous articles on the economic, social, and cultural history of the high Middle Ages. His publications include *Reichsabtei Salem: Verfassungs- und Wirtschaftsgeschichte des Zisterzienserklosters von der Gründung bis zur Mitte des 14. Jh.* (1974), *Grundherrschaft im Wandel: Untersuchungen zur Entwicklung geistlicher Grundherrschaften im südwestdeutschen Raum vom 9. bis 14. Jh.* (1991), and *Peasants in the Middle Ages* (1992). He is the editor of *Strukturen der Grundherrschaft im frühen Mittelalter* (1989).

HANNA VOLLRATH is Professor of Medieval History at the Ruhr University Bochum. She has written two monographs on Anglo-Saxon history: *Königsgedanke und Königtum bei den Angelsachsen* (1971), and *Die Synoden Englands bis 1066* (1985). Many of her more recent publications deal with the social implications of orality, especially in the field of medieval law. Her contribution to *Rassow, Deutsche Geschichte* (1987, 2nd edn. 1993) covers the Middle Ages from the beginning of the tenth to the end of the fifteenth centuries, and she writes on the century of the Salians in the new *Cambridge Medieval History*. Currently she is working on a parallel biography of Frederick Barbarossa and Henry II of England.

ALFRED WENDEHORST is Professor of History at the University of Erlangen-Nuremberg and the University Archivist. His research interests are the history of universities, and the history of the old

Imperial Church which he has been pursuing as an associate member of the Max Planck Institute for History in Göttingen. He has published four volumes on Würzburg in the series Germania Sacra, and together with Erich Freiherr von Guttenberg, one on the medieval bishopric of Bamberg.

Index